DATE DUE

Niko's Nature

The Life of Niko Tinbergen and his Science of Animal Behaviour

Hans Kruuk

With drawings and photographs by Niko Tinbergen

OXFORD
UNIVERSITY PRESS

OXFORD

UNIVERSITY PRESS

Great Clarendon Street, Oxford OX2 6DP

Oxford University Press is a department of the University of Oxford.
It furthers the University's objective of excellence in research, scholarship,
and education by publishing worldwide in

Oxford New York

Auckland Bangkok Buenos Aires Cape Town Chennai
Dar es Salaam Delhi Hong Kong Istanbul Karachi Kolkata
Kuala Lumpur Madrid Melbourne Mexico City Mumbai Nairobi
São Paulo Shanghai Taipei Tokyo Toronto

Oxford is a registered trade mark of Oxford University Press
in the UK and in certain other countries

Published in the United States
by Oxford University Press Inc., New York

British Library Cataloguing in Publication Data
Data available

Library of Congress Cataloguing in Publication Data
ISBN 0-19-851558-8

1 3 5 7 9 10 8 6 4 2

Typeset in Bembo
by Footnote Graphics Limited, Warminster, Wilts

Printed in Great Britain by
TJ International Ltd, Padstow, Cornwall

To Jaap, Catrina, Dirk, Janet, and Gerry

Preface

Over the autumnal reds and yellows of dwarf shrubs I was looking at an overwhelming backdrop of glacier. Snow buntings came close, there was a lake with white-fronted geese, and a reindeer disappeared over the hillside. There were no people within many miles. Greenland is magnificent, gigantic, and awesome.

Seventy years earlier Niko and Lies Tinbergen had lived there, for a year. The grandeur of the country, and the Inuit views of life deeply affected Niko, scientist and naturalist. Greenland showed him what wilderness really was, and made him realize that he was a hunter at heart. The Inuit people, closer to nature than he was, made him view animals as objects, as machines, which are part of their environment, not separated from it. Niko's later ability to study animals as machines that had evolved in their own context and environment was vital for his development of the study of animal behaviour, ethology.

Experiments with free-living, wild birds, without disturbing them, were one of Niko's innovations which now seem commonplace. At the time when he began this, however, in the 1930s and 1940s, the idea rocked the world of animal behaviour studies. It was one of his simple approaches that built up a new branch of science, for which many years later he would be rewarded with the Nobel Prize.

Some forty years after I started as one of Niko's students, studying gulls in the dunes of north-west England, I met Marian Dawkins, Professor of Animal Behaviour, on the stairs in the Zoology Department in Oxford. She was also one of Niko's disciples, and we exchanged some reminiscence of the good old days. 'Isn't it sad', she said, looking at me, 'that no-one has ever written a biography of him?'

The story of Niko Tinbergen is a fascinating one. He grew up in Holland, as a fanatic naturalist from his earliest years onwards, and as an athlete. He came from a highly motivated intellectual background: his eldest brother was to receive a Nobel Prize before Niko did – and two in one family is still a record. There was his magical year in Greenland, his period as a hostage of the German occupation of Holland in the Second World War, his emigration to England. And there was his extraordinary friendship with Konrad Lorenz, which led to the establishment of ethology.

To Niko's enthusiastic group of students in Oxford he was 'The Maestro', who wrote the book that established ethology as a science: *The study of instinct*. He also wrote many others, made prize-winning films, and his bird photography and drawings were legendary. For scientists, Niko's main contribution lay in his clear logic, and in the simple questions he asked about animal behaviour. It was this that enabled him to design the beautiful field experiments, with animals in their own environment, and it was this that put ethology firmly in place as one aspect of biology. Those of us who worked with Niko watched the birth of a science, and later its absorption into other sciences. All of us remembered ourselves spellbound by his teaching: he was an arch-communicator.

There were several arguments that made me realize that I was probably the obvious person to write Niko's story. Most important, perhaps, was that I had known him well, and Niko was a friend and a mentor to me. Of course this could pose problems of one-sided reporting, as I am indebted to him. However, objectivity is what Niko always wanted himself, and he would insist on being treated without favours. I think that just as, in previous books, I have written objective descriptions of behaviour of animals I love, I can also be objective about the life of a person I was close to, now many years ago. Moreover, in this biography I present not just my own insights, but especially those of others, and I have tried to assess Niko's contribution against general scientific standards.

There were also other circumstances which put me in a favourable position to write about Niko. Because I am Dutch, the language of sources presented no difficulties. Like Niko I emigrated from Holland to Britain, and I can appreciate some of the problems, perceptions, and emotions involved. I can look back at the Netherlands and see some of the distinctive characteristics of its people, in a way that would be more difficult for either a Dutch person who does not have an outside vantage point, or for someone not Dutch. This also added interest for me to the process of writing the biography, as I saw some of my own history and emotions unfolding in Niko's transition across the North Sea. Finally, and perhaps at least as important as any of the other reasons, was that I am a naturalist in the mould of Niko, not with his abilities as an observer and scientist, but equally absorbed by birds, insects, and mammals anywhere in the world. I think I understand that part of him.

Many people have helped me tremendously, and I am, as someone who had never written a biography before, deeply grateful for their confidence in me. There is a slight feeling of guilt, because much of the detail I learnt from people has not been expressed in this book. It has nevertheless been highly important to me, as it provided vital background. I have had to select what I thought was most relevant, and leave out many events, as well as people who have played roles in the story. I take full responsibility for such omissions. I admire the forbearance of the Tinbergen children, who tolerated my probing into sensitive aspects of their parents' lives without complaints, and who corrected many false impressions. Where their recollections disagreed, it was me who chose between them.

Whenever needed I have provided translations of Dutch and German material in the text. For the sake of authenticity, I have kept such translations as literal as possible.

For visiting several important witnesses, all around the globe, I received a generous grant from the Royal Society of Great Britain. A number of libraries and archives kindly gave me access to their collections, including the Bodleian Library in Oxford, the British Library in London, the archives of the Heimans and Thijsse Stichting, Amsterdam, the 'Naturalis' Institute of the University of Leiden, the Dutch State Archives in The Hague, and the libraries of the University of Chicago and Harvard University. Several people have been extremely generous with their own collections of Niko's letters and photographs: amongst many others, especially Els Barendrecht-Baerends and Rudi Drent (with access to the archives of the late Gerard Baerends), Lary Shaffer, Jimmy Rose, Irenaeus Eibl-Eibesfeldt, and, of course, Niko's children, especially Jaap and Catrina.

During this project I thoroughly enjoyed the hospitality of Sim Broekhuizen, and John and Hanneke Videler in Holland. I am indebted even more to Prof. Nick Blurton-Jones, Dr Harvey Croze, Prof. Mike Cullen (who sadly died soon after), Prof. Richard Dawkins, Prof. Juan Delius, Catrina Loman (née Tinbergen), Prof. Lary Shaffer, Dirk Tinbergen, and Dr Jaap Tinbergen for their hospitality, as well as for large amounts of information.

Lary Shaffer, Sheila O'Clarey, Irenaeus Eibl-Eibesfeldt, and the Tinbergen children (as executors of Niko's estate) generously allowed me to use their own and Niko's photographs and drawings.

Other sources who generously gave of their time and/or correspondence with Niko, and who either wrote to me or were interviewed, are (in alphabetical order):

Prof. Colin Beer, Prof. Tim Birkhead, Dr David Blest, Dr Luit Boerema (who sadly died soon afterwards), Derek Bromhall, Gerry Carleston (née Tinbergen), Mrs Jo Casimir-Jonker, Dr Rob Casimir, Prof. Carel ten Cate, Dr Malcolm Coe, Dr Marga Coesel, Prof. Stella Crossley, Dr Esther Cullen, Prof. Marian Dawkins, Prof. Irenaeus Eibl-Eibesfeldt, Benedikt Foeger, Prof. Ernst Gombrich, Dr Hans Gorter, Dr Fae Hall, Dr Mike Hansell, Prof. Robert Hinde, Prof. Peter Jarman, Dr Adriaan Kortlandt, Mrs Jane Kruuk, Dr Robin Liley, Mrs. Jeannie Maclean, Dr Gilbert Manley, Frans Makkink, Prof. Aubrey Manning, Prof. John Maynard Smith, Prof. Ernst Mayr, Dr Desmond Morris, Dr Bryan Nelson, Dr Mike Norton Griffiths, Miss Sheila O'Clarey, Dr Ian Patterson, Dr A. Perdeck, Prof. Chris Perrins, Dr Graham Philips, Dr John Richer, Major Jimmy Rose, Dr Hugh Rowell, Prof. Leen de Ruiter, Prof. Bill Russell, Mrs Pat Searle, Prof. Piet Sevenster, Dr John Sparks, Klaus Taschwer, Miss Jacomien Tinbergen, Mrs Tilde Tinbergen-Frensdorf, Dr Joost Tinbergen, Janet Tinbergen, Dr Niko Verbeek, Dr Verwey-Jonker, Dr Rita Weidmann, Mrs Ann Wilson, and Jaap Zwier.

Dr Jaap Tinbergen, Dr Loeske Kruuk, Jane Kruuk, Prof. Marian Dawkins, and Prof. Richard Dawkins read the entire manuscript and provided much thoughtful commentary and criticism; I could not have done without this, and I am deeply grateful. Shorter sections were improved by the comments of Janet Tinbergen, Catrina Loman, and Gerry Carleston, and they also deserve many thanks. Responsibility for the final product, of course, is entirely mine.

My wife Jane's support was, as always, wonderful and indispensable.

Aboyne, Aberdeenshire   H. K.
October 2002

Contents

Photos in the text

CHAPTER I

Wild birds and science

One cold, April morning I was perched on a dune, somewhere along the west coast in the very north of England, a student at work, diligently making notes on birds and beasts. In front of me, right across the wind-swept landscape of dunes and beach, tens of thousands of gulls were nesting: the sky was full of them, and their noise competed with that of the sea. There was an endless backdrop of clouds, sand, and waves, miles away from roads or houses.

A solitary figure emerged from the distance. Along the beach a small, khaki-clad man approached, carrying a floppy rucksack, on his shoulder a tripod, binoculars around his neck. His grey hair bristled in the wind, his spectacled face followed the birds, and he searched the sand in front of his feet for animal tracks. A man in his element.

Forty years later, I still carry with me this image of Niko Tinbergen in the early 1960s. He was then about 55, a quiet, unceremonious field man. But it was that same small man who had made watching wild animal behaviour into a science, the grand old maestro of ethology, and at the height of his creative energy. A few years later he would be celebrated in universities around the

Niko Tinbergen, out in the field at 69. Photo Lary Shaffer.

world, and be made a Nobel Laureate. Yet he always remained a field man at heart, a naturalist with the wind in his hair, who watched and wondered.

It is difficult to realize how far we have travelled from the early days of studying animal behaviour. Before Niko arrived on the scene, behaviour science was focussed largely on white rats and pigeons behind bars. Things that happened out in the wild were rarely respectable subjects for scientific enquiry. Now we see this fabulous richness of displays, gestures, attacks, and courtship in all creatures around us, and we simply cannot imagine not asking questions about that. Much of this change is due to *ethology*, the discipline of Konrad Lorenz and Niko Tinbergen.

The label 'ethology' is rarely used these days. It is the science concerned with *the biology of animal behaviour*, and the more usual term now is just 'animal behaviour', as in 'Department of Animal Behaviour'. Aspects of ethology live on in new disciplines: in behavioural ecology, sociobiology, cognitive ethology, neuro-ethology, and others. Ethology is not psychology, it is more concerned with evolution, less with learning processes, and it explicitly does not take animal feelings into account. Ethologists (and especially Niko) argued that we cannot know what an animal feels or what it intends, so scientists should not speculate on its subjective experience. This does not mean that one assumes animals to be without subjective feelings: almost certainly many have a rich palette of emotions, as anybody knows who keeps a dog or a cat at home. But scientists like Niko believed that these feelings are not accessible to us, and that one cannot experiment with emotions – we cannot really *know* about them.

What we do know is that animals show patterns of behaviour which have a biological purpose, and they have evolved, just as much as the animals' feet, coat colours, or internal organs. Often they are at least partly genetically determined, or they may be acquired during their lifetime. Behaviour is caused by physiological changes within the animal, and by external stimuli. The real skill of the early ethologists was to demonstrate that these aspects of animal behaviour can be addressed by research, and by scientific questioning. However, this can be done only if we set about it systematically, by carefully phrasing our questions.

Niko Tinbergen's greatest contribution to biology was probably the simple logic that he applied to disentangle our questions about behaviour. We hear the cock crowing at sunrise, and over the centuries many a mind has wondered why it does so. It was Niko who reasoned that we will never know whether that cock crows because it is 'happy', or because 'it wants to wake the hens', or because it 'hates' its neighbour. But he argued convincingly that, as a biological scientist, one can ask that question, *Why does it crow?*, with four fundamentally different meanings. They are all scientifically important, and they have gone down in science history as *Tinbergen's 'four whys'*.

Firstly, *causation*: what is happening inside him (the physiological state of the cock) and what is happening outside (the external stimuli) that make him crow? Secondly, there is the *ontogeny* of the behaviour: why and how did the individual develop it, what are the genetic factors involved, and how is crowing affected by learning and environment in the cock's lifetime? Thirdly, there is the why of *function* or biological purpose: we want to know what the consequence is of crowing, and how it affects the cock's own survival or fitness. And finally, there is the why of *evolution*: why and how has crowing evolved in this species? In principle the four questions apply to all animal behaviour, and we will hear much more about these important aspects of scientific methodology in later chapters. We will also see that our questions now reach well beyond these early approaches.

On that April morning, as I was walking down the dune to meet him, I wanted to tell Niko about what I had seen, about the attacks of the gulls on crows, and about my experiment with eggs in the colony. He was always bubbling with enthusiasm, and for a student there was nothing more gratifying than getting his comments, and to feel his interest in such observations as a pat on the back. I had come to him from a Dutch university, where professors sat next to God on a cloud. For me it was a magically stimulating experience to have this accessible scientific giant discuss problems of mutual fascination. He made one feel on the same level with him, which was extraordinary for a student like me. Being used to the Dutch academic hierarchy, it took me quite a while to get used to calling him Niko, as he told us to.

'I got a wonderful shot', he greeted me, dropping his tripod onto the sand. He had been filming with his old Bolex camera from a hide in the gull colony, and in great detail he described a meeting ceremony between a pair of black-headed gulls. The male lands next to the female, and standing parallel to each other both bend down into a horizontal posture. Then both heads go into an upright stance and exactly at the same time both face away from each other, the 'facing away posture' or 'head flagging'. Niko mimed the whole thing, his face smiling but very intent, using his hand and arm to show the head flag. 'Fabulous, and I was rolling before the male landed!'

We were on the beach just outside the gull colony. The birds were circling above us, and just as I was about to tell him my tales, one gull did a dive-bomb attack on us, one of those alarming swoops with a scream at the bottom. These birds do it when defending their nest, usually just missing the target. This time the gull let fly a large accurate splash, hitting Niko on the side of his face, and covering the inside of one of his glasses. A look of astonishment, then we both crumpled up with laughter, Niko slapping his leg. Afterwards, I tried to imagine one of my professors in the Netherlands in that kind of situation.

Together we walked back to camp, to our field base in the dunes, far from civilization in a stunning landscape of dunes and mountains. A large, old caravan served as common room, a group of tents as our personal retreats. That year we lived there with three D. Phil. students, and a 'slave' who kept the show on the road and helped all of us.

Niko came up frequently, escaping the confines of university life in Oxford. He loved those dunes, the exciting work of his students, and the tracks in the sand. He came back to the fabulous light for photographs and filming, and to his own field experiments with gulls and crows. We had sessions with Niko in the bird-hides or blinds, where for hours on end he would point out the small changes in animals' actions or postures.

I often think of these times in the hide. I remember sitting crouched next to Niko, overlooking a broad sweep of dunes, and the hills of the English Lake District behind them. Everything was quiet in front of us, nothing much happened. Above our heads, on the roof of the hide, was a gull, calling. Through the canvas Niko, slightly bored, tickled its feet. He rolled another cigarette, and with a smile on his face he mumbled, 'How much wood would a woodchuck chuck if a woodchuck could chuck wood?' It was one of those magic, nonsensical interludes.

Soon afterwards two crows appeared; they circled and looked down, then landed right in front of us, very close. One of our experimental nests was there, with a greenish, mottled egg of a gull next to an old eggshell. Within seconds the crows flew off with the egg – having demonstrated, again, how quickly they could find it, if the egg's camouflage was betrayed by an eggshell. We had made one more observation in a long series of experiments, to find out why birds remove empty eggshells from their nests. It was magical how Niko could predict what would happen next, keeping an eye on what the neighbour gulls were doing, or an over-flying crow. He was a quite incredibly good observer.

Often there were discussions in the camp about the fieldwork, with some heavy science as well as nonsense. Niko sat in the corner in the caravan, drinking endless cups of instant coffee, holding forth whilst rolling his cigarettes, an awesome and alert presence who never let up, at times full of jokes and reminiscences.

When he was in the mood, we got fascinating, small glimpses into his past, words from the oracle, with a fair amount of proselytizing to his students about the bliss of the good old days. His time in Greenland often came up, adventures with Eskimo dogs, or watching birds on the Friesian isles in Holland. He talked about the bird-hides he used with his friends near Rotterdam in the 1920s, taking pictures with his plate-camera, bicycling huge distances to get to his birds. There were the long skating trips on the Dutch lakes and canals, and he talked about watching insects in Holland in the summer.

He loved life in his tent and in the caravan, leaving Oxford academia behind him with a sigh of relief. He loved roughing it, and didn't really approve of things that we organized in the dunes to make our existence more comfortable, like a proper seat in the bird-watching hides in the gull colony, or occasional trips to the pub, or non-essential foods. Spartan was how he wanted it: that is how it was in the old days, and that is how field life really should be. We felt some slight resentment about this, of course. It was only much later that I realized how much of Niko's lifestyle, of his success as a scientist and as a communicator, was derived from that same spartan simplicity.

When meeting in the camp, Niko's first words would often be aimed at some results or other that were due in: 'How did it go?' Life centred around

Fox tracks across dunes in Ravenglass. Photo Niko Tinbergen.

results, and we students desperately wanted results to go some way or other, demonstrating a hard-argued hypothesis about the birds' behaviour, or continuing some trend. Maddeningly, the data as collected in the colony often went in the opposite way from our expectations. When I or one of the others arrived back at the caravan, crestfallen because of those damn birds, Niko's eyebrows went up excitedly: 'But that is *interesting!*' Yes, of course it was interesting, but we did not want that, we wanted some regular, expected outcome. Niko loved being with his students, arguing with them, and training them. Time and again, he dragged our complicated interpretations of observations down to basic levels, to common sense.

Somehow, it was often difficult to associate Niko as the man in the field, or in the corner of the caravan in the dunes, with theories of animal behaviour. He was keenly interested in every practical aspect of natural history in the dunes, in the tracks of a fox or a badger that we had spotted across the Big Sand, or in the exact posture of a black-headed gull just after mating, or in the nest of a wheatear in a rabbit hole just outside a tent, or in the caterpillars of cinnabar moths on a ragwort. Every detail was shown to anyone who cared to listen, and he spent hours on his knees taking photographs. Straight natural history was his passion, and it was hard to realize that this was the same man who a few years earlier had published the famous book *The study of instinct.*[1] That was about methodology, about behaviour as an outcome of conflicting 'drives', about the hierarchical organization of behaviour; it was where he theorized about 'displacement activities' and other phenomena.

There were changes in Niko in those days in the early 1960s. He was gloomy at times, and his interests in animals began to take a different direction.

His previous interest in 'causation', in the mechanisms that made an animal perform, had begun to wane, to be replaced by a different one. We, his students, witnessed it happen during the course of a series of experiments that he did with us, in which he studied mechanism and function of one brief piece of behaviour of the gulls. Before that and for many years Niko had studied displays by birds, where one judged whether some behaviours were associated with aggression, fleeing, incubation, sex, or whatever. Then one drew conclusions about what happened inside the bird, about the bird's underlying motivation or 'drive'. One treated the bird as a 'black box', of which it was known only what went in, and what came out, and one had to deduce the inside mechanism. Everyone was talking motivation, and furious debates were raging, as we will see in later chapters.

Gradually, Niko dropped out of discussions on motivation, and it became much more important to him to find out what the biological function was of just a small piece of behaviour. He wanted to know about the benefit of it to the animal itself, rather than about the internal mechanism. He began to notice that there are conflicting requirements on a bird, for example when it has to protect itself against predation, as well as incubate a brood. With that he began to realize that an animal needs to balance these requirements, it needs to optimize, not maximize, in order to be as successful as possible. Optimization was to become one of the focal points of a new science – ethology's main later offspring – behavioural ecology.

In the early 1960s, in the caravan in the dunes, behavioural ecology was in the distant future. It could have developed much earlier, it was waiting in the wings. Rather surprisingly, ecology itself, the study of relations between organisms and their environment, was miles away from the gull research group. However obvious, the connection between the two sciences, ethology and ecology, refused to be made just then. Niko had little contact with ecologists, despite the advances in that science of his late brother Luuk, and despite the presence of his Oxford colleagues David Lack and Charles Elton. It was one of the Niko enigmas.

One of Niko's big passions in fieldwork was to do experiments with wild, unrestrained animals, without disturbing them and without causing suffering. The driving force in these experiments was not so much to prove or disprove hypotheses, although that came into it, of course. Rather, what moved him personally, more than anything else, was that with his experiments he could fool the birds, that he could make them do things that revealed their biological secrets. Niko was a stalker, a hunter, in his experiments just as much as with his camera. He was trying to get the better of nature, and felt immensely proud when he succeeded. Much of this had started in Greenland, where a close encounter with Inuit culture had profoundly changed his attitude to animals.

Every time, while driving back to Oxford after a stint in the dunes, Niko would sit humming behind the wheel of his Land-Rover, thinking about the fieldwork. Inevitably afterwards, often immediately when he arrived, he would

fire off letters to those he called 'his boys' back in the field, letters with comments and reinforcements, practical suggestions, and bits of theory. Sometimes
these comments were annoying to us (such as when he told us to get up earlier
in the morning), just as teenagers are annoyed by interference from their
parents. But usually he was right in his judgements about our life and work in
the field, and whatever their immediate effect, they made students feel almost
part of a family. Even at a distance he had a penetrating presence.

The fact that Niko was a very high achiever was, inevitably, part of his
personality. Even in those early days in the 1960s, before his Nobel Prize and
many other awards, one was aware of his role in starting what we felt was our
science. By then he had published scores of papers and several books, was a man
of exotic experiences, and had spawned lots of exciting ideas; he was a popular
lecturer, a great raconteur, and always the centre of attention during conferences. To us students, he was the living image of his successful book, *The study
of instinct*. Later, his successes would expand over other fields, over cinematography, and over studies on children.

Behind all that, behind the naturalist with the authority, the jolliness, and
the charm, was a person with an unusual background, forever a foreigner, and a
man who suffered intensely from deep depressions. There was his upbringing in
a highly charged family, the fanaticism of a Dutch youth movement, his own
relentless drive for achievement. There was the year in the wilderness of Greenland, the war, there was his own family — always second to his single-
mindedness — and a background of Calvinism. His success was rooted in a
multitude of influences, and some fortuitous events.

When Niko first started with independent research in the late 1920s, the world of science was very different from what it is now. Most people take the importance of behaviour science for granted, and it has its tentacles in many other areas. But before 1930 there was no such science. There was animal psychology, which studied animal intelligence and learning of a few species in cages, always with mankind as the central point of reference. There were naturalists who described some behaviour of wild animals. Darwin's *The expression of the emotions in man and the animals*[2] was a major landmark, but no real animal behaviour science got off the ground until the years of Konrad Lorenz and Niko Tinbergen.

On a superficial level, discussion of animal behaviour and its mechanisms started long before Charles Darwin. Several writers in the eighteenth century addressed observations of birds' nesting habits and song, and the differences in behaviour of wolves and rabbits. Even the term 'ethology' was used in those early days, by people such as the Frenchmen Charles Leroy and Etienne Geoffroy-St-Hilaire in the eighteenth and early nineteenth centuries. However, it was Darwin who began to do the subject justice, taking 'instincts' into account when comparing species and considering their evolution. It was not altogether clear what he meant by instinct as he did not define the term, but with it he did refer to behaviour patterns that had evolved in animals and humans. He recognized that behaviour was a major force in the adaptation of animals to their environment, subject to natural selection. Darwin himself did not specifically study behaviour or its organization, but he was interested in it as part of animals' mechanisms for survival.

The fact that Darwin put the behaviour of animals and people under one umbrella was of importance in the birth of the science of 'comparative psycho-

Pair of black-headed gulls during meeting ceremony, Ravenglass. Photo Niko Tinbergen.

logy', which pursued its interest in learning processes, especially in rats and mice in laboratories. The interest of comparative psychologists in the processes of higher intelligence, in various forms of learning, left instinct behind. There was little in the manifestations of intelligence that was affected by instinct: philosophically it was uninteresting. Biology was not touched by this science. Comparative psychologists focussed on problems of learning in just a few species, and only very recently has their field widened.

Darwin's interest in animal behaviour was not followed up immediately by other scientists; in fact it was rather ignored. He had watched wild animals during his *Beagle* voyage, he watched the behaviour of people in Tierra del Fuego, and of dogs at home, but it took many years before such naturalist activities became respectable science. However, during the end of the nineteenth and in the early twentieth centuries a number of biologists in different parts of the world began to be interested in behaviour, people such as Charles Whitman, Jacob von Uexküll, Oskar Heinroth, Lloyd Morgan, William McDougall, Julian Huxley, and others. The names of Anton Portielje and Jan Verwey will come up later, people who described bird behaviour in often ethological terms in Holland in the 1920s. It would take us too far here to discuss their individual contributions, and they have been reviewed elsewhere.[3] The important point is that, despite efforts from several sources in different countries, they did not breed a concerted science focussing on animal behaviour.

The name of Konrad Lorenz will come up repeatedly in this biography. His ideas started off the systematic study of ethology, because he showed, first of all, that one can classify animal behaviour into separate units, into behaviour patterns, just as one does with organs in anatomy. It was Konrad Lorenz who suggested that these patterns evolve like organs. Secondly, he suggested that there are generalities, rules underlying those behaviour patterns which can be applied across species, and one can compare the behaviour of species and study evolution. Together with Tinbergen's, Lorenz's ideas created a 'biology of animal behaviour'.

Lorenz had many other inspirations about behaviour, some of which fell on less fertile ground. Often he expressed himself in a rather laborious, bombastic-German fashion, which did not greatly impress readers, especially anglophones. When Niko Tinbergen and Konrad Lorenz met and became friends, it was Niko who could sift Lorenz' chaff from the corn, and explain this in simple terms. At least as important, of the two it was Niko the naturalist who could bring these ideas to bear on the study of wild insects, birds, and other animals. Konrad was someone who kept animals at home and related to them, while Niko was out in the wilds and showed that one could use the new concepts on animals in the environment in which they had evolved. It was Niko who could make science of Konrad's ideas, and who could design experiments to test them.

Both Konrad and Niko were masterly observers of animals, each in his own way. Between them, these two started the science that attempts to systematically unravel the many different aspects of behaviour of animals, now firmly embedded in many other branches of study. Behind each of these two men, with their radically different histories and personalities, is an extraordinary story. Friends through adversity, they were in opposite camps during the Second World War, one in the German army, the other a hostage. One was flamboyant, noisy, egocentric, and pompous, with an encyclopaedic mind, the other was described as 'pathologically modest' with a narrow interest, but an inspiring communicator. One could not live without a retinue of domestic animals and admiring people around him, the other was the quiet outdoor naturalist.

Later students of the two scientists could reflect that you sat at Lorenz's feet, admiring his incessant flow of words, whereas with Niko you stood up and watched the world, with him firmly behind you, pointing out and encouraging. This biography is the description of the latter, of the brilliant birdwatcher who became a Nobel laureate.

CHAPTER 2

A Dutch upbringing

Home, siblings, friends, and school

Some 40 years before I met Niko wandering across the northern English sands and gulleries, he had been in a setting a long way distant, but not very different. The beaches near Scheveningen in Holland were just as huge, with the North Sea breaking into foam and noise, the dunes as a solid backdrop, sand drifting everywhere and gulls hanging in the updraughts off the dunes. Then in his early teens, Niko walked or cycled there from his nearby home, to watch migrating chaffinches and sparrow hawks following the coastline, and combing the beaches for anything the sea had brought in. The grey-haired man I met in the 1960s, roaming the dunes with his film camera, had not moved far from his roots, despite the geographical shift.

Niko was born in The Hague, the Netherlands (or 'Holland'), on 15 April 1907, and christened Nikolaas. He grew up in that country and was to spend more than half of his life there. Not surprising, therefore, that in his character in adult life Niko was very Dutch, even after living in England for almost 40 years, and speaking English with almost no accent. But that was many years away. Initially, the family into which Niko was born lived in an upstairs flat, but after 1912, when his first memories began to take hold, Niko's life revolved around a larger parental home in that heartland of the Netherlands, The Hague: 146 Bentinck Street.

Seeing the house now, it looks somewhat oppressive and provincial, a terraced house surrounded by a bourgeois, and at the time probably censorious, neighbourhood. Tall, three-storied, built of the brown-red brick that is ubiquitous in Holland, without a front-garden but with a neat pavement, it was one of very many, in several parallel streets. It must have been a highly respectable area, and just from its looks, it could have been a very restrictive place to grow up in. But by all evidence it was not, and all of the Tinbergen children, Niko and his brothers and sister, stated at some time or other that they had a really happy childhood.

In Niko's own words, his parents were 'healthy, happy middle-class city dwellers', and 'we were a truly happy family, our father a liberal-minded, very hard-working man with many intellectual and social interests and a fine, if at times somewhat prudish sense of humour; a man of total honesty; our mother the ever-cheerful, understanding, caring centre of "hearth and home"'.[1]

On the face of it, the Tinbergens were a very average Dutch family, having lived for generation after generation in The Hague and before that in nearby

Bentinck Street, The Hague, in 2000. Number 146 is on the left, with chimneys. Photo HK.

Rotterdam. A family tree goes back to the fifteenth century, when they were known as 'Engbergen' from an estate that still exists near Doetinchem, in the eastern part of Holland. The name changed several times and it came to be what it is now, via Tengbergen, Tingbergen and Timbergen.[2] In that line a Nicolaas Tinbergen was born in 1759 in Rotterdam, and the name Nicolaas returns several times in the family records before our Niko arrived.

Niko's parents were Dirk Cornelis Tinbergen, born in 1874, and Jeanette van Eek, born in 1877, and they were married in 1902. Dirk and Jeanette soon produced a fairly large family: they had six children, of whom five survived. The first was a son, Jan (1903), followed by a daughter Jacomiena (known in the family as Mien, 1905), then another boy who died of convulsions in infancy, then came Niko (1907), another son, Dik (1909), and finally, eight years after Niko, another son Luuk (1915). Apart from the Tinbergen children themselves, there were frequently other children staying for long periods, such as children of friends of the parents who lived in the Dutch East Indies, and for some time they had Belgian refugees from the First World War, and a girl from Austria. This full, restless community provided a very tight and fascinating backdrop to Niko's life, and almost every single member influenced him in one way or other. Despite its ordinary appearance, one can now see that they were no ordinary family, but an almost unparalleled intellectual powerhouse. Niko and his siblings were founding fathers or driving forces in several major sciences, with two Nobel prizes between them (Niko and his brother Jan: two in one family is still a unique record), numbers of honorary doctorates, and medals too numerous to recall. Niko in his youth, he once told me, was always considered the dim one in the family.

In those early years when Niko was growing up, his father was very much the centre of the family: it was a solid, patriarchal set-up. There was nothing particularly enforced about this arrangement: his family considered their father to be something of a superman, and perhaps he was. He was a small, rather portly person, with a moustache, quiet but with natural authority. When I see his achievements, and hear from people who knew him, he was almost too good to be true: well-read in many fields, an experienced writer and artist, working from morning till night but very much the family man, very unselfish but kind and helpful, thorough and careful. Dirk Cornelis was a school teacher of Dutch language, and at the same time a respected scholar of Medieval Dutch. He had a PhD, and was the author of several books, including a widely used Dutch grammar. He edited numerous volumes of Medieval Dutch literature; the one that later especially caught Niko's eye was his annotated volume of 'Reynard the Fox' in Old Dutch. Niko was as pleased as a little boy when in 1963 he wrote, with me as junior author, a popular scientific article on foxes in Dutch, which he could title 'Of the fox Reynard'.[3] Later, when he was retired, Dirk Cornelis had been planning to edit another Medieval Dutch book, Maerlant's 'Der Naturen Bloeme' (Flowers of nature, about 1270), jointly with Niko, but that was not to be. He was acknowledged for his thorough and precise editing work.

Dirk Cornelis had a full-time job in the Gymnasium of The Hague, at the same time doing four evenings per week as head teacher of the Business Evening School, and during the weekends teaching various other classes. People taught by him emphasize what a nice person he was, someone whom they remember seventy years later, and who managed to instil a love of language into many.[4] He was very keen on drawing as a hobby, and he was an admirer of the arts, often visiting museums and himself possessing a large collection of reproductions, especially of medieval paintings. At Christmas he used to arrange private exhibits of medieval Christmas art at home. He was also keen on science, particularly physics, and both he and his wife were fascinated by natural history, especially plants.

Dirk Cornelis wrote long poems in Medieval Dutch; one, for instance, celebrated Niko's appointment as a lecturer in Leiden University in 1940 – great fun to read. His grandchildren still remember his skills in producing rhymes at St Nicolas day, a celebration in Holland on 5 December, when writing personal rhymes is a national pastime. Niko also excelled at it.

Despite his wide professional activities and interests, Dirk Cornelis was very much a family man, who took his wife and children out into the countryside whenever possible. From 1923 they rented a holiday cottage every summer in Hulshorst, in the centre of Holland, where there were woods and moors, and sands and streams. He took the family on long walks through the polders, woods, dunes, and beaches near The Hague, collecting plants in special botanical cases to identify at home, and visiting the large and wild local parks (Scheveningse bosjes, where there were colonies of herons and cormorants, and 'Zorgvliet'). Often he took the children to museums. Heaven knows how he could have found the time to do all these things, with the teaching and writing workload that he took on. But that is how people remember him. Niko described him as 'devoted to his family, a very hard worker and an intellectually stimulating man, full of fine, quiet humour and joie de vivre'.[5]

Perhaps Dirk Cornelis' secret was that, apart from being a very gifted and energetic man, he was also extremely well organized. Everything was planned in advance, and carefully carried out to perfection. Typically, even a walk was mapped out beforehand, and if ever his wife suggested an exploring detour along the way, he demurred because it was not in the arrangements. He lived carefully and deliberately – he planned even the sharpening of a pencil.

His family's achievements at school were a prime interest. The children themselves were aware of and participated in activities he was keen on, and he took time over whatever they were doing. Somehow he made it understood that everybody had a moral duty to work hard. But the children were not nagged, they just wanted to do well 'because of father and mother'. For Niko this came at considerable cost: he hated school, but he put in just enough effort as was needed to scrape through.

There was no doubt that Niko idolized his father, as he showed in later life by emulating him in writing and drawing, and setting his standards by him. Normally in Holland in those days, children addressed their parents with the formal and respectful 'U', like the French 'Vous' and German 'Sie', but in the Tinbergen household the parents were called 'jij' and 'jou' ('tu' or 'du' in French and German). This was quite unusual, and showed a deep friendship rather than disrespect. There was no enforced discipline, but when Niko came home with a bad mark in his school report (not a rare occurrence), 'his asking "was that really necessary?" was enough to make me squirm – for a while', as Niko remembered seventy years later.[6]

When the children were small their father used to read them stories, and he used to read them the Bible. He was not fanatic about religion, but *comme il faut* he was a member of the Dutch Reformed church – he even belonged to the Reformed Brotherhood – and used to go to church until about 1940. All his children went to confirmation classes (although only the eldest two, Jan and Mien, were actually confirmed). Later on he would see all five of them through university, despite his financial constraints.

Niko's mother was the heart of the family, later described as a 'quite formid-able woman',[7] and by Niko himself as 'a warm and impulsive person',[8] the mother who worried at night about her children. She came from a teaching background, as her father taught maths, and she herself had been a school teacher. She still did some private teaching after she was married, to earn a bit extra. She was the more mathematical of the two parents, but also she was clearly fond of literature, and as Niko's sister told me, father Dirk Cornelis often asked for her opinion on matters of style.[9] She read a great deal, and tried to improve her knowledge in languages, speaking German, French, and English as well as Dutch. Clearly, the children of these two intelligent people grew up with a language background from both father and mother, who were two articulate teachers intent on stimulating their offspring into expressing themselves.

Niko at age four, with his sister Jacomien.
Courtesy of the Tinbergen family.

Niko took after his mother more than after his father, being impulsive rather than meticulous. He was also closer to his mother than any of the other children, although, according to his sister Mien, nobody was ever jealous.[10] In his later years he rarely mentioned her (he talked much more often about his father). Perhaps Niko had a special place in his mother's heart, to make up for the baby boy who died before Niko was born. Also, as Niko was not a great scholar in his early years, and with all those clever brothers and sisters around him, he may have had some extra appeal to maternal instincts.

One can imagine the turmoil of that household, with five children and both parents intensively busy, often with other children staying as well, and friends of the children dropping in all the time. When Niko and his friends came back from a weekend birdwatching, tired and dirty, interested people and a large pan of rice would be waiting – and in their old age, the boys still remembered this.[11] The home was simple, without frills or luxury, a bare linoleum floor rather than carpets, with a long table in the back room to seat everyone for meals. But it was a place full of life, love, and interest. Perhaps the only thing that was not tolerated was wasting time: everybody had to be busy, always.

One should view this family in the Holland of that time, a generally bourgeois, protestant society, with a deeply engraved Calvinistic lifestyle of centuries-old standing.[12] Without many exceptions, Dutch people in a town like The Hague conformed, and made sure they were seen to conform: they polished their doorbells and swept the pavement in front of their houses, and the houses had angled mirrors (called spies) at the windows so one could check on what was happening in the street. The work ethic dominated, the pursuit of pleasure was considered somewhat sinful, and thrift and austerity cleared the path to heaven. It would have been difficult, even for the most rebellious youngsters, to escape totally the heavy boot of conformity. But the Tinbergens managed it to some extent, especially Niko.

The family's interest in natural history did not stretch to pets. The Tinbergens never kept dogs, because they would take too much time and also could have been expensive,[13] but at times there was a cat. Niko never felt very comfortable in the presence of dogs, and did not keep any himself in later life. It is quite possible that if he had grown up with one, it would have been more difficult for him to see animals mechanistically as he did in his later science, and it would have been more difficult to sideline animal emotions and feelings.

Each of Niko's siblings was a high flier, some more than others, and their lives were to be enormously different. Jan, the eldest brother, stood out above the others in academic achievements right from a very early age, as first-borns often do. He finished his primary school with a certificate of 'most excellent pupil', and his life was to continue along those lines. He ended up with 20 honorary doctorates, the 1969 Nobel Prize for Economics, the Erasmus Prize, a knighthood in the Order of the Dutch Lion, and the Order of Orange-Nassau, amongst other honours.[14] Not only was it unique for two Nobel Prizes to land in one family, but also, by remarkable coincidence, Jan shared his with another economist called Frisch, whereas Niko shared his with a biologist called von Frisch, as well as with Lorenz.

Jan was clearly highly intelligent, but his achievements were also based on hard work and more work: he would always be the person who toiled without

The Tinbergen family during a walk near Bredero Castle in Holland, about 1923. Left to right: Niko, his mother Jeanette, father Dirk, a young niece, sister Jacomien, and brothers Luuk, Jan, and Dik. Courtesy of the Tinbergen family.

let-up. In later years, even when family came to visit, they would be talking to his wife, with Jan in his study,[15] and no doubt this was also his life as a boy. He was a huge contrast with Niko: he worked hard (Niko was always larking about), achieved excellent reports from school (Niko just scraped through), and was fascinated by indoor science (which bored Niko); and later more striking differences developed. Not surprisingly, the two boys were not particularly close; had they been so, science might have developed differently.

In his late teens, Jan went on to study physics at Leiden University, as a student of the well-known Paul Ehrenfest. Even early in his academic career, and before obtaining his PhD, he had the opportunity for discussions with famous physicists such as Albert Einstein, Heike Kamerlingh Onnes, and Hendrik Lorentz. However, when it came to his PhD, he had already decided that he wanted a direction to his life that would have more implications for people's well-being than he could realize in pure physics, and this was expressed in the title of his thesis: 'Minimum problems of physics and economics'. After that economics became his specialization. Jan's social conscience and his involvement in socialist politics were to colour the rest of his life. He was a moving force in the Dutch socialist party in the 1920s, he designed the economic policy for the Dutch government after the Second World War, he became head of the Central Bureau of Planning in the country, and later he was the author of an influential report on 'International Order' of the Club of Rome. What people remember about Jan even from his early youth is his commitment and enthusiasm, and his total command of the subject he was working on.

On a more personal level, Jan was a conscientious objector to military conscription in the early 1920s, which in those days was a very courageous decision to take in Holland. Instead of military service he had to spend most of his early conscription days in the prison service, later (and much more to his liking, after some string-pulling by his father) in the Central Bureau of Statistics. Because Jan as eldest brother did his bit for the country, his younger brothers were not called up, following Dutch law. Jan married Tine de Wit, also a committed socialist and a well-known instigator of charity committees.

Jan was a quantifier. Everything could be expressed in figures, somehow, in physics or in economics, and it was this strength that led to Jan's role as founding father of the celebrated 'econometrics'. He promoted his highly quantitative approach to science or private business or national economic policies everywhere, and one can only wonder what would have happened if Niko had been of a mind to take on board what his brother preached. But Niko did not; early on in his life he played hockey, watched birds, and combed the beaches, and later he continued this more respectably, but consistent with what he did as a boy.

Theirs was a lifetime of differences, a fundamental split between the two brothers, and after their early youths it did not help that their wives were also not particularly close. The two boys, and later the two couples, were in no way hostile to each other, but they followed their own courses. Only in Jan and Niko's declining years was there a rapprochement between the two brothers, when both came to global problems of conservation, each from his own angle (Chapter 9).

Of the other siblings, Niko's older sister Jacomien ('Mien') and younger brother Dik did not follow prominent academic careers. Mien studied German in Amsterdam and became a teacher (head of languages in a large school), and Dik read engineering in Delft and ended his career as Director of The Hague's Public Energy Industry (he was the author of a handbook for gas-fitters). Dik was a very modest and friendly person, much loved by the rest of the family. As a boy he often felt inferior to his elder brothers, who excelled either at school or at sport. Later Dik said of himself that his only claim to fame was being the only man in the world who had two brothers with Nobel Prizes, but he always felt some inferiority.

For Niko the most relevant and closest was his brother Luuk, eight years younger. When Luuk matured, Niko thought he was the most intelligent of the family, clearly destined for great things. The age difference between the two boys was large, and effectively Niko grew up without Luuk. They only really started to do things together when Niko was already in his twenties. However, because of their later close affinity, and also because of the contrast between the two brothers in their relations with the eldest sibling, Jan, I want to mention Luuk here in some detail.

Luuk had more in common with Niko than any of the other siblings: both were fanatic naturalists. But by the time that Luuk became effective in this passion, when he must have been about 15 years old, Niko had already left home. Remarkably, Luuk became interested in things natural very suddenly, when he was about 10, and by then Niko was off to university though still living at home. Until that time Luuk had been fascinated by cars, nagging his older sister to take him window shopping to car showrooms in The Hague. Then, one day after he had been on a family holiday in Hulshorst, he tore down all the car pictures from the walls of his room, replacing them, to the amusement of his father and Niko, with pictures of birds, and that was it.[16] It set him off on a brilliant, though sadly short, career.

Luuk was very thorough and careful, and especially later he became known amongst his friends and colleagues for his tenacity, worrying away at a problem without let-up. After he started bird-watching, in his early teens, he began with systematic observations on bird migration, and of waterbirds of the canals and dykes around The Hague. Initially this was largely independent of his older brother. He also began to develop his gift for drawing birds, for summarizing their characteristic features with a few strokes of the pencil, and he was only 19 when he published his first, beautifully illustrated, small book on how to identify waterbirds.[17]

Bird migration became a focal interest for Luuk, and later, when still in his early twenties, he became director of the Dutch Bird Migration Station. But before that he and Niko started a series of research projects on the food of owls and raptors in their family holiday area, Hulshorst. I will discuss this work in

Niko (left) and Luuk on De Beer, 1929. Photo F. P. J. Kooymans.

more detail in Chapter 3; Niko moved on to quite different pastures, whilst Luuk developed the simple project on diet composition into a much more interesting question. Eventually this became his PhD subject and the field of his main claim to fame: the effect of predators on their prey populations.

Luuk's PhD project focussed on the relationship between sparrow hawks and their prey, and at that time he took some advice that was exactly in line with the future course of ecology. He developed intricate statistical analyses for his observations, something that we now take for granted in almost every research project, but which, at the time, was an innovation. His mentor and advisor in this was his brother Jan, 12 years his senior, and ever the enthusiastic advocate of quantification. There was to remain a regular contact between Jan and his youngest brother for the rest of Luuk's life. Luuk became one of the most numerate ecologists at the time, having an enormous effect on colleagues and students. By the age of 36 he was professor in the university of Groningen, setting the pace in ecology internationally. But always he was full of self-criticism, and more and more plagued by self-doubt. Like his brother Niko in his later life, Luuk suffered deep, horribly black depressions. At the age of 39 he took his own life.

The ecologist Jan Verwey, who taught both brothers at Leiden University in the 1920s and 1930s, made an interesting comparison between them.

> *One could say that both Niko and Luuk started with an interest in ecology, and whilst Niko very soon specialized in behaviour studies, Luuk stuck to the road they had taken together and became an ecologist. This despite the fact that Luuk had shown to be able to do excellent work in behaviour, and Niko similarly good ecological research. I felt that it was the very different nature of the two brothers that decided this, a nature that manifested itself so strikingly in Luuk's tenacity and carefulness, and in Niko's spirit of adventure.*[18]

During Luuk's lifetime and afterwards, Niko was in awe of him. I don't think there was any jealousy, though there may have been some elements of competition in the 1930s. Luuk realized the need for quantification in ecology, prompted by Jan, and this same need would arise later on in Niko's field, ethology, but be unanswered by Niko. Looking back, it seems all the more regrettable that Niko did not use his brother Jan as Luuk did: Niko's own research, and ethology in general, would have benefited. This was not to be, probably due to the difference in character between the two eldest brothers from their earliest childhood.

It seems unlikely from these relationships, as we see them now, that Niko's development as a naturalist was in any way instigated by his family. This is in contrast to Luuk's, who followed in the footsteps of a sibling. Niko mapped out his own course, encouraged by his parents but not guided. This course started at a very early age: for instance, even as a five- or six-year-old, Niko already had a couple of fish tanks, which he was allowed to keep in the garden of the new house. With his small hand-net and a jar, the little Niko caught his first sticklebacks in the polders nearby, along with robber beetles and newts, and brought them back home.

Niko's life was about roaming around, watching little creatures, walking and messing about with nature, often ineffectively trying to identify birds and nagging teachers with his finds from the beach, and throwing himself into sports. He brought in oiled birds from the beach, to clean them with petrol. At home he talked endlessly about his exploits. Escaping school strictures may have been an important part of his frantic motivation, and his sister remembered Niko for his

restlessness when he was little, worrying his parents. He was a tease to his sister Mien and younger brother Dik, who both were livid with him at times. There was a brief period of piano lessons from an aunt, which was an absolute disaster, as Niko hated it.

An interviewer who talked to Niko in his retirement, remarked:

> *Had Tinbergen been born in 1968 instead of 1907, the course of ethology might have been very different. Young Niko could never remain still for long. Although his mother resorted to tying her toddler into his highchair, the result was always the same: Niko wound up hanging by his heels. His understanding kindergarten teacher allowed him to leap to his desk top every 20 minutes, do a little dance and sing a song. As a child today, he might be diagnosed as hyperactive and doped with Ritalin. The new science of ethology might have lost one of its brilliant pioneers.*[19]

Not surprisingly for such an active character, life was full of accidents. On the way to school he once shot under a lorry with his bicycle, but landed between the wheels and escaped unharmed. On another occasion he was attacked by a man who was after his briefcase; in the scuffle Niko managed to pull the valve from the man's bicycle tyre and police caught him. At home he once came headfirst down the steep stairs, which gave him a serious concussion. The doctor said that in later years this might possibly cause a blood clot – significantly perhaps, he was to die of a stroke. Despite all these and other accidents, however, little Niko was no hero, and more than once he nearly fainted at the sight of blood.

The secondary school that Niko went to, from 1920 to 1925, was a government grammar school in The Hague, the '2nd HBS' (Higher Burgher School) in the Stadhouderslaan. It was a day school; boarding schools are a rarity in Holland, and there are very few private schools. In any case, a private school would have been financially out of the question for the Tinbergen family. From the moment of his starting school, the range of his escapes from everyday drudgery increased. Having a bicycle helped enormously, and getting to know other boys with a similar outlook on life did the rest. Nor was Niko much obstructed in his quest to be out; his parents allowed him a lot of freedom. He had to be home in time for dinner and keep school ticking over, but they did not hassle him, hoping that he would get onto the straight and level at some stage.

Starting during these secondary school days, some of Niko's energy was channelled into sports. He loved hockey, and played until well into his student years; he was so good at it then that he briefly played in the Dutch national team (in a draw against Germany). He once even considered taking up sport as a career. Hockey suited him, it is fast, tough, and exhilarating; and ever the ethologist, he once told me that what he especially liked about it was fooling the other players with feints. It was a sport that allowed him some fast manipulation of human behaviour. At a later age he was an admirer of the Dutch footballer Johan Cruyff, similarly a master of the feint.

Another sport that infatuated him at school was pole-vaulting, and during a training session he once exceeded the national record. He was mad about ice skating, which was a Dutch national passion. Centuries earlier old Dutch painters like Avercamp had captured the mood of the whole community out on the ice, on their typical Dutch, long curved-up skates, and the importance of ice skating had not changed much in Niko's days. When conditions were good, skating could (and still can) take over the entire country; schools closed, and one made long trips with friends on the canals and lakes, visiting other towns along the way, or watching birds, or whatever. The speed and excitement, the swishing noise of skates over ice, the beautiful winter landscapes – nothing could be more wonderful in those low countries.

The infatuation with skating was something that never left Niko for as long as he lived, and throughout his career in Holland he would play truant from almost any commitment when there was skating to be had. Seeing him whizzing across Blenheim Lake near Oxford, even when well into his fifties, one saw him as happy as he could possibly be.

Another life-long interest that started at school was drawing, in which Niko showed his interest in birds as much as he was allowed to. His school sketch book from 1921, when Niko was 14 years old, has many a very able portrait of thrush, robin, wren, nuthatch, and others, amidst various objects he had obviously been told to draw.

Messing about with nature was to some extent encouraged when he was at school by people like his biology teacher, who must have had a wonderful influence over Niko. As Niko later wrote:

Sketch of nuthatches, made by Niko at school, 1921.

> *I owe a great deal to my biology master Dr. A. Schierbeek, who accepted my*
> *lukewarm interest in morphology and taxonomy and encouraged me in 'my'*
> *studies of wildlife in its natural surroundings … encouraged every interest in*
> *natural history that I showed and taught me much about how to keep aquaria,*
> *how to collect seashells and other tideline treasures, how to keep records of my*
> *observation, and so on.*[20]

However, school reports specifically chastised him for lack of diligence during
natural history lessons.

In the first decades of the twentieth century, teachers in Holland had begun
to take pupils out of school to see nature, in response mostly to the writings of
two teachers and naturalists, E. Heimans and J. P. Thijsse. Heimans started it
(but died very young, in 1915), and Thijsse especially was to have an enormous
effect,[21] not just in schools. His beautifully illustrated 'Verkade albums' came
out annually, cleverly distributed by the largest Dutch biscuit manufacturer
(pictures to be glued in, and available in packets of biscuits), and they were
hugely popular with titles such as 'Toadstools', 'Woods and moorland', 'My
aquarium', 'Coloured pastures', 'Spring', 'Summer', 'Flowers in our garden',
'Texel' (a Friesian island), and many others. Niko read and collected almost all

of them. Thijsse also wrote many other naturalist books, often jointly with Heimans, that later appeared to have had a large and lasting impact on Niko. Several times Niko, as a schoolboy and later as a biology student, went to see Thijsse, and they became mutual admirers.

Thijsse died after the 'hunger winter' in Holland, in the last year of the Second World War. In an appreciation in 1949 Niko wrote (trans.):

> *The present generation of biologists consists of people, all of whom, with very few exceptions, have been brought up with the books of Heimans and Thijsse and with* De Levende Natuur *[Thijsse's Dutch naturalist monthly, see below]. … I believe that the influence of Heimans and Thijsse was very large. Yet they did not train researchers, they did not educate scientists, that was not their aim. I think that the root of the spirit of biologists is their interest in all that lives, an intensive, honest and selfless interest that makes people observe for the sake of the enjoyment of observation itself. Only those with such an interest can be biologists, for one who does not have it will never want to dedicate his life to the study of living organisms, however sharp, critical or learned he may be. … Present-day biologists may be modelled by scientific teachers, but the sparks of the inner 'holy fire' were set off by Heimans and Thijsse, they kindled the first glow of fire and blew on it.*[22]

Not only was Niko's fascination by things natural encouraged and inspired by Thijsse, but several of his later behaviour research projects were based on ideas from Thijsse, even his PhD project on bee-hunting digger wasps.

> *Thijsse's* Intimate life of birds *and articles about digger wasps in* Living Nature *gave me an enormous push in my growing interest in studying the behaviour of animals in the field. Remarkably, with hindsight it was not the scientific content of those articles that fascinated and stimulated me, but more the tone, the atmosphere and the mood that somehow resonated and strongly stimulated my slumbering urge to relate to living nature.*[23]

At that time, however, in the early 1920s, Niko's scientific interest was still some way off; he was a fanatic teenage naturalist, and not yet much more. But things were moving fast, encouraged by Schierbeek, by the interest of his parents, by the books of Heimans and Thijsse, by the annual holidays with his parents in the Hulshorst area – one of Holland's natural jewels – and by new company that he found amongst young people of his own age. His and their interest found in Holland a wonderful display of biodiversity, a fantastic richness of flora and fauna and beautiful landscapes, much of which has now disappeared.

Youth organized for nature

Holland is a small country, about one-sixth the size of Britain, proverbially flat but at the same time very varied in its landscapes, and with very rich soils. Some of the 'typical' Dutch country is low-lying grassland or arable on clay, with numerous drainage dykes permanently full of water, as well as lakes. It is the landscape of calendar pictures with windmills, the countryside that we knew with its high diversity of pond life with masses of fish and invertebrates, as well as many water- and marshbirds and other animals. The Dutch coasts have many tidal sand- or mudflats with extensive dunes, all very rich in plants and animals. But about half of the country is sandy, with woodlands, small brooks and broad rivers, large heather moorlands, and some shifting sands. The Tinbergens' holiday retreat in Hulshorst was in that wooded, sandy part of Holland.

Lapwings, avocets, spoonbills: in Niko's days the country had an unusually rich bird life breeding even close to towns and villages, augmented by massive numbers of migrants large and small, with flocks of millions of waders. There were dozens of species of fish, frogs, and newts in the dykes, and marvellous plants, such as 38 species of orchid. It was a paradise for any naturalist, and some of that richness is still there. But much of it has fallen under the scythe of progress after a tremendous population increase, and the country is now inhabited by an average of 370 people per square kilometre. It now has the highest population density and road density in Europe, with all the trimmings of intensive agriculture and industry, and booming with prosperity. The country was developed entirely at the expense of the environment.

Stimulated by the writings of Heimans and Thijsse in the early decades of the twentieth century, there was a major upsurge of concern with nature in Holland. Many people developed an interest as general naturalists, enthralled by the rich Dutch countryside that contrasted with their urban existence. Such a general interest in all animals and plants is still there. I see a clear contrast with, for example, Britain, where many more people with a biological interest tend to be more specialized: they are ornithologists, or botanists, or entomologists, to the exclusion of interests in other aspects of nature. Niko in his later years was mostly a bird man, but with this Dutch background he was also keenly interested in and knowledgeable about plants, insects, and mammals.

Around the 1920s quite a few Dutch boys and girls became infected with a passion for nature, and in many schools, including Niko's, they started nature clubs, encouraged by teachers. The one in Niko's school was called 'E. Heimans', and Niko soon became involved in it, as the beginning of a phase in his life that was of great significance for his later development. This phase was his time in the Dutch youth movement.

Just at the time that Niko began secondary school, the natural history school clubs throughout Holland formed the Dutch Youth League for Nature Study, the *Nederlandse Jeugdbond voor Natuurstudie* or *NJN*. The society soon attracted other youngsters as well, and it took on a life of its own that became highly

influential, and which still continues to the present day. There has been remarkably little change in the organization, though perhaps some of the original
vigour has now gone.

The NJN was never very large, with usually around one or two thousand
members nationally in Holland. But its effects are quite out of proportion, and
not just for the few in its ranks. For its young members it became almost like a
religion, and this was as true for Niko and his friends as it was later for me and
thousands of others. Because of what it meant for him, it is worth describing the
NJN in some detail, and there is a considerable body of literature about its
history and significance.[24]

Later in the 1960s Niko often talked to me about his NJN years. Curiously,
though, he does not even mention it in his autobiographical 'Watching and
wondering' (1985). There is no doubt about the huge impact the organization
had on him; the reason he did not discuss it more publicly could be that he
simply forgot, but it is more likely that the NJN was such an intense personal
and emotional experience, so difficult to explain to outsiders (especially non-
Dutch) that he just avoided it. Similarly, he only once mentions his wife Lies in
his autobiography, just recording the fact that he married her, although she was
very influential in everything he did.

To those involved, to Niko, to me, and to the many others who went
through its ranks, the NJN had the force of freemasonry. It took over one's life
for several years just during the period when school should be of prime concern,
often to the dismay of parents because it happened under their very eyes. Seeing
the NJN world through young teenage Niko's eyes, it was wonderful, he lived
for it. He was outside with interesting people of his own age, he watched and
stalked and admired birds and beasts, he taught others what he knew and he was
taught by them, he even did research! They made inventories of animals and
plants in natural places, lists of bird migrants, records of when and where birds
were nesting, finds of rare animals in the tide-line on the beach, whilst friends
were looking at butterflies and beetles, and they were finding out which plants
grew together and where. The young NJN members were studying anything
natural that caught their eye, they had a scientific purpose, and they were
appreciated by their friends for doing it well; they were 'experts'.

As NJN-ers we felt a strong sense of belonging, and were different from the
rest of the world, with a fanatical enthusiasm. A different lifestyle took over; we
got dirty (which was admirable), wore different clothes, thick socks and sandals
when this was not done by anyone else, and we felt mocked by the rest of
humanity. NJN-ers relaxed with their own repertoire of folk songs and country
dances, and there was a large, exclusive vocabulary. The atmosphere was egalitarian and democratic, a spartan existence was de rigueur, luxury was out,
alcohol was out, nicotine was allowed only in pipes. Boys and girls mixed freely
(highly unusual, even as late as the 1950s), but anything sexual was frowned
upon. We were very chaste, and established couples were not expected to even
hold hands in company (nevertheless many people found their future spouses in

the NJN, including Niko). This was, of course, the only way to have a mixed, unsupervised society of teenagers, with camps and other outdoor pursuits. We all expected to work hard on our nature study, or at least we walked or bicycled hard; loafing around was out.

NJN-ers were, and are, between 12 and 23 years old; when they reach the age limit, they become 'old socks', and they leave, even fifty years later thinking back on those years with great nostalgia. Adults are not involved in any way, and NJN-ers have a fierce contempt for organizations such as the Scout Association. The youngsters themselves run a highly organized league, with branches throughout the country, a national executive, and local committees. There are branch field excursions every weekend (usually on bicycles or walking), national camps during the holidays, and a four-day national conference after Christmas. There is a publishing bureau, producing a magazine (*Amoeba*), a calendar, and small books (mostly keys for various groups of animals). People learned not only their plants and animals, but also how to organize, debate, and run their own lives as well as those of others.

It has always been a moot point, heatedly discussed, whether nature study or socializing with like-minded people is the main driving force for NJN members, but there seems to be room for both persuasions. The organization has been somewhat ashamedly elitist, a breeding ground for biologists and teachers (more than half of its members continued their nature pursuits as academics or in the classroom), and numerous well-known names in ethology and ecology in Holland, people who rose to great heights in the conservation organizations (as well as several prominent politicians and others), all made a start in the NJN. NJN-ers who will recur in this book are Luuk Tinbergen, Gerard Baerends and his wife Jos, Adriaan Kortlandt, Jan van Iersel, Piet Sevenster, Leen de Ruiter, and many of Niko's students. Lies Rutten, later Niko's wife, found a place in

NJN history because, in a camp on the Friesian islands, another NJN-er (Niko's friend Kees Ittman, a medical student) diagnosed her with acute appendicitis. She was transported to hospital on the mainland where she had an operation.

Within the NJN, and independent of the various branches, there were 'working groups'; one, for example, specialized in plant sociology, while others focussed on freshwater biology, marine life, insects, and birds. Niko, of course, was a lynch-pin in the bird group, which consisted of mostly hard men braving wind and weather, full of bird secrets, and by its nature rather cliquish, as it has always been throughout NJN history. Niko, however, was more inclined than most other birders to be outgoing, and even as a teenager he often lectured to non-NJN young people.

Local NJN groups went on excursions every Sunday, and Niko joined in. There were also the 10-day summer camps on the Friesian islands (Texel) or in the wild, boggy areas and woods near the German border, in Denekamp. It was these occasions that resulted in serious friendships with boys of similar age and interest, with people like Gerard van Beusekom, Martien Rutten, Frans Makkink, Kees Sipkes, and Kees and George Ittman, mostly other bird fanatics. Niko was intensely involved with the central organization of the NJN, for two years as 'leader' of District 5 (which included the branches The Hague, Leiden, Delft, Gouda, and Rotterdam), and he attracted others to the NJN in his public lectures (with 'lantern-slides'). One of the people who became hooked by Niko's lectures at that age was the later grand-master of ethology in Holland, Gerard Baerends. The 1920s was a very exciting time in the NJN, in a country that was doing well and had been far less affected by the First World War than its neighbours.

Niko never saw the NJN as a serious scientific organization, despite his activities within it. As a 19-year-old in 1926, he wrote in the NJN magazine *Amoeba* that 'The one and only thing that matters for us, is to open the eyes of young people that are still closed to the world, for problems of general human concern, and in that way to broaden their vision' (trans.).[25] In his own, often somewhat clumsy, teenage fashion Niko's aim was to bring young people into the field, in the long run to get their support for wildlife conservation. It was a 'Look, how wonderful' exhortation, with Niko very much aware that birds were declining in Holland and persuading people to argue on nature's behalf. But he also showed some very youthful, pure missionary zeal (trans.): 'With careful observation of the intimate life of the birds, you recognize yourself in all their expressions, and that is the value of birding. However strange it may sound, everyone best recognizes his own faults when he sees them made by someone else. End of sermon'.[26] He calls on others to join in the excursions, he nags and rebukes: 'I have to express my surprise, and really also some irritation, that so few people joined our excursion of 4 January [to the beach]'.[27]

His early writing aimed to convey the interest and beauty of his subject. Several of his articles have nice, simple drawings of birds, beautifully clear and immediately attractive. The acquisition of a camera sometime during his teens was a major milestone in his life, and photography, especially of birds, became an instant passion, fitting in well with his aims of furthering nature-appeal.

Niko's early photographic exploits are remarkable, especially now we have such sophisticated equipment ourselves. His first camera was big and heavy, with a bellows, and large, fragile 16 × 21 cm glass plates that had to be inserted and removed individually. All development and printing had to be done by him, in the darkroom in the cellar at home. When Niko was in full swing, the camera was installed under a wicker fish basket near a nest or a dead porpoise on the beach or whatever, and the shutter operated from 30 m away with a string, Niko hiding flat on the ground or in some cover. Later the wicker basket became larger and supported on turf, so he could sit under it himself with his camera. But whatever he did, the problem was that after every exposure a new plate had to inserted, with major upheaval, birds disturbed, and exposure corrected – all a far cry from our present-day automatic transport, focus, and exposure.

He regularly submitted photographs to be published in the widely renowned NJN nature calendar. Once, in 1926, Thijsse remarked in a review of the calendar that surely now we had seen enough portraits of birds sitting on nests, and it would be nice to get some more interesting stuff. Niko took this remark to heart with a vengeance, and he would repeat it to me almost 40 years later. In response to Thijsse he wrote an article called 'The task of bird photography', in which he admitted that with all the pictures of nests and birds on nests 'we, arriving photographers … are getting to the end of our subject … However there are other chapters in the life of birds outside their life during the breeding period, and now it is the turn of those chapters. … One is the migration of birds in spring and autumn, another is foraging, so very different in summer and winter.'[28] The article shows the 19-year-old proselytizing, as he so often did in those days. He did not yet think of the displays and other behaviour of birds near nests, subjects that would consume his interest later.

Niko had already made a start with writing for the NJN magazine *Amoeba* several years before his piece about the purpose of the NJN. Almost immediately after its birth *Amoeba* had become a quite respectable natural history outlet, although it also carried articles about the NJN itself, and announcements. Niko's publishing debut was a half page entitled 'Live Venus shell',[29] in *Amoeba*, Volume 3, 1923, when he was 16 years old. The little paper recorded his find of a live specimen of *Venus gallina* on the beach, its successful transfer to the school aquarium and its habit of leaving deep furrows when moving through the sand. In the same issue of *Amoeba* he wrote 'Dangerous buds of horse-chestnut',[30] about great tits getting stuck on the sticky buds of the tree, and escaping with the loss of several tail feathers. Not yet ethology, but a first published sign of interest in animal behaviour.

Soon after this *entrée* more contributions by Niko appeared in *Amoeba*, mostly about birds. In 1924 he wrote two detailed articles about bird migration along the coast near The Hague. One is about bird movements mostly at night,[31] in which he describes oystercatchers, redshanks, curlews, terns, wheatears, geese, thrushes, swifts, and many others during August and September. It comes with an honest warning that many observations were made in the dark and based on birds' calls, so there may be the odd mistake. Another paper from Niko's hand at that time contains a list of beach findings during an NJN meeting near The Hague, of various molluscs and birds in the tide-line.[32]

No doubt he considered these pieces as a fairly serious contribution to natural history in Holland, aimed at his naturalist peers – but he also went popular. As early as 1924 he had written a couple of articles in one of the more serious Dutch broadsheets, *Het Vaderland*, about seabirds along the beaches, and about squirrels in the woods in the dunes.[33] He was always convinced of the need and the moral requirement of writing for the general public – in this case it had the added attraction of providing much needed cash, which he used to buy his first camera.

By the age of 16 Niko had produced his first publications, and he had made a go of photography. It was all very small beer, of course, but at least he now knew he could do it. He knew that, with the wind around his ears in the middle of nowhere, he could produce something worthwhile that was appreciated by other naturalists, and even by his teacher Schierbeek. He loved that kind of activity, as he loved hockey and skating, and he was rather suspicious of academia, the habitat of his older brother. In 1925, at the end of his school years (where he had done only moderately well except in sport, where he excelled) Niko could not see biology as a career. He knew it as a subject dominated by morphology and lists of names, and he was never very good at it in the class room. He had a flair for languages, an excellent command of Dutch and school had given him a good working knowledge of German, French, and English. But he disliked any of these subjects in the disciplined, formalized context of school. Not surprisingly, he was full of doubts about what to do later in his life.

A trip abroad

Niko's parents wanted him to continue at university, as they wanted all their children to do. Niko vaguely thought about emigrating to Canada into forestry or agriculture (away, away!),[34] or of becoming a professional photographer, or of doing something in sport. The Tinbergens used to see Jan's professor in Leiden, Paul Ehrenfest, and they were also friendly with Abraham Schierbeek, the teacher, and these two men became involved in the discussions about Niko's future. As a result, Niko was persuaded to spend a few months in the nearest thing to a biological field station that existed at the time, and Ehrenfest wrote to the director of the world's first bird migration institute, Professor Johannes Thienemann of the 'Vogelwarte Rossitten' in Germany.

Later, Niko himself would say that it was these few months that sent him on towards academia and towards ethology,[35] but after reading what he wrote at the time, I think that this was a slight embellishment of the decision-making process. In the many letters home from Rossitten,[36] and in articles he wrote about his stay, there is hardly any mention of science: he wrote mostly about photography, the landscape, and some spectacular adventures with elks and the locals. He did not get on particularly well with Professor Thienemann; in fact he was rather critical, as he had to hand over some of his best photographs, and Thienemann was often away. Consequently Niko saw little of him and did not learn much about science. On the other hand, he took in many ideas about photography from Thienemann's assistant and photographer Rudi Steinert.

Rossitten was located in the Kurische Nehrung, a dune peninsula 90 km long separating a large freshwater lake from the Baltic Sea, in what was then East Prussia. It is now known as Kaliningrad, and part of Russia. Millions of birds migrating to and from a large part of northern Europe funnel along the coast there, hence the bird station. Niko stayed for two months from the end of August 1925, and the 18-year-old obviously had a tremendous time there, his first real trip away from home. His letters, affectionate, often very home-sick yet quite detached, are full of a boy's adventures abroad, with a great deal about money. He justified every expense to his parents. The letters showed him mostly busy with his camera, and very proud of getting some good shots of bull elk.

The Vogelwarte Rossitten is where bird-ringing started as a scientific method. Niko learned it there, too, and later he would often use leg-rings on his herring gulls. The trip resulted in his first two papers for Thijsse's monthly magazine *De Levende Natuur*,[37] the first of a very large number, produced almost until the end of his life. In these first pieces he described his exciting trip and the wonderful area of the Kurische Nehrung, people with different habits, and ploughs being pulled by six horses. The landscape with the spectacular moving

Elk in the Kurische Nehrung, 1925. Photo Niko Tinbergen.

dunes was especially interesting to him: throughout his life Niko would be fascinated by the structure of dunes, in many parts of the world. He described his narrow escape from an attacking bull elk, and the training of goshawks and peregrines for falconry sport at the bird station. He was taken especially by the custom of 'crow biting': the locals used to catch masses of migrating hooded crows in nets (to pickle them for food), and killed them by biting their heads.

The nicest Kurische Nehrung observations that Niko wrote about were on the migration of nightjars, in an article for *Amoeba*.[38] The dunes were full of them in the daytime, and in the evening they started moving, very gradually, in small groups and quite high. They did a lot of insect hunting: one heard bill-snapping, sometimes the birds circled a large moth before grabbing it. People tried to catch them by throwing small nets in the air to entangle the birds, but the nightjars just circled and followed the nets all the way down, clearly attracted. The explanation from not-yet-quite the expert: 'they cannot control their nerves' before discovering that this is not food!

Apart from this, Niko sent a list of birds to his teacher Schierbeek, and that was as much natural history as he did there. Rossitten had been a great experience, but I doubt that it was as decisive as Niko later claimed, and there is nothing in the correspondence between Niko and his parents to suggest this. His mind must have been made up earlier, and immediately after his return to Holland, early November 1925, he began his study in Leiden, several months late, but no matter. The university had caught up with Niko.

CHAPTER 3

Student years and Greenland

Playing truant

Leiden was only some 15 km from The Hague, a short trip by train, and Niko studied from home. He did not have to leave his stamping grounds and his friends, and for him the change from school to university was not the upheaval that it was for most other students. But what he found himself studying was something different, and totally new territory.

Students arriving at a university in Holland in the 1920s did not have the option of studying zoology or botany: the subject was biology, a five-year course. In Leiden, after two years of lectures and practicals in taxonomy, morphology, and physiology of animals and plants (with some additional geology, palaeontology, physics, and chemistry) one sat the 'candidate' exams, and then as a 'candidate' one spent another year on practicals in various subjects, and then, in the fourth year, one had to specialize in a main subject (one-year course), and two subsidiaries (half a year each). After these five years the student proudly finished with the 'doctoraal' exam (not a PhD, but something more like a masters degree) and acquired the degree of 'doctorandus' or 'doctoranda'. Then, if the mood took you, you could begin a PhD study.

All subjects in this course were very dependent on the interests of the teaching staff, and at the time of Niko's arrival in the Leiden of 1925, staff, resources, departmental obligations, and plans were all in a state of flux. Niko's interest, of course, was in zoology, and there the turmoil was greatest. The reasons were that the Zoology Department had just been given the additional responsibility for teaching morphology and anatomy to the medical students, which was a huge workload given that annually there were about one hundred medics arriving (compared to nine biologists in Niko's year). Added to this, the new science of animal physiology came into the curriculum in 1926 under Prof. H. Boschma, and the head of department, the comparative anatomist P. N. van Kampen, was seriously ill and was replaced by Boschma in 1931. C. J. van der Klaauw did most of the teaching during those years, finally succeeding Boschma as head of department in 1934. In general, the old comparative morphology dominated zoology in Leiden. Physiology was just beginning, but fieldwork in subjects such as ecology or ethology was still a long, long way off.

Niko arrived in this chaotic world of, for him, very new, difficult, and often unattractive subjects, several months after term had started, and still somewhat shell-shocked after his exciting time in the Kurische Nehrung. Later he wrote 'I started my studies in Leiden at the tail end of the most narrow-minded, purely

"homology-hunting" phase of comparative anatomy, taught by old professors'.[1]
For him, biology within university consisted of lists of facts and dry comparisons, contemplated in endless lectures in stuffy rooms; but outside, his biology
involved stalking birds and bright flowers, along beaches under drifting skies. At
the time people must have wondered if he was going to persist with it: Niko was
a wanderer, an outdoors man, charming, but he could also be quite stroppy, and
critical of the establishment. Clearly, the potential for disaster was there.
However, what saw him through this uneasy time was high intelligence and a
good head for learning, his sense of duty to his parents, and the knowledge that
he had to bite through the skin of the apple in order to get at the contents. He
stuck to the rigid menu of the course by spending a minimum amount of time
on it, just making sure that he would pass, while all the time doing exciting
extra-curricular field projects in order to keep sane, and keeping up with the
NJN and his hockey, training in the Dutch national hockey team. Not surprisingly, the undergraduate study itself had very little impact on him, but his
activities away from the university all the more.

A telling Niko article in *De Levende Natuur*,[2] dating from about mid-way
through his undergraduate study, begins (trans.): '25 April 1928. Glorious sunshine and a gentle east wind. My good intentions of working the whole day in
Leiden do not take well to this kind of weather. I therefore decide to take a few
photographs before going to Leiden, as they have been planned for a long time
but never had their turn.' Later it continues '... the pictures only take a quarter

Hockey training: Niko (front right) as a student, 1926–27. Courtesy of the Tinbergen family.

of an hour. What next? At this time of year it is always difficult to attend lectures regularly, and this beautiful weather is usually too strong for me, as it is today. The nightingales soothe my conscience and my bike wants to go to the beach at all cost.' Then follows an account of sandwich terns against blue skies and hazy horizons, and a report of the stranding of a very rare squid.

The man who really shoe-horned Niko into academia was the latest addition to the staff of the Leiden Zoology Department, Jan Verwey. The student arrangements were rather informal, as there were only nine students on the course. Jan Verwey was appointed by the Head of Department Van Kampen to look after the interests of Niko the late arrival, so he could catch up. They clicked; within a very short time into his first year Niko caught Verwey's attention by giving an excellent, illustrated lecture on his trip to Kurische Nehrung. This was the beginning of a life-long friendship.

Jan Verwey was to become one of the patriarchs of Dutch zoology, and thirty years after Niko I was also taught by him, a wonderful, enthusiastic, and exuberant ecologist with a very warm heart. By then he had become a marine biologist, but the love of his life was birds. He played many different roles in Niko's career. Initially Verwey was there only during Niko's first two years (he moved to a job in the Dutch East Indies in 1927), but later their paths were to cross again and again. Verwey was eight years older than Niko, and much more thorough, careful, and exacting. But like Niko, and despite his earlier PhD in parasitology, and subsequent involvement with the then very new field of animal physiology at Leiden, Verwey was very much a field man.[3]

At the time when Niko turned up in Leiden, Jan Verwey was studying a colony of herons close to his house, a piece of research that became the first substantial Dutch research on bird behaviour, published briefly in 1926, and as a large monograph in 1930.[4] He did not continue in this field (concentrating on marine ecology, and watching birds as a hobby), but in those early days of the late 1920s Verwey demonstrated to Niko that bird social behaviour, not just migration or feeding ecology, was a wonderful subject. The spectacular displays of herons on their nests were just asking for explanations, and for the young undergraduate this was a stunning revelation. Jan Verwey thought in terms that later would be common currency amongst ethologists, for instance of ritualized movements, and of behaviour out-of-context. The later, purely ethological analyses were clearly just around the corner.

In their spare time the two went birdwatching along the beach and in the dunes, Niko learning fast from Jan. Seeing himself as quite an athlete, Niko was very annoyed on one occasion when, after they had stripped for a swim, Jan challenged him to a run and completely outran him. It was not just heavy science on the beach; they also had a wonderfully unfettered free life, light-years from the (in their eyes) stuffy science of the laboratories.

Then Gerard Tijmstra, 'Lange Tijm' ('Tall Tim') as the boys called him, came onto the scene, meeting Niko also somewhere around 1925. Tijmstra was an amateur naturalist, one of these larger-than-life figures, with an immense

Niko during fieldwork on the beach, 1930. Photo J. P. Strijbos.

charisma, about 38 years old. He had a career behind him as a captain in the Dutch East-Indian army, then assistant-governor of the (few and minute) Dutch Windward Islands in the Caribbean, during which he fell out with the Dutch government over colonial policy and became a taxi-driver in Detroit. After a few years of that he became a maths teacher (later director) in The Hague.[5] Birds were his main hobby, and he was a critical and conscientious observer.

Around 1925 a group of young bird enthusiasts gathered around Gerard Tijmstra in The Hague, people like Niko and Luuk, Gerard van Beusekom, Frans Kooijmans, and a dozen others, calling themselves the 'Hague Club of Bird-migration Observers' (Club van Haagse Trekwaarnemers). They had monthly meetings at Tijmstra's house, and occasional excursions (he, as well as the boys, playing truant from school); one of the things that people remember from those days is that Tijmstra somehow imbued all of them with the need for total reliability and honesty with their observations. Niko became a personal friend, and later described Lange Tijm as 'a truly great teacher' and 'a man of great calibre.'[6]

The days and weeks spent with Gerard Tijmstra and 'the Club' in the late 1920s had two immediate consequences for Niko. Firstly, Tijmstra had a very soft spot for gulls: Niko caught the bug from him, a very productive infection that lasted the rest of his life. Secondly, the boys of the club started working on 'De Beer', a large nearby nature reserve and that work resulted in Niko's first book (jointly with several others). We will take the gull story first.

Herring gulls, now ubiquitous anywhere near our shores, originated in North America, and they had only just started their great increase in Europe in the

1920s, after they caught on to the use of man-related resources. In the dunes of Meijendel, very close to The Hague, a few pairs started breeding at that time, and Gerard Tijmstra, who had published a key for the identification of gulls in 1925, counted and watched the new arrivals intensively, especially their mating behaviour. However, around 1927–28 he decided that he just could not keep this up together with his other work, and he suggested that Niko take over.[7] Clearly he could not have asked for a better successor: the Meijendel observations were the start of a massive volume of studies in gull behaviour by Niko and his later students, and many of the most important ideas in ethology started in hides in colonies of gulls. In his first report on the Meijendel gulls (1932) Niko acknowledges that 'Tijmstra's work helped me into the saddle'.[8] And ride he did.

But Gerard Tijmstra and Niko Tinbergen were not the only soldiers on the gull front. Another, and at the time very well-known Dutchman, had in a way beaten them to it: this was the zoo man A. F. J. (Frits) Portielje. In 1928 Portielje published a long paper in German on 'The ethology and psychology of the herring gull'.[9] This was mostly about wing-clipped herring gulls breeding in the Amsterdam zoo, but it also contained some observations on free-living gulls, on their worm-catching behaviour, and their opening of mussels by dropping them from the air. Portielje's paper was concerned with captive birds, courtship behaviour and pair formation, copulation, nesting, intention movements, calls, ritualized behaviour, and juvenile behaviour. It presented a gallery of terms, mostly new, that would stir ethology in later years, and it contained many of the batons that would be taken up by Niko.

Not, however, in that first period after its publication: somewhat surprisingly, in his first few years with the herring gulls Niko showed little interest in the issues stirred up by Portielje, and he largely ignored them. In his Meijendel paper in 1932 he described the spring arrival of the gulls with its protracted to-ing and fro-ing of the flock, and the territorial system of mated pairs, and he gave detailed observations on the presence of a 'club' of singles. He was interested in differences between sexes: Niko distinguished males from females mostly by their faces. He explained that females have a smaller head, shorter beak, a different shaped front, and different eyes. The paper is also dotted with moving descriptions of the scene: 'It makes a powerful impression, to hear that beautifully clear courtship call from dozens of throats high up in the air, now swelling, then dying away, resounding over the wide landscape of dunes. Then, after some time we begin to hear another sound, a long-drawn, plaintive "au …!"' He provided several field protocols of his observations on copulation, and territorial behaviour of males and females, but he commented only briefly on the role of ritualized behaviour. He also presented some spectacular photographs of the gulls' behaviour (more than just portraits, as he had promised himself in earlier years).[10]

This, the early student-truancy in Meijendel, was the beginning of Niko's gull saga, of the next forty years of research on their behaviour. It did not start with the serious study of psychology of zoo animals, as in the case of Portielje. It was a birdwatcher's angle, taken by a boy with experience of flocks of birds, of spatial arrangements, of returning migrants, with a birdwatcher's eye for differences between males and females, and for territories. Portielje's behaviour observations may have made some impact on Niko's early writing, but not much: they took a very different line.

In later years, however, Niko was to move in on Portielje's niche in gull behaviour, and he would sort things out in a quite different way.[11] At the time it was mainly his love for the Meijendel dunes, with their huge sand-blown faces and rich fauna of birds, and he wrote an interesting paper with splendid photographs about the mechanisms behind dune-formations there, comparing it with the Kurische Nehrung.[12] In the 1930s Meijendel would become a frequent stamping ground for him and his students. Sadly, since then the dunes have changed quite dramatically; first, gull numbers increased in leaps and bounds to more than 5000 in the Meijendel of the 1980s, then they crashed to zero after the arrival of foxes in the dunes, after which the birds never came back. The entire area is now managed for the supply of drinking water.

The other large undertaking, in which Niko got involved alongside his rather despised undergraduate studies, was the joint venture on De Beer. There is nothing left of De Beer now, either, but once it was a magnificent island, created in the late nineteenth century when a direct shipping lane was dug to cut off the Hook of Holland, so traffic to and from the North Sea could avoid the maze of currents and sandbanks at the mouth of the Meuse and Rhine. Between the muddy delta and the new shipping lane about one thousand hectares of dunes, scrub, marshes, and sandy flats became an unbelievably rich bird paradise. It was well-guarded Crown property and visitors were not welcome, but somehow Niko and his friends managed to ingratiate themselves with the keeper and get access. It was no more than a good hour's cycling plus a boat ride from The Hague, and they realized that they were on to a gold mine.

Their regular visits to De Beer started in Niko's first year at university, around 1926, first a visit in summer, then a week around Easter, then more week-long camping trips, and, just to show that their playing truant was no half-measure, day trips every week on Thursdays. The main gang leaders, apart from Niko, were Beus (Gerard van Beusekom, another biology student), Frans Kooymans (a keen and brilliant bird photographer), and Martien Rutten (a geology student). Later other, non-Hague people got in on the act, especially Frans Makkink (biology student in Utrecht), and they frequently brought visiting friends.

Initially their main, or perhaps even only, interest was photography, and soon they got such (for those days) spectacular pictures that Tijmstra argued them into publishing. He saw it as their moral obligation to share their results with the world, because they were in such a privileged position. He also encouraged them to study, observe, and write down what happened around the nests of common and little terns, of avocets and shelducks, of harriers and oystercatchers, and they became even more impressed by the scientific possibilities when Jan Verwey visited and spent some time with them. The boys were totally overcome by the wealth of biology of De Beer, and they felt only marginally impeded by their commitments at the distant laboratories in Leiden.

Soon all this translated into Niko's idea of producing a full-blown book, written jointly by the four main instigators. The large, very respectably bound and well-presented *Het Vogeleiland* [Bird island] appeared in 1930,[13] with an Introduction by their idol Jacques Thijsse. The publisher only wanted to do it if they would forego royalties; the book had a print run of 2800 copies, and Niko *et al.* were over the moon.

Niko did the majority of the work for the book, writing more than half of the chapters and contributing almost half of the 85 photographs as well as many drawings. Beus did most of the rest. Curiously, however, the first author was van Beusekom: with their youthful idealism of equality, they decided to have the authors on the cover in alphabetical order, and no matter that Kooymans and Rutten contributed very little, they were on the list before Niko. It was a book bubbling with enthusiasm, natural history, and description of a fabulous area, with splendid (though rather static) photographs, but without science: it did not ask questions. The style of both Beus and Niko was, of course, very dated, and would tend to put people off now. 'Look there, what is that strange bird?', and 'Let us cross this dune here, and see ...', with many excited exclamations. It was an exuberant account of their wonderful discovery of De Beer.

There were lovely observations in the book, and the authors knew that they were valuable. Niko had just got his first pair of binoculars, and he said in one of his chapters, 'Field ornithology is not just a sport, but an indispensable part of science.' He obviously took their activities very seriously indeed, but he did not do much with his data, he just reported. He wrote about oystercatchers systematically preying on young terns, the sparrow hawk that specialized in field fares, the masses of different waders on the mudflats, the peregrine attempting to dislodge crows from their hiding place, the many different ducks displaying, all these were subjects that in later years would be the focus of intensive research by scientists all round the world. At that time the boys felt intuitively that it was a scientific treasure, but as yet they were unable to exploit it.

Bird island revolved around photography, and clearly the authors' minds did the same thing. They would spend any amount of time and effort to get that one good shot; their cameras were very primitive and heavy: working with glass negative plates was murder – although they saw it as the ultimate in technology. The plates were fragile, 16 × 21 cm, and the number that could be exposed on any one expedition was limited by the number of (expensive) plate holders that one owned. Niko saw himself as a lucky capitalist by owning three double plate holders, enabling him to make six pictures per trip. And as he told it, the most exciting pictures were always on the plates that would get broken on the bike ride home.[14] But it worked, somehow, requiring tremendous youthful energy. 'We were as proud as cocks on a farmyard midden!'

Building a bird-hide, Loosduinen, 1928. Photo F. P. J. Kooymans.

Nor was their birdwatching made simple by the use of the easy canvas hides that we nowadays have to watch birds: for them, old fishing baskets and pieces of turf had to do, involving a large amount of effort. The challenge they faced was enormous compared with what I have to do to quickly get a few bird photographs, and it is not surprising that they were so completely taken up by it when they walked away with such beautiful results.

As one could expect, life in the dunes for the boys themselves was also a great lark, and they had tremendous fun together. After some time they were allowed to stay in the warden's hut (when he wasn't present), sleeping on straw, taking turns over the cooking. Niko with his sparkling, alert wit, full of ideas and initiatives, was the recognized leader, but all felt that they had an equal part in the project. There was a great deal of banter, the odd smutty joke, NJN-politics, vegetarianism, sometimes sport, and whatever else young men talk about. But never was the subject girls or sex, because that, in their rather puritan society, was out. Often they talked birds, and according to Frans Makkink,[15] it was there that 'our ethology' was born, in the hut on De Beer in the late 1920s. Makkink concentrated on avocets and oystercatchers, Niko on terns, and there were long, exploring discussions about displays and what we now call ritualized behaviour and displacement activities. There was the hesitant feeling that they could make generalizations about what 'their' birds were doing. It was far too early for publication, but the process of germination had started.

The NJN was still a very important reference point for Niko and, with all its field trips, would remain so until, in 1930, he reached the leaving age of 23, when he became an 'old sock'. Nor did he spend all his time outdoors when he was away from the university. In his student years he published scores of small contributions to the NJN magazine *Amoeba*, as well as papers in *Living Nature* and the magazine *De Meidoorn* [The Hawthorn] of the Arbeiders Jeugd Centrale [Labour Youth Centre]. His friends at the time, just as we who knew him in later years, were astonished at the ease with which he penned these articles, usually getting every phrase right straight away, without any editing.[16] Some of the subjects he covered were bird photography, causes of dune formation, weather systems and cloud formations, bird reports for various areas, flotsam along the beach, observations from bird hides, birds in towns, observations on wheatears, on storks, on common terns, on herring gulls, black-headed gulls, lapwings, falcons, buzzards and harriers, sparrow hawks and goshawks, on the effects of severe winter on birds, and many others, as well as various book reviews.[17] Despite his young age, here was an author/naturalist in full swing.

The year 1929 was engraved in the memories of many people and in the history of almost every country. Throughout the world the disastrous recession resulted in massive unemployment and hardship, and Holland was no exception. But on Niko's life the impact of the recession was more or less zero, though that of several other events was all the more marked. The first major happening started in the early months, with one of the most severe winters that people remembered. Hundreds of waterfowl and waders concentrated at one or two places with open water near The Hague, and many succumbed to the weather. Niko and his birdwatching friends got little rest, and Niko wrote up the collective observations of himself, his little brother Luuk, and nine others, with fine pen drawings by Luuk (then barely 14 years old).[18] Usually, their mode of transport was the bicycle, but in that winter with those conditions, Niko and his friends gave in to the Dutch national passion of skating. They covered enormous distances on their long, straight Friesian skates, along the canals and on the many lakes within easy distance, watching birds as they went. Then one of Niko's friends, Martien Rutten, came with an invitation that Niko could not refuse.

The Ruttens lived in Utrecht, a large town in the centre of the Netherlands, and fairly close to the huge inlet of the North Sea in the centre of Holland, the Zuiderzee (later enclosed as the IJsselmeer). Being an inlet, the Zuiderzee was rather brackish, and in the severely cold winter of 1929 it became largely covered in ice. Martien asked Niko to join his family on a few skating trips along the shores and across the Zuiderzee, and Niko, skating maniac that he was, jumped at it. With half a dozen good skaters, vast distances were covered in traditional fashion, one close behind the other, each joined to the party by the one long stick under the arm, synchronizing their strokes against the fierce wind that cut across the icy plain. One of those other skaters was Martien's sister Lies (pronounced 'Lees'), then 17 years old.

Like her brother, Lies was in the NJN; in Chapter 2 I mentioned her appendicitis adventure in one of the summer camps. She was a good-looking girl with a laughing face, an enthusiast like Niko, and some people remember her as being very forthright, even as a young girl. The Ruttens were a lively geologist family, their father a professor in Utrecht University, and Martien was studying geology at the time. Later Martien would succeed his father, and I attended his lectures in the 1950s. I remember him as a small man, with a large domed head and little spectacles, and rather cynical. Lies was set to start university that September to read Chemistry, which she did. In the end, her chemistry career came to rather little, due to those skating expeditions: she and Niko fell in love, head over heels.

That summer of 1929, Niko would write in one of his regular letters home to his parents, from a summer camp with the NJN in the east of Holland (trans.):

> *I have important news. Last week I have asked the sweetest girl in the world to be my wife, and I had an in every sense satisfactory reply. Because of her really very young age (not yet 18) she asked if she may answer definitely at Christmas, but we believe and hope that no change will be necessary and we consider that in fact it is all arranged. She is Lies Rutten, the eldest sister of Martien. I hope that this is a good excuse for my sluggish writing at the beginning of the camp. My first question now is: what do the parents think about it? You do not know her, so I have to arrange for an introduction soon. ... You will understand that I rather like it here. But we both take care not to let our work in the camp suffer under this ... [Signed] Niek.*[19]

It is a strangely distant letter, especially since he was still living at home, at least in term-time, and he had known her for some time. Niko is 22 years old, he asks for approval from his parents, but in what way could they possibly react? There was nothing in the letter to say what Lies was like, nothing to show what

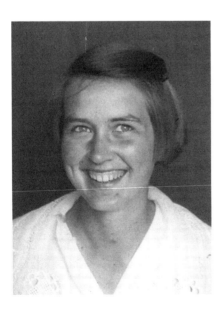

Lies Rutten, about 1931.
Courtesy of the Tinbergen family.

Niko really felt for her. The 'work in the camp' that he refers to was essentially birdwatching, and I am sure that there would not be many people who took that as seriously as did the two love-birds. Lies was Niko's first girlfriend, and so was Niko for her. But work was more important.

During the spring before the end of his undergraduate study, in 1930, Niko did his first, short but serious and concentrated scientific study, as the main research project he had to do towards his degree. This was officially under his lecturer Boschma, but Jan Verwey did the actual supervision. It resulted in a paper[20] that, because it was Niko's first proper scientific product, deserves a close look. It was controversial enough that, thirty years later, Niko's scientific lieutenant Mike Cullen would tear strips off it.[21] As Niko saw it, this was quite a compliment.

'The biology of mating in the common tern' is written in German, which at that time in Holland was the most commonly used international language for scientific papers in biology. It does not even have an English summary; in fact, Niko's friend Frans Makkink published a study alongside Niko's, on shelduck copulation, which was also in German but with a summary in Esperanto.[22] Clearly, at that time the influence of English in Niko's circle was still small.

Niko's maiden paper is largely descriptive, reporting on 3+ weeks of observations on terns, for which he had a soft spot. He watched them in their large colony on De Beer from a hide as well as from vantage points. He watched the beautiful displays on their territories, their mating behaviour, and the relations between chicks and adults. His special interest was that well-known, exciting behaviour that he called 'fish-flights', in which two birds, one often with a fish, pass and zigzag alongside each other with two distinctly different roles and ways of flying, and calling loudly.

In the discussion at the end of the paper, Niko says modestly (trans.) 'In a beginner's work such as this the value lies especially in the reported facts, and the discussion would be better left to experienced people.' Nevertheless he enters with some wide-ranging interpretations; he notes that male and female terns are virtually indistinguishable, and that both sexes perform the same behaviours (although there may be quantitative differences). He also suggests that in early courtship the main function of these behaviours is to stimulate partners to transfer from their 'social phase' (in winter) to their 'sexual phase' in spring. He discusses the significance of mutual courtship feeding, and considers the distinct possibility that either male or female may be the one that mounts during copulation. He believes that during the fish-flights, the roles of males and females are interchangeable.

In 1960, Niko's student Mike Cullen showed that the roles of males and females are more distinct than Niko suggested. The complication is that some males may often behave like females (though the opposite happens very rarely), especially during the fish-flights. Mike suggested that Niko had not had enough ringed birds to draw his conclusions about males and females. The main problem, of course, was that none of the data were in any way quantified (but

Common tern on nest, 1928.
Photo Niko Tinbergen.

neither were Mike's), and Niko's conclusions were drawn from just a few observations. The culture of quantification was very late in arriving amongst students of animal behaviour.

Also in 1930, Niko did three other research projects towards his degree, one on the phylogeny of echinoderms (that is, sea-urchins and starfish; mostly taxonomy), a literature study on gall-wasps and the galls they cause, and most importantly, under van der Klaauw, one on 'The phenology [that is, seasonality] of digger wasps'. We know little of Niko's echinoderm and gall projects; nothing was published on them and they disappeared. But the digger wasps would leave an indelible mark: they later became Niko's PhD subjects.

There are many species of digger wasp. They live solitarily, females dig deep tunnels where they lay their eggs and provision the larvae, and all of them prey on other insects. I will refer to them variously as 'digger wasps' or 'hunting wasps'. Niko's speciality was a species that hunts honeybees, known as the bee-wolf or bee-hunting wasp, *Philanthus triangulum*.

Why he chose digger wasps for his student project is not exactly clear, but I suspect a certain amount of opportunism. Niko's mentor Thijsse had written several popular accounts of some of the digger wasps, in one of the 'Verkade' albums and in *Living Nature*, including some of their behaviour: for example the wasps 'orienting' themselves when going into and out of their burrows. Thijsse even suggested some interesting questions about these wasps that needed answering; for example, how they could find their way back to their nests again? But that had been almost 30 years earlier.[23] Niko also remarked that he had been impressed by the book on hunting wasps by Henri Fabre, the famous student of insects, published in French in 1915, and later also translated into Dutch.[24] But what may have been much more important in deciding the topic of his project was the fact that, every year, the Tinbergen family spent their summer holidays in the village of Hulshorst, where spectacular inland sand dunes provided an optimal, and for Holland quite unusual, habitat for several species of digger wasp. The holidays were just at that time of year when the digger wasps were active. Purely by chance, therefore, digger wasps were almost presented on a plate to Niko – but more about that later.

Two months later Niko went on a two week expedition with eight other ornithologists, to observe bird migration in the Kurische Nehrung. They visited the area along the Baltic in eastern Germany, where he had been before he started his studies. The expedition was led by a senior ornithologist Jan van Oordt, but Niko was the local expert, and he was joined by several friends including Martien Rutten (but not his sister Lies) and Jan Strijbos.

Thus came the end of his undergraduate studies, in December 1930 when

Niko with herring gull, during expedition to Kurische Nehrung, October 1930.
Photo probably J. P. Strijbos; courtesy of G. J. van Oordt family archive.

Niko was 23 years old, a normal age to finish in Holland. What he had gained from the Leiden lectures was a large collection of biological facts, including a sound knowledge of animal anatomy (morphology). There was as yet little scientific questioning, and large themes, such as evolution, had been presented to him as no more than strings of facts. But some of his small student projects, and especially his extra-curricular activities, had stimulated curiosity, largely because of his own initiatives. Slowly the idea arose that, somehow, he could dress his passion for fieldwork and watching animals in a cloak of respectable science.

Niko knew what he liked doing but, just as before he had entered university, he was dithering about his future. He was offered an assistantship in the Leiden Zoology Department by van der Klaauw, who was keen on the idea of field biology (though did not want to be involved himself), but Niko had little respect for what was happening in Leiden. Also, he was not sure that he should continue in the university, as the salary would be puny, and with the economic slump there was little chance of promotion. He applied for jobs, writing to his friend Jan Verwey who, by then, had settled in the Zoological Museum in Buitenzorg on Java, Dutch East Indies (now Bogor, Indonesia; but they had no funds, either). He even applied for a vacancy in an anti-malaria bureau in Friesland.[25]

PhD time

In the end he overcame his objections and decided to stay where he was, to become an assistant in the department, and to do a PhD. This was to be his now well-known study on the bee-hunting wasp (more attractively called 'bijen-wolf' in Dutch, or 'bee-wolf'), a continuation of his earlier student project. It was a major change for Niko, in which finally he began to take academic science really seriously. But even this was tempered by his various projects on the side. For most of us a PhD project is a 100% commitment, but not for Niko. Birds continued to take up a lot of his time, and his relentlessly restless character kept pulling him from one piece of nature to the next.

His new spare-time passion was birds of prey, and owls. Even during the time on De Beer he had had close encounters with harriers, peregrines, and sparrow hawks, and one could feel his excitement from the description of chases by these spectacular hunters of terns and chaffinches. In the following years this went much further, and before he obtained his PhD he followed up this interest with observations that would produce a dozen papers and popular articles, as well as several joint ones with Luuk. There is little doubt about what moved Niko; it clearly showed in his writing.

> *Quietly the peregrine sits on the cross on top of the steeple. Every small flock of starlings that passes is reviewed, often you see him hesitate when a small troop gets close, he lifts his wings but no, folds them again and waits. The*

*smaller the flock and the closer, the more ready he is to pounce. He then shoots
down and before the starlings can take cover between the houses he is there, and
smacks into the one that he had his eyes on. With the starling in his claws he
whizzes along, rises a bit, a few times hanging still in the air to kill his prey,
and then flies up to his eating post. But it is nowhere near always that he hits
the target, and then we have the opportunity to admire the enormous speed
when he overshoots. (Trans.)[26]*

Writing decades later about that time with the raptors, Niko described a
brood of hobbies, a male returning to the nest with a prey,

*calling loudly in the distance, a clear quew-quew-quew! The sound of it would
rouse the female as well as us. She jumped from the nest and flew out to him
with strong, quick wing beats. She often met him a couple of hundred yards
from the nest and, while he slowed down, she threw herself on her back, in
mid-air, and with her talons took the prey from his.[27]*

Niko was a repressed hunter at heart, fascinated by these feathered killing
machines. He grew up in a society that did not shoot or kill in the wild, but he
got a tremendous thrill from watching animals hunt. Later, when he lived
amongst hunters during his stay in Greenland, he himself also used a rifle, and
that touched him very deeply. He acknowledged that his bird photography,
as well as his later field experiments with free-living animals, was surrogate
hunting.

His observations of male and female hobbies on and around their nest, of
the hunting of sparrow hawks and goshawks, and the speed and expertise of the
birds, were the really exciting things that motivated him. But around 1930 his
interests began to go further, and he started to put in a tremendous amount of
work to analyse the diet of birds of prey and owls from prey remains and pellets.
He had some inspired support in this from Luuk, who was then just in his

middle teens. Between them, and within a couple of years, they looked at well over 24 000 prey remains in pellets of long-eared owls alone, as well as those in pellets and heaps of feathers left by other species. The amount of work involved and the dedication of those two brothers was mind-boggling. Interestingly, of the two it was Luuk to whom this kind of work appealed most; Niko gave up the raptor and owl work after two years when he went off to Greenland, and never came back to it. Luuk continued, and eventually developed the relationship between sparrow hawks and their prey species into a justly famous PhD study.

The scientific value of those first Tinbergen raptor projects was rather limited even at the time, despite the mountain of work that went into them. The diet of many of the birds of prey had already been studied very thoroughly (with tens of thousands of samples) in Germany,[28] and Niko often referred to that work. The main scientific paper that resulted from Niko's observations was pure ecology: a large volume in the *Ecological Monograph* series,[29] written by Niko without Luuk. Interestingly, this was again written in German, although in it he often quoted British ecologists such as Middleton and especially Charles Elton, his later colleague in Oxford. The paper expresses an interest in ecology similar

to that of the British school rather than that of the Germans, in population fluctuations and cycles, and the role of predators therein. However, the quantitative analyses left much to be desired: results were expressed in tables often not even calculated into percentages, and in this and some other papers he did not mention the area where the work was done, probably for fear of the birds' safety. Niko concluded that the food of raptors and owls consists mostly of those prey species that are most abundant at the time, and he suggested that this contributes to the stability of ecosystems. It was a great deal of speculation with little in hard data that was actually relevant to population fluctuations. It was to be the last of Niko's efforts into ecology; but for his assistant Luuk it was only the very beginning.

Occasionally in these ecological papers one feels that Niko liked making sweeping statements, trying to present things smoothly and in a simple way, and I rather suspect him of sometimes being a bit economical with the truth for the sake of easy presentation. For instance, when the same data (on the food of long-eared owls) were presented simultaneously in Dutch in a naturalist article and elsewhere in a scientific paper in German, he referred in Dutch to finding 23 'house or field mouse', whilst in German this became firmly 23 *Apodemus* (field mouse),[30] and there were more of such short-cuts.

Niko's spare-time exploits into ecology were soon forgotten, while those of Luuk bloomed. The project that propelled Niko himself into science and later fame was his doctoral research that he did at the same time.

The story of Niko's PhD has been told and retold, of the wasps in the Dutch sand dunes and the neat little field experiments, ending in an embarrassingly short and hurried thesis. In the course of time discrepancies have slipped in, and after reading the first, presumably most truthful report in his published thesis, it is clear that the account that Niko gives of it and of the study itself, some 28 years later in his very engaging *Curious naturalists*, has to be taken with a pinch of salt. I will show some examples of this; presumably, the memories of early days evolved in Niko's mind, and he just did not bother to go back to the original descriptions to verify them.

Niko's student project on hunting wasps, in 1929 near his parents' holiday cottage at the inland sand dunes of Hulshorst, was his first exposure to those fascinating solitary insects. He watched the comings and goings of one species, the bee-wolf; he timed their flights around the entrance of their burrows before they flew off hunting, and noticed that if he moved some of the surrounds of the nests, such as pine cones (as Henri Fabre had done before), these orientation flights lasted much longer. He must have seen the experimental potential of this, and wrote an enthusiastic piece for the NJN magazine,[31] spurring people on to spend time watching behaviour, rather than collecting the insects.

I think Niko would rather have done a PhD project on birds, as they were his passion in life. In those days, however, and certainly in Leiden, that was not feasible: fieldwork on birds would not have been a respectable subject for a PhD student. So, despite his enthusiasm for birds, he decided to continue with

Bee-wolf (Philanthus triangulum) with prey, returning to its nest. Photo Niko Tinbergen.

a PhD study on wasps under Boschma. In Leiden there was a lot of research on insects. By focussing on the solitary hunting wasps he had a subject that lent itself well to field experiment rather than to mere observation, and one can imagine that the exciting hunting behaviour of the bee-killer wasp *Philanthus triangulum* was a phenomenon that would attract someone like Niko. Coincidentally, just during the early 1930s there had been a kind of population explosion of these insects on the Hulshorst sands; a few years later there were few left and they would have been very difficult to work with.

Niko's supervisor, Prof. Hildebrand Boschma, specialized in taxonomy and physiology of invertebrates. He was interested in fieldwork but not in doing it himself, and so he gave Niko a free hand in his work. The two were to become friends in later years, and they continued to exchange long letters until Boschma's death in 1976. One aspect that must have given people like Boschma confidence in Niko's choice of research project was that in recent years a considerable body of comparable studies had been developed in Germany by Karl von Frisch, Ernst Wolf, and colleagues, focussing on such questions as how honeybees find their way back to their hive and whether they can see colours.[32]

Philanthus, the bee-wolf, is one of the larger solitary wasps, yellow and black. It feeds on nectar. In sandy dune country, the female digs a tunnel about half a metre deep with a few chambers at the end, which she supplies with dead honeybees (and only honeybees), several per chamber. She lays one egg in each chamber, and the larva feeds on the bees. Bees are hunted and caught away from their hives, and killed by a sting under the chin. Before transporting its prey to the burrow, the wasp squeezes the nectar out of the bee's stomach and eats it.

Henri Fabre had actually done some rather rough and ready experiments on the vexing question of how a wasp finds its nest on its return with a prey for its larvae. He did this with another species, *Bembex*, but his approach was obviously applicable to any digging wasp: he removed landmarks around the entrance, alternately putting a stone or some horse dung over the entrance, and saw that wasps had no problem in finding their way back to their home. He removed wasp antennae to check their sense of smell during homing: it had no effect. He was baffled by the subject, so he left a fruit ready to be picked by someone more scientifically alert.

Niko's first question was the same as that of Fabre: which senses does *Philanthus* use to return to its burrow, and how does memory play a role? His second question was about hunting behaviour, which was directed entirely at one prey species, the honeybee: how does the wasp recognize a bee from all the other insects? He probably would have expanded on the basic questions given time, but he was cut short: he had to end his project about one year after he started, because of the sudden opportunity, that he felt he had to grasp, to go to Greenland. With his supervisor, therefore, he decided to finish and write it up, and submit the still rather meagre results as a PhD thesis.

In Holland at that time, the awarding of the PhD degree was in large measure in the hands of the supervisor (called 'promotor'), though in consultation with the rest of the faculty. In fact several members of the faculty judged the thesis as lacking in stature, but Boschma convinced them that here was a special case, and that a great deal more was to be expected of Niko in the future. Right he was, but Niko told me years later that he himself was rather amazed to get away with it. In 1958 he wrote, playing the dare-devil in his *Curious naturalists*:[33] 'I had to produce a doctor's thesis dealing with my work on *Philanthus*. I am afraid that this little matter was dealt with in a rather cursory way'.

The result of all this was a PhD thesis 29 pages long, in German: 'Über die Orientierung des Bienenwolfes (*Philantus triangulum* Faber) [About the orientation of the bee-wolf]', published in 1932 in the *Zeitschrift für vergleichende Physiologie* [Journal for comparative physiology].[34] It must have been one of the shortest theses in the history of biology, at least in this field. For comparison, once in the 1970s I was examiner to a PhD thesis of 1340 pages, and theses of several hundred pages then were the norm. Nor was Niko's that outstanding in content; at the time, it was quite a good paper, but nothing more.

But what made the thesis striking was the systematic, scientific use of simple field experiments carried out by an excellent and shrewd observer. It was the account of a scientist who sat somewhere out in the open, watching his wasps come and go, making little changes around the wasps' burrows involving a simple circle of pine cones. It sounds like child's play, but in Niko's hands it gave some lovely insights into the behaviour of the wasp.

Question: Does the bee-wolf recognize the immediate environment of its nest to help it return? In the morning, you put a rather rough 30-cm circle of 20 pine cones around the conspicuous sand patch in front of the wasp's burrow and leave it for a few hours 'training'; you come back in the afternoon, make another sand patch about 30 cm away, take the pine cones from the burrow to the new patch and see what happens. The wasp flies in with a bee, lands smack in the new circle, and searches for where the hole should be but isn't. Chase the wasp away, put the cone circle back around the burrow, and as the wasp flies back in it lands directly in front of the burrow, with its bee. Niko did this with 17 different bee-wolves, repeating it several times with each individual: invariably and in all cases, the wasp was totally taken in by the pine cones.

This was one of the results, probably the most important one. However, when Niko wrote about these same experiments in 1958[35] there were a lot of changes. He described a neat 20-cm circle of 16 pine cones, which he put down just at the time when the wasp was inside its burrow. After the wasps emerged and later returned with a bee, some were fooled by the new arrangement and came to the area to which Niko had now shifted the pine cones, some wasps returned to the burrow itself, and again others vacillated between them. He explained this rather less clear-cut result by the wasps also using other landmarks apart from the pine cones. Clearly the details of the experiment are very different in his two descriptions. Also the accompanying drawings are at variance with each other, but they appear more 'presentable' in the later version. The start of the *Philanthus* PhD story became rather different; in the *Curious naturalists* version Niko graduated in 1929 without a job, found himself walking over the sands and bumping into the bee-wolves, watched them a bit and 'My worries were over; I knew what I wanted to do. This day, as it turned out, was a milestone in my life' (rather than the 1931 return to an earlier student project).

Whatever the presentation of the results, there is no doubt that Niko did some excellent detailed and very shrewd observations on the bee-wolf: he was a natural fieldworker, biologist, and observer. In his thesis he first gave a good general description of *Philanthus* behaviour, based partly on his own work, and he emphasized the elaborate 'orientation flights' of the wasp. After the first orientation experiments described above, he then tested the role of scent in the wasp's recognition of the burrow site. Again a very simple experiment was used: he put two pieces of cardboard dipped in pine-oil next to the entrance, and compared that with non-smelly cardboard next to the dummy entrance, with and without cone circles. The wasps were disoriented when the pine cones moved, but the position of the scented cardboard was immaterial. Niko demonstrated, from the behaviour of the wasps when they met the pine-oil, that they could smell it perfectly well, they just did not use it for orientation. In a further experiment Niko cut off the antennae of wasps, in which their scent organs are located: it made no difference to their homing abilities. In his more popular description of this work in the magazine *De Levende Natuur*, he made a large effort to morally justify this 'vivisection' (his term).

Niko probed further into the wasp's visual orientation, by using sheets of coloured paper in the same kind of experimental set-up. The bee-wolves did not respond to changes in the position of the papers, but only to three-dimensional objects. Finally, he could show that when the pine cones are more than a metre away from the nest, the wasps stop using them for clues, although for that test he only used observations on one bee-wolf.

Turning then to the hunting behaviour of the bee-wolf, Niko put one under a large glass cheese-cover, together with one or two honeybees or other insects, using exactly the same method as Fabre had done earlier. This told him that, as expected, bee-wolves only catch honeybees, killing them by a sting neatly under the chin. Remove the antennae of the wasp, however, and it no longer responds to honeybees. If one crushes a honeybee and rubs that onto an ordinary bluebottle, it immediately becomes an attractive target to an undamaged wasp. For good measure, at the end of the thesis Niko added a description of the anatomy of the bee-wolf's scent organs on the antennae, not so much because of its relevance, but obviously because this was a popular subject in the Leiden department.

This was the entire thesis. There was no discussion of theoretical implications of the behaviour, only a brief statement to categorize the observations in terms of the current theory on animal orientation,[36] of what one called 'tropisms' and 'forced movements'. Niko wrote: 'We are dealing here with an example of optical mnemotaxis (Kühn 1919)' [by which is meant an orientation towards something that the wasp has remembered]. Also, 'From the experiments [with flat and cone-shaped objects near the entrance] it can be concluded that [the wasp's reaction] does not depend on the structure of the receptors [that is, the eyes], but is psychological'. Clearly, the more ethological concepts that would occupy him a few years later were still a long way off.

I believe that, if Niko had been taken on for a PhD in some strong research group, it is unlikely that he would ever have developed the idea of field experiment in the way he did. In his PhD project Niko was taught very little by others. He followed his own lead, set his own questions, and used his own arguments: the Leiden professors tolerated, but hardly guided him. He also learned little from the literature; for instance, in his thesis he quoted publications by Von

Frisch, but mostly for simple methodological points, such as the use of coloured paper. Niko himself developed the much-lauded field-experimental approach in the project, by carrying out the ideas of Henri Fabre in a systematic fashion. Niko's PhD work was one of the independent beginnings of the field experiment in studies of animal behaviour.

With the thesis finished, early in 1932 everything seemed to be happening at once. Niko Tinbergen became Doctor of Philosophy on 12 April 1932, and a married man on the 14th, a few days before his 25th birthday. Elisabeth Amélie Rutten and Niko were married in the Town Hall in Utrecht, in a small family affair with only a few friends. Everything seemed very hectic; at the same time Lies completed her undergraduate 'candidate' exam in chemistry in Utrecht. They were frantically preparing and stocking up for their imminent departure to Greenland in mid-July. Greenland was to be their honeymoon, an audacious adventure, and a major contribution to science: work was never far from Niko's mind. As it turned out, the Greenland experience had a tremendous effect on Niko, on his outlook on life and on his science.

Greenland

What had happened was that, through the influence of his friend Tijmstra, Niko had managed to be selected as one of a small contingent of Dutch scientists to be funded by the government for an expedition to east Greenland. The expedition was in the context of the International Polar Year 1932–33, and consisted of six participants, including four meteorologists, who were to spend a full year on the east coast of Greenland. Niko, 25 years old, was extremely keen to go (hence the speedy thesis), and just as keen that Lies should join him: adventure beckoned. He was ready for something like this, a fairly wild enterprise with the chance of interesting biological work and photography, which would give him a reputation and establish him as the seasoned field man. At that time a journey to a far, difficult-to-get-to place like Greenland carried much more significance than it would now.

Before Greenland, Niko had had very little experience abroad, apart from his trip to Germany; Lies had spent her early childhood in Indonesia. They arrived from a highly sheltered urban environment, from a country with beautiful nature but on a small scale, where wilderness was enveloped by culture. They were nature-lovers, admiring, and sentimentally involved with, the animals they watched, imbued with ideals from the NJN. Niko had written articles about the need for just watching butterflies, rather than collecting them. Then, at a sensitive time of their lives, they were to be struck by the vastness of Greenland, by its size, its overwhelming landscape, its beauty, dangers, and their own abilities to cope with it. They would be captivated by the way the people lived there as part of the wilderness, and especially by the totally different relationship between people and wildlife.

The scientific observations during their Arctic interlude were interesting, and they are still referred to in the literature. But more significantly still, I believe that the Greenland work marked a watershed for Niko the scientist: he came of age. Greenland conferred a maturity that began to show in the papers on the bird work during the second part of their stay. He also began to publish in English, and after Greenland, he began to theorize. His views of animals had changed, and he became confident of his scientific approach to animal behaviour.

On 23 July 1932 Niko, Lies, and the others were dropped off in Angmassalik by the *Gertrud Rask*, a sail and steam vessel belonging to the Danish government, after a nine-day voyage from Copenhagen. Their subsequent stay in Greenland is well documented; Niko kept a diary of his observations (300+ typed pages),[37] and wrote two scientific[38] and several popular articles[39], as well as a book in Dutch, *Eskimoland*.[40] From the book, with its magnificent photographs, one gets an impression of the impact the country had on him, despite its being written in a curiously impersonal style. He described what he saw and what they did, but never what he felt about the people or the landscape. He only occasionally referred to 'my wife', and never even mentioned her name.

Greenland is a land of fjords, mountains, and ice, a country almost the size of Europe when one includes the inland ice cap; without the ice it is about the size of Britain. The climate is severe, and, especially in the time when Niko was there, one had to be really fit in order to survive, to move around, to kayak to places often long distances away, and generally to remain on top of things. To him it was no problem, and it was also fortunate that Lies could keep up. Niko

Lies spearing salmon, east Greenland, 1923. Photo Niko Tinbergen.

was an athlete, and living a primeval life with hunting and fishing gave him enormous satisfaction. Also, more than would have been possible almost any-where else in the world, he was overwhelmed by the magnificent solitude and beauty of the natural landscapes of Greenland: this is what nature was, and what it should be. There were times, many years later, when Niko would be severely depressed by what we do to our planet, and a 1970s visit to Holland literally brought tears to his eyes. In a way, perhaps, Greenland set him some rather impossible standards.

Since Niko's visit, the people and all signs of their presence have changed and increased. But that same beauty in the landscape is still there, largely unscarred, the awe-inspiring mountains with snowy tops even in summer, the gigantic glaciers, the crystal-clear water with the ice floats, and in the autumn the bright yellows and reds of the dwarf shrubs. People still hunt the many thousands of seals of various species, one still sees the gigantic whales blowing and diving in the fjords, the flocks of snow buntings in numbers that are like sparrows elsewhere, and the different gulls and ducks, the peregrine and the gyr falcon. It still is an icy, threatening paradise.

Most of Greenland's very sparse population lived along the west coast, and along the east side there were only a very few, small settlements of Inuit; inland Greenland is solid ice. Contact with modern western civilization was hardly 30 years old at the time the Tinbergens went there, and things had not changed much over the previous centuries. Life was concentrated along a strip of high, spectacular mountains and many fjords, against the massive glaciers inland. Icebergs and drift ice covered the sea and fjords for much of the year.

Angmassalik (now Tassiusaq), the area where the Tinbergens went, is in the south-east. It is just below the Arctic Circle, so even in midwinter there are always a few hours of daylight. The local population subsisted on hunting several species of seals as well as polar bears, and fishing for salmon, char, cod, halibut, and many others, using many traditional methods, harpoons as well as guns, and they were dependent upon dog-sledges and kayaks for transport. Contact with the outside world consisted of the odd ship that called in.

Full-blooded Inuit, who look rather Asiatic, now make up about 80% of the population, and the rest is mostly Danish; in Niko's time there were even fewer Europeans. Even today, first and foremost the people are hunters, and every-thing revolves around hunting and fishing. To us, people there seem totally careless about animal life; for instance, one commonly finds Inuit shooting many times more seals or birds than they can retrieve. Shooting animals, whether it is muskox, seals, whales, or kittiwakes, comes naturally to these people, like cutting grass or picking flowers for us. Niko's Dutch conservation mentality must have had a severe knock when he got there.

Interestingly, he never criticized or protested, not even in his own personal diary: he was totally in awe of the people's relationship with nature. At least partly, the explanation for this lies with the Tinbergen's Inuit host in Greenland, Karale. After Niko and Lies landed in Angmassalik, they separated from the rest of the expedition and moved up the fjord to a small settlement, Kungmiut, which they used as a base. It was there that they spent the winter with Karale Andreassen, a man in his early forties who sadly died a year later. His house was small, of a relatively modern, wooden Scandinavian type, one of the very few of such in the area, and Karale lived there with his wife, and daughter Elisa. He was a fascinating person, still well known in Greenland today as an artist of contemporary Greenland life, with a large book of his drawings and paintings published recently,[41] and even the design of a 1984 Danish stamp to his name (a polar bear killing a hunter). Karale came from a family of shamans, who were highly important in the community. It was he who, 17 years before the Tinbergens arrived, had established the community of Kungmiut up the fjord, a measure of his place in society.

A shaman intervenes between the world of people and the world of the spirits. There are guardian spirits that control every object, person, and animal, and for everybody, the individual relationship with the spirit world is expressed through amulets, custom, and taboo. Some of the spirits dominate the others, and amongst the spirits everything is in process of transformation: they move between past and future, and between the dead and the living. Direct contact with them takes place through the shaman, who is also responsible for organizing seances, feasts, and celebrations, for instance at the occasion of the emergence of seals onto the ice, and the beginning of winter darkness. Many of Karale's drawings were of spirits, animals, and hunters.

Karale taught Niko, he was his guru. He showed him how to paddle a kayak, how to hunt and fish, and how to survive in the cold; he passed on his knowledge of animals, and of people. From a protectionist, Niko became a hunter, like an Inuit. He was immensely proud when, using the traditional Inuit white

Niko at 26 in east Greenland, with shotgun. 1933.
Photo F. P. J. Kooymans.

screen to hide behind, he stalked a seal and shot it, arriving back in Kungmiut with the seal on the back of his kayak. The hunting experience affected him deeply.

His own diary showed that Niko threw himself into his new existence with complete abandon, and the Tinbergens would talk about their time in Greenland until the end of their lives. They dressed the part, had no problems in living on a diet of ship-biscuits, seal meat, and fish, and honed their field skills. Niko was especially proud of his mastery of the art of righting an overturned kayak ('toppling'), and even wrote an article about it later.[42] But, to his intense embarrassment, when he paddled up to meet the ship that collected them at the end of their stay, he capsized and got soaking wet, in full view of his two friends on board and the crew.[43]

Karale and the Tinbergens got on tremendously, and when 70 years later in Greenland I talked to Karale's daughter, Elisa, who was about 14 when the Tinbergens were there, she remembered the Tinbergens warmly. She talked about Niko's early-morning trips to the snow buntings, his long periods spent writing in their room upstairs after he came back, and the friendship with her parents, and she was full of admiration for the way they integrated with everyone as part of the family. Both Lies and Niko learned Greenlandic (very unlike, as she commented, the arrogant Danes who governed the country), and she recounted how Lies was concerned with women's issues and learned to make kamiks (leather boots) of seal-skin, a very difficult thing. People thought Niko's activities a bit strange (why come all that way to look at those little white birds?), but then that was his business, not theirs.

Through Karale, it was especially the Inuit relationship with animals that affected Niko, and I believe that this went to the heart of Niko's views of the

animal world, and therefore of his science. The Inuit saw animals as no more special than plants or rocks; they felt it as a normal duty to kill them. Animals were to be treated with respect, but a respect different from that which our society would recognize. Animals were not accredited with the subjective feelings that we have ourselves: they were objects, highly complicated yet objects, as are plants. This view of nature was very different from what Niko had grown up with, but it became an important aspect of his scientific, ethological approach to his animal subjects.

From their base in Kungmiut the Tinbergens went on long camping trips in pursuit of birds. Before he set out, Niko had planned several ambitious studies for his year in the wilderness, in which he showed his interest in ecological theory and comparative behaviour studies. He intended to study food cycles of birds, to explain the cyclic nature of animal populations in the Arctic following Charles Elton's work (and obviously inspired by his own earlier studies on long-eared owls and voles). He also had detailed plans for comparing the breeding behaviour of glaucous gulls with that of the herring gulls he had observed in Holland, and he wanted to observe the relation between gulls and terns, their aggression, and a comparison of their ways of coping with weather conditions during the rearing of chicks. Finally, he planned a study of the behaviour of the snow bunting, concentrating on territoriality and inspired by previous observations of Elliot Howard on buntings in Britain.[44]

It was an impressive programme, but drawn up at a time when he knew little of what to expect, and consequently, once he was there, Niko (ever the opportunist) switched most of his objectives. Of the programmes on the initial list only the snow bunting research would be realized. Apart from his scientific aims, he wanted to take many photographs, and he also undertook to collect indigenous artefacts for the School Museum in The Hague, and biological specimens for the Museum of Natural History in Leiden.

During the first half year in Greenland he and Lies spent a lot of effort on one science project that was conceived on the spot, which seemed to have little structure to it and did not bear much fruit. This was a study of the local sledge dogs. In the area where the Tinbergens were, every hunter had a team of sledge dogs, at least six of them. Sledge dogs were treated as I would treat a bicycle, maintained as useful objects but not revered, and kicked or whipped if obstreperous. They were mean beasts, punished hard and finding their only reward in food, and when they got too old they were killed. About one hundred typed pages of Niko's diary describe their observations on the interactions between dog packs, and between named individuals within packs. There were long descriptions of who mates with whom, rank orders between the animals, fights between males, and changes in the packs and pack territories.

Interestingly, Niko's were exactly the kind of observation that others produced in the 1960s and 1970s, to describe the social structure of societies of wolves, lions, hyenas, and other carnivores. But he never did anything with it, and there did not appear to be any underlying question in his observations. In the hands of a later scientist these dogs could have produced a good story. Perhaps Niko felt intuitively that this kind of data might be useful, and later they were overtaken by other field projects. It was one of the very few occasions that Niko did not write up his work, though in later correspondence, articles, and lectures he used to refer to his unpublished observations of the dogs' group territories and social rank order. In any case, however, it was not very likely that he could have spent his time much more profitably during the Greenland autumn and winter: because of the weather and very short days fieldwork was almost impossible, and most birds were gone.

Niko was intrigued by the way the locals handled and treated their dogs, which were often left to roam for months on end, having to fend for themselves almost like wild animals. The Inuit relationship between man and beast was also evident here, and he saw all this in close-up. He tried his hand at running a team with a sledge. Thirty years after, he amused his students with the problems of an unfortunate sledge dog: it urgently needed a comfort stop with the sledge at full speed, and the handler lifted the dog to the outside of the team with his whip, dung flying over the occupants of the sledge. Just like the people around him, he was never personal with the sledge dogs, although he spent a lot of time watching. Later he never felt easy with dogs, perhaps because of this time with huskies. He never owned a dog as a pet himself, nor were his children allowed one.

Once spring arrived and once the birds returned from their migration, Niko more or less abandoned the dogs, and he pulled out all the stops to record bird behaviour. The main objects of his interest, snow buntings, are common in Greenland, small and strikingly beautiful white and black or brown. At the time one of their claims to fame was that, after Eliot Howard had described the strictly territorial system of the closely related yellowhammer and reed-bunting,[45] the ornithologist Max Nicholson had visited Greenland and found snow buntings to be non-territorial.[46] Niko had begun to take a close interest in the problem of territoriality, and here was a potentially interesting handle on the subject.

A territory is a well-defined area that a bird or other animal defends against others of the same species, often around its nest. Why should it do that? That is how the question was framed at the time; now it is considerably more refined (see later). It is a theoretical problem of fairly universal importance, with Niko involved at many stages of the discussions well into the 1950s. He had observed territories in his herring gulls in the Dutch dunes, but it was during his Greenland period that he started to take an interest in the theoretical aspects, by setting out to compare closely related species with reputedly different territorial habits. He did not publish this study in English until six years after his return from Greenland[47] (as well as a fairly detailed account much earlier in Dutch[48]), but his interest in territorial behaviour of birds started even before the preparation of the fieldwork there, and not as a result of what he saw in Greenland.

The observations on the snow bunting took about three months. It soon became clear that they were just as territorial as any other bird, and that Nicholson had mistakenly concluded to the contrary because he visited at the wrong time of year. Niko described the birds' behaviour during the entire breeding cycle, and especially territorial behaviour in detail, defining it as 'sexual fighting in a restricted area'.[49] He suggested that its main function is defence against sexual competitors, as well as the reservation of food close to the nest. There are exciting accounts of the long-drawn out flutter-fights between the white-and-black males in the snow-covered landscape, and he also described various other aggressive and courtship behaviour patterns, and several different types of song. Niko concluded that song serves both to attract a partner and to repel competitors. Interestingly, in this study he looked at the birds as individuals, not just as representatives of a species; he gave them names, and recorded individual differences and peculiarities. But he never took the next step of asking why these individuals should be so different. That kind of question was to come later, and not asked by Niko. Nevertheless, the snow bunting research was an important contribution to the study of behaviour, and it set the pace for much that has been done since.

The snow bunting study, published in 1939, provided a fairly detailed *ethogram*, that is, a description of territorial and reproductive behaviour, with relevant conclusions. The discussion was somewhat rambling, and it lacked the clarity of Niko's later writings. For instance, he defined a sexual territory as an area defended by sexual fighting, then stated that the function of sexual fighting is protection against competitors, and that the function of the sexual territory is to protect food sources around the nest: it is rather confused. The paper is also written in a somewhat cocky style, slapping down other authors, often using words such as 'undoubtedly' and 'certainly'. He wrote:

young birds that do not beg for food are not fed. This *proves* that with some species it is necessary for the parents to make but short foraging excursions. It is therefore *proved* that a foraging area around the nest is a necessity with some species. It seems to me, therefore, that it is idle to argue against a food value of territory in general.[50] *[Italics are Niko's.]*

Quite likely this over-assertiveness developed in the years after the Greenland time, but it later disappeared again, fortunately.

Right in the middle of the snow bunting period, when the Tinbergens were camped on a small island (to protect their camp against marauding sledge dogs), Niko hit on another diversion, when the red-necked phalaropes arrived back from their migration, close to the tent. Phalaropes are amongst the most curious species of wading birds: not only are they brightly coloured, but these are also the colours of the female, the male being the drab sex. To anyone with an interest in behaviour, this would have been a major challenge: how does this state of affairs affect the birds' territorial behaviour (in other species the job of the brightly adorned male) and breeding (normally mostly the work of the camouflaged female)? Phalaropes were not on the Greenland project plan, and Niko had much to do on his snow buntings. But these fascinating birds, right on the doorstep, were impossible to ignore.

In the end Niko spent three weeks watching the magnificent little waders whilst Lies continued with the snow buntings. The diversion was justified,

because the phalaropes produced a lovely story that Niko published in English and Dutch as soon as he got home.[51] The female, with deep-red sides of the neck and a smooth grey back, established a territory on arrival, patrolling it very conspicuously, and she vigorously attacked any visiting female. She courted visiting males, stopping her conspicuous display as soon as a male became established; after mating she visited a number of nest scrapes, finally producing first one, then three more eggs, closely witnessed by the male. From then on the male, nicely camouflaged in his drab outfit, did all the incubation.

In his study Niko was concerned with the relation between coloration and various aspects of breeding behaviour, and clearly the observations were very relevant in the discussion of the function of territoriality. For some reason he also focussed on aggressive and sexual reactions of the phalarope to other species of bird, a subject that would not particularly interest us now. He never asked the obvious question of why there was the role reversal; quite likely this is related to the male and female sharing the costs of reproduction in such an extreme habitat, rather than having the female cope with it all herself. Fifty years later it would be a typical concern of the science of behavioural ecology.

With snow buntings and phalaropes Niko should have had enough to occupy his time in the spring and summer of his Greenland year, yet he kept casting a wistful eye at the colony of glaucous gulls high up on the mountain above them. He climbed up once or twice, but finally decided that he just couldn't start any serious work there. He also played around with nests of Arctic terns, which are very similar to the common terns he had looked at in Holland. He put up a hide, and experimented somewhat haphazardly with eggs of different species to see how terns recognize their eggs. Terns accepted eggs of any colour when presented with them close to their nests, and they rolled them in, but a large duck's egg was less attractive than a tern's egg. Niko spent a few days on these small experiments, but he soon gave up, deciding that these were things he could also do at home with herring gulls. He published the results only rather superficially in Dutch.[52] Later, such egg-rolling experiments would play a very important role in the ethology of Niko and his scientific offspring, but the idea originated in Greenland.

Apart from giving Niko a new confidence and a new outlook on the animal world, the Greenland trip produced data for several scientific papers, and it resulted in a beautiful collection of photographs. He returned with a famous assemblage of Inuit utensils, clothes, tools, carvings, artefacts, and drawings for the School Museum. In 1999 the anthropology museum in The Hague, now called the *Museon*, organized a national exhibition of their Greenland collection named after Niko's book, *Eskimoland*.[53] It proved very popular and attracted a great deal of publicity in Holland. More than half of the exhibits came from the Tinbergens collection some 65 years earlier, and it used many of Niko's photographs, taken with the Rolleiflex that he had bought specially for the expedition, and with an old plate camera. There were also drawings by Karale, and Niko's own drawings of the Greenland story, made for his children during his confinement in a hostage camp during the war. The ethnographic part of their expedition had been obviously successful, all the more so since only a few years after they left the country, east Greenland was thoroughly westernized by the Danes.

Throughout Niko's accounts of the Greenland expedition one finds an overwhelming fire and enthusiasm. He had an awe for the country and its wonderful nature and people, and his writings showed how the experience of real wilderness, and the basic connection between people and animals there, touched him to the core. Later, he commented wryly (trans.): 'in Holland, where I grew up, my ancestors had killed all the worthwhile game, so I couldn't become a hunter (for that is what I really am).'[54] Greenland had a profound effect on Niko's science, causing a transformation from a young, somewhat sentimental naturalist to a hunter who saw his animals as objects, as things.

What would have happened to his later career if Niko had not gone to Greenland, had not met Karale, had not been a hunter, and had not lived in real, unfettered wilderness? Of course one can only guess, but quite possibly his overall scientific approach to animal behaviour would have been less mechanistic, and more subjective and sentimental. In later years he would be in the forefront of the use of scientific analyses of birds and other animals as 'behaviour machines'. It was this approach that, at least initially, set him apart. It was stimulated by Karale in Greenland: without it, Niko might never have been a leader of behaviour science.

Early in September 1933 the *Gertrud Rask* came to collect them again, and on board were two Dutch friends who had come for the ride: Niko's old photographer friend Frans Kooymans, and the 19-year-old Jan Joost ter Pelkwijk ('Pelk'), friend of both Luuk and Niko, and later student of Niko. In Pelk's diary of that trip[55] he recorded Niko's plans for another big expedition to Greenland, but once back in Holland this idea was never mentioned again. Pelk captured the Greenland effect on the party, Niko's feeling as much as his own (trans.): 'More than ever at this moment I feel how intensely wonderful life is. What lucky swines we are, to experience this!'

CHAPTER 4

Ethologist in the 1930s

Leiden after Greenland

The Tinbergens returned to Holland on a high; many people knew about the expedition and admired the pluck of Niko and Lies. Their arrival back home in September 1933 was soon followed by articles in the Dutch popular press and pieces written by Niko himself,[1] and obviously they could capitalize on their stories for a long time. In the world of birdwatchers Niko's tales of phalaropes, snow buntings, and gyr-falcons made news, and as far as his Dutch friends were concerned, he had become an ornithological world authority. There was the fabulous collection of Eskimo art and utensils, and his first-hand knowledge of life in the cold. It was something like fame, with all its time-consuming trimmings.

However, it was not just the aftermath of the Greenland trip that occupied Niko's mind. Lies and he also had to find a place to live, to set up house in Leiden and to start married life in Holland after their long honeymoon in Greenland. They wanted to get settled properly: both were ready to become part of the establishment, each in his or her own way, and Lies (probably more than Niko) wanted to start a family, soon. In November 1933 they moved into a rented, small, terraced brick house, 5 Meloenstraat (now gone and replaced by other houses), a typical Dutch urban street in Leiden, about 10 minutes bike ride from the Zoology lab. About one year later, in December 1934, their first son, Jaap (Jack), was born.

Niko and Lies were intensely happy together. Lies had no career herself, but through endless discussions and participation in field trips she was closely involved (although second-hand) in Niko's interests, successes, and concerns, and she knew the people. Despite her university degree in chemistry she never felt that she was badly done by in becoming a housewife; she determined at an early stage that what she wanted out of life was to support Niko's career. This decision was based not only on love, but on a deep admiration; she knew that he was a great man and she saw it as her undisputed duty to see that he did what he wanted. She never wavered from this throughout the rest of her life. Lies was also intensely maternal: she loved children, and wanted to have many under her wings herself. Husband and children were her mission, although she had a scientific degree herself.

One remembers Lies as a friendly and jolly person, with strong opinions that she usually kept to herself. She was a good manager of people, firm, yet pleasant and understanding. She could be somewhat disconcerting at times, especially in

*Niko's son, Jaap (Jack), playing with
grandfather Dirk's watch, 1936.
Photo Niko Tinbergen.*

her way of observing people intensely and remembering their characteristics in detail, including their foibles and inconsistencies. One sometimes felt on trial. When Niko had friends, colleagues, or students at home she was often working or sitting somewhere in the corner, reading or doing needlework, taking in every word and discussing it all with Niko afterwards. Niko left the running of the house, and later the running of the family, entirely to Lies. She did everything, all domestic details down to the last nail to be hammered in or bill to be paid, ever cheerful and energetic.

Even during their early married life in Holland Lies and Niko were not great socializers. They did not go out, and visited rarely. Niko had that outward appearance of jolliness, but often he would brood, and in later years the brooding developed into deep depressions. His science was his life, family holidays were spent at the sites of fieldwork, domestic issues were peripheral, and if he had a hobby it was his rummaging around in nature and photography, both intimately interwoven with his work. Only when older did he become a keen gardener, interested (passively) in politics, and an avid reader of detective novels.

Back in Leiden Niko slipped again into the none-too-glorious job of assistant in the Department of Zoology, under van der Klaauw. Apart from his own research work, duties included a course of lectures in comparative anatomy, and he had to design a course in behaviour, with the emphasis on experiments. Surprisingly for an outdoor natural history fanatic, Niko was very taken by anatomy, not just by giving lectures in it but by the subject itself, probably because it gave him a first acquaintance with evolutionary problems, with differences between species, and with homologies (similar organs with common ancestry in related species). The connection of all this with behaviour was waiting in the wings.

In his own research Niko only slowly began to be aware of the need to rise above the mere collection of behavioural data. His head of department, van der Klaauw, frequently emphasized the central importance of theory in their efforts,[2] but Niko was very much a field man, and not particularly interested in behaviour theory. He had been aware of the then standard textbook of psychology by William McDougall[3] (he had a copy in Greenland), he read Portielje's interpretation of herring gull behaviour in detail, by 1933 he had begun to correspond with the Dutch psychologist Bierens de Haan, and he had quoted the first papers by Lorenz on jackdaws, with their behavioural analyses. He himself had a background of ecological interests in birds, in their feeding and spacing in the colony (territory). He had produced some descriptive studies of mating behaviour, and some pure and simple behaviour experiments in insects, but his Greenland work was yet to be written up. As Niko later admitted, there was nothing systematic in his knowledge, it was an almost accidental accumulation of experiences.

However, an awareness was emerging, and in the next couple of years these experiences resulted in an analysis of territoriality in terms of behaviour patterns, whilst he left the purely ecological aspects of territoriality to his brother Luuk. In Niko's review papers on territoriality (see below) we find his first attempt at posing fundamental questions. Niko, therefore, entered behaviour questions about birds from the strong ecological angle of his previous fieldwork, and it was in coming from this direction that he contacted animal behaviour problems as discussed by psychologists.

These studies of territoriality were the real beginning of Niko's ethology. He was searching for a theoretical base, and for scientific respectability. He needed both at that stage; he had harvested much kudos from his trip to Greenland, but he would have been well aware that, academically, he had not been doing particularly brilliantly until then. He had had success in the NJN and with other bird friends, but his school and university results were thin. He only scraped through his PhD, in a way that even many years later caused him to feel rather embarrassed. He had few substantial publications to his name (but then, he was only 26).

With his background in birdwatching and ecology, in counting, and in observations on habitat and food, it was not surprising that Niko was taken by the subject of territoriality, rather than by the 'pure' behavioural issues that animal psychologists got worked up about, issues such as learning and intelligence. The 'territory' concept straddles the border between ecology and behaviour, and it was much in vogue at the time, especially after Elliot Howard's 1920 book *Territory in bird life*. Niko had not addressed it with any specific observations, but in the two years following Greenland he wrote discussion papers in Dutch and English. The subject of territory never completely left him, and some twenty years later he published papers about it again.

The 1930s territory papers discuss fighting, song, and territory of birds. They are clear and decisive in some parts, but rambling elsewhere. Niko dissects some of the fuzzy confusion surrounding the concepts, and here for the first time, he states explicitly (trans.): 'Instead of: what are birds fighting for? it would be better to ask: what drives (and what stimulates) birds to fight, what do they fight, and what is the effect of fighting?'[4] On the other hand, he still struggled with semantics throughout, and like many other scientists against whom he fulminated, confused the issue of what we mean when we say 'territory'. His own definition of the term ('an area which is defended by a fighting bird shortly before and during the formation of a sexual bond')[5] is not particularly helpful, and in later papers he would broaden the concept (now it is generally understood as any 'defended area'). In the end, Niko's intervention did little to advance the discussion on the function of territory in the 1930s.

Niko's style at that time had a certain patronizing cockiness, though one cannot help but feel that he himself was still something of an upstart. He upbraided the then famous bird author Elliot Howard for not clearly distinguishing between the questions of cause and effect of the actions of animals, and he judged Howard's observations as being too general. He similarly approved and disapproved of other authors; one hapless scientist he even described as 'useless'.[6]

He was aware of his occasional high-handed attitude, and (appropriately) explained it in animal behaviour terms. In a letter to Adriaan Kortlandt in 1939 (in which he criticized the latter's high-handed and aggressive attitude in a manuscript that Kortlandt gave to Niko for comments) he wrote (trans.):

> Now I believe that I understand very well how you arrive at this. It is your 'overawing' [in German 'Imponieren'], a form of male display. As it derives directly from your instincts, you will have difficulties in detecting this yourself, and subduing it. I can say all this quite easily, because I did have it strongly myself and still have. As in animals, such 'overawing' is to show your superiority over other males, in which the displaying male does his best not only to appear big and strong himself, but also tries to make the opponent and rival appear small and insignificant, for instance by stirring up a quarrel and then punching him in the face. In the present case this happens not with the fist, but with the pen.[7]

Niko later referred to the 'arrogance of youth', and he obviously knew what he was talking about. Fortunately, his over-assertiveness disappeared later, perhaps in the hostage camp during the war. But he never quite lost his tendency to frequently use phrases and words like 'I am sure that', 'undoubtedly', 'clearly', 'there is no doubt that' (or Dutch or German equivalents), when arguing a case in situations where there would have been room for other interpretations. For scientists this kind of usage goes against the grain: one likes to use terms like 'suggest', 'maybe', or 'perhaps'. Later I and other students often nagged him about it. He in turn used to tease us about our pussyfooting caution. Contrary to what I thought at the time, it may well be that his simple, assertive approach was one of the attractions of Niko's writing: sometimes it may have raised a few scientific hackles, but it carried a clear and easy message.

In trying to find a single, scientific framework for his interests in the early 1930s, Niko had available to him several theories and methodologies for approaches to animal behaviour that were doing the rounds. Often, these theories were not explicitly expressed as such, because as yet there was no separate science of animal behaviour. To provide a very brief overview and history of this background, I need to mention some of the ideas and terminology being discussed at the time. They stood in sharp contrast to the science that was soon to find a name for itself: ethology, the biological study of animal behaviour.

The first writer who struck Niko with his ideas about generalities of animal behaviour must have been Frits Portielje. Dutch, and known as a very pleasant and friendly person, Portielje was a highly popular writer and radio-figure, and inspector and later director of the well-known Amsterdam zoo 'Artis'; once he was called 'the apostle of animals.'[8] He wrote many scientific and popular articles and books, mostly about mammals and birds in the zoo, but what was initially most important for Niko was a substantial paper[9] on the behaviour of herring gulls in 1928. This appeared just at the time that Niko, still an undergraduate, developed his interest in these birds in the dunes near The Hague.

In this contribution Portielje described the 'ethology and psychology' of the gulls, in which 'ethology' referred to the behaviour as we observe it, especially the innate, stereotypic behaviour such as mating, fighting, courtship, and threat. 'Psychology' addressed the inner processes, that is, the emotions of animals that caused the behaviour. Portielje gave detailed descriptions of calls and postures, then assumed that a bird could feel, and be aware of the purpose of its behaviour, for instance of its call, though not as much as a person would be. A gull mew-calls 'in order to show anger'. He talked of a 'tenderness call' of the herring gull, and a 'rejoicing call'. He also described a category of behaviour patterns that he called 'symbolic actions', which included redirected behaviour and what we now call 'displacement behaviour', which I will discuss later. He suggested that such symbolic gestures would be carried out by a bird, for instance in order to stimulate its partner into the right mood. Portielje described as his method of approach: 'contemplating as much as possible, including observation, consideration and intuitive feeling about animal behaviour'.

Right from the beginning the scientist in Niko felt uncomfortable with the subjectivity of both method and conclusions. He and Portielje visited each other and corresponded, they discussed their observations and quoted from each other, and they checked with each other on how to distinguish male herring gulls from females.[10] But there was a wide gap on many different levels; Portielje was more than 20 years older, he was a zoo man, and although his writings were very popular in Holland, his scientific writing was convoluted and full of jargon. When the British Association for the Study of Animal Behaviour considered a translation of Portielje's main book[11] from Dutch, it was advised that 'the author's style was so extraordinary as to be virtually untranslatable'.[12] Portielje's impenetrable psychological jargon, with many words between quotation marks, put Niko off as much as his own conviction that one cannot know about an animal's deeper feelings or its insights into the purpose of its behaviour. Some years later Niko wrote a friendly, but rather negative, review[13] of Portielje's *magnum opus*.

Portielje had been strongly influenced by the views of two main movers in animal psychology in Holland, Buytendijk and Bierens de Haan; all three were born in the 1880s. The doyen of Dutch animal psychology was the deeply religious Buytendijk,[14] who was active in this field until about 1940. He was a laboratory man, and compared the performance of many different kinds of animals in perception, problem solving, and learning. Initially he saw the 'psyche' of animals as the (God-given) central force, denying a more physiological and mechanistic view, but later he changed his mind and saw instinct as growing during an animal's lifetime. He often changed his religious as well as his philosophical outlook on life. Buytendijk was a loner. His writing was replete with philosophical jargon and psycho-babble, and it was hardly surprising that he had little following, despite his considerable written output. He left Niko totally cold.

Much more influential generally was Johan Bierens de Haan. He and Niko became friends despite a large difference in age (and it took them 14 years to call each other by their first names). They exchanged many voluminous letters,[15] mostly about their work, thoroughly disagreeing with each other but maintaining a pleasant, friendly discussion and with many personal details added, over almost 20 years. Bierens de Haan was a gentle character, a former student of Buytendijk, and a man of independent means as well as a lecturer in Amsterdam. He was an armchair biologist who was obviously delighted to let someone tell him about research on animals in the wild, whilst the young and eager Niko was only too keen to enter into debate about any idea that Bierens de Haan produced. And ideas there were many; Bierens de Haan wrote seven books about animal psychology as well as many papers. He was also the editor of the fairly influential Dutch *Vakblad voor Biologen* [Journal for Professional Biologists], in which Niko succeeded him in 1940. Niko admired the other's extensive knowledge of literature and his clear writing, but balked at his interpretations.

In Bierens de Haan's world, an animal's instinct had a clear purpose: it was innate and specific to a species. Instinct involved first of all an 'awareness', followed by a 'feeling', and that followed by a 'striving'. This striving produced overt behaviour, and for the observer it was important to be able to recognize this chain of events by intuition.[16] However, Bierens de Haan's own data, observations, and experiments had little to do with such theory. They were involved mostly with mazes, tool use, and reactions to artificial environments. In Niko's many letters to Bierens de Haan (some more than seven large pages long) he discussed, amongst other things, his observations on rank order and aggression in sledge dogs in Greenland, as Bierens de Haan was especially interested in the higher mammals, and he criticized Bierens de Haan's writing in detail. After

Greenland Niko was inclined to ignore the subjective ('psychological') aspects of animal behaviour: he urged that the physiological question be separated from the psychological one, and left little doubt that he was interested only in the former.[17] Years later he would state: 'Because subjective phenomena cannot be observed objectively in animals, it is idle either to claim or to deny their existence'.[18]

What appeared to exercise both men a great deal in the 1930s was the recognition in animal behaviour of different kinds of 'tropisms', of mechanisms used by an animal to orientate itself. As a topic initiated by Bierens de Haan, they endlessly discussed phototaxis (attraction towards light), mnemotaxis (towards remembered objects), klinotaxis (relative to a gradient), phobotaxis, and several more, mostly concerning invertebrate animals. There was a large earlier literature on the subject dating from around 1920, mostly concerned with classification and semantics and, to us, rather uninteresting (although Niko still took it fairly seriously even as late as in his *The study of instinct* in 1951).

Niko's criticisms of Bierens de Haan could be quite hard-hitting, but this much more senior scientist always put up with it. In a long letter apropos of the latest of his books that Bierens de Haan had sent him as a present,[19] Niko wrote (trans.): 'for judging performance during the experiment, knowledge of innate ways of moving should be the basis for species comparisons. Especially in chapters 5–8 it is striking how little this has been the case (from necessity, I admit), and these chapters therefore have become a rather fragmented and incoherent compilation.'[20] Then he added: 'I hope that you appreciate from these remarks how much pleasure your book has given me.'

Bierens de Haan took it in good spirit. He visited Niko in his fieldwork, and gently chided him for his mistakes (especially when Niko referred to existing literature). Bierens de Haan was a friendly character – although neither Portielje, nor Kortlandt (see below), who both worked in or near the same place, could get along with him. Both he and Niko were deeply involved in the search for answers and understanding of animal behaviour, and in their discussions one does not find point-scoring, but serious arguments that did not spare the opponent.

The most important contribution made by Bierens de Haan to Niko's development was probably not his philosophy of the animal psyche, but his great respect for and command of relevant literature. More than anyone known to Niko, Bierens de Haan excelled in knowledge of the written word about animal behaviour in Dutch, German, English, and French, and in letters Niko several times expressed his admiration for this (or had to excuse his ignorance). In later years, Niko himself obtained a wide grasp of anything written that was even remotely connected with animal behaviour.

These Dutch animal psychologists, who were Niko's first contacts with theories of behaviour, often represented the views of scientists writing and working abroad, in America, Britain, and Germany. Bierens de Haan's ideas were broadly in line with those of the British psychologist William McDougall, who regarded 'instinct' as an innate tendency to react to a situation with a specific *emotional excitement*, leading to a specific kind of reaction.[21] Instinct and intelligence acted in 'intimate co-operation'. He was more theorist than observer, but his work was widely read, especially in Britain, though much criticized in the USA (where he taught at Harvard from 1920 onwards). Niko saw McDougall as the representative of animal psychology, and at the time his most important book was part of the curriculum in Leiden.[22] In letters Niko referred to 'mcdougallism'.

Almost diametrically opposed to McDougall and Bierens de Haan were the ideas of J. B. Watson from Chicago, the man behind *behaviourism* in the 1920s and equally an anathema to Niko. Watson initially defined 'instinct' as behaviour that had not been learned,[23] but later abandoned the term altogether, arguing that there was no need for it as it could not be measured. He came to consider that all behaviour was acquired in various ways, and that every animal was a trained response machine; any behaviour could be taught.[24] Obviously, this was a point of view in which there was little to attract a naturalist. The greatest heresy of the behaviourists (in Niko's eyes) was their preoccupation with white rats and monkeys in cages, pressing levers in learnt responses. In Niko's own words: 'I wanted wild, not domesticated species and those that could be kept in the laboratory under reasonably natural, richly 'patterned' conditions. Definitely *not* white rats, to which behaviorism had given me a mental allergy from which I have never fully recovered.'[25]

A different approach again, similarly firmly rejected by Niko, found an exponent in the Englishman E. S. Russell.[26] Here, animals were assumed to direct their behaviour to a certain goal *on purpose,* or, as Russell wrote, 'the objective aim or "purpose" of the activity controls its detailed course'. This *vitalism* suggested that, for instance, animals fight 'in order to' remove opponents from their territory, and they mate 'in order to' produce offspring. Niko objected that this went against any physiological explanation of behaviour.[27]

There were many other important players in the animal behaviour game before and up to the early 1930s, but few appear to have been of much interest to Niko. He did not read much. He wasn't even concerned about the grandmaster of all, a biologist with much to say about animal behaviour, of whom he wrote: 'Of Charles Darwin's work, I read at that stage only *The Voyage of the Beagle* and, without being much influenced by them, the three volumes of Darwin's life and letters.'[28] Nor did his regular reading matter include the influential British animal psychologist Lloyd Morgan (working mostly in the 1890s), whose famous canon would have been balm to Niko's soul: it told that no behaviour should be explained by a higher psychological mechanism if it can be accounted for in a simple way.[29] Lloyd Morgan was another scientist considered to be a 'founding father' of ethology and animal psychology (there were rather many); he certainly was someone with a great deal of common sense. He considered 'instinct' as species-specific behaviour, advocated the use of operational definitions to prevent misunderstanding, and stressed the need for replication of experiments. Most of his interest went out to observations on dogs, especially on learning and conditioning.[30]

In later life Niko expressed much admiration for Julian Huxley, whose scientific papers (1914, 1923)[31] on the behaviour of grebes and divers were frequently quoted, even fifty years later. Niko first met Huxley at an ornithological conference in 1930 in Amsterdam; at the time, language was something of an obstacle, as Niko was fluent in German but not quite yet in English. Huxley was not that much of a field man, despite his publications, and altogether he did not spend more than forty or fifty hours on field observation in his entire lifetime.[32] But what impressed Niko was that he treated behaviour patterns of birds as species characteristics, especially behaviour related to mating, and he discussed the evolutionary implications in terms of sexual selection, a topic that twenty years later would fascinate Niko. However, somehow Huxley did not make much impact on behavioural science. Apart from his few early bird papers he published little in this field, and although he saw himself as one of the founders of ethology, his 'primary accomplishment in this area was to make the contributions of writers like Selous and Howard more accessible to the scientific community. ... [Huxley] was a master at organisation, synthesis and presentation.'[32]

Not a single scientist amongst all the behaviour theorists was a field man who sat and watched his animals in their own habitat, not even Charles Darwin. They did not know what animals *normally* do. Howard and Selous were field people, but they did not theorize much. Clearly, there was an open niche here.

However, although at that time Niko felt a need for a theoretical base for his own work, for example, for a theory underlying territoriality, he was not yet interested in a general psychological theory that explained animal behaviour as an overall objective. When fifty years later he looked back at his interest of those early days, having received a Nobel Prize for 'work on the elicitation and organisation of behaviour patterns', he remembered:

this did not truly reflect the haphazard, kaleidoscopic attempts at understanding animal behaviour done by the future ethologists. Rather than being far-sighted ventures into the unknown, with the intention to 'map' that unknown territory systematically, they were in fact no more than tentative, groping attempts at seeing some sense in the variety of animal behaviour systems that fascinated, yet bewildered us, and the understanding of which had in many ways been made difficult rather than facilitated by the many early brands of psychology to which we turned for enlightenment, but which disappointed us so bitterly.[33]

Niko's somewhat half-hearted searching for a theoretical underpinning to his observations did not proceed with much success, at least initially. In the meantime, however, his involvement with a group of enthusiastic students pushed him forward with observations on the organization of behaviour on a quite different front. Niko was an inductive scientist: reading about behaviour theory did not suit him, but getting a set of observations and making sense of them came much more naturally, especially when in the company of keen students. In fact, students gave a major boost to his own role in science.

In the first few years after his return from Greenland, his work developed slowly. He worked non-stop and produced several papers, but bright ideas were lacking; partly, perhaps, because he was too occupied by his departmental duties. There was also a lot of activity at home, with the arrival of their firstborn, Jaap, in late 1934. But Niko's domestic duties were never very onerous, and he was not a great changer of nappies: Lies did it all, and made sure that Niko was distracted as little as possible from his work. Still, home must often have been on his mind.

Soon after Greenland, in the spring of 1934, Niko was out again in the herring gull colony near The Hague, every early morning of the breeding season. Students, who had just started in Leiden as undergraduates, came along to help, like his brother Luuk, and Luuk's friend, the same Jan Joost ter Pelkwijk ('Pelk') who had gone to collect Niko and Lies from Greenland. There was also Gerard Baerends, a new enthusiast from The Hague, and one of the few girl students, Jos van Roon. They beavered away for that season and the next; yet afterwards, Niko admitted: 'Although all of us gave quite some time to the gulls in both years, we did not get very far. But we did bring to light some facts that seemed very much worth the trouble' (trans.).[34]

Facts, yes, but deeper insights, not quite. There were observations on individual recognition by gulls, and experiments on recognition of nest site, eggs, and chicks. (Birds recognized the nest, not the eggs and not the young chicks, but they did recognize the older chicks. One could exchange eggs or young chicks for others with, for example, different colours, and birds would accept them.) Theory in that study did not go much further than a statement that (trans.) 'monogamy is important, because through it every set of chicks is cared for by a *pair* of adults.' Nowadays a pronouncement like that would be rubbished by behavioural ecologists, and altogether, the results of the gull work in the mid-1930s were not very inspiring.

Camping with the wasps

Later in the summer of 1934, in July, Niko was again out in Hulshorst, haunt of the digger wasps, where he developed studies on new species and followed up some of the many loose threads left hanging from his PhD thesis before the Greenland trip. Again, he went with a group of students; his boss, Professor Boschma, allowed him an annual two months in Hulshorst, in which students could participate in the fieldwork as part of their course.

The Hulshorst area had long been a favourite with Niko. Situated in the centre of Holland, its sand dunes, pine woods, streams, and heather moorland were home to a rich fauna. When I visited there in 2000 with Niko's son Jaap, there were tracks of fox and badger, a black woodpecker calling, and ravens flying about around the beautiful old, bent pine trees and wide sweeps of sand. Since the early 1920s the Tinbergen parents had taken their children to a holiday cottage there, every summer. After Niko's earlier exploits there with owls, birds of prey, and bee-wolf wasps, he had recognized the potential of the place; besides, there was a moral obligation for him to delve much deeper into the bee-wolf behaviour, after his disappointingly brief PhD thesis on the subject. As he wrote later:

> my plans for the summer vacations for years to come were made: I had to keep going back to Hulshorst and find out more about the bee-killers. As it turned out, this decision fixed the summer plans of my wife, of all our children, and of several 'generations' of students as well: for the fieldwork on the sandy plains went on for many years.[35]

The Tinbergen family plus students[36] set up a tented camp in Hulshorst, which they would revisit every summer until the war, and for several years after. It was work for Niko (although he included in it his two-week holiday allowance), and it was seen as a holiday for Lies and the children, although it involved much hard work for Lies. Over the years, this side of Tinbergen family life, whether in Holland or in Britain, would change rather little, and this mix of work and outdoor activity was how almost all family holidays were to be spent ever after. When the Tinbergens moved to Britain in 1949, the Hulshorst custom transferred for another few years to Niko's successor in Leiden, Jan van Iersel, until the camps stopped in the late 1950s. Now, almost 70 years after they started, the campsite is still there in the pine wood, off the beaten track and marked by little more than an old pump.

The set-up was run more or less like an NJN camp (and many of the participants were current or old NJN-ers), with everyone eating together and helping out, except that it was ruled by a firm hand: not Niko's, but Lies's. There were always children around, the Tinbergens' or later the children of doctoral students, which enhanced Lies' position as camp matriarch. She did the cooking and organizing and could be quite strict; sometimes students rather resented her regime, having to polish Primus stoves or wash plates on order. Everyone bathed in the stream, in fact a regular dip in the cold water was mandatory; people were called back from their nearby study sites for meals (in later days by Jaap blowing a conch shell), and there were many other little routines.

These camps were no luxury, but they were fondly remembered by most. They were exciting and intensive, and a great deal of enthusiastic work was done. They also attracted visits from established scientists, such as Bierens de Haan and Portielje, who came to see the small and crafty field experiments with the wasps (though Portielje was kept away from the most exciting places, as Lies was worried about him publishing ideas).[37]

As soon as the Hulshorst (what was to become) routine had started in 1934, Niko attacked his bee-wolf digger wasps again. This time the research was done together with several undergraduate students, and it resulted in three sizable scientific papers,[38] all in German. They studied which stimuli a wasp used to catch a bee (visual, or scent, or noise), and how it recovered one that it had dropped near the nest, and they discovered a complicated interplay of several orientation mechanisms, different for each behaviour. This first part was written up by Niko on his own, descriptively and with little quantification. In the second of these studies (jointly with W. Kruyt), the results of the many experiments were presented in tables. They gave a more detailed analysis than Niko had done in his PhD thesis, of general characteristics of objects used by the wasp to find its way back to its nest: large objects were more important than small ones, objects with contrast more than even-coloured ones, three-dimensional ones more than two-dimensional, near more than far, tall more than short, and

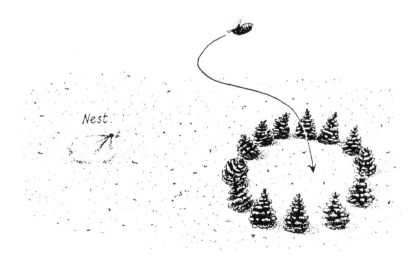

Bee-wolf homing experiments (note landmarks around nest entrances). Hulshorst, about 1938. Photo Niko Tinbergen.

so on. The third paper (with R. van der Linde) described experiments in which wasps were transported over distances of up to one kilometre in all directions, to see if they had some kind of sense of direction towards their nest: they had not, so the conclusion was that they had to learn the location by experience.

In their spare time, when the sun wasn't shining and the wasps were inactive, Niko, Luuk, and one or two others picked up the observations on hobbies again, spending hundreds of hours in hides near the nests of these wonderfully fast falcons. Niko's hunting instincts were stimulated again: 'To see a hobby whiz straight down from perhaps 1,000 ft., wings almost folded alongside the streamlined body, and grab a swallow in passing so you can hear the impact 100 yards away is really an experience. The rush of air as the hobby shoots through it like a meteor is almost frightening.'[39] The observations produced a long, descriptive paper on parental behaviour,[40] demonstrating that the male would hand over food to the female in flight, but only if the prey was of sufficiently large size (not, for instance, a dragonfly). The female would then feed the waiting chicks. Chicks would beg from any adult (but only from an adult in flight), and adults would feed any chick, not just their own.

All these Hulshorst observations and experiments in the early and mid-1930s were done with a tremendous enthusiasm by Niko and his students, and no doubt everyone learnt a great deal from the experience, and enjoyed it madly. Niko was at the centre of it all, which was no mean feat for someone in his twenties. He and his students did not cover a great deal of new ground. They addressed the sort of questions about orientation with which various digger wasp-watchers and birdwatchers in Germany, France, and Britain had been

occupying themselves for over thirty years. Niko was aware of this, as shown from the references he quotes. He was more precise in his arguments and experiments than the work that had been done with solitary wasps before, but a new approach it was not.

Niko's experiments at that time showed resemblance to those of a German scientist who was very active at that time, Karl von Frisch, with whom Niko would later share his Nobel Prize. Von Frisch worked with honeybees, and did outstanding research in the field on the performance of different sense organs by bees. Niko greatly admired the elegant, clean work of von Frisch and his associates (including Mathilde Hertz).[41] He was fascinated and inspired by their experiments, 'methodologically faultless and beautifully elegant in their sophisticated simplicity,'[42] and it showed in the kind of experiments that Niko himself set up with his students.

The Hulshorst work also did not continue with any deeper questioning of animal behaviour by Niko himself. There was 'a quite respectable chunk of truly new facts about the behaviour of these species,'[43] such as the observation that bee-wolves used certain kinds of landmarks. Just so. There was no further link-up with sensory physiology or ecology, and there was no follow-up in terms of further questions about the organization of behaviour (that was picked up later in another study by Gerard Baerends; see below). If one were to judge by scientific results alone, Niko's own Hulshorst projects were rather a dead end, not groundbreaking. But they gave the students involved a wonderful start in research.

Another, perhaps important, factor that motivated Niko in these Hulshorst studies showed through later. In 1958 he looks back at this period in his *Curious naturalists*:

When engaged in such work, it is always worth observing oneself as well as the animals, and to do it as critically and as detachedly as possible – which, of course, is a tall order. I have often wondered why the outcome of an experiment delighted me so much. A rationalist would probably like to assume that it was the increased predictability resulting from the test. This was a factor of considerable importance, I am sure. But a more important factor still (not only to me, but to many other people I have watched in this situation) is of a less dignified type: people enjoy, they relish the satisfaction of their desire for power. The truth of this was obvious, for instance, in people who enjoyed seeing the wasps being misled without caring much for the intellectual question whether they used landmarks or not.

Niko probably realized that it was the hunter in him that drove him on.

Experiments in Leiden

In that same period around 1934, Niko started his academic career with lectures in ethology, and from the next year onwards he was responsible for organizing a series of practicals in the lab. It was here, with his students, that Niko made real scientific progress, partly through the involvement of one particularly gifted individual (see below). The 6-week block-practicals were for third-year biology students,[44] with the aim of exposing them to real research, with experimental techniques. Most of the practicals were done with aquatic animals such as robber beetles, water scorpions, water boatmen, and sticklebacks, all subjects that Niko used to keep himself as a boy in his aquarium in his parents' garden in The Hague. Gerard Baerends, who was in the first batch of students exposed to this, remembered:

At the beginning of the course the students were asked just to observe the behaviour of their animals and record it as carefully as possible, with pencil and paper. Following this introductory period, they were encouraged to start asking questions, and thus to wonder about the behaviour they had observed. These questions were then critically discussed and where necessary corrected and refined. Finally, the students were invited to design and carry out experiments for testing their own hypotheses.[45]

Some of the practical projects were reported in the magazine *Living Nature*, for instance one on the feeding behaviour of the very large robber beetle *Dytiscus*.[46] Niko described the way in which these animals catch their prey (tadpoles), then analysed this with ingenious little experiments to see at what stage the sense of smell is important, when vision and when tactile stimuli are used, and where the relevant sense organs are located. This was new stuff, exciting work for the students, and even now it is still fascinating to read these clear and simple results, with their expert, explanatory drawings.

The most exciting observations and experiments by Niko's flock were done with the small, most common freshwater fish in Holland, the three-spined stickleback. In spring, the males of this fish are brightly coloured with a red belly; they vigorously defend a territory, and in that area they build a nest on the bottom. Males are attacked, but females are guided towards the nest with a specific way of swimming. The nest entrance is pointed out by the male with a specific posture, the female swims through the nest and deposits her eggs, and he follows and fertilizes them. Afterwards, he guards the nest and maintains a water current over the eggs, and when they hatch he guards the young fish, picking them up and spitting them back into the nest when need be. This much of the intricate life-story was already known, but in the practicals Niko and the students took it considerably further. One student stood out in all this, Luuk Tinbergen's friend Joost ter Pelkwijk, who took the lead, invented several of the experiments, and wrote all the results up jointly with Niko,[47] in a paper beautifully illustrated by Pelk himself.

Pelk was, like Niko, a rather wild outdoors person, highly intelligent and original, a gifted naturalist, with a great ability for drawing animals and people. He did not fit in well with formal education, having gone through eight different secondary schools.[48] He was known to have been refused service by a hairdresser because of all the sand in his hair. But he was on the same wavelength as Niko, and they were close; Niko felt Pelk had great potential as a biologist. Unlike, for instance, his contemporary, Gerard Baerends, of whom more below, Pelk was not one to worry about minute details of experiments, but he was full of enthusiasm and good ideas, and he was generally considered to be the brightest student around by far.

Niko, Pelk, and the other participating students showed that one could induce a male stickleback to attack a model-fish (for example, a dead one on a piece of wire, or a wooden stickleback hand-crafted and painted by Pelk). They showed, for instance, that a male attacked a model more often if it had a red belly, and males were said to be so ardent towards red bellies that they attacked in the direction of a red postal van driving past the window of the lab! Males also showed most courtship behaviour to female models with the largest bellies (full of eggs). Furthermore, if the model approached in the typical female 'courtship' posture, that is, pointing upward at an angle, then the male would guide it to the nest, and it would show its characteristic entrance-pointing. The students did a series of such experiments with models, also using fish kept inside test tubes and presented to the sticklebacks to react to, thus manipulating posture and movements. In this way they showed that the entire courtship sequence of the stickleback can be broken down into simple, separate elements, one leading to the next by each partner responding to particular stimuli of the other (called *sign-stimuli* or *releasers*), to particular colours, positions, and behaviours of the partner.

This result was a vitally important next step, leading to an understanding of animal behaviour that was one stage more complicated than had been achieved before. It came after the simple stimulus–response cases provided by the wasps in Hulshorst, and by the gulls rolling eggs into their nests. Here was a marvellously simple analysis of a *social interaction*.

How much of this new development was contributed by Niko, and how much was conceived in the ideas of Pelk or other students? It is difficult to answer this. I have experienced this problem at first-hand in Niko's group, and Niko acknowledged it in his later autobiographical notes.

> *Looking back, it is as impossible for me as it is for many of them to know with certainty which of the many ideas that have in my lifetime contributed to the growth of 'naturalistic' ethology, and later to a primitive kind of eco-ethology, originated in whose mind(s). Much has undoubtedly been the result of group work, of communal, often at first vague 'wondering'.*

All of us students, other researchers, and Niko himself took part in the intense, informal discussions during and after the work with animals, discussions including students and senior people on an almost equal footing. Niko was never one for pulling rank. There were ding-dong arguments, people coming up with ideas and others developing them or chucking them out. Niko guided the discussions almost imperceptibly, and sometimes not at all. Nobody could claim priority for ideas in those circumstances, and we all took it for granted that they would be used by Niko. It was quite likely that many of the insights in the stickleback story were Pelk's, and (as a rare occurrence) Pelk was also the senior author on the resulting papers, though only 22 years old and 7 years Niko's junior.

The stickleback study was to become an all-time classic, 'providing much of the evidence on which the concept of sign stimuli, releasers and the innate releasing mechanism are based.'[49] The research showed how an interaction between animals can be dissected into a series of changing stimulus and response relationships, each element of which is open to experimentation. Stickleback research was one of the backbones in the development of ethology, a paradigm forever associated with Niko.

Looking back at the stickleback story with all the benefits of hindsight, one can see that vital details were wrong. The researchers drew conclusions from inadequately controlled experiments. Almost half a century later, one of Niko's own former students, Piet Sevenster, then himself a professor in Leiden, repeated some of the work with a visiting American colleague. Sticklebacks responded somewhat reluctantly to models such as the ones used by Pelk and Niko, and when they did, males did not attack red-bellied models more than grey-bellied ones; in fact if anything it was the other way round (although there was a lot of variation between individuals). The experiments suggested that males were slightly more frightened of the red-bellied models. Also, males responded more to female horizontal models than to ones in head-up or head-down postures, unlike what was stated by Pelk and Niko. The original experiments were vindicated in the case of reactions to a big-bellied female.[50]

The case was discussed from many angles, and many more scientists joined the fray in the 1990s. The stickleback story that emerged was highly complicated: the reaction to models of red-bellied males depends on whether an encounter takes place inside or outside a territory. Inside, more attacks are released the more intensive the red is, just as Pelk and Niko showed. But it works only if two models are presented and compared simultaneously, and it does not work if a single model is presented as they described. Outside a territory the reaction from the fish is the opposite.[51] The real advantage of male red bellies appears to be a quite different one: the redder a male's belly, the more a female responds to it (and the biological function of this female reaction is that males with bright red bellies have fewer parasites and produce more offspring).[52]

Perhaps the reason for Niko's different results was that the earlier experiments had been badly controlled, and models had been presented manually by young experimenters who had an interest in the outcome. They (no doubt subconsciously) 'wanted' a male to attack a red belly, because it would fit the story, and they did not bother to quantify numbers of tests with different animals. The repeat experiments in the 1980s and 1990s were done with mechanically controlled models, were run many times, and were rigorously tested statistically.

Reading accounts of the original observations by Niko and Pelk, it was surprising that nobody tried to check the different reactions of the fish to involuntary movements made by the experimenter with the dummy. After all,

Male stickleback (Gasterosteus aculeatus) in threat display before mirror.
Photo Niko Tinbergen.

one of the results of the tests was that movements of the model were highly important. And when thinking about the lack of quantification in this work, I could not help but notice that at that same time Niko's brother Jan (then professor of statistics and mathematics in Amsterdam, a world expert in statistical analysis, founder of the science of econometrics) was insisting on quantitative analyses, stressing the overriding importance of a quantitative approach to scientific problems.[53] It was a call ignored by Niko, to his detriment. This lack of contact with his elder brother perhaps went right back to early childhood rivalries. As mentioned earlier, the youngest brother Luuk developed a much closer contact with Jan over statistical analysis,[54] and his later pioneering of a quantitative approach to ecology has been of fundamental importance.[55]

At the time, however, the stickleback story stood, and it became a classic well before the later reservations made any impact. Furthermore, even severe critics now would concede that the exact details of the results were not that important. It was the method that counted, the approach, the way of analysis. It was quite right, therefore, that the stickleback research was later prominently used in Niko's *The study of instinct*, in his *Animal behavior*, and in many textbooks by other authors. In 1936 it provided solid, basic support for the understanding of social behaviour.

Just at that juncture, Niko came in contact with Konrad Lorenz.

Niko and Konrad

The relationship between Niko Tinbergen and an intellectual giant, Konrad Lorenz, provides one of the strangest stories-within-the-story of Niko's life. It played an overriding role, and it profoundly affected the course of his career and the course of behavioural science. The Niko-and-Konrad tale is one of a deep, lifelong attraction and friendship between two totally different characters, one a wildlife-lover and the other a keeper of animals, two people who were not just accidentally but vehemently on opposite sides during the Second World War, who were socially very different, who agreed and disagreed over their science, and who complemented as well as annoyed each other. When they were in the same room the air would be full of their tales, and roars of laughter. Together they were, in Konrad's words, two 'Lausbuben' (street urchins).

Konrad was four years older than Niko. He was a large man in every sense, with a big shock of hair and a beard, an ebullient extrovert, always the life and soul of the party who needed to impress. Desmond Morris commented that 'his style was as flamboyant and colourful as Tinbergen's had been gentle and persuasive ... unashamedly anecdotal, and tables or figures were nowhere to be seen ... living proof that eccentric, inspired guesses are frequently the basis of scientific progress ... his whole life-style seemed to be an animal-infested chaos.'[56]

Lorenz bubbled with ideas, was well read in many fields around his own subject, including philosophy, and a brilliant linguist (he once claimed to me to know at least the basics of 23 languages, and he was fluent in several). Konrad grew up as a German living in Austria, in a large and rich country house called Altenberg, close to Vienna. His father was a surgeon. Unlike Niko, Konrad was not a naturalist in the narrow sense of the word, but he kept animals of many kinds at home (mostly birds, fish, and dogs); he bred them, lived with them, and knew them intimately. Konrad was always surrounded by many different pets and aquariums, but Niko never even kept a dog. Like Niko, Konrad had the gift of the observer: he saw in tremendous detail, and felt in his fingertips what was going on between the animals he kept.

The difference in character between the two men shows strikingly in their respective autobiographies, which they contributed to the volume of 19 biographies of prominent animal behaviourists, edited by Donald Dewsbury in 1985. Niko's 'Watching and wondering' is hesitating, often somewhat self-deprecating, and wise, looking at and enjoying his own history but rarely justifying himself, only showing a little pride here and there, without claiming more for his contribution than was his due. He conveyed 'Haven't I had a lucky life'.[57] Konrad, on the other hand, wrote a piece with a title that (characteristically) he had copied from another author ('My family and other animals', G. Durrell), in which he showed himself hugely pleased with his abilities and intellect, displaying his achievements (which were many), and promoting his own genius with supporting anecdotes. Typically, he describes his first boyish looking at the behaviour of fish and birds at home, and concludes 'This is actually the discovery on which all ethology is based'.[58] Modesty was not his strongest virtue. Nevertheless, the minds of these two opposites somehow slotted into each other.

Lorenz had published a few papers in the late 1920s and early 1930s,[59] describing and interpreting the behaviour of his jackdaws. Niko had read them, but they had not stirred him greatly, and the two exchanged a few formal, polite letters. Then, in 1935, came Konrad's enormous and best-known contribution, 'Der Kumpan in der Umwelt des Vogels',[60] all 200 pages of it, with an index of 17 pages (translated from German into much-abridged English as 'The companion in the bird's world', in 1937).[61] It was a paper that had a lasting effect, perhaps surprisingly so. The impact was not instantaneous, but took years to build up; it may well have been partly Niko's influence that helped to put it on the map.

The 'Kumpan' was a long, rambling piece, written in difficult prose. The often convoluted style with many long words was only partly due to the difference in writing style between German and English; partly, it was just Konrad. Nevertheless, between the long descriptions of observations on his birds there were ideas on the organization of behaviour that made instant sense to Niko. Perhaps the most important aspect of Konrad's approach was that he thought of behaviour patterns of animals, of 'instincts', as if they were organs that evolved, and which could be compared between species as one would compare wing structures or feet or bills. One could analyse their structure and function. This especially appealed to Niko, who in Leiden was assisting with a course in comparative anatomy in which the search for homologies (similar organs in related species, with common evolutionary ancestry) was central.

Lorenz argued that each instinctive behaviour pattern was 'released' by a combination of species-specific stimuli, like a key that fitted a lock. Some of these *releasers* are behaviour patterns or structures in partners; for instance, almost all striking colours and shapes of feathers act as releasers in some way or other. The instinctive behaviour patterns released in this way are fundamentally different from 'learnt' or 'intelligent' behaviour. He called them 'innate releasing schemes'; later, Niko and he would change that to *innate releasing mechanisms* (IRM). However, he showed that some instinctive behaviour patterns have a learnt component as releaser: Konrad described *imprinting*, in which, for example, the following response of goslings towards an object (usually their parent) is learnt during a very short period of their life (and cannot be changed thereafter).

As another important point, Konrad referred to behaviour as occurring in different functional classes ('Funktionskreizes'), such as breeding, fighting, etc.: an inkling that there might be some kind of systematic arrangement of behaviour inside the animal (although Konrad did not take this further). A highly important aspect of animal behaviour that Lorenz recognized was, what he termed, *appetitive behaviour*. This was often spontaneous and could bring an animal into a position where it could respond to environmental stimuli with a *fixed action pattern*, a *consummatory act*. For instance, searching for a mate is 'appetitive behaviour' that may lead to the consummatory act of copulation.

Because behaviour patterns are species-specific, just like organs, one can also use them as taxonomic characters when comparing species. About 20 years earlier Oscar Heinroth, who was Konrad's mentor, had already pointed this out in his enormous study on (captive) ducks.[62] Konrad elaborated on this extensively. It was, incidentally, Heinroth who first used the term 'ethology' as we use it now, and through him it was passed on to Konrad. Lorenz also recognized that animals have emotions that accompany instincts, but he did not appear to be greatly interested in these. His suggestion of selected stimuli (*sign-stimuli*) from

an animal's environment, triggering specific behaviour patterns, originated from another one of his heroes, famous at the time also well outside Germany. Jakob von Uexküll had previously considered the difference between the environment of an animal, as it could be assessed objectively, and the selected part of this environment that the animal subjectively perceived, its 'Umwelt'.[63]

As they stood, Konrad's suggestions in the 'Kumpan' paper could be seen as arm-waving, as good but unfounded hypotheses, not backed by hard evidence and put forward rather noisily. However, they struck a well-tuned chord with Niko, who just at that time was emerging with his (highly relevant) stickleback story from the Leiden student practicals. Konrad's paper had an immediate effect on the work in Leiden. It was intensively discussed and even used as exam material, and everybody involved felt the need to test these ideas, to do experiments, to study different species. Niko wrote to Konrad, and a discussion started. About a year later and purely by chance, Lorenz had to go from Vienna to Belgium on a business errand (to collect some vehicles for the business of a relative), and Niko persuaded his head of department van der Klaauw to organize a symposium on 'Instinct' (what nowadays we would call a workshop), where Lorenz could discuss his ideas. It took place in Leiden on 28 November 1936. Others present included Bierens de Haan, Verwey, Portielje, and the British animal psychologist E. S. Russell, as well as the local students who had been so much involved in Niko's work.

In Niko's words,

> I was fascinated both by Lorenz's paper and by what he said during those few days of discussions; from his side he immoderately enthused about our stickle-back work: 'That is just what we need!', was his often repeated comment. I was frankly astonished at his undue admiration for our work; in my view the experiments were so common-sensical and so much dictated by the relative rigidity of the hundreds of mating sequences we had seen ... that, although I felt of course greatly flattered, I honestly could not see what all the fuss was all about![64]

Konrad was right, of course: Niko's experimental approach was indeed just what he needed, as he was totally non-experimental himself. Niko, on the other hand, had suddenly been given the theoretical underpinning essential for his work.

The two also hit it off immediately on a personal level, during their first meeting in Leiden. Konrad and his wife stayed with the Tinbergens, and discussions and jokes flowed well into the night. Further plans were made, and during that time the Lorenzes invited the Tinbergens to come over to Altenberg for three months, lock stock and barrel, for more discussion, and for joint work.

In spring 1937 the trip happened: Niko, Lies (pregnant with their second child), and little Jaap went over to Austria. Niko had negotiated an absence from Leiden with van der Klaauw, he received a grant from a Dutch foundation ('Donderfonds'), and, clearly, everybody had a tremendous time. To quote Niko again, in the same, modest retrospective almost 50 years later: 'Those delightful spring months at the foot of the Vienna woods in early 1937 laid the foundation for our lifelong friendship and collaboration, even though we each chose our own course and in some respects drifted apart scientifically (with Konrad always in the lead in theoretical and philosophical matters)'. Whilst Konrad, writing at the same time as Niko, confessed 'this summer with Niko Tinbergen was the most beautiful of my life. What we did scientifically had the character of play and, as Friedrich Schiller says, "Man is only then completely human when he is at play." Niko and I were the perfect team. … I missed Niko Tinbergen most dreadfully when he left Altenberg in the autumn of 1937.'[65]

During Niko's stay another long paper by Konrad appeared in print, this time in the flagship German science journal *Die Naturwissenschaften*.[66] In this, he reviewed various behaviour schools and their philosophies, defended his own ideas of instinct against alternatives, and discussed the occurrence of instinctive behaviour at times when it is non-functional. Again he described *vacuum activities* (behaviour performed for no apparent reason), imprinting, and the comparative behaviour of related species. It was the material for long discussions with Niko, who also accompanied Konrad when the latter gave his weekly lecture to students in Vienna. And when they were not talking or studying the birds, they would be digging ponds for the geese (literally; especially Niko was keen on this), or Niko would be prowling around with his camera (taking many now-classical pictures of Konrad and his goslings).

Konrad Lorenz and his 'imprinted' goslings, during Niko's visit to Altenberg, 1937.
Photo Niko Tinbergen.

From Altenberg Niko wrote to his Dutch friend Bierens de Haan (trans.):

> *My mother-in-law, who always very endearingly writes everything that might interest me, passed on a remark by you, which suggested that I would not have much to learn from L., but rather that I should provide him with criticisms and guidance. That is not correct. Lorenz is far ahead of me in thinking through observations and results of experiments, his mind is enormously mobile and sharp, and as regards shaping hypotheses and combining conclusions I have learned a lot here. He is also a sharp observer, at least as good as I am, and I believe better. But as an experimenter he is superficial and uncritical (for instance in tracing sources of bias); moreover, he is bad in designing experiments. He will never learn that – but I am convinced that he is a great man; he will certainly play an important role.*[67]

Although Niko and Konrad were to see much more of each other over the following decades, the one and only publication they ever produced jointly resulted from this first stay in Altenberg. It became a celebrated paper, on egg-rolling by geese, and it was published immediately after the work was done.[68] In a footnote, Konrad is credited with the theoretical parts of the work, Niko with the design and operation of the experiments. Briefly, when an incubating grey-lag goose spots one of her eggs outside her nest, she will stretch out and roll it back in with the underside of her beak. Konrad and Niko recognized an instinct movement which, once set in train, runs its complete course even if someone takes the egg away in the process. At the same time, however, the goose adjusts the position of its bill to movements of the egg, thereby steering it. These lateral movements stop when the egg is taken away, but not the main rolling-in. Replace the egg by a similar-sized wooden cylinder and the lateral bill movements adjust to this. So there is an instinct-action with its specific releaser, and a separate direction-component, also with its own stimuli.

It was a nice set of small experiments, showing details of a behavioural mechanism that made a good story. The experiments did not include any repeats, and most of them were probably done with just one bird. Clearly, they found their origin in some of the egg-rolling experiments Niko had done earlier with terns and gulls, but, less clearly, they enabled Konrad to hold forth with long-winded theory. The paper is dominated by Konrad's deliberations about instinct movements and taxes; Niko's parts dealing with the experiments are written much more simply.

The goose paper announces further research, but nothing ever came of this from either Niko or Konrad. I believe that the reason why the two never again published together was Konrad's very German style of writing, in his case also domineering and rather bombastic, which must have been anathema to Niko, despite his warm affection for Konrad as a person. Niko once quoted Mark Twain (in guidelines for students about writing reports) 'Whenever the literary German dives into a sentence, that is the last you're going to see of him until he emerges on the other side of the Atlantic with a verb in his mouth.' Ernst Mayr was also dismissive of Lorenz's writing: 'to a layperson apparently the big-sounding words and poetical sentences are very appealing, but that there is nothing behind it is not apparent to outsiders.'[69]

Another toy for the two enthusiasts in Altenberg was a long piece of string. It was tied high up in a tree, and ran over an enclosure with small goslings and turkeys; along this, Niko, perched on a branch, could send cardboard models of birds whizzing down. Niko struck upon the idea that the same piece of cardboard looked like a goose when flying one way (long neck, short tail) and like a hawk when going the other way (short neck, long tail). The goslings noticed the same: they ignored the goose shape and were highly alarmed by the hawk. Other shapes of model did not affect the goslings and turkeys. It was a lovely, simple demonstration that a small change in the stimulus situation, in the 'sign-stimuli', caused a large difference in behaviour, and it was textbook material for years to come. It is one of those typically simple Niko experiments for which he was so admired.

Unfortunately, however, the story did not stand up to scrutiny, and things were more complicated than Niko made out when he finally wrote it up in 1948.[70] Many years later several other researchers tried, but could not repeat the result with well-controlled and quantified experiments.[71] Some were working with hens, some with turkeys, some with ducks, and there was little evidence of the purported sign-stimuli: birds showed no systematic differences in responses to any of the models. The problem was solved in the 1960s by one of Konrad's former students, Wolfgang Schleidt, who showed that young turkeys reacted with alarm to any slow-moving shape overhead, even a very small one (as long as it moved at 5–10 model-lengths per second) and they rapidly lost this reaction to a specific shape if the test was repeated.[72]

Niko later admitted that maybe his result was due to Konrad's goslings and turkeys being used to the shapes of flying geese, and showing alarm for any rare model.[73] Somehow, it did not matter that much. The idea behind the results, the field experimental analysis of shapes and their effects on birds, was more important than the results themselves.

Some other experiments that Niko did in Altenberg were with nestlings of birds. In the previous two years he had started a project with one of his students

in Leiden, Don Kuenen (later to become professor there), on the begging behaviour of young song thrushes and blackbirds. They watched nestlings in the wild and also brought them into the lab to be fed by hand, to find out exactly what set off the spectacular screaming and gaping mouths of the chicks. Niko continued with some of these observations in Konrad's set-up, and he wrote it up. In this paper, as so often with the early ethological studies, his general approach and methodology were especially appealing: Niko saw a behaviour pattern (begging by very young chicks), separated this behaviour into different, simultaneous components, and analysed how they change over time and which stimuli elicit them. There is no reference to feelings of 'hunger' or 'wanting to eat' of the young chicks, just a straight, almost physiological analysis of observable movements.[74]

Niko and Don concluded that there are two separate mechanisms underlying begging behaviour, one that releases and one that directs (just as in the egg-rolling geese). In very young chicks the releasing mechanism is vibration, but at later age the necessary stimulus becomes 'a moving shape above eye-level and larger than 3 mm'. The directing mechanism is initially based on gravity (throats pointing upwards), while later it operates visually and chicks point at the head of the parent bird, and the researchers experimented with cardboard models to discover the characteristics of 'head' (relative size, placed high up on model, etc.). The paper by Tinbergen and Kuenen dealt with a problem rather

similar to that of Lorenz and Tinbergen on egg-rolling in geese, but it was far less pretentious and more elegant.

At the end of the Tinbergens' stay in Lorenz's comfortable surroundings, Niko had a foundation of theory for what he felt he wanted to do with animals. He may not have been entirely at ease with Konrad over all the latter's theorizing and over his style of writing, and he was clearly much happier dealing with wild animals than with tame ones. But the Altenberg period gave Niko the theoretical base needed to satisfy his urge to play tricks on wild animals.

On his way back from Austria to Holland Niko called in on the laboratory of a man he greatly admired for his experimental skills: Karl von Frisch, in Munich. This became a remarkable trailer for the future: coming back from the broad visions of Lorenz, to combine these with the sharp experiments of von Frisch. It was to be Niko who pulled the skills of the two older scientists together in his own work, and it was the three of them jointly who were to be awarded the big prize.

The visit to von Frisch in 1937 also presaged other changes. In the corridor of von Frisch's lab, a student threw a 'Heil Hitler' salute at the professor, which von Frisch acknowledged with the more friendly 'Grüss Gott' of southern Germany.[75] It worried Niko at the time, and as he expected, von Frisch's life would later be made very uncomfortable under the Nazis. A more striking contrast with Konrad Lorenz could hardly be found: Konrad became a member of the National Socialist party in Austria less than a year later. Given their friendship and close contact, Niko must have been fully aware of Konrad's sympathies when he left for Holland.

Leiden after Lorenz

Niko was bouncing with energy after his stay with Konrad, and there was a lot to do. Almost immediately after getting off the train in Leiden in June 1937, he and Lies moved to another small house in the same street (now 45 Meloenstraat). Their son Jack was not yet three years old, and Lies was well along in her pregnancy with Toos (Catrina), who was born in August. Later the family was to move again, to another, larger terraced house but this time on the corner, in the more quiet, up-market bird-area of Leiden: 8 Leeuwerikstraat (Lark street). That was where Dirk, the third chick of the brood, was to be born two years later, in November 1939.

Leeuwerikstraat in the 1930s was a time of salad days for the Tinbergen family, probably their happiest in Holland. Work was going well, they lived in a pleasant part of town, Lies had her children playing in the street unthreatened by traffic, and friends were right next door. They knew Henk and Jo Casimir from NJN days and camps; Henk was in the physics department of the university, and he was later to become head of research of Philips Electronics, internationally known for his discovery of the Casimir force in electrodynamics.

Their children and the Tinbergens' were of similar age; coincidentally, many years later the two eldest Casimir children were to become my friends, also in the NJN.

Small flashes of reminiscence still survive. The Tinbergen and Casimir toddlers dominated the two adjoining gardens, picking flowers and joining hands, shouting 'wedding!', and running in and out of each others' houses. Jo Casimir described her friend Lies: 'she did everything that Niko wanted, she was the old-fashioned mother-hen'. Their families spent feast days like Christmas and Easter together, and Niko and Henk used to go skating on canals and lakes. Together they bought a very large pike from a fisherman they met, in 1941 after war had broken out, and it became a monumental meal for both families. Lies stockpiled eggs in the attic, to cope with frequently ailing children's stomachs, and she struck disaster one winter when everything froze.

The children still remember Niko's riotous games at home, he as wild as a teenager himself. Jaap (Jack) told: 'He'd sit on one of those living room chairs after dinner, Toos [Catrina] and Dirk on his knees, myself standing on the back of the chair. Niko would make steamboat noises, rock the boat suggestively, point out flying fish, the Statue of Liberty, icebergs, etc. At times Lies made him stop, as she was getting seasick just from watching'. Catrina wrote:

> *we would perhaps all be talking at the same time and we would not realize how noisy we were, and father would start banging his hands on the table chanting: 'And now we all make noise, noise, noise, noise, hey hopsasa noise, noise.' We would of course all join in with great glee banging the table and screaming with laughter, and then we would finally all be quiet.*

Pictures of family life: Niko taking Jaap skating, the little boy only five years old; working away on a doll's house for Catrina (he was hopeless at carpentry), and helping the seven-year-old Jaap with the fretsaw, to make furniture for it. Making funny drawings for everybody, writing poetry for the annual St Nicolas events. All these are snippets of a happy time, not always easy but complete, a time of family sunshine before the storm. It linked in with Niko's professional success; he was still a mere assistant, soon to become a lecturer in 1939, but already his research and lectures were drawing attention. Every week students used to come to the house for discussion meetings, where observations, experiments, and the latest animal behaviour literature were on the table. These meetings were contact points between personal and professional life, where students got to know the personal ground of their teacher, and where Lies had the opportunity to take part in Niko's interest. Students occupied much of Niko's mind at that time: he talked to them formally and informally, organized practicals, and arranged their participation in exciting research projects.

Niko was an excellent, and very popular, lecturer. One could never forget his soft-spoken and gentle delivery, wide-open eyes looking at the audience, a smile on his face, the odd hand movement emphasizing his points, shining with

Father Niko and children, just before his internment. Hulshorst, 1942. Left to right: Toos
(Catrina), Dik (Dirk), and Jaap (Jack). Courtesy of the Tinbergen family.

enthusiasm throughout, and packing in the odd little joke. Students loved it,
and ethology could not have had a better advocate.

He was ambitious, but he was not interested in acquiring influence for its
own sake. Niko was keen to get promotion, but he avoided appointments to
committees, obviously rather enjoying it when he could cock a snook at an
invitation. When asked to become honorary treasurer of the Dutch Zoological
Society, he replied (trans.): 'although of course I would have grasped with joy
the opportunity to give a loose rein to my passions for the treasury, I cannot
even consider giving in to these (almost insuperable) urges.'[76] He did accept the
job of editor of the (Dutch) Journal for Professional Biologists in 1940 (following Bierens de Haan), a journal that reached mostly teachers of biology, because
this gave him full opportunity to popularize his own field.

During this time Niko made a long trip to America, from July to October
1938, his first visit there. It was a trip on a shoestring, although he got some small
grants, but he made some money on the way by lecturing; his $100 for a lecture
in Cornell was a fortune. He visited many of the great names in animal
behaviour research, and these contacts had a large effect on his understanding of
current thinking, on the perspective of his own position, and on what he
wanted out of research. During his three months there he wrote numerous long
letters home and to colleagues, of which several survive to document Niko's
thinking at the time.[77]

He enjoyed the boat-trip across, watching whales, dolphins, flying fishes,
and birds, and America struck him, as a conventional European, in classical

fashion (letter to Bierens de Haan, 22 September 1938, which tells as much about Niko as it does about America) (trans.):

> *Everything here happens so totally differently. Money, land, space and materials are in plenty, perhaps even in super-abundance. People, at least in New York are also too many, and the high urban population density goes together with the well-known phenomena of degeneration: enormous luxury next to great poverty, unhealthy people, beautifully painted but childless women, dirty and dusty streets full of rattling marvels of technology.*

He found it all fascinating, but soon he had seen quite enough of it, and was longing for his birds. Even in the middle of a city like New York, what interested him especially was that gulls flying along the Hudson River would go over a 100 m-high bridge, rather than under. But he had a tremendous time, he was feted by his hosts, and he marvelled at the luxury of expensive beach-clubs, his ice-cold beers, and the movies. And he learnt a great deal professionally.

He first spent a considerable time in the American Museum of Natural History in New York, mostly with two people: G. K. Noble and Ernst Mayr. Noble's main interests were in the roles of conditioning and of hormones in behaviour, and he also experimented with such problems as the use of colours as stimuli in courtship of lizards and birds. He should have had much in common with the Dutch ethologist, but Niko was rather critical. He found Noble very knowledgeable, but secretive about ideas and results, and also messy, hasty, and superficial in his experiments.[78] Niko stayed for some time at the home of Mayr, then still a 'young upstart' in Niko's eyes, 'but clever, a polymath with critical views of animal behaviour', who provided valuable criticisms on Niko's manuscript of the snow bunting work.[79] Some forty years later Niko would reflect about his interests in evolution: 'I remained an ignoramus until I met Ernst Mayr (1938), and his *Systematics and the origin of species* gave me a real push.'[80]

At Yale Niko briefly met the famous R. M. Yerkes, zoologist and pioneer in comparative psychology, whose pursuit was 'intelligence' in many different animals, and he visited Yerkes' chimpanzee research in Orange Park, Florida. In a conference at Cold Spring Harbor Niko contributed a substantial paper on social behaviour[81] (he called it 'social organization', but he dealt with signals and responses between birds). It was published in the USA, but he would soon expand this into a much larger paper to be published in Europe.

'I now have a bit of an idea of American psychology', Niko wrote (trans.), 'also by looking at some of the textbooks. I had never expected that methodologically one would be so strict here, and I was pleasantly surprised to see how consistently one strives for objectivity. ... strongly tied to methods and whatever-one-can-do with them'. He noted

> *a resistance to thinking about problems and to shaping an organisation of problems. ... From the beginning they all focus on man, monkey and rat, Yerkes as an exception. I believe that in their own problems they are ahead of*

us, that is in those problems that roll out of maze-experiments etc. Yet I think
that we are on a better path by starting from problems that are dictated to us by
the [animal's] behaviour, then finding an appropriate method.

In Niko's opinion the work that he and Pelk had done, or the *Philanthus* (bee-wolf) work, would be quite out of place in America at that time, 'and if anyone ever does something like this, it is methodologically so childish that one cannot understand why a journal would publish it.' He saw the lack of experience in this type of work amongst American scientists as the reason why Noble's work was so superficial.[82]

The trip to America had two immediate consequences. Firstly, it gave Niko a large boost in confidence in the research of himself and his group. Comparing his own work with what was going on elsewhere in the world, he felt satisfied with his Leiden performance. He knew that he could counter criticisms, that his approach was valid, and he was in a position to criticize other views of animal behaviour. This increased confidence shows in his scientific papers, and in letters. Secondly, and more tangibly, his American hosts were impressed, and he was being considered for a couple of upcoming positions in the USA: one as head of a new animal behaviour field station in Albany, and the other as head of a department of ornithology being created in Wisconsin. Niko was tempted though not bowled over by these ideas; in the end, he used the offers to excellent effect by asking his Leiden superior Boschma for advice,[83] and not many months after that the Leiden faculty offered him a lectureship.

Research at Leiden was going well, as testified by several important papers from his hand, and by the continuing stream of popular articles in *Living Nature*. With Pelk and several other undergraduates he designed experiments for a student practical on a small fish, the bitterling, the male of which defends a freshwater mussel as a moving territory. The female deposits her eggs in the gills of the mussel (and later, the mussel expels its planktonic babies which attach themselves for some time to the fish: an interesting symbiosis). The experiments (with models, mirrors, and tubes of scented water) showed, amongst other lovely little details, that it was the mussel's scent that was a critical stimulus for both males and females, whereas it was the mere sight of another male bitterling that drove a male to attack.[84] In another series of practicals Niko and his students studied the feeding and courtship behaviour of the smooth newt, again with elegant little experiments.[85] Pelk collaborated intensively in all this, and many of the ideas and later illustrations were his. He was closer to Niko's work than anyone else at the time.

Summer activities in the Hulshorst camp still focussed on the bee-wolf *Philanthus*, but other projects were also started there. For instance, Niko and his students performed an interesting demonstration on animal camouflage and how natural selection operates to maintain it: small stick caterpillars were exposed to predation by jays, and they showed under what conditions the birds were successful, and when not.[86] (Some 10 years later this was to be the subject of

a major PhD study under Niko by Leen de Ruiter.) Niko began to become
enthralled by animal tracks in the sand and what he could deduce from them, as
shown in his article on the natural history of central Holland, the 'Veluwe'.[87]
Tracking animals was to become a passion in his later years. The major student
project that Niko started in Hulshorst at that time was on the behaviour of the
grayling, a rather inconspicuous butterfly and a common occurrence throughout Europe in dry, sandy areas. The result of this study was another classic paper
that came out in 1942, standard material for many later textbooks, and Niko's
last substantial publication in German.[88] More than eight students worked on it
over several summers.

The grayling is dark greyish brown, with some lighter and yellow patches
and a few eye-spots, and the sexes are slightly different in colour. The male sits
on the ground and chases passing females; when successful, the female lands,
followed by her suitor, and they sit opposite each other with several displays. At
some stage the male squeezes the female's antennae between his forewings, after
which he walks round, hooks his abdomen onto that of the female and mating
takes place. The researchers analysed different phases of this procedure, which
stimuli caused what, just as in the stickleback work. After noting that males,
when they were on the job, chased almost any kind of butterfly, the students
flew butterfly models at the end of a rod-and-line held by an observer. By
varying the model they studied the success of shape, size, colour, and movement
in releasing the reaction of the male.

Results showed that the darker the model, the more likely that the male
would follow it, but it appeared that shape was of little consequence (a round or

Camouflage of grayling butterfly (Eumenis semele). Hulshorst, 1938. Photo Niko Tinbergen.

square disc was just as good as a butterfly shape). Size mattered; in fact larger
models were followed even more often than natural-sized ones: they were
'super-normal'. Especially important was the model's way of flying: it needed to
'dance' or tumble about, rather than fly smoothly. All these characteristics acted
simultaneously in a cumulative fashion, so they were co-ordinated somewhere
in the grayling's central nervous system. One thought about that as a 'black
box', where one knows input and output but not what goes on inside. With
other experiments, the researchers showed, for instance, that in the behaviour
following the chase, the male causes the female to touch a patch of scented scales
on his forewing with her antennae, and this was a necessary stimulus for
copulation to proceed.

The conclusions from these experiments probably assisted a great deal in
establishing ethology as a sound science, and they found their way into many
textbooks. The experiment suggested that here was scientific rigour, with experimental field tests of ideas, something that was lacking in the theories that came
from Konrad Lorenz. Nevertheless, it is difficult not to be critical of the charming simplicity of Niko's method. It must have been terrific fun for the students
pursuing heavy science with their models on rod-and-line, in the beautiful
wilds of pre-war Holland. But as one of the results of the experiments showed,
the manner of movement of the models was critical for their success in eliciting
the male's response. Did that not leave a great deal of room for (unconscious)
observer error in almost all of the results? The presentation of data in graphs was

Student Luit Boerema dangling models before grayling butterfly. Hulshorst, 1938.
Photo Niko Tinbergen.

also rather mysterious; for instance, average values lay inexplicably outside the range of individual observations. Nowadays, this paper would not have passed the scrutiny of referees. But in the end, it was the innovative idea behind it that mattered, rather than the execution.

During these activities with students Niko still found time to finish the write-up of his Greenland snow bunting work, and he produced a batch of popular articles in *De Levende Natuur*, such as the three on the language of animals,[89] small ones such as on a bumblebee that learns the route between flowers,[90] on the opening of food items by gulls by dropping them in flight,[91] and on nest-building by long-tailed tits.[92] He wrote extensive reviews of the work by the American Margaret Nice[93] (which he admired greatly), and of Portielje (whom he gently took to pieces for his subjectivity).[94]

Interesting in a different manner was a piece he wrote for the *Vakblad*, the professional journal for biologists, of which he himself was the editor at the time. In it, he expounded on the need for biologists to explain their work to non-scientists,[95] a subject that stayed very close to his heart throughout his life. Despite its title (trans.) 'On the value of popularizing biology', he did not address the question of why it was important that a layperson should know about biology. He took it for granted that they should, and he criticized biological scientists for not providing the wherewithal.

He stated that society saw us, biologists, as people who did little more than enjoy themselves passively, at a cost to themselves and the state, and that the value of biology for the mental and material welfare of people was insufficiently realized. This was our own fault, he argued. He described 'nature minstrels' who write lyrically about animals and plants, but whose knowledge was third- or fourth-hand: people needed the accounts from biologists themselves. Biological scientists look down on popular writing, he alleged, but this condescension hides their own real or imagined inability. This was quite understandable, he felt, because the writing of scientific papers easily damages one's sense of language proper. Biologists should write for a more general readership in simple terms, which should be possible when their ideas are based on common sense. But often a scientific train of thought, without frills, appears to be what he called a 'bare baron', and only the really clear arguments will also be well-presentable in simple words. A popular publication is more demanding than a scientific paper. At the end of his plea he said disarmingly: 'Perhaps all this sounds rather bitter, and one could rightfully say: do better yourself. Perhaps I myself am not able enough, but there are biologists amongst us who decidedly can do it, yet they won't.' This from one of the best popularizers of behavioural science.

Niko also felt critical about the lack of popularizing of his science by his own students, although he never said so publicly. One was his most brilliant follower, Gerard Baerends, who in the late 1930s was completing his PhD study on the caterpillar-killing wasp *Ammophila*. It was an excellent piece of science, and Niko later confessed to feeling greatly embarrassed (envious?) by its fascinating results, produced whilst he himself had been on the spot but looking the other

way.[96] But Baerends was not a popularizer of science, and it was Niko, particularly, who brought Baerends' work to the layperson in his *Curious naturalists*.

Baerends and his wife (Niko's former student Jos van Roon) carried out a
very thorough, neat, and well-quantified study,[97] in which they showed that
their species of *Ammophila* made several burrows, holes in the sand with a chamber at the end. A caterpillar was deposited, an egg laid, and the hole closed again;
several days later the wasp would return, check the nest and provision it with
more caterpillars, and over the following days another check would be made
and a larger quantity of caterpillars added if the larva needed them.

In the meantime a wasp would start and maintain up to five other burrows
with larvae; it would remember the exact sites over several days, and especially,
it would remember their state of provisioning. The Baerends' subtle experiments (for example removing or adding caterpillars from nests of marked wasps
in between visits) showed the complexity of the behaviour of even such small
insects. A wasp would come for an inspection visit and perceive what was
needed, and this would decide the following series of provisioning visits; during
the provisioning visits themselves the burrow's content was irrelevant to whatever the wasp did next. The inspection visit brought the wasp into a given state,
and that state for that burrow would spark off a set of further actions irrespective
of changes after the inspection. One is reminded of the egg-rolling goose in
Niko and Konrad's experiment: once in a given mode, the wasp continued the
full behaviour regardless. With these observations the Baerendses demonstrated
the basis of a hierarchical organization of behaviour, with the wasp's actions for
each burrow going through a series of states, and that again interspersed with
other types of behaviour such as hunting, which could also be seen as organized
at a number of levels.

Gerard Baerends, in an autobiographical sketch,[98] related that the conclusions of his study in his main paper, and the realization of the hierarchical
structure of behaviour, were written jointly with Niko, his supervisor, who had
come to realize from his own work that the organization of the behaviour of
animals in general could be best understood in such terms of hierarchy. For
Niko, the Baerends' wasp study provided a beautiful and very opportune analysis, demonstrating a highly important concept. For Gerard Baerends, this was
his first acquaintance with a principle that would occupy much of his scientific
interest for the rest of his career.

During the previous few years Niko had been closely involved in studies of
many different kinds of behaviour in a variety of animals. Enormously helped
by his contact with Lorenz, he had started to think in terms of generalities of
cause and effect and function, and of common patterns in behaviour of all
animals and humans. In America he had presented a paper to a symposium that
started to outline such generalities, but that was only a beginning, and around
1940 he began to take this much further, just at the time that war shook
Holland, and when he had been appointed lecturer in Leiden. The result of this
was an important, 60-page scientific paper, 'An objectivistic study of the innate

behaviour of animals'.[99] It became the Credo of ethology, and although 10 years after he greatly expanded and improved it in *The study of instinct*, the landmark was this 'Objectivistic study' in 1942. It is a small monument, despite the forces of war that minimalized its impact at the time. Niko was in his early thirties.

Reading it some sixty years later, I find the 'Objectivistic study' a strangely moving paper. Published in an obscure Dutch series, *Bibliotheca biotheoretica*, it was printed on now brittle and yellowing war-time paper. It shows Niko's abilities as well as his weaknesses, more than any other document from that period. He saw it as a 'programme' for ethology, not a review, and he wrote it in terms of often strong advocacy, sometimes rather schoolmasterly and very assertive, in as-yet somewhat clumsy English. He frequently pronounced strong judgements on other studies, and talked about proven facts and absolute imperatives. Because of all this it now comes over as endearingly immature, but at the same time fresh and convincing.

Niko's aim was to outline the organization of behaviour in such a way that it would be opened up for observations and experiments. He contrasted his cause–effect (what he called 'objectivistic') methodology with the subjective approach: seeing a herring gull attack another, he would ask which stimuli of the opponent, which part of the environment (territory), and which internal characteristics would cause the aggression. What he rejected was assuming that the bird attacked because it 'felt angry' or 'disappointed'.

Niko's position on subjectivity versus objectivity was tolerant:

> once the question has been asked 'what causes this process?', these causes can only be detected by the usual objectivistic method of the natural sciences. On the other hand, once the question has been focussed on the problem 'which subjective phenomena can be detected in the animal?', research has to follow this line of thought, applying the appropriate method necessary to obtain the appropriate answers. Both these viewpoints, and others too, can enrich our picture of Nature, and I cannot see the use of a-priori rejection of one of them. However, failure to keep methods consistent and pure, such as starting to search for the cause of an animal's movements and ending with a statement about its emotions as intuitively felt by the observer, leads to confusion.[100]

In his 'Objectivistic study' Niko argued that animal behaviour has internal and external causes, and can be arranged in hierarchical fashion. For instance, environmental factors cause a stickleback to be in 'reproductive mood', which he more or less equated with 'reproductive drive'. Other such major drives would be, for example, a fleeing drive, or a feeding drive, and different drives exclude each other. Once in reproductive drive, given stimuli would cause 'sub-drives', such as a 'nest-building drive', a 'courting drive', or a 'fighting drive'. In each of those 'sub-drives', stimuli would cause the fish (for example, when in 'courting drive') to perform a zigzag dance, or to show the female the nest-entrance, or to fertilize eggs, etc.

It was Niko who suggested that a step-wise organization would apply to all behaviour, and that causal analysis of such a *hierarchy* is compatible with a physiological, exact scientific approach. Later authors would agree; Richard Dawkins, for instance, in a paper on hierarchical organization 35 years later, called it an 'indispensable classificatory device ... a generally powerful explanatory concept'.[101] Dawkins reviewed other (often better) hierarchy models that were proposed, including several by Adriaan Kortlandt at the same time as Niko (see below), and many later ones. It was especially Gerard Baerends who made the hierarchical structure of behaviour a cornerstone of his lifelong contribution to ethology.[102]

Following Konrad Lorenz, Niko assumed that all the drives and behaviour patterns included in his model were inherited, innate, and he referred to them as 'stereotyped movements' (later called fixed action patterns), each set off by a 'releasive mechanism' (the later innate releasing mechanism). However, within this arrangement there are searching phases, 'appetitive behaviour', as part of the drives and sub-drives. As Niko put it, the activation of a major drive (for example reproduction) leads to appetitive behaviour (for example the process of finding a nesting site), and this behaviour is continued until a certain stimulus (a suitable site) inhibits the searching and releases appetitive behaviour of a lower order (finding building materials), etc. 'The types of behaviour included under the term "appetitive behaviour" ... are of a perplexing multiformity and variety. In fact, they offer the real challenge to the ethologist', he wrote.

> *Appetitive behaviour includes the highest forms of conduct. We are not impressed so much by the sneezing, walking, sleeping, eating, copulating, etc. capacities of our fellowmen, but by the means, the detours, the endurance, the cleverness, etc. displayed by their appetitive behaviour. At the same time, the stereotyped movements are very small in number in comparison to the enormous variety of movements performed during appetitive behaviour.*[103]

The 'Objectivistic study' contained many definitions and categorizations, and there were long discussions of what are rightly or wrongly called instinct actions, reactions and reaction-chains, reflexes, vacuum activities, intention movements, substitute activities, and many others. It also singled out the importance of the study of function of behaviour, especially in communication: animal behaviour that is designed to carry information to another animal.

Much of the terminology and some of the principles outlined in this paper came from others, especially from Lorenz. The smallest units of behaviour in Niko's model corresponded with Konrad's 'Erbkoordinationen' (instinct actions), and the largest ones with McDougall's 'instincts' or von Uexküll's 'Funktionskreise' (function-circles). Niko gave structure to the previous chaos with his hierarchy, and he cleared the way for exact observations, experiments, and analyses.

This contribution, which is one of the peaks in Niko's output, firmly established ethology as an exact science. To support his cause–effect approach, he drew a comparison with physics, then seen as the highest achievement of science: 'As regards our older, or rather, more thrifty brother, Physics, we ought never to forget that he was applying strict and consistent objectivistic methods long before we began to do the same.'[104] Interesting, especially since his own older brother actually was a physicist. Expressing the principles much more clearly than Lorenz had ever done, Niko now became the mouthpiece of the new science, a role that he expanded in the 1950s with his books and papers.

In the process leading up to this major paper, his Credo, Niko had written one other, long theoretical review, published in German in 1940. It was on a much smaller subject, and he also included the gist of it in the 'Objectivistic study'. Since then Niko's name has been very much associated with the main behavioural phenomenon described in it, 'Übersprungbewegungen' or 'substitute activities' as he termed them then,[105] *displacement activities* as he called them later. Displacement activity is 'behaviour out of context'; for instance, in the middle of a fight a herring gull may perform nest-building actions, or an oystercatcher may adopt a sleeping posture. Or, in a tricky situation, a person may scratch behind his or her ear. Such behaviour had been remarked upon by several authors well before Niko (including Portielje, Selous, Huxley, Kirkland) and also by Niko himself in his observations on herring gulls and sticklebacks. It was nothing new, therefore, and Niko certainly did not 'discover' displacement activities. But he put them on the map as a special category of behaviour, and suggested a causal mechanism.

He pointed out that when two mutually conflicting drives (such as attacking and fleeing) occur in an animal at the same time, for example in a fight on the border between two territories, an animal will perform a behaviour from a totally different major drive, for example nesting, or feeding, or preening. There are also a few other situations in which displacement behaviour occurs, and Niko argued that in such cases an animal is unable to perform an immediately relevant behaviour (attack, or flight). When that happens, a surplus in 'drive' enables a quite different action to be realized. However, this different action always varies slightly from the original behaviour in its normal functional context. For instance, the nesting movements of a herring gull during a fight are much more vigorous and directed than when the bird is really making a nest. In such a case, the displaced behaviour has acquired a new function, secondarily in its 'new' environment: as a signal, a display, it becomes more conspicuous and stereotyped, and it acquires its own internal motivation. The grass-pulling of the herring gull has become a threat display, and is recognized as such by the opponent.

Niko finished the paper as he often did, in a rather self-effacing way: he admitted to many gaps in the story; it was not a finished product, but was meant as an invitation to further research. Despite such modesty, it had a large impact and was often quoted. Interestingly, in the same year as Niko's displacement paper appeared, another Dutchman published a long contribution with a review and analysis of hierarchies of behaviour organization, and of displacement activity.[106] This was Adriaan Kortlandt, and the relation between him and Niko was remarkable enough to warrant comment.

At the time these papers were published, Kortlandt was still in his early twenties. He was born in 1918, and as a teenage schoolboy started to photograph and study cormorants. Like Niko, he was a product of the NJN, encouraged first by Portielje and then also by Niko, in person and by letter. His contributions and career have been described in detail by Röell in his *De wereld van instinct* [The world of instinct],[107] and I met Kortlandt on several occasions and interviewed him in early 2001. Niko once summed him up: 'A new star in the sky of animal psychology is A. Kortlandt, a young fellow, very clever, very original, very "cormorant-minded"; for years he has lived among the Lekkerkerk cormorants, most of the time in a hide in the nest-trees, where he often stayed for one or more weeks day and night continuously, receiving his food by a "téléférique" '.[108] Kortlandt was an excellent and totally dedicated observer, with interesting ideas about behaviour. Obviously, he and Niko had much in common in interest and background, and there could have been a very productive collaboration between them. It was not to be; differences between the two men were huge and insurmountable, both in science and on a personal level.

The main scientific difference was that Niko confined himself to analyses of causes and biological function of animal behaviour, whereas Kortlandt wanted much more, he wanted to know, in his own words, about animal emotions and the purpose of life. A passage in a letter from Niko to Kortlandt, 14 November 1940, reads (trans.):

> When you people say that with causal analysis one does not discover the essence of life, OK, that is true; therefore we only want to know the mechanisms being used by life. A causal question can never get further. And I admit that someone who does not want to know God from his Works, but directly, may achieve much more satisfaction and insight. But he does not get to know the mechanisms that are God's Works. There are countless ways of approaching God; mine is one of them, and that of the artist is another. That of the 'emotion-psychologist' is another again. But I stick to my idea that all of us in our own way will get furthest if we keep our question and method pure, and not try to answer the question from one point of view with the reply from another.[109]

The letter showed Niko's specialism, and his tolerance towards others; he felt that Kortlandt was expecting the wrong answer (subjective emotions) from his objective observations.

Kortlandt wrote many polemical and haranguing letters to Niko about this and other topics: he sided firmly with McDougall, Portielje, and Bierens de Haan in ascribing animal feelings as the cause of their behaviour. If gulls float in the wind above the sand dunes (my example), one could say that they do this 'because they like it'. Niko, however, argued in the same letter to Kortlandt that

you scupper the problem by such a vitalistic baling out, just at the point where
we run to a stop with our analysis (because of the lack of facts at our disposal).
History of biology is full of such evasions; as soon as analysis hesitates to find a
new way, a lot of guys desert and are content with the easy vitalistic conclusion.

Over and above the scientific differences, the long-running controversy between the two was fuelled also by personality and other problems. Niko was very patient with the younger, awkward student who had some brilliant ideas, and helped him with writing his publications and later by providing references. But Kortlandt did not present well; he wrote in a difficult, unclear, and convoluted style (for instance about hierarchy as 'concentric purposiveness'), he was aggressive towards others (often presenting their ideas in a slightly modified way, so he could attack them), and he did not use English until well into the 1950s. Add to this his vitalistic views, and it was not surprising that at the time his work did not impress ethologists. He was critical and negative, and bitter in letters and publications about the lack of attention that his work achieved (especially when Niko ignored his views about displacement and hierarchy in the *Study of instinct*).

The coincidence of timing of the review papers by Kortlandt and Niko has inevitably led to suggestions that one or the other would have 'borrowed'. However, both Kortlandt and Niko stated explicitly that they were convinced of each other's integrity: they were both working on the same problem at the same time. As always, there was much discussion of ideas between them and with others (especially with Baerends), and as in so many instances also within Niko's group, the origin of the very first suggestion of an idea is impossible to establish. It is not unlikely that Niko was prompted by Kortlandt's manuscript, which he saw before submission. What proved to be decisive in the end was the clarity and authority with which Niko presented his ideas and reviews. Kortlandt lost out, and he has been largely ignored (which is a loss to science).

On 24 January 1940, at the age of 32, Niko sealed his authority in ethology with a public lecture in Leiden University, on the occasion of his appointment as lecturer in experimental zoology a few months earlier (in Holland a lectureship then had an authority similar to a personal professorship now). It was obviously a big occasion, with many Dutch colleagues interested in animal behaviour in the audience, as well as old friends and students. Under the title of a Dutch expression 'Every bird sings to the shape of its beak', he justified his own causal analyses next to other views of the animal world.[110] He did not claim to occupy the only road to truth, but he did argue that his was the right approach to behaviour as a natural science, specifically adding (trans.):

Fortunately the causal question is not the only one to occupy our mind. Pity
the scientist who recognizes only cause–effect relationships in his contemplation
of nature! … also the artist, the religious thinker and the naturalist have their
own opinions about the essence of nature that surrounds them, opinions that
are very different despite being founded on the same objects.

He then continued with a description of how behaviour can be analysed at different levels: a hierarchy of research strategies.

Niko ended with an admonition to students, which was equally a guideline that governed his own life:

> *Millions envy us the advantage of being able to develop our natural gifts with a great measure of freedom, and in favourable material circumstances. Let continuous awareness of this be a stimulus for dedicated work! However, let us not forget also that a sense of duty is not everything. If you are not inspired by a great enthusiasm for your profession, if you are not set alight by a spark of holy fire, then your sense of duty will be sterile.*

During the celebrations afterwards, in an old Leiden restaurant 'Den Ver-gulden Turck' [The gilded Turk], Niko's father Dirk contributed a splendid poem[111] to the occasion, eight pages in medieval Dutch, unfortunately not translatable without losing its magnificent flowery beauty. It marked the planting of Niko's flag of ethology.

CHAPTER 5

The Second World War
and after

German occupation

On 10 May 1940 German ground forces invaded Holland. It was expected, and when it happened the Dutch army, small as it was, put up an honourable resistance for a few days, but obviously did not have a chance. Niko was not directly involved in this; in 1939 there had been a mobilization of young males, but he had escaped it, as his elder brother Jan had been an approved conscientious objector, and under the law all his siblings were exempt from military service. On 14 May, Rotterdam was destroyed by the Luftwaffe. It was fire-bombed, with many thousands killed; this was the end of the fight, the army capitulated, and German jackboots overran every corner of Holland. The country had not been involved in the First World War, and this was the first invasion since Napoleon, a huge blow to a fiercely independent people.

In the months that followed, the Germans established their staff and their organization, trying to be friendly at first, then becoming increasingly bloody-minded when, at every turn, the people figuratively spat in their faces. Persecution of Jews began. The underground resistance movement established itself throughout the country. Acts of sabotage became common. On the other hand, some of the Dutch collaborated with the invader, greatly despised by the rest of the country. Despite all this, for most people life continued more or less as before, but with deep resentment stamped on the entire community.

Niko was one of those for whom things did not change much in the first two years of the war, at least not on the surface. University life continued for a bit, and he lectured and produced several important papers, some of which he published in German journals; he did not feel that German science should be held responsible for the atrocities of its government. The field camp in Huls-horst was not far from an important railway, which later in the war was bombed six times, and the Tinbergen holiday house in Hulshorst had all its windows blown out. They decided to move the camp to another site under large beech trees, so it could not be seen from the air. But such changes were relatively small; basically, Niko kept his head down and worked, keen to build on his success.

At home in Leiden the Tinbergens, together with their neighbours the Casimirs, took in many patients from the nearby orthopaedic hospital, people who had been evicted by the occupying forces to make way for German casualties. The two houses were more or less joined up and turned into a tiny field hospital, with the women taking on the role of nurses, and the children having great fun with all these excitements. Otherwise, civil life was little affected initially.

The quiet time could not last, of course. The occupying forces became more and more restrictive whilst being attacked from outside and inside the country, and problems were building up. But it was not until late 1942 that this came to a head for the Tinbergens. Immediately after the war, Niko wrote to Margaret Nice in the USA:

> *During the first year of occupation the Germans did not interfere so much with our life ... Soon however, the Germans began to register the Jews and to outlaw them, then to influence the schools and the teaching. Interference went on progressively and soon a point was reached where we felt we ought to stiffen and resist as much as possible. Our University was, by accident, the first group of Dutchmen to be tackled by the Germans as a group, and the first to refuse to surrender. The Germans wanted to 'cleanse' our corps of Jews and of anti-Nazis and proceeded to fire one professor, then another, step by step, on wholly irrelevant grounds. Soon we saw no other way than to resist by refusing to stay in the service of the German-controlled government, and soon after the University was closed by the Germans because of anti-German 'irregularities' sixty of our professors including myself laid down their function. This was at the same time our protest and our means to prevent the Germans to nazificate the University by dismissing only some few of us, for whom they had a nazi-replacement, and to keep the rest as 'flags' to adorn the planned nazi-university.*[1]

Things were not going to plan for the occupying forces in the Netherlands generally; military trains were being blown up, German soldiers were being shot at, public registers (with ancestry information) were destroyed, and generally, life became more and more uncomfortable for the 'moffen' (Boche). In response the occupying forces decided to meet the increasing incidence of sabotage with the establishment of hostage camps, accompanied by the threat to shoot hostages in return for any blow delivered by the resistance. Prominent people were selected for the hostage pool: ex-ministers, members of parliament, journalists, academics, famous writers and musicians, trade unionists, and others. The official German statement announced the arrest of 460 Dutchmen (trans.) 'who used to be in public life and of whom one can assume that they sympathize with the intrigues directed at the occupying force ... their lives a surety against violence instigated by the clique of emigrants in London'.[2] The first several hundred were rounded up on 4 May 1942 and put behind barbed wire, and smaller groups were added at later dates.

Although only a lecturer, Niko was picked up on 9 September,[3] whilst he was in Hulshorst with his family. At the same time as several Leiden professors who had resigned, he was collected at home by the police and transferred by train to the hostage camp Beekvliet. In peacetime this was a large seminary (training college for Roman Catholic priests), a neo-gothic complex of buildings in St Michielsgestel in the south of the country, some 100 kilometres from

Leiden. By chance I visited it some 10 years after Niko resided there, unaware then of the association it would later have for me. Even then Beekvliet struck me as a place with a frightening, choking prison atmosphere.

Over 1200 men were interned in Beekvliet in total (out of 1900 hostages in Holland altogether), some 500 to 800 at a time, for an average of about 12 months each. Over two-thirds of them had been prominent in some way or other (including Mr Schermerhorn, who was to be prime minister immediately after the war, and other leaders of political parties, directors of large organizations and businesses, as well as 12 Leiden professors). A great deal has been written about the camp[4] (partly because of the kind of people who were incarcerated), so one has a fair idea of what went on during this side-show of wartime Holland. It was a fascinating set-up: Beekvliet was definitely not all misery.

The organization of the camp was left entirely to the hostages themselves. There were hostage camp leaders, who had to deal with the German command, and generally Germans did not come inside the buildings, but only into the central office in the entrance hall. Of course there were armed guards (Germans or, worse, Dutch in German service), and of course there was barbed wire. The hostages themselves were responsible for room allocation; they organized the meals with the food provided, the cleaning and maintenance, post, a camp shop, and a system of communication with loudspeakers, and there was a great deal of home-made entertainment.

On the face of it the hostages had a life of modest luxury. Food and hygiene were reasonable, personal space was fairly generous, and there was much intellectual stimulation. But one had to manage oneself, and there were large differences between the men in their responses to the kind of stress generated there. Niko thought that those who did not have some project or other to work on, like he had, were finding life pretty difficult.[5]

There were clouds over the hostages, clouds that affected everyone, and there were the personal ones. There was the real threat of the firing squad. Three weeks before Niko arrived three men from St Michielsgestel (and two from elsewhere) had been taken from their beds by the German camp commander, given two hours to write to their families, and shot at dawn, in revenge for railway sabotage. One month after his arrival another hostage (as well as 14 from other camps) died similarly. That was the last time it happened, and, frightening as it was, the inmates did not feel execution to be a likely fate. But there were the worries about home, about the effects of war on the families, and there was the boredom of it all, the inability to be involved and to do things, the impossibility for someone like Niko to be out in the wilds and feel the winds, watch birds, and take pictures.

Niko was to be locked up in St. Michielsgestel for two full years, much longer than the average hostage. Nobody knew why he was treated that way, least of all Niko himself: the release strategy for hostages was totally chaotic. Every so often a group of people or some individuals were set free again, and every so often some others were locked up. Escape was not an option, because if anyone did the Germans would have taken it out on his family or on the remaining hostages in the camp. Nobody even tried it.

In his first weeks of internment Niko's life was probably more relaxed and less demanding than it was at home. Of course, all his letters from the camp were censored (they carry the German stamp 'Geprüft' (checked)), but his lack of concern sounds genuine (trans.): 'If you did not know that you are a hostage, you would think yourself at some interesting conference', in a letter to his sister.[6] He described the many people he met: acquaintances, politicians, writers, and musicians, and the various courses and lectures he attended, all the parcels he received, his sport (hockey, twice a week), and how to his surprise he began to like listening to music.

Later, when the months ticked slowly away, it must all have become very stale, and he missed his family (Jaap, Toos, and Dirk were eight, five, and two, respectively, when he was taken by the Germans), his students, and his birds in the wilds of Holland. Only his early letters from the camp survive (mostly to his parents), from the time when he still had mail three times a day, and he could write and receive as much as he liked (free, no postage needed). But the separation became more difficult − after a month the Germans only allowed two letters per week per person: one in and one out. These were to and from Lies. Later in Oxford, after he had died, Lies destroyed all personal letters from Niko.

He did take a fairly active part in the camp life of Beekvliet. Over the years there was a huge variety of lectures from the many experts; Niko himself gave illustrated talks on (trans.) 'Experiences with East Greenland Eskimos', 'Camouflage in the animal kingdom', 'Warning colours in the animal kingdom', 'The way home for bees and wasps', and 'Kleew for grown-ups or the sociology of a gull colony', and he did an 11-lecture course on 'Animal sociology.'[7] There were lectures on subjects as far apart as Arabic, car engineering, theory of bridge, trade management, colloid-chemistry, Sophocles, economic policy, hieroglyphics, electromagnetism, human physiology, Dutch history, Russian, agriculture, and literally hundreds of others. Courses in portrait-drawing were given by the well-known Karel van Veen, which Niko avidly attended and where he became a skilled portrait artist. Beekvliet was like a reasonably sized university, of many diverse faculties.

The camp inhabitants were very conscious of the need to prevent boredom and depression, and they made a conscious effort to keep minds busy. There were frequent concerts by several world-renowned musician hostages, and the camp actually had an excellent Steinway grand piano sent up to one of the interned. And there were poetry readings, there was theatre, serious and humorous; Niko went down in history for his performance as a French lady (with a perfect accent). Typically, a group of the men (including Niko) had noted that many inmates absorbed the contents of lectures rather uncritically, and they designed a delightful spoof 'The Spark papers', which was performed

Caricature of Niko in the hostage camp, by Karel van Veen. 1943.

on 24 June 1943 and later published.[8] It commemorated the death of a mythical composer William Spark (derived from the Williams–park Road), with many speeches, drawings, and his compositions. To everybody's joy many of the audience were completely taken in.

Niko was also part of the team of shoeshine boys[9] (one of whom would go round pointing out to people the inadequacies of their footwear maintenance), operating often without polish but with great verve. About his life and activities he wrote (trans.):

> *I am working nicely on my book, sitting quietly in a corner of the large auditorium, where there is complete silence. Because of all the brain-work here, that order is totally respected. There are several regular customers. Prof. Huizinga sets an example for all, the whole day he works on a new edition of Homo ludens. Prof. Geyl sits in another corner, in the meantime his portrait being drawn by an artist. … Several people are hanging around the case of handbooks (including the Brockhaus encyclopaedia). Every so often I attend a lecture or course, e.g. one course on Dutch history by Algra, teacher from Leeuwarden, which all of us enjoy because of the clear way in which he depicts things 'psychologically'. … Days fly, and people who have been here longer say that this goes faster and faster. Very strange how easy it is here to put all responsibilities aside, which of course is good initially in order to relax, but soon it becomes dangerous, for we all want to emerge from here fit and full of zest for work, and not weakened. One sees the different possibilities realized in those people who have been interned for a long time, like the 'Dutch East Indian group' who have been inside since summer 1940.[10]*

In his letters about the camp Niko liked the absence of ranks and class that otherwise plagued Dutch society, and he referred to the homely atmosphere. Everybody talked to everybody, ministers and professors were queuing up with him for breakfast and took part in fatigues, cleaning the corridors, and washing up. His Leiden boss Professor van der Klaauw was there, and so for a short time was his former mentor Jan Verwey, as well as the co-author of their 1929 bird book, Gerard van Beusekom, who was working on his PhD thesis and regularly consulted Niko. So there were at least some biology contacts. Mostly, however, he worked alone, writing away in his corner of the auditorium.

Niko shared a room with five others, and in the morning he rose at sevenish, showered (in warm water, as he mentioned delightedly) and went for a walk, then from nine onwards spent the rest of the day working, with a short break for lunch. He was very well organized therefore, but obviously conditions for writing and thinking were not optimal, and his main product of that period, a book with the title *Inleiding tot de diersociologie* [Introduction to animal sociology],[11] was not a great success. It was a fairly short (184 pages) paperback in a semi-popular science series, published in 1946, just after the war. Niko illustrated it with many of his and Luuk's drawings, so visually it was appealing enough. But it was never reprinted, unlike the 1945 book by Bierens de Haan in the same series on 'Instinct and intelligence in animals'.[12] It seems amazing now that such books were published at all during that turbulent time, in a battered Holland. Niko wrote his almost entirely in the hostage camp, with only a few finishing touches added after the war.

In his *Inleiding* Niko wrote in a rather formal style, never in the first person, his tone somewhat schoolmasterly. He used the book as a plea to others to take up his kind of observation and experiments, especially in the last chapter on methods. One feels a certain emptiness in it, Niko out of his usual element writing in the corner of that large auditorium, in a hostage camp in a dusty seminary, needing to cover his unease by writing with a certain stuffy formality. The book could have done with some friendly criticism; for instance the title is strange. Niko defined sociology as the study of 'society and community in the wider sense, and we will take this to mean every result of co-operation of two or more individuals'. There was an entire chapter on superficial similarities between human and animal societies, highly uncritical (comparing languages, social morals, including reactions to homosexuals, the role of laughing, territorial defence) and rather out of line with anything Niko wrote before or after.

In his book Niko insisted that animals behave for the maintenance of the species. He went even further, by describing processes that are for the good of the entire community (trans.): 'Everywhere we see co-operation, to the benefit of the family, or to the benefit of the colony, in both cases to the benefit of the community, of the super-individual relationship' (about herring gulls).[13] And elsewhere: 'Species make sacrifices for the welfare of the larger community, similarly individuals make sacrifices for the welfare of the species, and within the individual its organs make sacrifices for that individual.'[14] It would seem more than a coincidence that Niko, in his hostage camp environment, would uphold this philosophy. However, such views were quite common then, and perhaps one should not read too much into it. Thirty years later Niko's student Richard Dawkins summarized and emphasized with great clarity the evidence that animals behave for the good of themselves and their offspring, but never sacrifice themselves for the benefit of the species (let alone for other species in their natural community).[15] Niko kept his good-of-the-species belief for at least another 20 years. One of his main interests was natural selection of behaviour, but he never thought out this discrepancy for himself.

It would not be fair to judge the *Inleiding* by the blemishes that we can now see with the benefits of modern developments. The book did provide a charming kaleidoscope of examples of social behaviour in different animals. It discussed many important phenomena such as imprinting, the learning and instinctive aspects of bird song, rank order, signalling, displacement activities, parental behaviour, and many others. Niko stressed the need for a physiological approach, and evidence that most animals have no insight into the purpose of their behaviour. It was quite interesting fun, though not exactly a tour de force. It should be seen against the background of the dreary conditions under which it was written, with an almost total lack of access to relevant literature.

But how different were the results of his other pastime. He produced some charming and brilliant small books for his family, in which one feels that he is talking to them through his pen and his pencils.[16] Only two of these were published, but the others were written, drawn, and coloured in small, landscape-format drawing books just for his own children, describing nature as he thought of it from behind the barbed wire. It comes across as the world seen by him but through a child's eye, as he felt his children wanted to see it.

Klieuw is the story of a herring gull. It hatches, grows up, and lives the full life of a herring gull on a Dutch beach, making a nest and rearing chicks. It socializes, combs the beaches, deals with foxes, hawks, farmers, and crabs. All the while it is being watched from a hide (blind) by a certain Mr Tinbergen, and it gets ringed (banded) by him. Mr Tinbergen chases a fox from the nest and in gratitude the gull chicks are named after his children Jaap, Toos, and Dik. The story starts: 'Klieuw is a gull. His father and mother live on a high sand dune. When they stand right on the top of the dune, they can see the sea, far away. Every so often they go there, to get food …' and 40, delightfully illustrated pages later it ends 'and like that it will continue, for ever and ever and ever, egg-chick-old-egg-chick-old-egg-chick-old- The end!'

In the hostage camp Niko met a well-known Dutch bookseller–publisher, Leo Boucher, who agreed to take on the herring gull story. This, as it turned out, took quite a few years and it was finally published in 1948. In the meantime Niko had visited America again, immediately after the war, where he showed the story to a publisher, who agreed to an American edition which appeared before the Dutch one. The lay-out is the same in English, but the line-drawings aren't quite as subtle as in the Dutch edition, and the text, translated later into

English by Niko himself, is somewhat abridged and slightly different, more aloof and less personal. The Dutch *Klieuw* is clearly meant for reading by an adult to four- to eight-year-olds (Niko's children were three, five, and eight at the time), whereas the American *Kleew* is for children from seven upwards, to be read by themselves. Both versions of the little book have been deservedly successful, being reprinted repeatedly until at least the 1990s.

'Het verhaal van Jan Stekel' [The tale of John Stickle], hand-written and drawn by Niko, was never published in Dutch. Only much later (1952) did it come out in English[17] as 'a simple picture book for children of 7–11, on the life history of the stickleback'. Superb drawings and about the same amount of text were adapted for British use – in the original version a little boy called Jaap lazes away on a bridge in the polders and spots a fish, but in English a boy called Bob does the same thing in the Broads. In 48 pages the booklet tells the whole story of the stickleback, the red-fronted males that make a nest and look after the young ones, the large-bellied females that spawn, and the pike that lets go a stickleback because of its spines, all this interwoven with the activities of the boy and his brother and sister, their little net, and their fish tank at home.

The other booklets that Niko did in St Michielsgestel remained unpublished, but they were at least as good as *Klieuw* and *John Stickle*. He may have been behind barbed wire, but his mind was miles away, watching the wonders of the world with his children, and here it all is, in his own clear print-

Drawing by Niko for his children at home. Hostage camp, St Michielsgestel, about 1943. Loman archive.

handwriting. There is the 'History of the dew drop', with the subtitle (trans.) 'A story for Jaap, Toos, and Dik by father in St Michielsgestel, 1943', well over a hundred pages, with a one-page drawing for every two pages of text. It is a set of weekly letters, several of them rubber-stamped by the German censor, describing the peregrinations of a drop of water as told to a butterfly. Niko must have written it whilst he felt the children sitting on his knee, describing to them some of his own adventures and the world that he loved. He is skating on the huge Dutch lakes with the speed showing in his drawing, he crashes through the ice and is rescued by Lies' brother Martien. Lies and he are kayaking over the high seas and Eskimos hunt seals in Greenland, with sledge dogs howling in chorus and huge glaciers 'calving' next to Niko and Lies' tent. In Hulshorst the family's tent is being washed out by a raging storm, whilst baby Jaap is crawling about in it; over New York Niko sees a gigantic thunderstorm, and from an ocean liner he watches the flying fishes. The children must have loved it.

'The old oak beam' is shorter, and later Niko apparently considered submitting it for publication, because the original Dutch manuscript has a typewritten English version attached. An ancient sheep barn somewhere near Hulshorst had a very rugged beam, and the beam told its story to all the animals. Once upon a time a large oak tree dropped its acorns, and one of them was hidden by a jay. That again resulted in a large oak that supported a community of all the familiar birds (lovely drawings and details) and that tree was finally chopped: it became the beam. Then there was 'The sand book', written for Toos' (Catrina's) birthday in August 1944 just before his release, and in it Niko's mind again wandered around the sand dunes in Hulshorst where his family was staying at that time. It is 43 pages long, with careful, almost calligraphic text on one side and colour pencil drawings on the other. As the story went, a property developer tries to persuade old farmer Hendrik to plough up the sandy land. Then a pine-cone talks to Hendrik, and changes him into a pine-moth caterpillar who understands the animals. He meets the caterpillar-killing digger wasp *Ammophila*, the bee-wolf wasp, a fox, rabbit, hobby, curlew, and dung beetle, and he sees the wonderful tracks in the sand. When he becomes farmer Hendrik again, he decides not to plough up the place.

What Niko wrote for his children was steam from a safety valve, and seeing these little books now one can appreciate what he felt when he was locked up. Niko may have taken part in the community life of the hostage camp, but sitting in his solitary corner of the large auditorium with his pen and his pencils, his thoughts were miles away in the wilds of the world, as well as in the abstractions of his ethology.

Only once was Niko allowed to go home for a few days, so he did see his children briefly. But this did not make life any easier for either himself or for the family he had to leave behind, and it did little to alleviate his two year sentence. Finally, in the autumn of 1944, Holland south of the main rivers Rhine and Meuse was liberated. Ahead of the advancing Allies on their way to Arnhem, the German jailers closed hostage camp Beekvliet, themselves escaping after

Drawing of a hobby by Niko for his children at home. Hostage camp, St Michielsgestel, about 1943. Loman archive.

transferring the remaining hostages (including Niko) to a notorious nearby concentration camp, in Vught. The hostages spent a few more days there and then, on 11 September 1944, exactly two years after Niko had been rounded up, the entire German internment machine collapsed. They were free again.

In his absence, Lies with the children had decided that war-time life in the countryside would be easier than in town, a decision that later turned out to be a very wise one. They stayed in their nice old holiday house in Hulshorst, 109 Oudeweg [Old road], a house in later years replaced by a new development of holiday villas. Large trees in friendly farmland, fields and wide horizons, other houses and farms scattered nearby, a village community, and woods and sands within easy walking and cycling distance – they were as comfortable as one could be in the Holland of that time. Importantly, too, life was cheap, which was a major consideration for a family without any income, dependent on friends and relatives for support.

But there were also risks. They shared the house with Lies' younger sister Tineke and her husband, Dick de Boer, who was a contact between two cells of the resistance. There was the railway nearby, an important supply route for the Germans in the west of Holland; this frequently attracted shelling and bombing raids by the Allies, which were not always very accurate. In the meantime, the Tinbergen house in Leiden was a shelter for people hiding from the Germans (looked after by some schoolmistresses). Later it was used by Niko's brother

Luuk and his young wife Tilde: she was half Jewish. Then there was the German army, often out to intimidate people. Lies was out on her bike with six-year old Toos on the back, and a soldier on horseback deliberately frightened her off the road: such incidents were common. People were shouted at, and threatened. With these daily risks, and the problems of often rather sickly children, Lies probably had a much more difficult time during the war than did Niko. But at least she could do something, she had a clear role to play, whereas Niko was helpless.

That September day after his release in 1944, Niko found a telephone that worked in Vught, and sent a message to his family – he was coming home! Ahead of the advancing Allies, he managed to get back to Hulshorst. There were a few buses and trains, slow and chaotic. There was no transport for the last few kilometres, and he had to walk, leaving his luggage at the station. I heard the story from Lies, who was still moved many years later: somehow she felt he was on his way. She cycled to meet him on a long, straight, and narrow road through the woods, in the far distance one single, small figure walking towards her.

Coming home was a huge relief, but also difficult, as for so many fathers returning from years of war. Lies had been through many problems with the children: their health had suffered and they had trouble with their metabolisms, and little Toos broke bones because of lack of calcium.[18] All such things took years to sort out, but fortunately there was a good local doctor in Hulshorst. In Niko's absence they briefly had a dog, which was soon killed on the road near the house; the family never had one again. Niko had missed out on all such dramas and all the lighter spots: he had been away from his children for two crucial years. He had felt absorbed by them when he was in St Michielsgestel, he talked to them in his booklets, and drew for them, but his children were abstractions in his mind, not active, flesh-and-blood and all that that implies. Like so many war-time fathers, he had been slightly alienated, both in his own mind and in theirs, and I think he never quite caught up again.

That last winter, 1944–45, was the toughest of the war, and in Holland it is still referred to as 'the hunger winter', when thousands starved to death. But the Tinbergens were together, and felt they could cope with anything. It was no time for science, the issue was survival. Hulshorst was only a short distance from Arnhem where, that autumn, some of the last ferocious battles were fought. There was also a steady stream of people from the large towns in western Holland, people who came to find food, to bargain their last urban possessions for a few potatoes or some flour. The Tinbergen house filled up; Niko's parents lived in another holiday house nearby, but that was badly damaged in one of the bombing raids, so they moved in with Lies and Niko's family. Lies' sister Tineke and her husband Dick were also there. The parents and brother of Tilde survived the bombardments of Arnhem but their house did not; they moved in, too (all three on false papers, as the father was a Jew). Altogether there were 12 people in the house.

There was no electricity, as the power station in Arnhem had been put out of action. The solution was a bicycle-dynamo: the men in the house took turns in pedalling an adapted bicycle wheel in the back room to power small lights in the kitchen. One could read whilst pedalling, and loud complaints would emanate from the kitchen if the lights dimmed, usually due to a particularly absorbing section in the book of the duty-pedaller. By the light of the fire in the other room they would play games, and sing old NJN and children's songs, with Lies' brother-in-law Dick on the guitar.

Food in Hulshorst during the war was scarce and bad, but by dint of fifty-mile bicycle trips to the east of Holland they managed to scrape enough together. One of Niko's self-imposed duties was at the local school in Hulshorst, where arrangements had been made to take the flood of people from Amsterdam, Utrecht, The Hague, and other towns, who came through on their way to forage in the east of Holland. The winter was seriously cold, with snow and ice, and people came on bicycles or with hand-carts, anything that could carry food back to their homes. People were desperate; sleeping on the crowded floors of the school provided ample opportunity for theft, and order was difficult to maintain. Niko was in charge of a scheme whereby people handed him their identity cards before bedding down, making it impossible for them to abscond with someone else's property. In the attic of the school a radio receiver was hidden, and that almost proved the undoing of him and his family.

The possession of a radio was one of the most serious crimes under the German occupation. One listened to the BBC to follow the fortunes of the Allies and the Germans, and coded messages were received for the resistance. Important information about the war was passed on to others, often on small typewritten slips of paper – and Niko did the typing. One careless man lost such a slip, right in the village, and it was duly found by a German soldier. Houses were raided, and typewriters checked against the fatal piece of paper. In the Tinbergen house the typewriter was found, a sample of Niko's typing was taken away, and all in the house were interrogated by the Dutch Territorials (Dutch nationals collaborating with the occupying forces, generally considered worse than the Germans themselves). All, except the old Jewish man (Luuk's father-in-law), whose German accent would have given him away immediately. If this had not been happening just a couple of days before liberation the consequences would have been too horrible to contemplate, and fatal to the Tinbergens. As it was, the interrogating menace left with threats, but did not return.

When the liberating Allied forces (here Canadian troops) reached Hulshorst in April 1945, the nightmare was over. 'We wept for joy and still, nearly 18 months after our liberation, we are easily moved to tears by remembrances of those days.'[19] For a few days Niko was part of a tank crew and visited farms with the Canadians, rounding up hiding German soldiers, Niko translating to and from English, Dutch, and German. They found one farmer with a German tied to a stake. Essentially that was the end of Niko's war. In May, when western Holland became accessible after the German capitulation, Niko and a friend (the famous astronomist Jan Oort, a professor in Leiden who also spent most of the war in Hulshorst) got hold of a tandem bicycle and pedalled the seventy-odd miles to Leiden, to find out what was left of their alma mater.

The country was cheering and shouting, Dutch flags were out everywhere, and there was a tremendous feeling of relief, hope, and optimism. Holland was running again, there was a frenzy of action and new initiatives, and Niko ran with all the others, organizing, attending meetings, writing letters.

The damage of the war to Niko's work environment in the widest sense had been considerable, and took many months to assess. Many areas for fieldwork were mined or otherwise inaccessible, and most people had no transport because all their bicycles had been stolen by the fleeing German soldiers. The university buildings, labs, and facilities were there, but they were in chaos, and there were no animals left. There was no word of his close young friend, student, and colleague, Pelk, last known to be in the Dutch East Indies. Somehow he learned that Konrad Lorenz was presumed dead on the Russian front, and his old mentor Jacques Thijsse had died in the hunger winter. Bierens de Haan had only just survived. Tragically, as he heard almost a year later, Pelk had been killed by a Japanese bullet on a Dutch mine-sweeper, in 1942, 27 years old and much mourned by his many friends. Niko organized a moving book with Pelk's writing and drawings, with the title (trans.) 'This beautiful world', with a tribute from Niko himself as a foreword.[20]

But the initial rumours about Konrad Lorenz were wrong: he was alive but out of circulation for a few years, imprisoned in Russia. What had happened to him during the war was, briefly, that in 1940 he had been appointed professor and director at the Institute for Comparative Psychology in the German town of Königsberg (now Kaliningrad) on the Baltic Sea. He was soon drafted into military service in 1941 as 'military psychologist', then as neurologist and psychiatrist in a military hospital in Poland.[21] In April 1944 he was appointed medical officer to the Russian front, and in June of that year taken captive by the Russians in Vitebsk (now in Belarus), not to be released until 1948.

Since Niko's stay with him in Altenberg, Konrad had become a convinced Nazi sympathizer and party member (1938). Self-preservation may have had something to do with it; in the Roman Catholic Austria of that time he had problems with the authorities over his Darwinistic views, and he could not get funds for research. After the German take-over of Austria and the *Anschluss* (joining), Konrad did not find it difficult to use his research as backing and scientific foundation for the Nazi ideology, and he openly admired the German state. He published papers on racial purity and the effects of domestication in animals and man, and attracted considerable research funds, helped by glowing references to his political attitude and uncontaminated descent.[22] He became a member of the Office of Race Policy, and he lectured at public events. He stood, wholeheartedly, for a regime that Niko loathed.

Soon after Niko was taken hostage in 1942, one of the editors of the German ethology journal *Zeitschrift für Tierpsychologie*, Otto Koehler, wrote to Niko. That spring Niko had finally submitted the grayling paper that he had promised

Koehler, but obviously reluctantly 'only because I promised you'; he wanted out of the German science scene. Koehler suggested that an effort should be made to get Niko released from his confinement, and Lies replied for Niko (trans.): 'Do not trouble yourself in getting him out. In the first place you would not succeed, and secondly he would definitely not want it. Please imagine yourself in our Dutch situation.'[23] When Koehler told his co-editor Otto Antonius about this, the latter's reaction was (trans.) 'As regards Tinbergen, I believe that only Lorenz would have enough influence over him to keep contact going. In the end also these people have to find the way into the new times.'[24] Lorenz did write, apparently, but his letter was later destroyed, and Lies' answer was pretty clear-cut: 'Er will nichts mehr mit ihnen zu tun haben' (he does not want anything to do with you any more).[25]

After the war, in letters to Huxley and Thorpe enquiring about possible jobs, Konrad justified his earlier pro-Nazi stance by saying that he was never active in politics, but that he told the powers-that-be whatever they wanted to hear.[26] However, he never publicly withdrew his former Nazi support, and resentment against his position rumbled on throughout his life, especially after the Nobel Prize award in 1973. Niko was also affected by this public anger, because of his association with Konrad.

However, all that came much later. Immediately after the war, Niko (and everybody around him) understandably felt a strong revulsion against everything German. In a letter to Margaret Nice, an ornithologist friend with strong behaviour interests in the USA, he wrote:

> Lorenz was in the army, Dept. of 'Heerespsychologie' [military psychology] since 1941. He was rather nazi-infected, though I always considered him an honest and good fellow. But it is impossible for me to resume contact with him or his fellow-countrymen, I mean it is psychologically impossible. The wounds of our soul must heal, and that will take time. … It is absolutely impossible to collaborate with nazi's, SS-men etc., who have murdered and terrorized so many of our dearest relations. This is not a result of a desire for revenge, but we simply cannot bear to see them. … It is not right to think that the atrocities were only committed by a minority of fanatical SS-, SD- or Gestapo men. Nearly the whole people is hopelessly poisoned; I can give many personal experiences![27]

It is not clear whether Niko ever knew the full extent of Konrad's involvement with the Nazis. What he did not know, perhaps he did not want to. But he knew at least part of the story. In June 1945 he wrote to Bierens de Haan (trans.):

> since my wife asked them [Koehler and Lorenz] not to involve themselves with the question of my internment, contact has been broken off, but not because they were offended about this, because they wrote that they could understand

our point of view. But at the moment I feel like waiting a bit also with purely
personal contact, especially because I cannot much appreciate the attitude of
both with respect to national socialism.[28]

Koehler was less involved than Konrad and, unlike Konrad, later publicly
admitted that he had been wrong.

These letters were written in June 1945, and, as always, time healed wounds.
A few months after his release in 1948, Konrad was invited to a behaviour
symposium in Cambridge, about which more later. It was July 1949, and one of
the participants was Niko. When the two met again, in Bill Thorpe's house,
after all those years and experiences, each having suffered behind the barbed
wire of the other's authority, they were overjoyed, and filled with emotion.
By all accounts it was for everybody present a very moving occasion. In their
science, it was the first time since the war that Germans and the others talked
again, with wounds still raw: but here the world saw that Niko, the former
hostage, totally forgave. The old, deep friendship was still there, and it provided
a tremendous uplift for all. Smiling, and with his gentle voice, Niko told Konrad
'We have won!'[29] Clearly he meant that their friendship had triumphed, and he
publicly forgave Konrad, a gesture that must have helped Konrad tremendously
in being accepted again by the scientific community.

Everyone had the feeling that ethology was back again, with a mission,
branching out in its first, properly international exposure, leaving the ghastly
war to history. Konrad was his old, ebullient self, with lots of stories about his
POW experience, probably quite exaggerated but eagerly lapped up by his
audience.[30] Soon Niko and he were at work again, and Robert Hinde recalls
one of their arguments about quantification:

Tinbergen and Lorenz were discussing how often you had to see an animal do
something before you could say that the species did it. Konrad said that he
never made such a claim unless he had seen the behaviour at least five times.
Niko laughed and clapped him on the back and said 'Don't be silly Konrad,
you know you often said it when you have seen it only once.'[31]

In his autobiography Lorenz commented that his time as prisoner of war,
and Niko's hostage camp 'had made no difference whatsoever'.[32] At least as far
as Niko was concerned that was nonsense; the war had a huge effect on his
outlook on life, he matured from a somewhat blinkered naturalist and scientist
to an emotional and more complete human being. Niko himself wrote, in
somewhat stilted English: 'The advantage of all different sufferings, though they
were not as serious as to give me a lasting set-back has been that I have
experienced intensities of emotions that I never had before during peace-time;
disagreeable emotions like anxiety and distress, but also the more pleasurable
emotions of seeing one's family back after black periods.'[33]

Leiden after the war

In the first few months after liberation Holland's table was bare. The most common and necessary things in daily life were missing: food was scarce, and clothing
very difficult to get hold of. Niko's family was hit like everyone else; after the
severe winter 'when we as a nation and personally, escaped destruction by a
miracle' they had almost nothing, no shoes for the children, no clothes for the
new baby.[34] International assistance swung into action with the Marshall Plan,
and many private institutions helped in some way or other. Switzerland, which
had escaped the war, took a special interest, and as just one example the
University of Zurich extended a helping hand to the University of Leiden,
offering hospitality and direct help to staff. In the summer of 1945 Lies and
Niko were two people who accepted, and they went to stay with the family of
a medical doctor in Zurich, farming their own three children out to grand-
parents. From Zurich Niko visited the University of Basel, lecturing the
students on the delights of ethology, and Esther Sager (see Chapter 6) first met
him. She vividly remembered the enthusiasm of his lectures;[35] to cover an

Niko and Lies after the war, on their way to Switzerland, August 1945.
Courtesy of the Tinbergen family.

obvious need, all the students clubbed together to get Niko a new pair of shoes, and the zoo director Heini Hediger gave them an ostrich egg, to make an omelette for the children.

In late summer 1945 the Tinbergen family left their Hulshorst hideout, and trekked back to their old house in the Leeuwerikstraat in Leiden. Luuk and Tilde moved into the Hulshorst house, for him to start his research on sparrow-hawks for his PhD. On the face of it, life in Leiden was taken up again at more or less the point where they left it. Just as before their friends the Casimirs were neighbours, the children went to school, and Lies was pregnant again. This was to be their fourth child; a second daughter Jannetje (Janet) was born in October, a demanding baby, weighing only 3½ pounds when she was born and causing Lies a large amount of work and worry.[36] Not the least important was that Niko received several years of salary, so they could repay their debts.

The war also had changed little in the contact with the rest of the family. There was always with Luuk the shared interest in birds and Hulshorst, and they often saw each other. That year and the next the two families shared a typical national festivity, the St Nicholas party on 5 December, a Dutch variant on the father Christmas theme. The white-bearded bishop St Nicholas visits houses with children, assisted by Black Peter – Niko filled the role of St Nicholas admirably, and a blackened Luuk did the rest, a ritual long remembered by the children. There was much less contact with Jan and his family, just as before the war; the spheres of interest of Niko and Jan did not overlap, unfortunately. Luuk saw much more of Jan than Niko did.

In the day-to-day running of the family Lies played a solo role, the house was her domain. Lies spent all her time, energy, and thoughts there, she laid down the discipline, took the initiative, and told the children what they could or could not do. Only as the ultimate threat for a misdemeanour, would the children have to tell their father when he came home. He was there in the evenings, he talked to Lies about his work, and amused the children; but gradually, nevertheless, Niko had become somewhat of an outsider at home. Perhaps as part of a vicious circle, he focussed more on his work, and on his students. More than one of Niko's children said to me later that Niko was more interested in his students than in his family. Niko would probably have denied this – though admitting that he loved being with his students – but there must be more than a grain of truth in the children's perception. He was an insider in the Zoology Department, but much more peripheral at home. Luuk's wife Tilde once remarked[37] that Niko's self-confidence was built mostly on his success in his work. It was a shrewd observation, and whereas for many other people families and friends figure large, for Niko they did not.

There was little room in Niko's mind for other, outside influences such as clubs, or the Church. Before the war Niko and Lies had been rather indifferent towards religion. They had been brought up in a Protestant environment, but their scientific rationality had never been encouraging towards a religious belief. In the hostage camp Niko had lent an interested ear to talks by the well-known

Protestant theologian Banning, but also he had seen the deep-running divisions and intolerance between the different Protestant sections in Holland, which reverberated in the religious political parties. The arguments of irrelevance of a god in the misery of war had impinged on both of them. Perhaps it was not surprising that they became strongly anti-Church, and anti-religion. Soon after their return to Leiden nine-year old Toos wanted to go to Sunday school, with her best friend. Despite desperate pleas her parents put their foot down: the answer was a very firm no. Niko came to hate church, to hate the sound of church bells, and rarely have I seen him so put out as 20 years later in East Africa, when he had to wait an hour for my wife and me to attend a Christmas service in a Swahili church: it was a total waste of time in the field.

Immediately after the war began a new period of work, work, and more work. The most essential things were still missing; for instance, Niko's bicycle had been requisitioned by fleeing German soldiers, note paper was impossible to get (in the end Niko obtained both these commodities from London, via his friend the ornithologist David Lack). Niko took on massive obligations, he chain-smoked cigarettes, and hammered away on his typewriter, before long hitting his first collapse from mental exhaustion. He was raring to go after three years of war-induced absence, three years of thinking about his ethology without being able to do anything about it.

However, irrespective of personal ambitions for his science and research projects, he was landed with a huge teaching load: hundreds of students had been prevented from going to university by the war, and they now descended on Leiden in droves. There were 700 medical students alone, all needing lecturing in animal morphology, and half of these lectures were thrown at Niko by his head of department van der Klaauw. There was all the re-building of his research facilities and his team, applying for new funds, reconnecting with the rest of the scientific world, replacing his dependence on German contacts and reinforcing Anglo-Saxon connections. 'Personally I feel the loss of contact with German zoology as a great void, the logical consequence of the changes in Germany, but … fortunately England and America offer sufficient possibility for international contact' (trans.), he wrote in a letter to Bierens de Haan.[38]

To help with the rebuilding of Dutch ornithology Niko took on editorship of the national scientific bird journal *Ardea*, and within a few years had put it firmly on the path to becoming the prime international journal that it is now. He was asked to be the successor of Jacques Thijsse, his former role model who had died in the hunger winter, as editor of *De Levende Natuur* [Living Nature]. That monthly magazine had always been close to his heart and would be for the rest of his life, and as Niko's many articles were clearly influential and more or less set the pace for it, he could hardly say no. He accepted on condition that he could do it jointly with others.

However, his main effort in the editorial field was entirely on his own initiative, the creation in 1948 of a new international journal of ethology, *Behaviour*. Until then the mouthpiece for the biological study of animal behaviour had been Koehler and Lorenz's *Zeitschrift für Tierpsychologie* [Journal for Animal Psychology], but that had gone defunct in the war. It was to arise again from its ashes a few years later, but immediately after the war there was a void, and in any case there never had been a journal in his field in English. It was a unique opportunity for Niko to jump in, and jump he did.

He negotiated with the Leiden publishers, Brill, who published other journals to which Niko had contributed. They were keen, and still have *Behaviour* now, more than 50 years later. He invited a small international cast to become joint editors, a process that took innumerable long, explanatory, and persuasive letters. Not everybody wanted to get involved; for instance Julian Huxley and David Lack refused.[39] But he roped in the Fin Pontus Palmgren from Helsingfors, the Swiss Heini Hediger from Basel, and the Englishman Bill Thorpe from Cambridge, the latter at the suggestion of David Lack as Niko did not know him. The promotion of *Behaviour* by the editors and publishers started in 1946, and the first issues were on the shelves in 1948. The editorial team was enlarged with other great names such as Frank Beach and Hale Carpenter from the USA, and Otto Koehler from Baden. When Niko left Leiden in 1949, his former student Gerard Baerends took over as managing editor, and continued in the post for almost 40 years. But it started as Niko's brainchild, it became a leading international journal in the field of animal behaviour, and, more than any other journal, it has published the kind of studies that were his main interest.

Niko probably worked harder in those years than at any time before. In Leiden his own students and field projects demanded a great deal of attention, apart from all his lecturing and other departmental duties. He was highly appreciated for his commitment, scientific output, and his clarity of argument in lectures and discussion; as a consequence, his colleagues must have been aware that, with so many foreign contacts and lectures in Holland as well as abroad, there must have been a danger of losing him. In 1946 he was offered the chair in zoology in the University of Groningen (after Jan Verwey had declined it), but he preferred to stay in Leiden, and suggested his former student Gerard Baerends for the job (who accepted). Niko certainly exploited his popularity (just as he had when, before the war, he had been considered for positions in America), and when he was offered a chair in Cairo in October 1946, the first thing he did was to go with the letter to the curators of Leiden University to see what they were prepared to put on the table in terms of research funds and assistants.[40] He did pretty well out of that: apart from an ample budget they offered him a head research assistant, an assistant, a caretaker for his animals, a secretary, a cleaner, and a technician. Niko's comment, in English, to Gerard Baerends, was: 'My darling, what more do you want?'

Within a year of the re-start of the university after the war, his Head of Department van der Klaauw had put him forward for a full professorship. Niko was only 39, very young for a chair in any of the sciences, for those days in Holland. In January 1947 he was appointed Professor in Experimental Zoology, one of three chairs in the department.

Three months after his appointment in Leiden he gave his inaugural lecture, with the title (trans.) 'Nature is stronger than nurture', subtitled 'In praise of fieldwork'.[41] The inaugural lecture was and is an important feature in Dutch academia, and it received much attention, with family, friends, and colleagues from afar attending. The Dutch expression in the title could have referred to his own absconding from lectures in order to watch birds, and it also implies that instinct is stronger than training. He told his audience (trans.):

> Self-observation has slowly made it clear to me that many of the new insights in ethology have emerged thanks to some primitive urges in the adherents of the profession. ... the dedication, even devotion to their profession which characterizes so many field biologists, can be explained by the fact that their profession satisfies a primitive, very human but also very general animal drive.

There is little doubt to whom he refers here, being aware of his own hunting instincts.

In the lecture he outlined the aims and methods of ethology. He then argued that insights into the organization of animal and human behaviour are useful scientific results, that humanity needs biologists for this kind of research, and that the proper training grounds for biologists (all biologists!) are in wild nature. Hence came the need for nature conservation (he did not mention impoverishment of our environment, only the needs of biologists). He warned against Christian influence (trans.): 'the emphasis by Christianity on our responsibility for our behaviour has had the consequence that the differences between man and animal are perceived as too prominent. The Christian, therefore – and the entire western world is still laced through with Christianity – feels much less related to the other animals than many other people do.' He wondered whether the Netherlands will be a place 'for breeding young biologists, as the country is developing into an ever more efficient, managed and regulated stifling culture-steppe'. Finally, he said that he intended to dedicate himself to the running of the zoology laboratory (although only a few months later he would be probing for a place abroad). He ended with a message for his students (trans.) :

> We biologists are a happy group in society. We carry out our profession from an inner desire, and because our work is important for society, we can even earn a living from it. ... Not only academic results, but also material advantages which biology presents to society can be delivered only by people who carry out their job with the pure motive of 'wanting to understand'. In that spirit I hope to continue my work with you.

Niko's promotion brought him a lot of extra work. Apart from his existing lecturing duties he became involved in departmental organization and, conscientious as he was, threw himself into it. He suddenly became aware, for instance, how much the students' exam load had increased since his own days:

in their first three years they had to do six exams in zoology and three in botany, as well as chemistry. He worried that students were not reading enough because of this load, and within months of his appointment he started campaigning in the faculty to get the exam burden reduced. He also strongly suggested a smaller lecturing programme (which, of course, would benefit him personally, too).[42]

Whatever pressures Niko was under, students were always tremendously important to him, as I experienced myself some 15 years later. In those Leiden years he put it explicitly in a letter to his friend Ernst Mayr:

> *Personally, I like teaching and especially discussing problems with graduate students and guiding their first steps in research very much indeed. It is so stimulating and it keeps you young, it also brings you in touch with interesting people in one of the most interesting phases of their life. Seeing one of your students you have worked with embark upon his own independent course and then realizing he is doing well because he has developed into an independent mind brings the highest form of satisfaction to me. That is also why I do not care to have especially ethologists among my pupils; I am just as satisfied when they become ecologists or systematists, provided they have had a good look at my field and used it for broadening their interest and their grasp upon biology as a whole complex of interrelated problems.*[43]

Niko had no more research projects for himself, but rather did everything jointly with students, almost all undergraduates. Just as before the war, his main contact with undergraduates was during their third-year practical course in animal behaviour. Apart from the camp in his old stamping grounds in Hulshorst, he took them out to a herring gull colony in the dunes near Leiden (Meyendel, after initial concerns about the area having been mined by the Germans),[44] or to the wonderful Friesian island Terschelling (along the north coast of the Netherlands), or they watched animals in tanks in the lab. Many of the projects were at the initiative of the students themselves.

His relationship with students was a curious one. He mucked in with them, very keen and enthusiastic, intent on sharing the delights and deprivations of fieldwork and observations, and showing his mastery of the subject. He also included his family in this contact, and asked students to his home. Students could argue with him, and there was nothing of the distance between him and them that plagued the rest of Dutch academia. He saw them as part of his circle and often admired their abilities. On the other hand he could madden students, in the same way that their parents would, by his nagging, insisting on them getting up very early and working hard, and sticking to exhausting field schedules. He did not tolerate luxuries, and expected full help with domestic chores from everybody. I don't think he ever realized that he caused some mild resentment, as he wrote later:

> *I used to wake up the camp between 6 and 7 a.m. by walking from tent to tent whistling the reveille and tapping each tent lightly with a stick. After some*

Hulshorst camp, about 1947. Gerard and Jos Baerends on left and right; Leen de Ruiter third from left (note clogs). Photo Niko Tinbergen.

> *weeks, our jays [captive birds] began to give wonderful imitations of the tune I used to whistle. One morning they started to perform at 4 a.m. – and two of my students woke up, dressed hurriedly and came out rubbing their eyes before they discovered what had happened.*[45]

In 1946 the Hulshorst tented camp lasted from early July until the end of August. There were 16 undergraduate students, who arrived on a lorry, with their food- and paraffin-coupons and various other requirements from a detailed list (rationing was still in operation).

> *For the novices it is emphasized that we are a work-camp. No invitations for visits from acquaintances without my knowledge. In principle all days including Sundays are working days. We will not buy food on the black market, but my wife will strive to get the best possible and diverse food for everyone. Every participant is requested to take Dfl. 10 per week and if required to hand this over to my wife. (Trans.)*[46]

Lies was again in charge of all domestic arrangements.

Student numbers were large because of the post-war student bulge, and the 1948 field camp in Terschelling, for instance, had 30 participants, a far cry from the half dozen that Niko was used to before the war. In Terschelling most of them were persuaded to do projects on herring gulls or oystercatchers, but they could branch out into other pursuits if they had ideas. Niko loved Terschelling, the miles and miles of dunes with the unusually rich flora, and the wide flats with the thousands of shore birds, the gulls, terns, oystercatchers, godwits, and all the others: 'the most beautiful and gripping landscape I know'. He used to potter around in his wooden clogs, a cigarette in his mouth and holding forth to his charges. They camped in the dunes, and the behaviour course started with each of the students spending a day in a hide, a canvas cubicle of about $1 \times 1 \times 1$ metre, next to the nest of an oystercatcher or a gull. They had to write down everything the bird did, without disturbing it. Someone would put them in the hide at 9 a.m., if necessary with a bottle to pee in, and get them out again at 7 p.m. and that was their introduction to fieldwork.

One student, Piet Sevenster, discovered on Terschelling that there were red-backed shrikes around, and he studied their predation on large insects. After being appointed by Niko as student-assistant, he also involved four other under-graduates in this mini-project[47] (more about him later). An interesting result of the students' oystercatcher observations was the now well-known 'super-normal'

Choice experiment with black-headed gull: bird rolling eggs into nest shows preference for the 'super-normal' stimulus of a giant egg. Photo Niko Tinbergen.

egg: given the choice between their own egg and one four times as large, the birds will choose the large one, though quite unable to incubate the monster. (Similarly, they prefer a nest with five eggs over their own normal clutch of three, despite being unable to cover such a cornucopia.) Niko published the super-normal egg findings in Dutch, within weeks of the observations.[48]

In the Hulshorst student projects the main focus of attention had shifted somewhat away from wasps, although they were still important in the pro-gramme. They studied the way in which the hunting wasp *Bembex* returned to its nest again[49] (rather different from the previous subjects *Philanthus* and *Ammo-phila*), the project on the grayling butterfly was still going, and, in particular, there was more work on the subject of camouflage, which was to fascinate Niko for the next 20 years. Internationally prominent scientists came to visit the site that had acquired fame through the pre-war publications, including David Lack from Oxford, whom Niko greatly admired because of his work on robins, Konrad Lorenz, and the German entomologist Franz Huber. Niko impressed them with his field experiments, and in the collective enthusiasm the students obviously had a very exciting time there.

Leen de Ruiter was one of the new undergraduates who began their career in Hulshorst. After a reluctant start on a project on camouflaged caterpillars (prompted by Niko) he became so involved that he developed it into a long PhD study on the subject of 'counter-shading', completed nine years later. The research had its origin before the war, with Niko's observations on jays in large cages in the Hulshorst camp, birds who were experts in finding the marvellously camouflaged twig caterpillars. This was his first project on the biological function of camouflage and behaviour, later to be continued in the early 1960s with the research on egg-shell removal by gulls. But after the war he handed the insect camouflage project over to Leen de Ruiter, and let him get on with it for his PhD. Perhaps this was generosity, perhaps he found that he himself had gone deep enough and wanted something new again.

Leen focussed his entire project on the beautiful camouflage patterns of caterpillars. He studied the importance of relevant behaviour of twig caterpillars (which look exactly like small twigs on a branch, of just the species of tree on which they occur) to prevent predation by jays and other birds.[50] He also studied the behaviour in counter-shading, that is, caterpillars being lighter in colour in that part of the body that is normally shaded. Those species that are dark on top and light below turn their back towards the light, and species which are lighter on top sit upside down. The overall result is that the caterpillar looks flat and not cylindrical, and disappears in the flat foliage,[51] so predators do not see it. Many of the ideas were Niko's; it all had very little to do with the theor-etical aspects of causation of behaviour, but everything with natural selection. Niko just loved the beautiful details of how such animal behaviour works and is selected for by predator pressure, and he found great satisfaction in teasing it apart.

I have often met people who are not sympathetic towards this approach. They argued that it made us forget the beauty of the things we analysed; they felt that we were tearing the wonders of Creation to pieces. This is an unfair accusation ... So long as one does not, during analysis, lose sight of the animal as a whole, then beauty increases with increasing awareness of detail ... I must stress that my aesthetic sense has been receiving even more satisfaction since I studied the function and significance of this beauty.[52]

Another project at that time in Leiden, a project that attracted much fame later on, was on the behaviour of herring gull chicks, again an ostensibly very insignificant subject. Why do these chicks peck at the red spot on the bill of their parents? As in many others of Niko's ploys, this started as a project in a camp for undergraduate students with Niko's enthusiastic involvement, and was then picked up by one of the students, Ab Perdeck, as a special undergraduate project.[53] Niko's real interest in this was embodied in the title of his first publication about it, in Dutch (trans.): 'The function of the red spot on the bill of the herring gull'.[54] This was followed up by a paper in English, jointly with Perdeck, in *Behaviour*, on exactly the same results but with a title more in line with current ethological theory: 'On the stimulus situation releasing the begging response in the newly hatched herring gull chick'.[55]

The study described herring gull chicks in their first few days of life: when a parent alights on the nest, chicks peck at a red spot on the lower mandible of the otherwise yellow bill, and this causes the adult to regurgitate food. The question

was, what exactly is the stimulus that makes the chick peck at the spot, and Niko and his students designed a series of experiments to find out. The idea for this project was by no means new; in 1937 the German ornithologist Friedrich Goethe had reported experiments using the heads of dead birds to answer exactly the same question.[56] But the Leiden work was much more thorough, employing many differently painted cardboard models of gull heads, which the students waved in front of newly hatched chicks, one model after the other, offered immediately after the experimenter had uttered the 'mew call', an apparently essential prerequisite.

First they tested the importance of the colour of the bill spot, and concluded that red was best in making the chick peck at it. Then they researched the effects of 'contrast' (in a scale of greys; the more contrast the better), bill colour (red was excellent, but yellow with a red spot was even better); they also discovered that a natural shape of head was best, but a long thin bill elicited even more responses than a natural one, and so on with a number of other characteristics. The uttering of the mew call was an important releaser, and so was the movement of the model (moving being much more stimulating than still). All results were attractively presented with pictures of the models, each with a bar graph next to it.

The overall conclusion was that there is a pattern of 'releasers' of the chick's behaviour, their optimal value usually coinciding with the bill and head characteristics of the adult bird. But one gets the impression that here and there

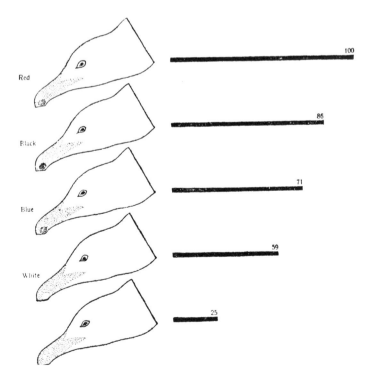

Red   100
Black   86
Blue   71
White   59
          25

Niko tried to fit the result into a pre-conceived idea, of everything in nature being totally adapted for the good of the species. If the optimal 'releaser' (stimulus that causes the chick to peck) in an experiment was not the same as what one saw in the adult bird, he argued his way around it. For instance, a model with a long, thin adult bill caused a better response from the chick than a normally sized one; this result was explained by the suggestion that the chick sees the adult bill from underneath, therefore not broad-side on (but if that were true, then it would also be impossible for the chick to see the red patch). When a black patch on the bill caused a greater response than a red one in one of the experiments, Niko explained it by a quirk of the experiment (that is, students had 'accidentally' used non-naïve chicks for the red test, which had had too much previous experience with 'red'), and he calculated some strange correction factors based on new experiments, showing that, really, the natural colour red was better. A similar argument was used to explain away an unexpected result with a grey bill. There were no statistical evaluations, but that was the state of the art in those days.

What worries me about these experiments, is that all models were presented and moved by hand, by observers who had certain ideas about what sort of results to expect. Model movement was demonstrably important in releasing the chicks' pecking, and the study was therefore compromised by possible (though unintended) observer bias ('I am expecting you to peck at red, go on!'). It is a criticism that strikes at the heart of the simplicity of the experiments, of exactly that which gave Niko so many admirers. The principle of Niko's experiments was to make systematic, but relatively small changes in an animal's natural environment and then to watch its reaction. It was a far cry from the then standard methodology of controlling the environment as much as possible (in the lab) and then making changes. But one potential problem with Niko's

Hand-held cardboard model of herring gull's head, testing reactions of chicks to bill spot colour. Terschelling, 1948.
Photo Niko Tinbergen.

approach was that the changes he made could not all be accounted for; for example, the observers' hand movements.

Such criticisms may be real, but they should not detract from the unique value of the principle of these experiments. At the time theirs was a new, innovative approach to biology – they were like a puff of fresh air through the dusty atmosphere of laboratories and museums. Here was bird behaviour being analysed scientifically, in the birds' own habitat, and next to observations on their life in the wild.

In 1946 one of Niko's students, Jan van Iersel, was appointed as his senior assistant. Jan had an excellent analytical mind and original ideas in designing experiments. He and Niko got on very well, and Jan was especially interested in the stickleback research that he later made into his lifetime speciality. Niko was obviously keen to have someone take the place of Pelk to continue with his beloved sticklebacks, and in van Iersel he had found a very able scientist. With him Niko did his first ethological experiment that was not concerned with simple 'releasers' or orientation; it was a study that went beyond that, aimed at the role of 'displacement' behaviour in the evolution of animal signals, one of Niko's established theoretical interests.

Almost immediately after Jan's appointment Niko and he wrote a paper on displacement activities in sticklebacks,[57] in which they detailed a number of behaviour patterns of the fish which occurred out of context (for example digging in the middle of a bout of fighting, and various others). They presented evidence that some of these 'displaced' behaviours had evolved into signals to other fish (for instance the digging movements signalled a threat to the opponent), but others had not. Exactly those displaced patterns that were used as signals had also become very 'ritualized' (slightly altered movements, more strikingly conspicuous), whereas the other, non-signalling displacement actions were never ritualized. Without any quantifying, this was a very elegant contribution to the understanding of the origin of various displays during fighting and courtship: the evolution of behaviour.

Jan van Iersel later went on to become Niko's successor and professor in Leiden, the driving force behind a large and long-lasting research group on stickleback behaviour. For Niko, this was almost the end of his involvement with sticklebacks; later he would supervise just one or two more student projects on this in his research group in Oxford.

Another well-known Leiden researcher who got involved with sticklebacks at an early stage was Piet Sevenster, whom I have already mentioned. I had known him from the early 1960s, and met him again in 2000 at the age of 76, quietly retired and living in a flat in a castle in Warmond, near Leiden.[58] Piet was a rather late student, held up by the war, and he was about 21 when he arrived in Leiden in 1945. He was fascinated by the opportunities for field research that were exposed by Niko, by the discovery that one could really do research this way. Niko took to him as someone who loved messing about in nature, and especially as someone who loved skating. Piet used to sit for many hours on end in front of his aquarium, watching the sticklebacks, and in winter it happened several times that he was interrupted by Niko: 'this is stupid, it is far too beautiful a day to be inside, let's go skating'. They often went together. Piet saw Niko really relax when skating: he was excellent at it, with long strokes crossing the huge Kaag lake and miles and miles of Dutch dykes and canals.

Piet Sevenster was a good experimenter with his sticklebacks, and other animals such as newts, impressed by and quickly picking up Niko's clear line of questioning, and good at designing equipment to do the job ('messing about with little tubes and paper-clips', as he put it). Niko admired that in him. But they never published anything together, and the development of the large, long-term stickleback programme in Leiden was largely the product of collaboration between Piet and Jan van Iersel: Niko left them to it. Many years later Piet was to succeed Jan van Iersel as professor.

Despite being terribly busy throughout those years, Niko did manage to escape quite often to get his fresh air, not just skating but in field camps with his students, or with friends on quick trips to his beloved bird dunes of 'De Beer', or on bicycle trips to the beautiful dune areas near The Hague. At this time also his first interest in filming emerged, when he accompanied his amateur-

As Dutch as they come: Niko during a student camp on the island Terschelling, 1948. Courtesy of the Tinbergen family.

cinematographer friend Olaf Paris: together they made their first, short educational film on herring gulls. Lies and the children usually could not come on
the expeditions (except to the Hulshorst camp). He was away a great deal, and
his absences from home within Holland must have been felt even more strongly
because of his frequent trips abroad.

Productivity, ideas, and travel

Once his research unit was a properly going concern again in late 1945, Niko
started to make moves towards a long trip to the United States. First he wrote to
his previous host there, Ernst Mayr,[59] and suggested that he was keen to visit,
although he needed a year of lecturing in Leiden, and to set up the field course
for his students and get the journal *Behaviour* off the ground. But before he went
to America again, he had arranged another trip over to Britain. David Lack had
attended a symposium in Leiden in February 1946; he stayed for a couple of
weeks, and when he returned to the UK Niko went with him. In Lack's home
base of Oxford Niko met the 'father of ecology' Charles Elton, and Mick
Southern. He went across to Cambridge where he made the acquaintance of
Bill Thorpe and James Gray, and he spent some time in London with Julian
Huxley. He was surprised about how much was going on in Britain that he did
not know about, and conversely, how little British circles were aware of what
was happening in Holland and had been happening in Germany before the war.
It strengthened his arguments for his new international journal.

After a summer full of fieldwork and students in Holland, in late autumn
1946 Niko set off to the States and Canada for a three-month lecturing trip. It
was a marathon, organized by Ernst Mayr: Niko presented an important paper
at the Wilson Ornithological Club in Nebraska,[60] he lectured in the universities
of Chicago, Wisconsin, and Alberta, he went across to California where he had
an exciting time in Caltech and Berkeley, and his trip culminated in a series of
six lectures in Columbia University and the American Museum of Natural
History in January and February 1947. Obviously, this highly charged visit
wonderfully stimulated his mind, and it was the six Columbia lectures that
became the basis for Niko's best known work, *The study of instinct*.

The rest of 1947 Niko spent at the home base in his new appointment as
professor and director of the zoology laboratory, working up his assembled
notes into a book, lecturing to the hordes of Leiden students, and taking part in
projects in the field camps. Some invitations he declined, and when his former
supervisor Boschma asked him to a large conference on Physics and Medicine
in 1947, he excused himself (trans.): 'I am afraid that people will start calling me
a travelling salesman in ethology!'[61] Soon, however, he was on the move again,
in Switzerland, where he gave a series of four lectures in Zurich in January 1948.

In those few post-war years Niko must have been on trips abroad much
more often than almost any of his colleagues and other scientists, despite all the

work he was doing in his own research group, all the writing, editing jobs, and his other projects. However, things were not what they seemed, and his travelling was not just a spreading of the gospel. Certainly, he was preaching ethology, passing on the message. But throughout that time he was also considering jobs abroad. Niko was obviously restless, wanting to break out and away.

Soon after he came back from Switzerland, in February 1948, he complained of exhaustion, and needing to lie down every so often: 'I am at the end of my strength'.[62] Yet he couldn't let go; at the end of that year he had organized another trip to Britain for early 1949, with a series of three lectures in London, and further ones in Oxford, Cambridge, Edinburgh, and Aberdeen, a journey on which Lies was to accompany him.[63] But at that same time he also finished the manuscript for his book, and with all such pressures on him he appears to have had a minor nervous breakdown, what he himself called 'a kind of collapse, just over-strained myself for some time'.[64] He cancelled his trip. His breakdown incapacitated him for only a short while, and in February 1949 he did travel to England, to discuss the possibility of a job in Oxford. And fairly soon after that in July, he was back in England again, this time to talk to a symposium in Cambridge, invited by Bill Thorpe.

Surprisingly, the post-war period was a time of great scientific productivity for Niko, despite the chaos, the upheavals, the departmental responsibilities, his frantic travelling, his unease in Leiden, and the loss of contact with his previous German colleagues. He was obviously at a peak in his career, and perhaps this is true for many scientists around the age of 40, when creativity, intelligence, and experience meet. The period 1945–49 saw in Niko a rush of blood, when he met the expectations surrounding his new position and responsibilities not just with all kinds of practical action, but also with clear formulations of his own science. In simple terms it was the time when he outlined how science should look at animals, and what he wanted with his career.

Niko's main products of these years were first and foremost his book, *The study of instinct*, and three papers[65] that mostly contained material which was also presented in the book. Significantly, all of these, the papers and the book, were based on and expanded from lectures he gave abroad. It was the preparation for a talk or a series of lectures that set Niko thinking and assembling his facts, which he then used for a publication. This may be one reason for Niko's assertive style when he was writing: he was not just putting together a scientific structure and argument on paper; rather, there was a sea of faces in front of him, and he was on trial. When reading his papers one can almost hear him: 'There is no doubt that …', 'certainly …', 'this can mean but one thing …'.

In his own observations and experiments of the late 1940s Niko was still mostly concerned with 'releasing stimuli', that is, aspects of the environment in the broadest sense to which animals reacted with specific behaviour patterns (for example the red spot on a bill, the super-normal egg). But his more theoretical interest in the entire organization of behaviour was almost separate from this, and it had made considerable strides since his 1942 'Objectivistic study'. Those strides were not made during his confinement in the hostage camp, if his small Dutch *Inleiding* [Introduction; 1946] was anything to go by. Niko's continued development of the 'Objectivistic study' came after the war, prompted by the series of lectures he gave in New York in early 1947, and the subsequent expansion of these talks into a book. Altogether, by 1949 this amounted to a general model of animal behaviour.

Many important elements in this grand theory had been contributed by Konrad Lorenz and others before him. However, Niko pulled it together into an all-embracing structure of the behaviour of all animals, into a science. The picture that he presented at that time looked something like this.

The behaviour that we see in animals is caused by (finds its origin in) physiological mechanisms. It may also be accompanied by subjective experiences, by feelings, but as scientists we cannot be interested in that. Niko's letters to Bierens de Haan were quite clear on this (trans.):

> *you use the word 'cause' for a different concept than I do, and than is current in all other branches of science … 'Walking' is observable, describable and measurable; 'fear' is not, that is the fear of the hare is not observable. To suggest a cause of an observable process, in terms of something that in principle is not observable and not measurable, does not take us one step further; after all, fear is a subjective phenomenon that can only be approached indirectly in a different animal. I know that there are all sorts of indirect observations which make it probable (in fact so probable that only a seeing-blind person can have any doubt) that every animal has subjective experiences, but despite all your arguments it is for me self-evident that the subjective phenomena are not causes in the scientific sense of the word. This is not a matter of emphasis, as you write, but definitely a matter of principle.*[66]

The physiological, causal mechanisms of behaviour develop in an individual during its lifetime (ontogeny); conditioning and learning may be involved but this is strictly separate from instinctive behaviour, and in the animals that we are

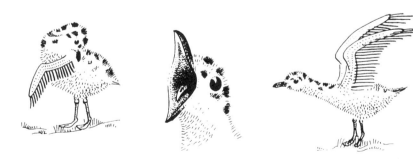

studying we are mostly interested in instinctive, species-specific actions. Behaviour has a purpose, although the animals do not know that, and it has been selected in evolution because it has a biological function that contributes to the preservation of the individual and the species, even of the species-community. Behaviour has evolved in species-specific ways, so one can compare species and study homologies (degree of correspondence or similarity of behaviour), as first pointed out by Heinroth and Whitman, and later emphasized by Konrad Lorenz.

The causal, physiological mechanism of behaviour can be considered in the same way as we look at an organ, it is a characteristic of the animal. It has a hierarchical, pyramid-shaped structure, in which higher 'centres' (for example, a reproductive 'drive') influence lower ones (for example courtship, fighting, or nest-building), and each of those influence lower ones still (for example courtship influencing different behaviours between the partners, fertilization, etc.). As Niko put it: 'This hierarchical system is a system of nervous centres, the higher centres controlling a number of centres of a next lower level, each of these in their turn controlling a number of lower centres, etc.'[67] These centres operate by initiating exploratory behaviour called appetitive behaviour, which continues until the animal comes into a situation that provides the sign stimuli necessary to release the motor response of one of the centres of a lower level. The final motor response, bringing the striving of the animal to an end, is called the consummatory act (the terms appetitive and consummatory had been coined about 30 years earlier, by the American Wallace Craig).[68]

> *To consider the part played by external stimuli. ... facts point to the conclusion that the releasing stimuli are not calling forth the response in the way of a reflex, however involved this reflex response might be. We must rather assume that they merely remove a block and thus provide free passage for the motor impulses coming from the activated centre. The instinctive centres seem to be in a state of readiness, they are constantly being loaded from within, but their discharge is prevented by a block. If there were no such block, continuous simultaneous discharge of all centres, and, as a consequence, chaotic movement would result. The adequate sign stimuli act upon a reflex-like 'innate releasing mechanism' (IRM), and this mechanism, upon stimulation, removes the block. Each centre, on each level, has such a block with corresponding IRM. As long as this block is not removed by stimulation of the IRM, the centre cannot 'get rid' of its motor impulses.[69]*

The IRM was the slightly modified idea of Konrad, referring to the response to highly specific releasing stimuli, and his idea was based again on the views of von Uexküll. This IRM was the subject of much of Niko's own research. Niko's model (although in those days it was not called that) went into greater detail than I present here; for example he fitted in phenomena such as displacement activities and others. It drew partly on recent physiological research into the nervous control of very simple animal movements, such as movements of fin rays, and research into behavioural reaction to electrical stimulation of parts of the brain.[70] The theory had the tremendous attraction of providing an explanation for the mechanism of all animal behaviour in a scientifically respectable way, suggesting many testable hypotheses for physiologists and ethologists alike. It connected directly with the sort of study one could imagine doing in the field; it made physiology touch on birdwatching, and the magic of behaviour on evolution.

Niko covered all of this in the set of six lectures he gave in Columbia University, to be written up over the following two years, again at Ernst Mayr's suggestion. In the talk in Nebraska, on his way to New York in November 1946, he had focussed on releasing stimuli (especially social releasers) and methodology,[71] which he later included in the Columbia lectures. About a year later he published an important paper that was the result of four lectures in Zurich in January 1948, which also more or less covered the whole subject; it came out in German in the Swiss journal *Experientia*.[72] Finally there was the talk he gave in July 1949 at a symposium in Cambridge: it described the model of hierarchical organization of behaviour as outlined above, in simple (and as we now know, very naïve) terms.

As always, Niko continued to publish at the same time popular articles in Dutch, in his beloved *De Levende Natuur* and some other magazines, a steady stream of easy writings that covered his current interests and casual observations (between 1945 and 1949 he wrote at least 27 of those: see list of publications). However busy and overworked he may have been, there was always time for this popularizing. He seemed to come to life when writing such articles, banging away at great speed on his old typewriter, without corrections or re-writing, a concentrated look on his bespectacled face and a cigarette in the corner of his mouth, usually humming some tune or other.

The Cambridge symposium in July 1949 on 'Physiological mechanisms of animal behaviour' was a climactic event for Niko, for several reasons, and it does not deserve to be dismissed in a couple of sentences. It was clearly a landmark in the history of ethology. Personally, Niko would always remember it as the occasion when he saw Konrad again for the first time since the war. But the papers presented there were also important, and the discussions perhaps even more so. The symposium was the brainchild of Bill Thorpe, after consultation with Niko and others; Niko was very keen on it indeed, as a first step in providing an international forum for his science. It was organized on behalf of the Society for Experimental Biology and the British Association for the Study of Animal Behaviour. Most of the participants were physiologists, many from Cambridge itself (amongst others E. Adrian, James Gray, J. S. Kennedy, Hans Lissmann), and also two from America (Karl Lashley and Paul Weiss), but in addition two Dutch and two German ethologists had been invited: Niko, Gerard Baerends, Konrad Lorenz, and Otto Koehler.

During the symposium there were intensive discussions with the physiologists about the new concepts of ethology, and the physiologists were not that much taken by the new science. There was no problem over contributions such as the one from Baerends about 'releasers', which was by then an established path. But as far as the overall organization of behaviour was concerned, the Cambridge people especially (foremost James Gray and Hans Lissmann) believed that ethologists underplayed the role of fairly simple reflexes, controlled not by the brain but much more peripherally, in the nervous system. Ethologists emphasized the central nervous organization as the control of behaviour, with Niko's hierarchy model as a paradigm.

In his contribution Niko attempted to bridge a gap, by presenting ethological evidence for a hierarchical organization of behaviour, which could be seen as an extension of an existing physiological explanation for the lowest units of behaviour (that is, single movements). This physiological model had been proposed by one of the participants to the conference, Paul Weiss.[73] Niko's paper was well received by everyone, especially because it was clear and to the point, and opened up many testable hypotheses. In later years, however, Niko's model would be totally rejected, after new insights into animals' physiology.

Lorenz's presentation was characteristically wide-ranging and full of ideas, arm-waving, and explaining it all with large but vague concepts.[74] It is remembered particularly because it was here that Konrad provided his famous energetic model of behavioural organization in hydraulic terms. He described it as a large reservoir of water providing the internal force that drives behaviour, what he called 'action-specific energy', running out through a valve, the releasing mechanism, which is controlled by a weight (the releasing stimuli). Both the accumulation of water in the reservoir and the weight of the external stimuli can open the valve. Water runs into a trough with different outlets, which represent the observed behaviour of the animal, and depending on the amount of water running into the trough different behaviour patterns emerge.

Konrad's hydraulic model was politely accepted (with many reservations), probably largely because of his authority. It has been more or less ridiculed ever since, but the idea of an organization of nervous energy as the driving force of behaviour stuck for a long time; it was also implicit in Niko's model. Another one of the many ideas that Konrad presented at the symposium, to him particularly relevant at that time after the war, dealt with human aggression, innate and dangerous. This he was to develop later in great detail, as one of the most controversial topics addressed by ethologists.

The Cambridge symposium is referred to as the first properly international conference of ethologists. This sounds rather ambitious: it was small, and ethologists were few. But all were convinced that more such meetings should follow, and the next year Niko, Gerard Baerends, and Bill Thorpe went over to Germany at the invitation of the behavioural physiologist Erich von Holst, joined by a group of German behaviour students in von Holst's laboratory in Wilhelmshaven. Cambridge was, indeed, the beginning of a long series of international ethological conferences, now held every two years with many hundreds of participants.

The study of instinct

The study of instinct was the outstanding result of Niko's post-war years in Leiden. More than anything else that he wrote or did, it was this book that brought him fame, and it was this book that put ethology on the map. It was written in Niko's hectic years of 1947 and 1948, finished just before Christmas, but not published until 1951. The reason for the delay was in its conception; it started in America, where Ernst Mayr prompted Niko after his January 1947 Columbia lectures to put them into book form. Niko immediately did some organizing, and the New York branch of Oxford University Press was happy to snap it up, but then dragged its heels. Two years later the Press decided that it would be much cheaper to publish it in Britain, and transferred it to Oxford, a process that took a miserably long time. On the flyleaf Niko is described as 'Lecturer in the University of Oxford'; in fact, he was when the book came out, but it was entirely the product of his Leiden years, and of his foreign lecturing trips.

It is not difficult to see why the book made such an impact. Its contents gave an outline of the entire structure of all animal behaviour, with the internal and external mechanisms behind it, its development, and aspects of its biological function and evolution. *The study of instinct* provided order in the perceived chaos of behaving animals, with simple and probable explanations and ideas about how to watch and study. The text flitted kaleidoscopically between examples from many species of animals that one can see in one's own environment, with easy-to-read graphs mixed between pleasantly natural drawings of the animals themselves.

Niko used an easy, direct vocabulary without jargon, helped by his child-hood indoctrination of the need for clear language, and as a non-native English speaker not encumbered by a need to use big words. The book was nicely presented, not too long (228 pages), an easy quantity of hard science but also lovely natural history. Later much of the structure of behaviour that Niko proposed in the book was dismantled again. But *The study of instinct* served its purpose, and it had an impact greater than that of any other book on animal behaviour before or long after.

The first of eight chapters is headed 'Ethology, the objective study of behaviour', and explains how ethology relates to physiology, animal psychology, to American behaviorism, to vitalism, and to other biological sciences, and it outlines the kind of questions Niko thinks are important. Following chapters describe the role of external, 'releasing' stimuli in causing behaviour, and the internal factors such as hormones and the central nervous system, and there is a detailed explanation of the hierarchical organization. The last three chapters look at the development of behaviour in an individual's lifetime (including learning and conditioning), adaptiveness ('biological function'), and evolution. It is the book of the 'four whys', although most of the emphasis on the 'why' of ontogeny was to come later.

It is interesting to see the progression from Niko's 1942 'Objectivistic study of the innate behaviour of animals'. That contained largely the same subjects, but *The study of instinct* is a great expansion, with a much larger field of literature covered; in particular, the 'Objectivistic study' contained even less on ontogeny and learning, and almost nothing on neuro-physiology. The influence of Niko's contact with Ernst Mayr is noticeable in *The study of instinct*, with a final chapter on the evolution of behaviour, lacking in the earlier work.

Underneath the broad picture of animal behaviour that was painted in *The study of instinct* there were quite a few blemishes, but most of those were happily accepted at the time. A great deal of the book's strength was in its simplicity, but that sometimes involved barely acceptable simplifications, arrived at by removing all the 'ifs and buts' from individual studies. There were some unwarranted conclusions from his own research, such as the effect of red stickleback bellies and the over-flying predator model. And the lack of quantification, which may have made the book very readable, also laid it open to criticisms. When Niko talked about 'facts', which he did often, he was referring to what were frequently no more than assumptions. In the years since *The study of instinct* we have become much, much more careful in our ways of describing observations and experiments. Two examples of Niko's style:

> *the function of these conspicuous colours is not merely that of social releasers in the service of actual copulation, but it is certain that part of their function is to bring males and females to well-timed and well-oriented co-operation (p. 175).*

Or:

> *Summarizing this paragraph on social releasers, it will be clear that although
> their function has been experimentally proven in relatively few cases, we can
> safely conclude that they are adaptations serving to promote co-operation
> between the individuals of a conspecific community for the benefit of the group.
> It is a striking fact that all social releasers studied seem to be beautifully adapted
> to activating an IRM, for a social releaser is always specialized in such a way
> as to send out stimuli that have the characteristics of sign stimuli. They are
> always relatively simple and at the same time conspicuous (p. 184).*

Nevertheless, if one did not look into too much detail of individual cases, if one
did not bother too much about the actual data, the overall story was extremely
appealing. Its success was that it showed a simple approach to explaining almost
all animal behaviour. When I read it as a young student, I thought this was
fabulous; I immediately felt that I wanted to be involved in this, to take it
further, to test it, and to put flesh on those bones. What more can one want from
a book? Despite its inevitable flaws, it was a masterpiece.

Move to Oxford

Niko had been highly successful in Leiden. He had become a professor at an
unusually young age, he had a great international reputation, his science was
going well, he had funds and good students, his *magnum opus* was about to burst
onto the world scene, he was editor of the main international journal in his field,

Niko, about 1949.
Courtesy of the Tinbergen family.

and he could obviously travel as much as he liked. Yet, in 1949 he upped sticks from Leiden, and climbed down from his chair to take a job as demonstrator (below the level of lecturer) in Oxford. What stirred him?

It is a question that many people have asked. The standard answer that Niko gave at the time, the one he mentioned in his autobiographical notes[75] and the reply that one still gets from others, was that he wanted to spread the message of ethology to the English-speaking world. It was a noble motive, much respected and with an element of self-sacrifice, but it was not the whole story. I also talked to him about it, perhaps sensitized after I had left the Netherlands myself, as a student. Niko's comments to me, some 12 years after his departure, revealed that missionary zeal was only a part of his motivation.

There was another, more important and much more personal reason for the move: he had had enough of Holland, he wanted out. As one of his daughters heard it from her mother, Lies: 'One evening he suddenly said "I can't stand it here any longer, we've got to emigrate"', which Lies countered with 'Oh, all right.' Apocryphal, perhaps, but Janet said that Niko never contradicted this story.[76]

To understand it, one has to go back several years before Niko took his decision. In the hostage camp many prominent politicians were locked up with him, and month after month there were discussions about what the country should be like when the war would be over, with detailed plans. Dutch pre-war politics, the government, in fact much of life in Holland (press, broadcasting, societies, charities, etc.) had long been based on religion, referred to as 'denominational segregation'. This resulted in a numbing small-mindedness of many totally intolerant factions. The political leaders in St Michielsgestel hostage camp planned an alternative, a democratic people's movement with a better, more principled and tolerant society. Niko was not politically motivated or even much interested, but the atmosphere of expectation rubbed off on everybody in the camp.

Within days of the liberation in 1945, a new national government was in place, manned to a large extent by former St Michielsgestel hostages under Prime Minister Willem Schermerhorn, himself one of them. Unfortunately, despite all their laudable intentions, it was soon business as usual, and the glorious optimism of liberation day became deep disappointment. Very little had changed.[77] Perhaps Niko would have accepted it if there had not been all this high-level discussion about alternatives – as it was, he felt contempt. Niko also could not shake down a resentment that the country had been violated by Germany, and he saw that not all those in the country who now had prominent positions again had been opposed to the German occupation: collaborators were still around.[78] Moreover, his pre-war scientific stimulation and contacts had come largely from German and Dutch sources, involving people like Lorenz, and he felt unease about continued dependence on them. He wanted some distance.

Recent history may have brought things to a head, but there were also aspects of the Dutch bourgeoisie that profoundly irritated Niko. It was a society that organized itself with choking rules and regulations – probably a *sine qua non* for that large (and relatively rich) population in a minute country. Niko was a freedom-loving character, who had seen much greater personal freedom in England and America, countries where people were also far less judgmental. In Holland he was living in a straightjacket. He saw the materialism of the country, its celebration of financial gain as it destroyed every notion of conserving the last areas of wilderness he loved. Holland's crowds, too, got him down,[79] which was understandable: the Netherlands was then the most densely populated nation in the world (never mind that he himself had already contributed four children).

Against the background of general dissatisfaction with his country, Niko also felt unease about his personal situation in the university. He had to spend a lot of time on administrative duties and faculty matters that did not really interest him, and he had to lecture hordes of medical students. All this kept him from what he really wanted to do – especially after he was promoted to a chair. More subtly, his older colleague van der Klaauw, who had spent so much effort in getting him promoted, was someone whom Niko admired, but who also demanded much help – and he found it very difficult to refuse this, especially since van der Klaauw was also an invalid (with use of only one leg).[80] There was really no way of modifying these chores – it was a matter of either doing them wholeheartedly, or leaving. The decision that Niko took was not surprising, really, as he was never a man for the grindstone but loved the challenge of something new.

This is not to say that his mission-argument for a move abroad was untrue. There was a strong element of veracity, it was a good excuse, and afterwards Niko probably came to see it himself as his major driving force. Very likely, also, the later consequences of his move for the development of ethology were profound and highly beneficial. But history suggests that the much applauded missionary idea emerged only later, well after he had made the decision for himself to leave Holland, and, to some extent, as a justification for his 'dis-loyalty'.

Niko hesitated for a long time, and not surprisingly: a move would be a major upheaval. He never even considered the possibility of a return; it would be a departure for good. He first mentioned a move abroad in September 1945, either to America or to the Dutch East Indies,[81] and the subject came back again and again in his letters. In March 1947 he told Bierens de Haan that he had seriously considered a job in America, but felt that his duties lay in Leiden.[82] But in August of that year, only months after he had been appointed professor, he was again writing to Ernst Mayr in America about the possibility of leaving Holland: he was tired of his country.

> *I realize that I have been very lucky to get one of the most attractive jobs I could hope to get – yet the considerations that have compelled me to stay in our overcrowded little country are losing strength. It is difficult to state in a few*

words why this has occurred; let it be sufficient to tell you that my motives are naturally complex, not altogether egotistic and certainly not materialistic. One important thing is that the general lack of vitality of our people is disappointing me, and also their self-satisfied conservatism. ... I now should like to let you know that I would be inclined to come over and settle in the New World when I would get the chance.[83]

In February 1948 the ornithologist David Lack was agitating with his head of the Zoology Department in Oxford, Professor Alister Hardy, to find a place for Niko. Hardy had said 'We must simply get him', and Niko used this to put a bit of pressure on Ernst Mayr in the States: 'I can quite understand that this might cause you to give up any attempts on my behalf, although I still think I would prefer a similar position in America.'[84] In September 1948 Ernst Mayr mentioned to Niko that there was the possibility of a post at Caltech in Pasadena, a place which had impressed Niko during his visit, and he was certainly interested. He wrote to Mayr 'When I was there Christmas 1946 I saw that it was a very active centre of research, and the presence of at least three Dutch biologists means something to me, in spite of the fact that I am trying to leave Holland.'[85] All this correspondence, and various remarks to me and others, suggested strongly that Niko's reason for a move was first of all to find a change, something more inspiring than what he had in the Netherlands.

In summer 1948 David Lack visited Niko in his field camp in Hulshorst, and brought with him a letter from Alister Hardy, offering Niko a job. Niko and Lies had endless discussions about it, and later in 1948 he went to stay with his brother Luuk and Tilde in Hulshorst, to get their advice. It was all this, and the finishing of his manuscript, that caused the small nervous breakdown, and the cancellation of his lecturing trip in Britain.[86] Fortunately he quickly got over it.

From his letters to Ernst Mayr it seems quite clear that Niko was more attracted to a job in the United States than in England, although he could be rather critical of America. There is 'much that is wrong there', he felt. David Lack suggested that he would 'lose his soul' in America, but when push came to shove, I doubt that Niko was that much attracted to the 'soulfulness' of Oxford and England. More likely, it was the fact that there was a firm job offer from Oxford on the table at the time that his need to get out was greatest, and the American post at Pasadena was still uncertain. He liked Oxford, he had developed a friendly relationship with David Lack, and he did have great respect for the ecological expertise of people like David, Charles Elton, Mick Southern, and the evolutionary geneticist Arthur Cain. Distance also played a role in the decision,[87] as both Niko and Lies did not want to be too far away from their Dutch relatives. Other universities in Britain were not seriously considered: for instance there was research on animal behaviour in Cambridge, but Niko did not feel greatly interested in its leader, Bill Thorpe, who was not a field man, and was an active Quaker. Robert Hinde thought 'they would never have got on'.[88]

In February 1949 Niko took the boat to England again, for a final detailed negotiation with Alister Hardy about the Oxford job. Hardy was an expert in marine biology who had only recently taken over as head of department, a lovely man with a gentle smile, full of adventure and an excellent artist, and he and Niko took to each other immediately. He gave Niko a firm offer of the job of demonstrator, at the bottom of the academic ladder, with the promise of a lectureship as soon as this could be wrenched out of the University (the demon-stratorship was, indeed, converted by the time Niko started in Oxford, by Hardy's 'juggling with two half-vacancies').[89] In addition, Niko would get a fellowship in one of the old colleges, which would provide extra pay and access to traditional Oxford academia. Niko could bring an assistant from Leiden for a year (on a special grant from the Nuffield Foundation). The department had some working space for Niko, but not that much; there was the assurance that he could do as much fieldwork as he liked, provided he would also do some lecturing. The department would help with some equipment (including a film camera), but here, too, provisions were not ample (though better than in Leiden). Niko noted that Oxford would be further from his beloved sea coasts than almost any place in Britain; Hardy, himself a man of the sea, countered this argument with the observation that there was no place in Britain from where you had equally good access to so many shores in all directions.

So the immediate prospects in Oxford were far from great. There were promises of better times to come, promises also of many good students to join him. But what really moved Niko was the enthusiasm he met, from Alister Hardy and the other staff, people whose interests touched his, and who were dead keen to have him in their midst. Niko's mind was made up there. After he returned from Oxford he discussed things again with Lies, and at the end of

February he wrote to Alister Hardy that he accepted. He would join the Oxford department in September of that year, 1949.

One thing that had bothered Niko about leaving Leiden was a replacement; having started what was effectively an ethological school there, he could not just abandon it. The obvious successor would be his first and oldest student, Gerard Baerends, but in 1946 Baerends had been appointed to a chair in Groningen, and although interested in the Leiden job, he decided to stay where he was. The next one on the list was Niko's then aide-de-camp in the lab, Jan van Iersel, and Niko wrote confidentially to him in October 1948 to ask if he would be inter-ested, so Niko could suggest him to the Senate.[90] After 1949 Jan the stickleback man, an excellent experimentalist and theoretician, became Niko's successor in animal behaviour research, later professor, and was to maintain Leiden's role as a bastion of ethology for the next few decades. Another former student of Niko, Don Kuenen, succeeded Niko in the chair of experimental zoology.

Niko expected the reaction from his Leiden colleagues to his departure to be censorious, and he was right. Initially, he thought that van der Klaauw under-stood his reasons for leaving and agreed with them,[91] but once the decisions were taken van der Klaauw was hurt and negative. He had gone through a great deal of trouble to get Niko a chair in the department, and this was the reward. Other colleagues were even more bitter; probably, they nursed an expectation of loyalty that Niko had failed to meet. Loyalty to your community and to the hand that feeds you was a vital ingredient of Dutch society, and Niko earned strong opprobrium, which took years to die down.

In response, Niko wrote a circular letter to all his colleagues, in March 1949,[92] in which he explained his reasons for leaving. It was all about the oppor-tunities for his science to be carried out in the Anglo-Saxon world, about research and teaching, and about the fact that there would be no problem over a successor in Leiden. He did not say that he wanted to leave Holland, but he admitted that there were some, unspecified conditions in the department that worried him slightly, although he said they hardly played a role. He was at great pains to emphasize that he did not leave for financial gain or promotion, because in the Calvinistic egalitarian organization of Dutch society in those days someone who sought promotion was a 'streber' (a German word, meaning pusher, careerist), and this was very much disapproved of. One did not try to do better than one's colleagues. No, Niko left for idealistic reasons, and he hoped that they could part as good friends. It was crying for the moon; Leiden did not even give him the option of having an honorary chair, as would have been customary. 'Our decision to say goodbye to Leiden and go to Oxford has given us a lot of unpleasantness' (trans.), he later commented. [93]

When the boat carrying the Tinbergen family to England departed from Hook of Holland, nobody from the university came to see them off, although Leiden was quite close. It was all rather bleak; there was family, and there was Piet Sevenster, who was to come along and work as Niko's assistant in Oxford for the next year. Piet was struck by the lack of warmth from Niko's former colleagues. The departure left Niko with a rather bitter taste in his mouth, and afterwards he rarely went back to Leiden.

Standing at the railing of the ferry from the Hook on that bleak September day, the Dutch landscape moved past Niko and Piet. They looked at the dunes of De Beer, Niko's old, magnificent stamping grounds. Niko, cigarette in his hand, was rather silent. Quietly he said (trans.): 'Perhaps the last time that I see this, it will all go, irrevocably.'

Sadly, within a few years he was proved right, and the entire sand-blown wilderness of De Beer was translated into the huge Europort harbour. In 1973, when he returned to the Netherlands to collect the Swammerdam Medal in Amsterdam, he had tears in his eyes when he said to his audience: 'I've just come here by train, and I looked at the landscape. What have you done to this country?'[94]

CHAPTER **6**

Starting again: Oxford in the 1950s

Arrival

Oxford is special. It and Cambridge are different, not just because of the historical universities, the old buildings, the style and traditions, but because these are the backdrops to excellence and power, academic as well as worldly. In the 1950s Anthony Sampson wrote of these universities:

> *For seven hundred years two universities dominated British education, and today they dominate more than ever, with a fame enhanced by their isolation, and their sheer hypnotic beauty. Like dukes, Oxford and Cambridge preserve an antique way of life in the midst of the twentieth century … students of Oxbridge make up, from the outside at least, one of the most élite élites in the world … Oxford is different from Cambridge, older, more worldly, more philosophical, classical and theological … and with a flair for self-congratulation and public relations.*[1]

More than any other universities, Oxford and Cambridge pride themselves on erudition. By joining Oxford, Niko entered academia *par excellence*, with a highly charged atmosphere of academic brilliance.

Later, one would usually associate Niko with Oxford University. However, by the time he started there, he already had more than half of his life behind him, and much of his work had been done. The 42-year-old man, who arrived in the city of dreaming spires in September 1949, was at an age of high youthful intelligence, and at peak performance, but he brought much pre-Oxford experience with him. He had had a successful career by any standards. He played a leading international role in animal behaviour science, he had produced a number of authoritative and trend-setting papers, he lectured widely in the most prominent universities, and his uniquely important handbook was about to be launched.

However, as he put it himself, he was ready for a completely fresh beginning. He had burned his boats. He still had his baggage of Dutch lifestyle and science, but he was now in a position to reject at least part of that. The person who emerged was the Oxford-Niko that the world got to know – the ethologist who earned the prizes.

Niko arrived with some exceptional abilities and characteristics. Foremost, he was an original thinker with ideas, and with an ability to formulate new questions in new ways. Combined with this, he was an excellent naturalist who had studied or watched many different animals, not just birds or some other single group. He was good at experiments with animals. He was totally charming, as well as a brilliant communicator with well-organized thoughts and perfect photographs, a good linguist, and genial with an infectious enthusiasm; he had a bubbling sense of humour and great appeal to students. Especially, he had vision, and missionary zeal: he knew what he wanted with his science – maybe it was intuitive and not completely thought through, but it was vision, and people were fascinated.

Niko's fame and student-appeal in university-England was magical, and not just in Oxford. As an example and amusing aside, at the time of his arrival in 1949 John Maynard Smith, now the most eminent evolutionary biologist in Britain, was a student in London. In the spirit of the time, he wrote a long poem *La femme à la Tinbergen*[2]. It refers to sign-stimuli, those very limited aspects of an animal or object to which another animal reacts:

> *… the thoughts which lecturers deserve*
> *Tended to dwell on female curves.*
> *He thought 'If only I could build*
> *A form so with the essence filled*
> *Of shapely ankle, rounded thigh,*
> *Of all that pleases, why then I*
> *Could earn my fortune on the stage*
> *And never learn another page …*

Niko also had his weak points. He was much more of a pragmatist than a theoretician, not much good at any quantitative aspect of science, and with only very limited interest in subjects outside his own field; one could not call him very erudite. Of course this did not go unnoticed in Oxford, and his new world may have been charmed by Niko, but there were also reservations. Especially some people who knew him well personally found his single-mindedness rather off-putting. Piet Sevenster, the Dutch student who accompanied the Tinbergens to Oxford for their first year, told me that one of his new disciples in Oxford, Martin Moynihan, commented that Niko could never relax: every discussion, even a light one, had to have a function as science, it had to have an aim. 'In the long run I couldn't stand it with him, however much I liked him.' Piet himself also found (trans.) 'an eternal tension, with even a single remark leading to moralizing. One always worked towards a goal, and one could never have a nice, light-hearted barmy nonsense conversation'.[3]

Niko would forever be affected by the legacy of Dutch Calvinism, despite his religious denial. It was fundamental to him that no one should be just messing about, one had to be busy with an objective, and even after an enjoyable session observing birds he would comment on this 'nicely playing truant'. Niko felt that all of us have a strong obligation to society. He was a workaholic with deep-seated feelings of guilt. Piet Sevenster felt that Niko's moralizing was a product of this, and observed that (trans.):

he lived with an ideology in which ease, enjoyment and luxury were evil; the simpler life was the better, and one should not enjoy things that were not strictly necessary. This was always in the background. He could not relax, except when skating or walking in nature, and when writing. Then he was in his element, perhaps because his guilt disappeared when writing, as he was communicating.

Niko was a classical case of a person often troubled by stomach ulcers, which frequently laid him up. The man who arrived in Oxford was a charming, brilliant naturalist with a vision for a science, but to those who knew him well, he was also a man with a burden.

Most people who met him on a daily basis (including many of his students) described Niko in superlatives of charm, enthusiasm, teaching ability, and biological insight. Only some, a small minority, were more cautious. One should not read too much into this, as there may have been some personal mismatch, yet such criticisms may be revealing. One of his students (who wants to remain anonymous) wrote:

I actually found his personality quite difficult in spite of superficial cheeriness and good humour ... I wouldn't ever claim to have known him well, and never really felt at ease with him, nor I imagine, he with me ... with hindsight, I see that having left Leiden ... and his students there, he was probably feeling very vulnerable in Oxford and probably needed the support ... He seemed to me to be at heart a very simple man and culturally quite unsophisticated, not in any sense your typical Oxford don.

With Lies and the children, he fairly quickly settled down in what must be one of the most delightful cities in England, with its beautiful old colleges, its parks and college gardens, the river, and the surrounding hills and woods. Peter Hartley, one of David Lack's colleagues, arranged for them to move into a former old pub, the 'Worcester Arms', in Islip, a small village six miles north of Oxford. Piet Sevenster moved in with them for the first three months. In December 1949 the Tinbergens moved to a more central place (29a Banbury Road), which was so much more pleasant that it worried Niko's sense of modesty: 'It really is far too beautiful for us, but nothing else was available, and it was quite a favour that we got this, the ground floor of a gigantic villa, with a large garden around it, five minutes walk from the lab.'[4]

A nasty complication with Lies' fifth pregnancy arose during their settling-in. Within a month of their arrival at Oxford Lies developed toxaemia, and for many weeks until the birth of Gerry, five months later, she was hospitalized. It meant that, for once, Niko had to spend a great deal of time with the other four children, 4 to 15 years old, who had to start school in a foreign language, with all the attendant problems. They had had special English lessons in Holland, but not much had prepared them for the huge change, and especially the youngest,

*Niko and his Leiden successor,
Jan van Iersel, during
International Ethological
Conference in Buldern,
Germany, 1952.
Photo I. Eibl-Eibesfeldt.*

Janet, had problems in the beginning and drove her teachers to despair. Tellingly, when she introduced a later visitor to her doll, she told him: 'You must be kind to her, she doesn't speak English very well.'[5]

The young Tinbergen boys were sent to Magdalen College School, where they were quite happy, and which, fortunately, was an understanding and relaxed place. The girls went to Oxford High School. Niko, knowing little of the education system in the country, had been advised by David Lack that private school was *de rigeur* for his children, despite the expense and despite private education going against the grain for a socialist from Holland.

Finance was a major problem for the family, and even fifty years later the Tinbergen children remembered their relative poverty then. They had not been allowed to take more than a few Dutch guilders with them from Holland (because of currency restrictions), and Niko's salary was puny. It affected almost everything: children's clothes, their food, their socializing, and it was all the more hurtful because, this being the Oxford University of those days, they were surrounded by relative luxury. Many of Niko's colleagues had private money.

Niko spent his first English winter finding his feet, both on the home and job fronts. He initially tried to settle into a routine of pub lunches with David

Lack, Mick Southern, and other ecologists, but could not keep that up for long. He still felt somewhat out of his depth, not being at the centre of a crowd from his own discipline. However, it did not take long before a group began to sprout around him.

Two years after their arrival in Oxford, Niko wrote (trans.):

> My work here is coming up to speed now. The first two years I could give much time to writing; I had only few students, as my specialization was practically unknown here, and therefore I first had to acquaint the aficionados with elementary principles, which is a long job – not because they have to know so many facts, but because it is difficult for most people to see an animal as a machine. Now things are going better, and I have seven PhD students working.[6]

Seeing an animal as a machine was fundamental to Niko's contribution to science.

The 'Hard Core'

Even before the first year was out, Niko had begun to attract students and researchers. He was aided by several generous student and assistant grants from a British charity, the Nuffield Foundation, obtained through the influence of Peter Medawar, a later Nobel laureate who was always a friend and admirer of Niko. It was the beginning of a unique surrounding group of high-calibre enthusiasts, bubbling with ideas and energy, who pushed ahead with the new science at speed. Before long, the group in Oxford was building on Niko's ideas and new insights in animal behaviour, and it became the engine of ethology. They called themselves the 'Hard Core', a label coined by Martin Moynihan, and later, many of its members would be moving on to great things, heading different fields of science and writing. Niko himself was in awe of his new students (trans.): 'The quality of the students is very high, because of the severe selection that Oxford and Cambridge can afford to exercise; I sometimes tend to feel an inferiority complex. Once every week all my people come for an evening to our house for a seminar, and every time I am amazed at the clever-ness of my small group.'[7]

The Hard Core members were mostly PhD students (in Oxford the degree of Doctor of Philosophy is abbreviated as 'DPhil', but elsewhere as 'PhD' which is what I shall use), with an extraordinary ethos of enthusiasm and dedication. As one of the early members of the group put it, 'Niko engendered an atmo-sphere of mutual support and interest, and the totally free and literally joyful sharing of ideas and information … all the time, so that even if Niko didn't himself have much input into one's work, one received close and very incisive supervision from everyone else.'[8]

The Friday evening seminars at the Tinbergen house became an institution. Lies was always there, and people used to sit around the room, smoking and drinking quantities of instant coffee. There was a frontier spirit, with the limitless enthusiasm of young, brilliant minds. It was an in-house affair, and mostly one discussed recent papers, or recent research. Niko rarely dominated the conversation, but he was always there to chip in, to keep the discussions on track, and to ask 'what exactly do you mean by …'. Everyone I talked to who had been one of that select band still refers to those evenings with great nostalgia.

Martin Moynihan was one of the earliest disciples in the team, a well-loved American ornithologist and one of several good artists amongst them. It was he who referred to Niko as 'The Maestro', a term that stuck through the years. One of the others who shared a house with him described Martin as 'likeable, very flamboyant, upper crust, intellectual and arrogant, with an appalling temper'. Martin launched his ideas about displays and defended them with verve, he shouted and threw his paint around if a result did not please him. His own focus within Niko's group was initially on the displays of black-headed gulls, then on comparative behaviour and evolution in gulls, subjects that went to the heart of Niko's interest. Martin was a thinker, with a wide intellectual reach.

A later key figure was Mike Cullen, who grew up in India and England, and who arrived in Oxford as an undergraduate to study maths. After a year he switched to zoology, was caught by Niko's brilliant lectures and, in 1952, started a PhD study with him, on the behaviour of the arctic tern. He was an almost ideal complement to Niko: an obituary of Mike refers to 'his razor-sharp, quantitative, analytical mind … would take our half-baked ideas, inadequately analyzed data, or the hesitant beginnings of a mathematical model, and transform them into a beautifully polished gem'.[9] Unlike Niko, Mike was not a visionary, but he picked up the ideas of others and moulded them. What made him so very essential in the Oxford group was his total selflessness. He would abandon whatever he was doing in order to explore the problems of his colleagues and later students, and come up with wonderful analyses. He was totally fascinated by science, figures, and quantification, and throughout his life attended any seminar that was even remotely relevant. But he did not like writing, and published very little himself. Mike was an eccentric, known amongst others for his fire-eating abilities at parties, for his knitting during seminars, and for his eternal red sweater.

Niko was lucky to get Mike. The young PhD student grew, and by the mid-1950s he had already become the main pillar of Niko's group. Throughout Niko's tenure in Oxford Mike was his right hand scientifically, and the person on whom PhD students always fell back after The Maestro (and they themselves) had provided the ideas. I think it is fair to say that without Mike, the results of the Oxford behaviour group would have been far less impressive. On his departure, more than 20 years later, Niko wrote to Mike 'I shudder when I try to imagine how the presentation of quantitative data would have suffered had not you, Mike, been there to advise literally everybody', and 'I have learnt a lot, though not enough, from listening to Mike's way of discussing the stories told by graduates during seminars. You showed me the value of putting all criticisms in the form of questions.'

Years earlier in America, Ernst Mayr had pressed Niko to expand his interest into the genetics of behaviour, and suggested that he look at the behaviour of the workhorse of geneticists, the fruit fly *Drosophila*. He now had the chance, and one of his first students in Oxford was a local graduate, Margaret Bastock, who was keen to take this up for a PhD: she compared the courtship behaviour of natural and mutant fruit flies. Niko felt that this was a necessary development, but his heart wasn't in it, and later he would comment about behaviour genetics, 'I tolerated it, welcomed it, but could not understand most of it.'[10]

So Margaret became a Hard Core member, as did Philip Guiton (research project on sticklebacks, male courtship behaviour), David Blest (eye-spots of moths), Fae Hall (sticklebacks, comparing species), Rita White (black-headed gull chicks), Aubrey Manning (bumblebees), and Desmond Morris (ten-spined sticklebacks). Two post-docs also joined the group, Uli Weidmann and Esther Sager, both from Switzerland. Robert Hinde was doing a PhD with David Lack (on great tits) but felt more at home with the behaviour crowd, so he was always around in Niko's first year, and often also Bill Russell, who was studying the hormones of *Xenopus* toads under A. E. (Bob) Needham in Zoology. Another student was Leen de Ruiter, who came over from Leiden to finish his PhD with Niko on 'counter-shading' camouflage of caterpillars.

It was a splendid collection of 'bright young things', who saw Niko as the father of the group – as did he. The relationship extended into the personal,

Eyed hawkmoth, wings closed, and open when disturbed. Research project by Niko's student David Blest, 1950s. Photo Niko Tinbergen.

with Niko taking a keen interest in the well-being of his charges. When Aubrey Manning seemed rather slow off the mark and about to leave for military service, Niko told him to stop prevaricating and marry Margaret Bastock (they had been an 'item' for some time, and Aubrey did, a bit later). Niko put Mike and Esther on one of the Farne Islands for their fieldwork, with a twinkle in his eye, and Esther Sager became Esther Cullen. Niko sent Rita White to Lorenz' group for a month, to expand her horizons; she found Uli Weidmann there, who subsequently joined Niko's group as a post-doc, and they married soon after.

The group atmosphere was helped tremendously by the far from comfortable facilities in the old Zoology Department, next to the University Museum in Parks Road (see later). It was a place with great character, with old bricks and nooks and crannies. There was an us-against-them atmosphere, full of ideas but with few facilities; everyone was desperately short of space, but never mind, they put up wooden prefab huts on the flat roof, as well as large bird cages in which to keep animals. Niko encouraged the do-it-yourself ideas, which fitted in exactly with his frugality ethos. This went to such lengths that he rather disapproved when Desmond Morris and Philip Guiton started to buy tubifex from an aquarium shop to feed their experimental animals: he expected them to catch earthworms themselves, and chop them up as fish food.[11]

One joint venture of the entire Hard Core, still talked about 50 years later, was their organization of the International Ethological Conference in Oxford, in 1952. It went down in history, not so much for its smooth running and exciting science, but for a wonderfully conceived and executed spoof, in which Niko was as involved as anybody else. It was based on the Konrad Lorenz model from the 1949 SEB Cambridge conference, of the nervous, causal organization

Rita White (later Weidmann) testing pecking response of gull chick, about 1952.

of animal behaviour like a hydraulic system, a water closet. The 'psycho-hydraulics' idea had met with considerable criticism and ridicule, and during the Oxford meeting and under the leadership of Desmond Morris, Aubrey Manning, and David Blest, a large hard-ware model was constructed illustrating it. There were water-filled balloons which were assaulted by 'sperm' launched along wires, an altogether ludicrous contraption of lavatory plus tank, flasks, tubes, levers, ropes, and chains; the machine moved coloured liquids, generated smoke, and spurted a great deal of water on the audience, while the perpetrators 'milked it for every possible sexual and scatological belly laugh'.[12]

The performance of the model, at the end of the conference, was introduced by Niko. He ably summarized the proceedings and analysed the significance of the progress made during the meeting, then referred to those fields where advance had been less conspicuous, and especially to the use of models. He gradually introduced some more outrageous, nonsensical ideas, all in deadpan style, and slowly the audience began to realize that they were being had, when the three ring-leaders were introduced with their machine. It was a gigantic success, and as Desmond Morris commented in his autobiography: 'they don't make ethology conferences like that any more, and, to the front rows at least, it must be a great relief.'[13]

The high spirits of Niko and his group of students were a direct consequence of their joint involvement. Niko himself took an active part in those projects that intuitively interested him, especially in the gull work, though the sticklebacks began to leave him rather cold. Soon after his arrival he started to look around for suitable field study sites, which he found more difficult than he had expected. Somehow he could not appreciate the beautiful woods around Oxford. It was a habitat quite different from what he had been used to in Holland, and he never really 'clicked' with any of the birds or insects that were the subjects of so much research from the groups of David Lack and Charles Elton. In the first years Niko often went for walks in the famous Wytham Woods, a university conservation area just outside Oxford; he photographed badgers there, he admired the magnificent oak woods, but he was not drawn to study any of its denizens (unlike his earlier involvement in the pine woods and sands of Hulshorst, where he thought up so many of his projects).

The gulls in the marshes and lakes of East Anglia were something different, offering tremendous potential for research with PhD students. In 1951 he began a project on the black-headed gulls on the marshes of Scoult Head in Norfolk together with his students Martin Moynihan and Rita White, but this proved a mistake: in the middle of the breeding season all nests were washed away during a high tide. Niko got a good story out of 'the fallibility of instinct', with gulls desperately building up their nests whilst the water was rising,[14] and researchers getting wet in the hide, but the situation did not lend itself to his type of behaviour research. The next year the team (augmented by Esther Sager) moved inland to a gull colony in nearby Scolton Mere, but disaster also struck there: all the chicks died from some disease. The landowner felt that science was to blame for this, and they were no longer welcome. However, that same year they drove north and discovered the Farne Islands, a group of 17 rocky islands in the North Sea off the north-east coast of England. There were thousands of tame kittiwakes, terns, shags, eider ducks, and many other birds, and from then on there was no looking back.

Niko was remarkably lucky with the sort of people who were attracted to his group, people he did not really seek out himself but who just turned up, on their own initiative. Beyond doubt, one such stroke of fortune was Esther Sager, soon to be Cullen; her study of kittiwakes on the Farne Islands became an all-time classic. Carried out under Niko's aegis, he got much of the credit for it, but it consisted almost entirely of Esther's insights and her own work. Niko's involvement added some further new ideas, and he filmed the project.

Esther had heard Niko lecture in Basel in 1945, whilst she was finishing her PhD study there (on peacock tails, under Adolf Portmann), and she asked if she could come and help with fieldwork. In 1952 he met her off the train near his field camp in Norfolk (she dressed to the nines, he thinking 'my god, what do we have here?'). Here she learned the trade of bird observation in a colony of black-headed gulls, and she was an excellent assistant to Martin Moynihan and Rita White. Niko was by now getting into comparative mode, and he wanted people to start studying other species of gull. They went off to see the Farne Islands, at the invitation of Eric Ennion, an ornithologist and artist who lived in

Esther Cullen with kittiwakes. Farne Islands, about 1955. Photo Niko Tinbergen.

Seahouses, on the mainland opposite the Farnes. That same season Esther was detailed to study the kittiwakes there, with no other brief than that.

It was the beginning of a three-year project: once Esther sat on the cliffs and watched those ultra-tame kittiwakes in close-up, with no need for an observation hide, she had what Niko called the 'Aha experience', something like 'Eureka'. She realized that many of the peculiar ways of the kittiwake were an adaptation to its highly unusual cliff habitat. It made a wonderful publication,[15] showing a long list of behavioural adjustments where kittiwakes were different from their gull relatives, all determined by the necessity for survival on the narrow, steep ledges on which the birds nested. For instance, the birds had specially adapted fighting techniques, chicks did not run away from the nest, there was almost no anti-predator response, they copulated sitting, used mud as nest material, etc. It was a highly successful study that greatly improved Niko's standing in the behaviour world. Regrettably, after this beautiful project Esther rather faded away from the research scene. She left on the crest of a wave, but stayed in the background and had children, still doing some research on sticklebacks for Niko but never publishing again. She always felt that she was not aggressive enough for a research career.[16]

Mike Cullen started his PhD project on the behaviour of arctic terns on the Farne Islands at the same time as Esther, whilst another student, Frank McKinney, began a study of the eider ducks there. Together, and in cooperation with Eric Ennion from the bird study centre in Seahouses, they started the Farnes Observatory, which now has a long history of ornithological research. Only a very small part of Mike's excellent study on terns was ever published. The project had started as a comparison between the behaviour of gulls and terns (they are closely related), but by the end of his time there Mike had lost interest in comparative studies, instead becoming totally immersed in problems of behaviour quantification, and of statistical techniques.

Niko's participation in the kittiwake project on the Farnes consisted mostly of filming. This was a rather new departure for him: he loved photography, and in Leiden he had assisted a technician in rather primitive films on the stickleback, and on the research in Hulshorst. He had also helped his friend Olaf Paris with some educational films on birds, for schools. One of the lures of Oxford had been a state-of-the-art Bell and Howell film-camera with tele-lenses, which came with the job, and Niko took to this new technique like a duck to water. Filming, he felt, could play a major role in communication of science to others, and in this way he satisfied not only his hunting instincts, but also his conscience, which told him that he needed to show others the results of his time in the wilds.[17] He had made three films on black-headed gulls in Norfolk before covering Esther's work: black and white films of about 20 minutes length, concentrating on birds rather than on people, on results rather than on the process of research.[18]

Another film, which he made soon after the kittiwakes, was on the research of a colleague in the zoology lab at Oxford, Bernard Kettlewell. Bernard had

Mike Cullen in mirror experiment with kittiwake. Farne Islands, about 1955.
Photo Niko Tinbergen.

discovered a most interesting piece of evolution in the making: the highly camouflaged peppered moth, which looks exactly like a lichen on the bark of a tree, had evolved a black form which was also beautifully camouflaged, but only on trees without lichens, blackened in industrial areas. This 'industrial melanism' was highly effective because small birds selectively took the lichen-like forms from the black trees, and the black forms from the lichen-covered trees. When published[19] the research met with some disbelief, and Kettlewell asked Niko to film the birds in action, to back his story. Niko spent weeks in a hide filming redstarts, flycatchers, and yellowhammers selecting moths from trees, and it resulted in a splendid and very convincing film.[20] It was exactly the kind of work he loved doing; somehow, I think Niko the hunter felt he 'acquired' a piece of research once he had filmed it. Many years later the industrial melanism project was severely criticized as careless, and for bending the facts. Peppered moths rarely sat on bark, and the bird predation was induced by presenting moths in highly unusual densities.[21]

One of the sparks in Niko's Hard Core was Desmond Morris, who later was to shine on many fronts, particularly as a popular science writer. Desmond was a clever, flamboyant, and passionate man of great versatility, and already as a zoology student he was a prolific painter. He had heard a lecture by Niko, decided that this was his future, and in 1951 Niko took him on for a PhD study on the ten-spined stickleback.[22] Desmond stayed for five years, studying fish and finches in captivity, before moving on to London Zoo – he wanted to work with tame mammals, and Niko liked neither mammals nor zoos. Desmond was full of ideas and published several scientific papers on the organization of behaviour. He was much more of a publicist than Niko, and there were times when Niko sent him to conferences which he did not fancy attending himself, such as an important one full of pomp in Paris, with Konrad Lorenz and J. B. S. Haldane. Desmond, following Peter Medawar, called Niko 'pathologically modest'.

Desmond captured the spirit of total youthful, loyal, and uncritical enthusiasm of the Hard Core when he told me:

> *We now forget the antagonism of the psychologists that existed at the time. There was a big Psychology school in Oxford when Niko settled in, and we as his students looked on psychologists as the enemy: not just another discipline using a different method, but they were monsters and idiots, fools who did not know what they were doing and we would be violently opposed to them in all aspects. It was an emotional response, because we were the new guys, Niko had only just arrived and published* The study of instinct. *The 'white rat maze runners' looked as freakish upon Niko's idea of letting the animal have a natural environment and keep a study as natural as possible … We forget today the huge hostility towards the simplistic approach … the differences were so huge they really weren't criticisms, it was like Muslims and Catholics, differences so basic that Niko's students said because these other disciplines make a fundamental error in studying an animal in a totally alien abstract artificial environment, the idea that the research results are of any value to anyone is nonsense. That was wrong, and I realize in retrospect that it was just youthful enthusiasm for what we were doing.*[23]

Desmond was often somewhat 'over the top', one of the secrets of his later success.

Aubrey Manning was another one of those people brimming with vitality and enthusiasm, arriving in Niko's orbit in 1951 with the hope of doing a study on birds, but as Niko felt he had enough students on the gulls he steered Aubrey towards insects. Aubrey's project was on bumblebees and their ways of finding flowers, and the effect of the 'honey-guide', the markings inside the flower that direct an insect towards the nectar. One of the interesting general results from this study was the way in which individual insects learn and remember their plants: they remembered locations of ones that were difficult to see, but not of those that were very obvious, such as foxgloves. There was less of a need to learn those, and it meant that 'an animal's learning ability evolves to suit its life-history' – they learn no more than they have to.[24]

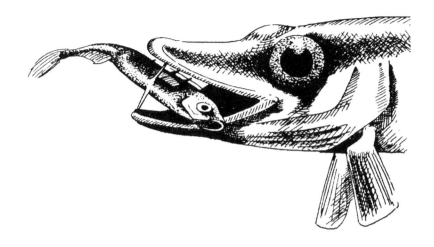

Winter was slack time for insect work in the field, so Aubrey teamed up with Margaret Bastock in her lab studies on fruit flies (so effectively that later they were married). It resulted in one of the classic papers in behavioural genetics,[25] in which they described in detail the mating behaviour of *Drosophila melanogaster*, the standard experimental subject of genetics; Margaret and Aubrey came up with an important model to explain the behaviour of the male fruit fly in terms of different 'thresholds' of excitation for each behaviour pattern in the sequence.

Another student in the early 1950s was Fae Hall, who compared the behaviour of different stickleback species, next to the more detailed single-species studies of several other students. All the stickleback studies in Oxford were obvious follow-ups to the research that Niko had done in Holland. After this flurry in the early 1950s, Niko's interest moved in other directions and he gradually abandoned the sticklebacks, with only one more doctoral study to follow a few years later. The stickleback had provided him with extremely fertile ground for behaviour studies, but he now left it mostly to his former laboratory in Leiden, under Jan van Iersel and Piet Sevenster.

Writing and science

The first year or so after arriving in Oxford, when he was still without PhD students and in the turmoil of the change, Niko was little inclined to fieldwork himself. So he wrote, fast and furiously, his famous *The herring gull's world*. It was published some three years later,[26] but written during that first Oxford year, miles removed from the Dutch herring gull dunes to which he would never return. Access to his beloved Dutch dunes was one of the boats he had burned behind him. He felt it, as he chain-smoked away in his room, banging on his small typewriter. The gulls, their calls, large white birds displaying near their nests, hanging in the wind, chicks pecking at parental bills, all of it came flooding back whilst he was laying out the magnificent photographs. He was surrounded by the walls of Oxford, but his mind, his writing, and the pictures on the desk were far away from it.

Of all his books, Niko always liked *The herring gull's world* best, and perhaps it did, indeed, reflect his abilities better than the others, in describing science and his own fieldwork to non-specialist naturalists. It came out in a popular English series of nature books, illustrated with his own excellent photographs, and to rave reviews. Without emphasizing his own enthusiasm Niko managed to convey the excitement of watching and studying the birds, by trying to answer the fascinating, and (once posed) very obvious questions about them. The book is miles ahead of most other single-species accounts one reads (there are many examples in the same series), because it introduces scientific procedure into natural history: valid and important questions in a beautiful context, with simple methods to sort them out, and with leads to further questions. He described his observations on displays, the theory of the birds' motivation for displays, the details of pecking behaviour of chicks, and the experiments he did with his Leiden students on how gulls recognize their eggs. And with all this he mixed a lot of general natural history from other literature. Even now, 50 years later, it still is an excellent read, remarkably and delightfully simple, however much later heavy science has modified and quantified the subject.

When *The study of instinct* finally came out in 1951,[27] three years after it had been written in the aftermath of his American trip, Niko had been in Oxford for almost two years, and his field research and student group had taken off. It was an immediate success, reprinted the next year, again in 1955, and many times since (most recently in 1989). It could not have come at a better time for him: he was getting established in Oxford, and there is little doubt that the book instantly gave him a huge reputation.

The reviews were very good. 'Tinbergen's fine book is an important synthesis and a valuable introduction to this actively moving field.'[28] 'A wealth of illustrative detail ... Its pages summarize much ingenious experimental work and present a point of view that is bound to have an influence on later behavior studies ... The concrete evidence of the book makes the American anti-instinct psychology of a few decades ago seem bizarre indeed'.[29] Not surprisingly, there were occasional reservations; for instance: 'In its current stage, ethology resembles a patchwork quilt, pieced together with bits of stickleback, wasp, cichlid, duck, herring gull, etc., the whole seeming to cover the reality better than any theory thus far advanced. Until more facts are available, some of the hypotheses may be viewed with scepticism, but they have stimulated much productive research and will continue to do so in the future.'[30] Or: 'Some scientifically trained objective students of behavior may wish for more rigorous definitions of some of the concepts ... may also feel that the failure of the author to provide information on controls and details of statistical analysis detracts somewhat from the value of much of the brilliant work he reports.'[31]

Overall the reception of *The study of instinct* was very warm indeed, except for the latest, 1989 reissue, which was hit by a rather more scathing review: 'By current standards the writing is uncritical, both in its treatment of other people's research and in its failure to discuss, or even define, terms such as 'instinct', 'innate' or 'drive'. The overall organization of the book and the style in which it is written often give the impression of an author groping towards conclusions'.[32] But that was much later, and on the whole the response to his *magnum opus* provided Niko with a great deal of encouragement.

Almost immediately the success of *The study of instinct* spurred him on to further writing on the central issues that were laid out in his book. Soon after, Niko published one of his few entirely theoretical papers, on 'derived activities', in a prominent American journal.[33] In essence it was a translation of his 1940 German paper on displacement activities, with some additions and modifications. It was rather imperial, with no hard evidence and rarely referring to published solid data, instead using mostly his own observations as generalities: 'this is how it is'. As a typical example, Niko just stated that 'internal factors activate a "drive" or an "urge" in an animal', and 'each drive is a hierarchical system, divided in subordinated drives of a more restricted type than the general

drive' (he therefore treated 'drives' as physiological entities). There are 'feeding drives', 'reproductive drives', and others. He demonstrated how one can fit existing observations and ideas into such a set of hypotheses, but without really testing any, or considering alternatives. He described how a combination of different drives produce displays, and how some behaviours occur away from their usual context as 'displacement activities' (for example grooming or feeding movements when the aggressive drive is thwarted) and are subsequently 'ritualized' to serve as signals between animals. The paper is a 'just-so' story, supported by Niko's authority and his enormous experience as a fieldworker and observer.

On all writing fronts Niko was tremendously prolific during these early years in Oxford, with dozens of popular papers and several books. He had the time to write, as he had not yet built up the many commitments that he had before and after this period. He was also cashing in on his popularity after the lecturing trips in America, and he needed to air the glut of new ideas and experiences. His international authority in ethology needed outlets.

The study of instinct was paralleled by a small, more popular version: *Social behaviour in animals*, which came out in 1953,[34] the same year as the gull book. Only about 150 pages long, it discussed many of the same topics as *The study of instinct*, but concentrated on interactions between animals. Again there were exciting photographs of a wide range of birds and other animals, and many pleasant, small, and simple drawings. Niko wrote it for 'non-professionals' in his usual effervescent style, and, just as in *The study of instinct*, skipped between species with his general principles. The behavioural generalities across different species are very attractive, but they may also be unwarranted and even dangerous. This becomes obvious especially when here, as in *The study of instinct*, Niko freely included human behaviour in his examples and generalities, which was highly appealing to a lay-audience. For example (p. 105):

> *Many birds begin to sit in the nest before the eggs are laid. What matures in the bird is not a mere readiness to respond to eggs, but an urge which may lead to overt behaviour even when the eggs are absent. We all know comparable behaviour in the human female: a childless woman often provides herself with a substitute with which to satisfy her maternal drive: either an adopted child or a pet. Many childless women develop a curious ambivalent attitude towards their own husbands and make them play the double role of mate and child.*

One now feels very uneasy about such unsupported statements, and ethologists have learnt to be more careful. Soon after Niko wrote it he was severely taken to task for his uncritical species-hopping (see below). Probably, with his references to human behaviour he merely meant to create an interest in the overall subject of behaviour. *Social behaviour in animals* was later reprinted in paperback, but it was never as successful as his other books from that time.

Much of Niko's written output in the early and mid-1950s was popular science. There was his delightful booklet, *The tale of John Stickle*, written in Dutch 10 years earlier during his time in the hostage camp, but now translated and adapted for use in England, and published by Methuen (who had also done his *Social behaviour in animals*).[35] He wrote *Bird life* for a more mature readership;[36] it was just sixty-odd pages, illustrated with photographs and wonderfully simple drawings on every page. It enthuses about how to watch bird behaviour and ecology, what to look for, and what kind of questions to ask. It is full of many lovely little off-the-cuff insights into the biology of birds, which nowadays often disappear in the mass of specializations (such as exactly how a sparrowhawk catches a tit; how lapwings have problems in walking in long grass because they do not bend their legs and toes, unlike redshanks; and how starlings have problems flying in dense forests because of their fast, straight flight, unlike jays). A little book like this could turn many a teenager into an ornithologist. It was short, but very effective, and it saw several reprints.

A few years later, in 1958, *Curious naturalists* appeared.[37] It was a much more substantial effort, a splendid, enthusiastic book in the vein of *The herring gull's world*, but ranging much more widely over almost all the research projects Niko had been involved in with his students. Illustrated with dozens of his own photographs and line drawings, it conveys the spirit of Niko's group, which enjoyed the questioning of nature, and I believe that for any naturalist, who was not merely interested in collecting lists of species, it would have been a great read. There was not much in it on herring gulls, as he had written about them elsewhere, but it covered Niko's time with other gulls, kittiwakes, hobbies, the work on insect camouflage and on the bee-hunting wasps, his studies in Greenland, and so on. However, for some reason it did not sell very well, at least initially, and Niko told me that he thought the reason was that the book covered too much ground. In Britain naturalists are birders, or insect lovers, or plant collectors, and rarely does their interest cover all these subjects. Nevertheless, many years later he revised and rewrote it, adding much new material and leaving out some of the old stories, and in 1974 it appeared again, as a Penguin paperback. It had changed: it had become somewhat more sophisticated and had lost some of its naturalist innocence, but it sold much better.

Alongside his books Niko continued to write quantities of natural history articles in Dutch, now even more than when he was in Holland. His list of publications has seven Dutch titles for 1950, four for 1951, five for 1952, and this continued: he hammered them out at great speed, next to his behaviour papers in English. The latter largely covered the same topics as his books, with further contributions on the origin and evolution of displays,[38] and in *Scientific American* on the behaviour of sticklebacks.[39]

With his prodigious output, his growing international reputation, the wide-ranging success of *The study of instinct*, an enthusiastic new group of bright students entering a new research programme, and the promising possibilities of Oxford, Niko was riding very high. Then, as a bolt from a blue sky, came a set of criticisms of his science so penetrating and so devastating that it would have felled a lesser man. It originated from a hitherto rather unknown source in America, Danny Lehrman.

Danny was a large, genial professor of psychology at Rutgers University, a relatively young man with a keen interest in birds and a splendid sense of humour. These characteristics hid a razor-sharp analytical and logical brain, exercised in highly disciplined scientific thinking. Originally a student of the psychologist Theodor Schneirla, his speciality was the development and physiology of behaviour, and he was not at all impressed by the theories and pronouncements of the European ethologists.

In 1953, prompted by other American psychologists, Lehrman published 'A critique of Konrad Lorenz's theory of instinctive behavior', as a long paper in the same American journal where Niko had published his 'derived activities' one year earlier.[40] Danny started by recognizing the importance of Konrad's theories, with Niko as collaborator:

> Lorenz's theory of instinctive and innate behavior has attracted the interest of many investigators, partly because of its diagrammatic simplicity, partly because of its extensive use of neurophysiological concepts, and partly because Lorenz deals with behavior patterns drawn from the life cycle of the animals discussed, rather than with the laboratory situations most often found in American comparative psychology.

He summarized the main tenets and then set to demolish them, one by one. Ethologists recognized a clear dichotomy between 'innate' and 'learnt' behaviour, but Lehrman argued that this was false and counter-productive. He suggested that the environment had demonstrably large effects on the development of 'innate' behaviour; for example, that even the 'innate' pecking behaviour of a chick was dependent on specific previous experience. There is no such thing as simply 'innate' behaviour. Niko had concluded innateness after sticklebacks showed the full range of aggressive and sexual activities even when reared in isolation, but Lehrman dismissed this, as isolation only excluded a limited range of experiences.

Another of Danny Lehrman's main criticisms concerned the physiological basis of behaviour, as suggested by Lorenz and Tinbergen. As they described it, an instinct has a fixed mechanism in the central nervous system, with specific 'centres' that produce excitation which is used up when particular behaviour patterns are performed. Such excitation is released when very specific 'sign-stimuli' unblock the centre concerned; Lorenz had illustrated all this with his hydraulic model. But Lehrman argued that there was no neurophysiological evidence for it at all. He demonstrated that the physiological research that Niko had cited in support was at best irrelevant (concerned with very simple swimming movements of fish, and not with much more complicated behaviour). Both Konrad and Niko quoted behaviour from a large range of animals that could be explained with the above causal structure, from courting butterflies to egg-rolling geese and foraging dogs. But Lehrman argued that the actual mechanisms of such examples might be totally different from one case to the next, and he suggested that categorizing them as similar would obfuscate the real underlying physiology. This problem gets even worse when one includes examples of human behaviour.

What many people saw as a strength of ethology was that it provided simple, similar models for so many different species and categories of behaviour. Danny Lehrman saw this as one of the dangers. For instance, Niko had argued[41] that a dog hunts when it is not hungry, and man indulges in sport and science when there is no immediate need: these are examples of 'vacuum activities'. Lehrman berated this 'most casual and unanalysed kind of comparison, and a lack of concern with the specific origin of the behaviour patterns at issue'. He was also especially concerned with Lorenz's extrapolation[42] of the complications in domestication of animals, to what he saw as the dangers of interbreeding between human races; this had been a justification of Nazi legal restrictions against marriage between Aryans and other races.

Apart from serious general theoretical objections to the work of Lorenz and Tinbergen, Lehrman also had many criticisms of conclusions drawn from Niko's experiments. For instance, he argued that Niko's joint paper with Don

Kuenen,[43] on the gaping of young thrushes, had not considered many ways in which the young thrushes could have learned to direct their gaping at visual clues.

It was a hard-hitting attack. Niko had to recognize that there was a great deal of truth in Danny Lehrman's assertions, and the paper was never rebutted. Niko's reaction was characteristic: he saw this as a battle, and he immediately invited Danny over to Oxford, where they talked. Niko had decided on a strategy (trans.):

> I heard that Lehrman's paper gave the impression in America of being emotionally-anti, unscientific in one respect, that is, that he is more interested in proving Lorenz wrong, than in honestly trying to synthesize what is good in the different approaches into a real insight. We will have to handle him tactfully, friendly but determined. His mentor Schneirla is incorrigible and can only be convinced if he dies, but Lehrman is not incorrigible.[44]

Astonishingly, Niko and Danny hit it off perfectly. Aubrey Manning described his visit to Oxford:

> He won us over by virtue of his personality. Danny was one of that rare type of human being that I would designate (following Evelyn Waugh) as a 'Life Force'. His warmth and kindness made all contacts with him a delight, while his enthusiasm and sense of humour were infectious. The story is that when Konrad Lorenz first met him, he exclaimed, 'Ach, but you are a large man!' He too had probably expected a wizened laboratory psychologist, but Danny mostly weighed in at 250 pounds plus, I imagine.[45]

Personalities clicked. Danny and Niko were both fanatically interested in birds, and in getting things right scientifically. Much of Danny's debunking may have been correct, but he had gone over the top in his criticism. As Niko pointed out, the word 'innate' was used flippantly by the ethologists, but whatever the mechanism, there were clear species-differences in behaviour, and there must be some genetic element in that.

Niko conceded that his neurophysiological interpretations were unhelpful. However, he did not want to go as far as Danny, who suggested that the entire idea of an 'innate releasing mechanism' should be abandoned, because it suggested similarities in mechanisms in different cases, similarities which were just not there. Niko countered this by saying that we also usefully talk about 'colour vision' in mammals and in insects, although the actual mechanisms in the two groups are totally different.

Only a few months later, Danny Lehrman and Niko met again to discuss the same issues. This was during a small, elite conference in Ithaca, NY, organized by the Macy Foundation to bring together American psychologists and European ethologists; Konrad was also there, as well as the famous animal psychologist, Theodor Schneirla, the evolutionary biologist Ernst Mayr, and others.

In response to a conference question, 1950s.
Courtesy of the Tinbergen family.

The proceedings were published verbatim, including the discussions, and they provide some very interesting insights.[46] Niko gave a presentation 'Psychology and ethology as supplementary parts of a science of behavior', in which he defended his and Konrad's contributions, but he also appeased by referring to their lack of data, basically saying this was only the beginning.

> *I consider as an encouraging sign of growing interest the sharp criticism that we have received recently from American colleagues, of which Dr Lehrman's blast in the* Quarterly Review of Biology *is perhaps the most valuable. That Dr Lehrman snipes at us shows that he is keenly interested in our work. That his sniping aims at an almost wholesale rejection of what we have done is, I think, only another case of the pendulum swinging a little too far.*

The discussion transcripts show Niko to be much on the defensive, making his points by 'we don't really know enough, but it looks as if ...', and sometimes he even goes so far as to actually hide embarrassing realities of his research. When discussing his research on gull chicks pecking at the red spot on the parental bill, the point is made that chicks could have been somehow conditioned and this would affect their (what Niko called) 'innate' behaviour, which Niko denied. Mayr asked: 'These are chicks which you yourself raised from the egg and which had not seen an adult gull?' (a point that was quite critical in the argument). And Tinbergen answered 'Yes.' However, this was far from the truth: the paper he published four years earlier described how they took chicks from the parent birds the morning after they had hatched overnight, and 'we think we succeeded in acquiring a fair proportion of inexperienced chicks.'[47] If he had admitted this during the Macy conference, he would have been severely criticized. He escaped by such bits of subterfuge, and by making pacifying noises, 'we did not really mean this'.

Later, Ernst Mayr would comment that Niko did not sufficiently stand up to the criticism:

> In all the years I had only one real disagreement with Niko, his 'pacifism', I remember a Macy conference where Niko was nastily attacked by Schneirla ... when Schneirla had finished, Niko did not jump up and refute vigorously all of Schneirla's nonsense ... but sat there meekly as if every statement against him had been true. Others (including myself) had to defend ethology.[48]

However, we can now see that perhaps Schneirla's criticism contained grains of truth, and had been more to the point than the loyal Ernst Mayr realized at the time.

During that meeting the herring gull chick-pecking paper provided Niko's main platform, and on many details his conclusions were demolished. As just one example, Niko said that he had demonstrated that the chicks peck at the red spot only when it is on the bill, not when it is on the head. From this he concluded that the chicks need the right configuration of stimuli for their pecking: it is not just red that is important, but red in the right place. But in the discussion he could not defend this. It was pointed out that, according to Niko's own observations, the chicks pecked especially at things that were nearby and moved, and with Niko's models the red spot on the bill-tip moved more than on the top of the head, and the bill-tip was also closer to the chick. Possibly, therefore, it was not place of the red spot that mattered, but proximity and movement. In many such details, his conclusions were demonstrably not justified. He had failed to convince his American psychologist audience, but his charm won through.

Niko's interpretation of these discussions was very different from what the official transcript of the conference showed, and nowadays he would be accused of spin-doctoring. In a letter to Robert Hinde, he wrote:

> Both Konrad and I reformulated our problems and results as cautiously as possible, and it was surprising to see how Lehrman and Beach, no doubt influenced by what they had heard earlier from you and Jan [van Iersel] and Baerendje [Gerard Baerends], dropped all their objections; we agreed on very much the same type of formulation of problems, and everybody admitted that 'ethologists' have tackled new phenomena, and had developed valuable new methods for studying old problems. It was amazing to see how our stuff clicked with all the human psychologists; they were really more interested in ethology than in American psychology.[49]

In the end, the Danny Lehrman episode ended on a positive note, though the ethological landscape would never be the same again. Lehrman became a friend of Niko, and ethologists learnt to be much more careful with their generalities, using a better formulation of questions. After this, terms like 'innate' became tainted words, 'releasing mechanism' was rarely used by the Tinbergen group, and in later years Niko often mentioned the cleansing effect of Danny Lehrman's intervention. Konrad was hit much harder; he was never able to get away from his innate–learned dichotomy, he hated people like Lehrman and Schneirla personally for their attacks, and he was quite unhappy about Niko's position.

There were assaults on Niko and Konrad from other quarters as well, although they did not have quite the same impact. Several researchers were unable to repeat the Tinbergen–Lorenz experiment that showed that a short-necked bird dummy (that is, raptor) alarmed ground-living birds, whereas other-shaped dummies were ignored, and they doubted the value of this observation.[50] It had been one of the cornerstone studies of ethology, the simple 'sign–stimulus' that set off a complicated behaviour pattern. Niko defended his work by pointing out that the repeat observations had been done on different species of birds (hens rather than geese or turkeys).[51] But in *The study of instinct* he himself had generalized from the original experiments to all land and waterfowl, and, as shown later,[52] there were indeed fundamental flaws in his work (his study birds were not naïve and had experience with raptors and other birds, and the experiment had been open to serious observer bias: there were no 'blind' controls).

Criticism did not come solely from America. Adriaan Kortlandt (see also Chapter 4) was smarting under a lack of recognition for his role in developing ethological theory, his substantial 1940 paper[53] on the hierarchical organization of behaviour and displacement activities having been virtually ignored. Rather than blaming his own, fairly impenetrable prose, Kortlandt decided on a full-frontal attack on Tinbergen and Lorenz. In 1955 he published a 130-page diatribe, in English but in a Dutch scientific journal,[54] a historical review and an analysis of the concept of instinct. It covered a large literature in psychology going back to Freud, aiming to show that ethology had ignored all of that as well as his own contributions. The paper is not easy to read because of its breathless style; it is bitter and full of jargon, and Kortlandt tore *The study of instinct* to shreds. No doubt there were important elements of truth in his contribution: for instance his ideas on hierarchical organization were probably more logical than Niko's. Twenty years later Richard Dawkins would refer to it as 'brilliantly erudite, if somewhat outspoken'.[55] But the paper was virtually ignored, whilst Kortlandt earned himself a reputation for being difficult and irrational. He told me that, since publication of that paper, the ethological establishment had sent him to Coventry.[56] Perhaps there was more to this than just one paper; Kortlandt sometimes lacked Niko's deftness in dealing with people, and he was often excitable and negative.

Reading through the theoretical treatises such as Kortlandt's, Lorenz's, and some parts of *The study of instinct*, one cannot help but feel a sympathy for Danny Lehrman's stance. The models of hierarchy of behaviour, of appetitive and consummatory acts, innate releasing mechanisms, and displacement and vacuum activities, have no firm base in physiology. They suggest similarities of mechanism between species in which such behaviour complexes have been observed, similarities which may not exist. What, then, is the point of such labelling? Admittedly, the models were an attempt to create order in the chaos of behaviour problems, but is such order in any way relevant? If one designs a taxonomy of plant species according to the colours of their flowers, does one end up with anything useful?

There were doubts about the theory underlying causation of behaviour within the ethologists' camp as well. On the one hand, for instance, there was the much-quoted example of an early paper from Niko's group by Margaret Bastock, Desmond Morris, and Martin Moynihan,[57] which is full of the terminology of drives and motivation as it expands and modifies Niko's visions from *The study of instinct* and his 'Derived activities' paper. On the other hand, from the same side also came Robert Hinde, who was critical and who effectively demolished the idea of simple 'drives' as a general explanation for behaviour. A few years later another member of the Hard Core, David Blest, was deeply critical of Niko's concept of 'ritualization', the process Niko suggested was responsible for the evolution of displays.[58]

Robert Hinde, who was to become one of the world's authorities in animal behaviour studies, had an interesting role in the young science of ethology of the 1950s. He started out as part of the Oxford group, but soon began to plough his own furrow. Robert, a tall gentleman with a background in the RAF, graduated late from Cambridge, and was one of David Lack's PhD students (studying great tits) in Oxford when Niko arrived there. He spent more time with Niko than with his official supervisor and, although they only overlapped for about a year, they kept in close contact and Niko had a large influence on Robert, at least in the 1950s. After receiving his doctorate Robert moved back to Cambridge, where Bill Thorpe had asked him to become the head of his new, small ornithology field station in Madingley. He stayed there for the rest of his career. He was a brilliant analyst and theoretician, interested especially in quantifying behaviour, and those were qualities that Niko lacked and which he greatly admired. Robert did most of his research initially with captive birds (chaffinches and canaries), and later with monkeys and children. He later developed his own school in Cambridge, and, however well they got on, he clearly did not want a role under Niko.

Robert would probably admit that he did not have Niko's ease with words and presentation (very few people did). Even in later years Niko felt he had to admonish him over texts for talks that Robert sent him for criticism:

> *I found it extremely difficult to follow the lines of argument … If you give the paper in this shape, nobody, except perhaps Lorenz, will understand it … try to explain it verbally to an imaginary fellow-ethologist, but in as few and as*

> *simple words as possible … write a very brief skeleton and fill in the facts …*
> *help the listener by frequent summaries of problems, of evidence, of argument,*
> *of conclusions.*[59]

Or:

> *The paper is not adapted to the audience. It is as if you have been thinking*
> *'damn the reader: I want to say something which I consider important, and the*
> *BOU [British Ornithological Union] has jolly well got to swallow and pub-*
> *lish this if they want me to participate in their silly symposium.' This paper*
> *can be understood at best by the very topflight people. I admit that I myself am*
> *pretty slow in the uptake, but … .*[60]

Such criticism is not easy to take, and I found Robert perhaps just slightly scathing about Niko, about his materialism and his simple experiments, as well as critical of his theories. As Robert said 'Niko did quantitative fieldwork and field experiments, but I am not sure how much of this came from his students, such as Baerends, who took things much further. But you cannot expect an innovator to do the whole of his science, he got people started, he got me started. I was counting in the field, but Niko developed me conceptually.'[61] Praise, but with a small sting in the tail.

In the 1950s Robert's papers, on Konrad and Niko's concept of 'drive' in behaviour studies, were important.[62] They were difficult to read but they did make an impact, and they were thoroughly dismissive of the idea of 'drive', without putting much in the place of the existing terminology. Hinde argued convincingly that for various reasons a 'drive', as a unit that energizes and directs behaviour, is an over-simplification and hinders analysis. Similarly, he concluded euphemistically that the usefulness of Lorenz's psycho-hydraulic model was very limited. His arguments (rightly) took away much of the appealing simplicity of the ethologists' structure of behaviour.

Robert Hinde was foremost in a posse of researchers of animal behaviour who had general models of behaviour in mind, who wanted to address the internal causes of behaviour without getting into physiology. They were people who at least as regards theories of animal behaviour may have had much more to contribute than Niko; they included Gerard Baerends, Richard Andrew, Adriaan Kortlandt, and several others. But because of his appealing clarity of expression and his accessible style, Niko left these others far behind when it came to communicating science to other specialists and non-specialists.

Students in the late 1950s

All the arguments and wrangling over ideas and theories about causality, and about the mechanism of behaviour, left their mark on Niko. Although he felt that he came out of the debates fairly unscathed (a feeling not shared by everybody), he felt tired of being shot at: his self-esteem had always been very dependent on his professional success. Probably mostly as a result of this, he began to lose interest in the issue of internal mechanisms, and saw that there were other, more rewarding sides to studies of animal behaviour. The change came gradually, and students were still encouraged to follow up some old lines of enquiry, but Niko himself began to cast his net in other directions.

The second half of the 1950s saw a new generation of students, involved in very different projects. All of them now also benefited from Mike Cullen's involvement, all of them becoming highly quantitative in their approaches. What turned out to be especially important was that, finally in 1957, Niko had found the ideal field-site for his gull interests, where he could start a programme involving several students: Ravenglass, on the Irish Sea coast in the north of England, in the Lake District. He started two new graduates there, Colin Beer and Gilbert Manley, to study black-headed gulls, and with that Niko was back in the dunes again, in his natural niche as in Dutch days. The next year he started another student, Juan Delius, first to act as 'slave' to Colin and Gilbert, later to start his own PhD project on skylarks. Ravenglass was a fabulous area, where I, too, worked under Niko in the 1960s, and I will relate the studies and vicissitudes of Niko's group there, and the Ravenglass rituals, in the next chapter.

At the same time several new people started up with Niko in Oxford, and the place was humming with projects. Some of the old interests were pursued by another PhD student on the fruit fly *Drosophila*: Stella Pearce (later Crossley). She started her research under one of the old Hard Core, Margaret Bastock, and when Margaret left Stella continued under Niko. She applied artificial 'selection pressures' on one single behaviour pattern in her fruit flies, and showed that one could dramatically change the inherited behaviour of a species within forty generations. It was a result that Niko was proud of, despite his lack of interest in genetics, because it suggested how natural selection pressures could affect behaviour. Stella in turn, though hardly finished herself, supervised one further *Drosophila* graduate student jointly with Niko, Dick Brown, who was the last in Niko's genetics line of research.

Genetics also played a role in another graduate project, but only marginally. Niko's well-known colleague at Oxford, Arthur Cain, was studying how different patterns of banding were inherited by the snail *Cepaea*. Associated with that, Niko's student Cliff Henty picked up on the snail-smashing behaviour of the song-thrush at special 'anvils', and by comparing the snail remains with live snails around the anvils he studied the thrushes' selection (or rather, the camouflage effect) of different types of banding in various habitats. Another type of camouflage was studied by Graham Phillips, who tried to answer Niko's question of why gulls are white. He flew gull models of different colour above tanks with fish (on the roof of the Zoology Department), showing that white was best in preventing the fishes' detection of a bird above them.

A Reading zoology student, Nick Blurton-Jones, had already done an undergraduate project on the causal organization of behaviour of Canada geese,

*Male eider duck. Farne Islands,
about 1955.*
Photo Niko Tinbergen.

with some lovely simple experiments. However, Niko felt it would be better
for him to do something quite different for his doctorate, more related to
function rather than to causation. So Nick followed up the earlier study by
Robert Hinde on great tits, this time concentrating on the role of the birds'
displays as signals and relating these to the kind of aggression that followed, and
to the context of the interaction. There were projects on the behaviour of zebra
finches in aviaries on the roof by Fae Hall, and on stickleback behaviour by
Esther Cullen (both now as post-docs); there was another PhD project on
sticklebacks by Trixy Tugendhat. Robin Liley, impressed by Guyanan fish life
during an expedition of Oxford undergraduates, persuaded Niko to take him
on for a PhD on behaviour mechanisms that separated species of guppy. Like
the early stickleback studies, this grew later into almost a guppy science, with
scores of publications. There was also the odd failure, for instance one girl who
came to Niko from Cambridge with good recommendations from Robert
Hinde and Bill Thorpe, but turned out to be quite unsuitable, much to the
chagrin of Niko, who blamed Cambridge.[63] In fact, Niko's own students felt
that he was not always the best judge of a person's quality and potential as a
scientist. The joke was that 'if you are known as a "good observer", then you
are in; the rest of your abilities or character don't matter'.

What former students especially remember from those days was the
excitement, the spirit of pioneering that discovered new principles, and that

showed the world how 'behaviour' worked. These people felt that they were not just studying the aggression of black-headed gulls or the courtship of guppies or great tits, they were uncovering the fundamentals of aggression and sexual behaviour in animals. There were endless discussions, in seminars or over lunch or coffee, angry arguments or proud conclusions, often with The Maestro just as much as between the students. It was a great discovery, for instance, that a particular bird display did not always carry the same message, but could mean different things depending on the situation: the context mattered. A gull might show the 'forward' posture to another male, or to a female: in the one case it announced attack, in the other sexual attraction. The significance of such a discovery for those young researchers went far beyond a description of behaviour in just one species. One felt that in those sometimes emotional discussions, what was being analysed and criticized went right down to the basics, to the ethological tenets of Lorenz and Tinbergen and other workers, and their methods.

At times Niko felt threatened by the criticisms of his students. He relied on his abilities in the field, which were amazing and usually clearly superior to those of his students, but the latter often saw a conflict with established scientific method and opted for experimentation. Niko expressed his concern in a letter he wrote in 1957, from the Ravenglass field camp, to Robert Hinde:

> I find it an uphill job to teach my 2 new people [Mike Cullen and Uli Weidmann] the real relevance, the possibilities and the limitations of the correlation method [that is related occurrences in field observations of birds]: careful selection of the simple situations (with snap decisions whether it is one or not) and then watch with the utmost concentration and score a significant observation. They either get confused by the continuous meddle of interfering events, or are too optimistic in concluding that a given situation was simple (as, I think, Martin Moynihan often was). After concentrating on this again for a couple of weeks, I am immensely reinforced in my belief that the method is sound and practical and that I achieve something really worthwhile by it, but I also realize that it takes both considerable experience and perhaps an individual 'knack'. But I notice that my power to predict is still increasing, and whatever formulation we develop, this power of prediction is a very real and significant thing.
>
> Please forgive this arguing; it is partly a reaction to doubts as to the value of the method which Uli Weidmann and even Mike raised now and then; they began to shake me, but now, after renewed experience, I see that their doubts are not sound; they concern the practical possibilities, not the basic soundness of the approach. ... I myself know the charm of experimenting and its value – but I remain convinced of the 'paramount' value of the naturalists' attitude – and people with the combined interest in the whole and partial mechanisms (or, translated in method: observation and direct experimentation) are too rare to be wasted. I want to prevent for example Mike from sliding into the relatively easy groove of just experimenting on 'basic issues'.[64]

Research projects

Throughout the 1950s Niko rarely got his hands dirty with research for himself, and he was personally much less involved, with any one project that was his own, than he had been before. There were no more field trips to study some bird or a problem himself; he became a supervisor, actively participating in fieldwork by several of his students and post-docs, but not holding the reins. He was looking over shoulders, commenting on and absorbing what he saw. It enabled him to provide broad background comments and overall observations, without providing detailed quantitative facts. For instance, summing up the work of his students, he wrote about aquarium experiments of undergraduates in Leiden and of Desmond Morris in Oxford, on the function of the spines of sticklebacks (they protect against predation by pike and perch, who refuse to eat sticklebacks after one or two exposures).[65] Several of his papers now showed a more distant and broader interest, a concern with methodology and organization rather than with new factual discovery. He wrote a general paper on 'appeasement gestures' in birds,[66] behaviour which has a function opposite to that of aggression. He focussed especially on comparative research, on the behaviour of related species, arguing the benefits of such an approach for the understanding of taxonomy and the evolution.[67] One of these more theoretical papers was written jointly with Robert Hinde.[68] He could follow his life-long inclination to generalize, and for the minutiae he could refer to the works of his students.

In 1959 Niko published a seventy-page review in 'his' journal, *Behaviour*, called 'Comparative studies of the behaviour of gulls'.[69] This article was special in several ways. It was his main scientific paper of the 1950s, and it was also his main contribution on the behaviour of gulls, to which he had a life-long

Lesser black-backed gull pair, courtship feeding. Walney. Photo Niko Tinbergen.

attachment that was stronger than to any other group of animals. He was 52, he had done research on insects, and on fish, but in his heart he was a bird man, and gulls were his speciality. The contents of the paper characterize much of his approach to ethology: it was typical Niko. And finally, the paper marked something of a turning-point in his scientific career. He subtitled it 'A progress report', but with it he ended his personal involvement in studies of displays and likewise his interest in the analysis of causes of behaviour, in the internal states of animals that produce displays. After he had published the comparative gull paper, he focussed on biological effects of behaviour rather than on causes, and he restricted his personal research interest to other, non-display types of behaviour.

The review is confined to the gulls' displays. Displays are striking, often exaggerated movements and postures, with the immediate appearance of showing off something, of signalling a message. They were prime objects of interest to ethologists, partly because they are amongst the most conspicuous kinds of animal behaviour, prompting the questions as to why animals perform these antics, and what their function is. Niko considered displays from three different angles, asking what caused birds to display, what the effect was on other birds, and how they evolved in different species. He gave descriptions of 14 types of display, with suggestions as to the information conveyed in their message, and differences and similarities between species.

The gull paper reviewed Niko's own observations and those of others, mostly his own students and post-docs, and it paid a great deal of attention to methodology. It was entirely non-experimental, based on observations of wild birds, and conclusions were derived from the way a display is associated with another behaviour, from what Niko termed 'correlation'. A display was called 'aggressive' if often associated in time with attack, 'sexual' if associated with copulation. Then it gets more complicated: especially in displays, he argued, we have 'dual or multiple motivation': in a single display one finds that a bird may be simultaneously inclined to attack as well as to escape and to stay where it is. Other behaviours, for instance feeding or copulation, have a simple underlying motivation. He cited observations where a bird in the middle of its territory always attacks another one, but when it is in the middle of the neighbour's territory it will always flee. However, when the two birds meet on the border they will each be inclined to attack as well as to escape. Then they show displays with clear elements of aggression as well as fear.

Niko described the causes of behaviour in terms of 'motivation' and 'tendency', such as 'a bird is motivated to attack', or 'it shows an aggressive tendency'. His discussion betrayed the considerable problems he had with this kind of analysis. He did not define either of the two terms, but used them more or less interchangeably, in an operational manner. He argued that all displays had a simultaneous, dual, or even multiple motivation of fear as well as aggression and/or sex. Such analysis gave the impression of physiological mechanisms, for instance of an 'aggressive system' operating in the animal at the same time as a 'fear system'. In fact these 'systems' were nothing of the kind, they were just correlations of different kinds of behaviour (but important nevertheless). Conclusions about internal mechanisms derived from such correlations have to be very tentative.

He was well aware of the problems associated with this approach. In the Introduction he wrote:

> However much Lorenz, Hinde, Baerends, Andrew, Marler, Moynihan, Morris and others have contributed to theoretical clarification, and however much of great interest has been found already, we are still far from knowing exactly what we are doing; much of our work is guided by intuition rather than by conscious and systematic thinking ... In the course of our studies it became gradually clear that much of the reasoning applied by us had often been vague, to a great extent intuitive, and less sophisticated than that which is now being developed in taxonomy.

In fact, almost all the reasoning behind comparative behaviour studies is intuitive: one sees a particular posture in a species of gull, a posture in another species that 'looks' very similar, and then draws a conclusion from that. This procedure is derived from comparative anatomy, but since we are dealing here with movements the comparisons are that much more difficult.

To study the effects of displays on other birds, experiments would have been necessary. But as Niko remarked, they were almost impossible, as the gulls were either frightened of dummies or tore them to shreds. He was aware that just recording what an opponent does after a display is not very helpful, and there are many problems. Niko concluded that the effects of displays on other birds depended on the individual (whether male or female, intruder or neighbour, etc.), and were usually dictated by the motivation of the displaying bird: for instance if this was an aggressive male, then the opponent would flee if it was a male, and might be attracted if female. As we can now see, the potential for circular arguments here is considerable; for instance if the opponent fled, then the display would be judged to be aggressive.

In the end, the main points that Niko made in this paper were of two kinds: firstly, he gave a description of the displays (which are rather similar in all gulls, with some species-specific differences); secondly, he provided behavioural evidence that all gulls have evolved from a single ancestor. The displays evolved from other behaviour patterns such as 'intention movements' or 'displacement activities', and through evolution became more conspicuous and unambiguous as signals. They are the outcome of simultaneous 'tendencies' or 'motivations' to attack, or to flee, or to mate, and are perceived as such by other gulls.

One old problem with Niko's review was the lack of quantification. His conclusions were intuitive, not measured or even estimated; the paper contained much use of 'must have', 'there is no doubt that', 'almost certainly', 'similar', 'roughly the same'. There were no recorded observations to back up the conclusion that birds attack or flee inside their territory and display on the boundaries, and there were no recorded observations to show that a herring gull in an upright posture with its bill down is more likely to attack than one with its bill up. All observations and 'data' were non-quantitative generalities. One feels they are valid because they come from a good observer, and his style of presentation has flamboyance. Nevertheless, the lack of exact support leaves the paper vulnerable to criticism, and in later years it would not have been accepted.

After the 'Progress report' Niko turned away from comparative and causal analyses, and several times in conversation he mentioned that they did not interest him any more. Perhaps he felt unhappy about the potential for criticism inherent in this approach, perhaps he just felt out of his depth. Causal analyses, the understanding of internal mechanisms in animals that produce behaviour, were popular with behaviour theorists in those days, and there was a glut of papers about drives and motivation, attempting to arrive at generalities about behaviour throughout the animal kingdom. There were time-series analyses, there were correlations and experiments, but real internal physiological mechanisms of behaviour were hardly touched by these approaches, and neuro-physiological explanations of displays and other behaviour remained somewhat of a holy grail. History has shown much of the analysis in terms of drives and

motivation, with a hierarchical organization, to be somewhat of a dead end, and interest in this approach waned and almost disappeared after the 1970s. Niko's first student, Gerard Baerends, with his group, was one of the last adherents.

Niko and academia

With Niko's appointment in the Zoology Department of Oxford came a fellowship at one of Oxford's oldest colleges, Merton. The college had everything that Oxford stands for: beautiful, age-old buildings and rooms, the style and erudition of its members, academic excellence, and a wealth of tradition and property. Anybody who is somebody in Oxford University belongs to a college, and some colleges are more prestigious than others. To be asked by a college as prominent as Merton was an honour, and Niko had to thank his professor Alister Hardy, also a Merton fellow, for this.

All would have been well if Niko had enjoyed college life: the traditional events and the dinners he was supposed to attend every so often, the drinks parties and the brilliant conversation. The trouble was that he did not, and thoroughly loathed all of it: college life was not his style. The reasons for this were several, and so were the consequences. Niko disliked pomp of any kind, with a disdain that is almost a Dutch national characteristic, but he had it more than most. He hated wearing a suit or even a tie, let alone a gown, and he gently mocked the college rituals of high table with all its silver and established seniority. Curiously, one of the reasons he gave for why he had felt unhappy in Leiden University had been its formality;[70] maybe it was naïve of him, but he had not anticipated anything like Oxford college life.

Apart from the appearance and ritual of traditional Oxford, perhaps one of the main reasons why Niko felt like a stickleback out of the water was his lack of erudition, the absence of the wide knowledge and keen interest in subjects other than one's own that makes an Oxford don. The fact that he was not English certainly did not help. Many of the subjects of conversation that make up English culture were quite unknown to him, and university politics, English literature, and the arts were alien. Nor was he inclined to belatedly take an active interest in any of these, and a certain shyness prevented him from bluffing his way through. At home he described a college dinner at which he sat next to a philosopher, whom he told 'I am always puzzled about philosophers, they are slagging each other off but keep calling each other "brilliant".' Seriously, his table companion answered 'Yes, to be a philosopher you have to be brilliant.' Niko was contemptuous.[71]

Soon, he reduced his college attendance to an absolute minimum, to the disappointment of Alister Hardy (with whom he nevertheless remained good friends). In later years he would abandon Merton altogether, becoming a fellow of the modern Wolfson College, which was much more down to earth, and which did not ask for a commitment on his part. But in the 1950s the lack of common ground between Niko and Merton effectively closed a door into Oxford academia.

Perhaps, if Niko and Lies had been used to entertaining in the English tradition, social contacts could have made up for a dearth of academic acquaintance through college. But being financially far from well off, and being thrifty Dutch, without the dinner-party tradition and with a handful of children to fill the house, entertainment was confined to Niko's students, and to the frequent stays of overseas friends and colleagues. Early on in the 1950s, Niko and Lies began to build their own world in Oxford, with children and students, with contacts in zoology, but largely avoiding the embraces of Oxford academia and England.

In his own world, in his science and with his group of brilliant students and collaborators, Niko was outstandingly successful. But other branches of the Oxford zoological tree he hardly touched, although his students made up for this. With hindsight, this lack of common cause was surprising especially with the ecologists, who had been an important aspect of Oxford's attraction for Niko. David Lack and his EGI (Edward Grey Institute of Ornithology),[72] and Charles Elton and his BAP (Bureau of Animal Populations)[73] were housed in a building separate from the main department, only five minutes on a bicycle away, but Niko rarely went there, nor did they come to the main department. In fact the BAP and EGI also saw very little of each other. They were in separate wings of an old building near the Botanic Garden, and the door between them was kept permanently locked. The three eminent men guarded their territories, and collaboration was not on their minds. There was little doubt that the lack of spark between these outstanding scientists was a consequence simply of human nature, of personalities just tolerating each other rather than jointly pursuing science.

One can only think wistfully of what could have been achieved in the interface between ecology and ethology as early as the 1950s, if Tinbergen, Elton, and Lack had put their heads together. The ecologists had no interest in animal behaviour: they could not see its relevance. Once, during a seminar at the BAP by Denis Chitty about population crashes in voles, someone asked about the observed increase in aggression of the animals during peak populations, clearly a highly important phenomenon. Charles Elton dismissed the question with 'sheer cussedness, I suppose'.[74]

One occasion when the differences in interest between Oxford ecologists and ethologists came to a head was in the mid-1950s, when the issue of animal territoriality was a hot topic. This had been one of Niko's hobby horses for some time, and it was particularly relevant to both ecologists and behaviour students. Territorial behaviour is an obvious interface between an individual and its environment. It is important to food supply, nest protection, population density, and in many other ways, and at that time these were topics high in the priorities of interest of Niko, David Lack, and Charles Elton.

Territoriality could have been developed into a major joint Oxford research interest, but it resulted in an unpleasant muddle. Elton was not interested at all

in behaviour, Lack was. Niko was dismissive of Lack's approach, for example when referring to the relevant sections of Lack's enormously important book, *The natural regulation of animal numbers*:[75] 'I think these chapters are loosely conceived and full of confused thinking. But somehow I cannot get David to go into details in a discussion – we never seem to get really in touch.'[76] Niko was clearly right about the muddled thinking of David Lack in these particular pages, but Lack did have a voice of authority.

A whole issue of the leading bird journal *Ibis* (edited in Lack's institute by Reg Moreau) was to be dedicated to the topic of territoriality.[77] An unedifying small row ensued; Niko had suggested that he himself write a general introduction, but he was left out of the plans altogether and Reg Moreau asked Robert Hinde to write a summing-up. Niko was rather offended and suggested to Robert that they write it jointly; Hinde thought better not. Niko then wrote a separate territory paper for another bird journal,[78] and finally he was also asked to contribute a paper to the special issue of *Ibis*, on just the territorial behaviour of gulls.[79] He consulted Robert Hinde about these papers, telling him what he planned to do in the face of the uncooperative ecologists. But Niko was not entirely honest with Hinde either; perhaps he suspected that Robert had gone behind his back. He had already submitted his papers to *Ibis* and *Bird Study* at the time when he wrote to Robert[80] that he was planning to write them. None of the great men came out of this bickering exchange of letters with a great deal of honour.

One can see that, at times, Niko must have felt the Oxford establishment as a cold shower, and he did not ask for, or get, an involvement from the Oxford ecologists. But that was just what would have been needed: Niko's 1950s and 1960s questions about the biological function of behaviour required ecological answers, and, conversely, ecological relationships needed to be explained in terms of behaviour. The next generation of Niko's students started addressing this, but it was to be another twenty years before the potential was fully realized, when behavioural ecology became a science.

The main Zoology Department in Oxford was housed in a wing of the old university museum, a Victorian building with many small corridors and spiral staircases, far too small for its purpose. Professor Sir Alister Hardy had lined the corridors with small aquaria and tanks for fish and frogs, and there was a small patio, where coffee was had when the weather allowed. Niko had been allocated a quite large room next to the back door, connecting with the room of his secretary through a small hatch. His students were mostly in a group of prefab huts that had been erected on the flat roof of the building, a world in itself, where they worked day and night, where finches were kept for study, where people slept (illegally) and played their guitars. Niko did not go there very often but left it to the students to sort themselves out. When he was in the department, he spent most of his time in his room behind his desk, rapidly hammering away on his typewriter, often sitting on a box rather than on his chair, smoking like a chimney, slightly annoying his secretary by wanting to do much of his mail himself. His room was a rather dark, dank pit, its view blocked by another large laboratory, but he seemed perfectly content there.

There were departmental coffees and teas, in which Niko was a happy participant, eloquent and funny, with an excellent memory for jokes, and there were often roars of laughter coming from his group. On that level he got on very well with everyone, with his own group and other students, with the other staff such as Alister Hardy, Arthur Cain, Bernard Kettlewell, Harold Pusey, Henry (E. B.) Ford, Bob Needham, George Varley, and with the technical staff. Scientifically, only with Bernard Kettlewell did Niko strike up a substantial rapport when he helped out with his filming skills, but in the life of the department outside his group, apart from his teaching of undergraduates, he participated only on a more superficial level. To the department he was the funny, charming, and easy figure, friendly with everyone. He used to pin humorous snippets onto the notice board; typically, once when certain beer adverts were popular, he put up one of his photographs, a natterjack toad that had died and dried on the sand: 'This will never happen to you! Why not? Guinness!'

Almost the only condition that Hardy had put to Niko when taking him on was that he should shoulder some of the burden of undergraduate teaching. In the 1950s and 1960s, Oxford zoology students had to take the Animal Kingdom lectures, the later demise of which was much lamented. Niko taught the Molluscs. It was a field that, with its morphology and taxonomy, was largely alien to him, but he loved to teach it, and must have kept it up for 12 or 15 years (9 lectures and 9 practicals every second year). He also taught 16 lectures per year as well as a 10-day block practical on animal behaviour, and to make his point that scientists should speak German, he did 16 lectures per year in elementary German. This was a pretty solid load of teaching by any standards, which he enjoyed and which was remembered by students for his clarity of explanation, and for the simple, appealing drawings on the blackboard. He excelled at it, and this teaching must have helped him greatly in his integration into the department, as well as giving him access to the undergraduates. In 1960 he was promoted to Reader in Animal Behaviour.

There was no doubt that Niko kept aloof also from the other sciences in Oxford, either from lack of interest, because he was so very busy with his immediate duties, or both. He also kept his distance from other researchers of animal behaviour in Britain, despite various formal roles that he accepted. For instance, there was and is the Association for the Study of Animal Behaviour (ASAB), which became very active in the 1950s with regular meetings, and which published the journal *Animal Behaviour*. Niko was its president from 1954 to 1957, but he very rarely went to the meetings, and he never published in the journal. He did not particularly like ASAB and its members (and he once actually said so to me); they were very English and tended towards white rats and pigeons, and he did not feel it his duty to make them see the light. One of the active figures in ASAB of the 1950s was J. B. S. Haldane, a very eminent Professor of Zoology, for whom Niko felt great antipathy.[81] But Robert Hinde, who had worked with Niko in Oxford in the early 1950s, was a firm adherent of ASAB and also published many important papers in the journal, including theoretical ones and such pure ethological studies as Niko himself had advocated in *The study of instinct*. Later, ASAB was to move entirely in the direction of ethology, but that change of interest was none of Niko's doing.

In contrast, Niko kept up enthusiastically with his international contacts. He was a great writer of letters, producing numerous epistles several pages long. There was a steady flow of correspondence with Gerard Baerends in Groningen, about his science, students, friends, about the journal *Behaviour*, and about the international behaviour conferences. With Konrad Lorenz he still maintained a regular contact, but their relationship had cooled a bit, especially after the Danny Lehrman episode. This was mostly because Niko saw that Danny was right in several of his criticisms, whereas Konrad wanted none of it: to Konrad, for instance, there was a very strict and sharp line between behaviour that was learned or innate, and he felt it as a betrayal of the cause that Niko accepted Danny's criticism and rejected such a sharp divide. The rift between the two was to deepen even further in following years, but in old age their friendship blossomed again.

Niko's many contacts with America showed that he was becoming the grand old man of English-speaking ethology, despite all the criticism that had been levelled against him, and despite the reservations from several behavioural scientists who did not know him personally. He was still not as well known as Konrad, who now had his own new Max-Planck institute in Germany, and who had become a household name with books such as *King Solomon's ring* and *Man meets dog*.[82] But Niko had the advantage of being in the Anglo-Saxon world, he was 'one of us', with a wonderful command of English and only a slight hint of a Dutch accent. He probably commanded more scientific respect in that world than did Konrad. When in 1956 an elite conference of the five most prominent American and five ditto European animal behaviourists was organized in Stanford, California, by Frank Beach, Niko was one of the invited, not Konrad (this was a tremendous high-science jolly, over three weeks on a lovely site – 'the most important conference I have ever been to' according to Robert Hinde).

The British and international contacts initiated a tremendous amount of travel, lecturing, conference attendance, and visits to new field sites. Just as a sample, between 1954 and 1958, at home he lectured in Glasgow, Edinburgh, St Andrews, Aberdeen, Sheffield, Exeter, and Reading; abroad he held forth in Helsinki, Berlin, Copenhagen, Leiden, Utrecht, Groningen, and Amsterdam, and was a visiting professor in Seattle for four months, and in Stanford for one month.

One episode he thoroughly enjoyed was a trip to South Africa, where for a couple of months he was hosted by a pre-war student and friend from Leiden, Gerry Broekhuysen ('Ponky'). In 1954 Niko and Ponky, with a group of South African students, did an intensive study of the courtship and territorial behaviour of the Hartlaub's gull in the Cape, which turned out to be remarkably similar to that of the black-headed gull. It made a great impact in South Africa and it certainly furthered the study of ethology there – apart from providing material for several papers by Niko in Dutch and in English.[83] It was Niko's first foray into Africa, and he was quite bowled over by its richness, by the close-up experience of elephants and lions. Some 10 years later he was to sample much more of the same in the Serengeti.

International conferences in animal behaviour became numerous, foremost amongst them the regular, biennial occurrence of what became known as the International Ethological Conference, IEC. First started when Niko arrived at Oxford, the IEC became a tradition that is still going strong at the time of writing and, with the journal *Behaviour*, is probably the longest-standing institution in the science of ethology. In the 1950s Niko was always there, as well as at many other conferences throughout America and Europe.

International Ethological Conference in Groningen, 1955. Some of the participants:
1. Desmond Morris, 2. Eric Fabricius, 3. Bill Russell, 5. Mike Cullen, 7. David Blest,
8. Konrad Lorenz, 9. Danny Lehrman, 10. Gerard Baerends, 11. Jaap Kruyt, 15. Leen de
Ruiter, 16. Esther Cullen, 17. Adriaan Kortlandt, 18. Paul Leyhausen, 19. Otto Koehler,
21. Niko Tinbergen, 24. Wolfgang Wickler, 27. Gretl Lorenz, 29. Peter Marler,
30. Margaret Bastock, 31. Klaus Hoffmann, 32. Bill Thorpe, 33. Renke Eibl-Eibesfeldt,
36. Monika Meyr-Holzapfel, 38. Piet Sevenster, 39. Jan van Iersel, 41. Tony Bannett,
42. G. V. T. Matthews, 45. Heini Hediger, 47. Eric Hess, 48. Frank Beach, 52. Robert
Hinde, 55. Jos Baerends, 59. Uli Weidmann, 63. Richard Andrews, 65. John Crook.

Home and career

When looking back at Niko in his Oxford environment, in the corridors of science and in his gull colonies, it is easy to forget that he had a home and a family. I think that he himself also often forgot, and his children accepted that home came second. There was some resentment, naturally, especially in his daughters, and when later I asked whether they were interested in their father's work, one said 'a little but I did not understand it', the other two 'couldn't care less'.

When the small, prematurely grey, bespectacled man arrived home after a day in his sombre room in the department and stepped off his bike, what did he come back to? In September 1956, just after a long joint trip to the USA, Lies and Niko had finally moved into their own house, their first property. They had to leave their flat on the busy Banbury Road (the owner, Oxford University, sold it to next-door St Anne's College), and went to live in a pleasant, detached house in a cul-de-sac in North Oxford, 88 Lonsdale Road. It was at the edge of town, a 10-minute cycle ride from the department, and the river Cherwell with its willows meandered just behind it with a lovely stretch for canoeing. Inside, the house was fairly austere (rather like Niko's parental home in The Hague[84]): in the first few years there was not even a carpet on the floorboards (except in the drawing room). The furniture was not very comfortable, and there were few cushions. Niko's Greenland photographs were on the walls, as well as the odd memento: I remember a harpoon, seal-skin boots, and Inuit masks. There were books, lots of them: decoration was unnecessary, but learning and interests came first, and even at table there could be reference books and dictionaries.

To some extent austerity came naturally to the Tinbergens, with their background of Dutch frugality. This must have helped them greatly, because, as I mentioned earlier, their finances were very far from ample. With their meagre funds they had to look after five children, and Lies, as a highly practical person, developed a great ability to make ends meet. They had to shop in the right places, use second-hand clothes for the children, and have newspaper in the loo; pocket money for the children was non-existent, and there were many other constraints. In their first year in Oxford they needed to borrow money from Niko's colleagues.

The children's interests were much in evidence in the Lonsdale Road house. A piano took a prominent place, and music played a large part, especially later. Niko was not at all musical (he had hated piano lessons when little) and was not interested, but the others were all the more so. Lies certainly was, she played the piano, and the children were not asked 'Do you want to learn an instrument?', but 'Which instrument do you want?'[85] Lies had grown up playing the piano to her father's singing of Schubert songs, and she massively encouraged her brood in such enjoyment. She was very successful in this: making music on violin, piano, cello, or recorder became an important part of the children's lives. Janet and Gerry later continued at music conservatory in Glasgow, with Janet becoming a professional cello teacher, and Gerry a professional violinist and teacher. Dirk is a keen amateur violinist, whilst Jack and Catrina learnt to play instruments in later life. Niko was left out of this, totally, though he was very proud especially of his daughters' achievements.

Lies was always at home for the children, with a smile on her round face, her hair in a classical bun. 'There was something matriarchal about Lies', commented one of the students. 'I was very fond of her, because her heart was in the right place, however tactlessly it sometimes came out.' 'In some ways, Mother was a single-parent family' was one of the views from the children. 'Mother laid down the law', took the decisions, and steered them through their new country, so Niko could see to his work. Rita, one of the early students, later reflected about Lies,

> We got on very well, she was an unusual person and I admired her managing skills, because they managed on a shoestring really. The money wasn't much in Oxford, they had five children to educate, and Lies was a brilliant housekeeper. She had to do the whole thing herself and was endlessly energetic. I admired her though she was a bit authoritarian, you could see that she couldn't really let go. She probably kept Niko on the straight and narrow, with her very strong character. It was a tough move coming over here, and she did not get out much, which happens with a big family, so she kept her very heavy Dutch accent to the end.[86]

Niko was the highest level of authority at home, and for the children 'having to tell Father' was the last line of any argument with Lies. But he was remote, which the children felt, however much they loved him. Many years later I had a sample of their comments: 'he was interested in us children to a certain extent', 'I don't think he ever asked me what I was learning at college', 'taking us out birdwatching wasn't his scene', 'he found it difficult to do father-like things with us children', 'he was so interested in his work that he regarded us as a

The family in Oxford, January 1951. Left to right: Catrina, Lies, Gerry, Janet, Dirk, and Jack. Photo Niko Tinbergen.

nuisance', 'he lived for his work, but if the family wanted what he did, we did it together', 'he was always thinking about evolution or something, he never let go', 'he felt terribly guilty about not being as strong a family man as he felt he ought to have been', 'he was interested in his children, but not in what they were doing'.[87] These were the more objective comments, made long after; but at the time the children took Niko's absence for granted.

However, despite such misgivings, most importantly they all considered themselves a very happy family. One of the youngest daughters told Lies, 'Mother I hope you don't mind, but really we love Father best' (Lies replied that she did, too).[88] The children interested Niko scientifically, and Lies also had that objective fascination about all children. 'I certainly had the feeling that they were observing me as an animal going through the courting–mating phase, and it wasn't a very comfortable feeling to have', said one of the daughters.

When Niko did partake of family life he was brilliant, funny, and full of verve. His little songs and ditties (all from various children's books) still had his children in stitches even fifty years later; they were in the style of 'Willy in his bright new sashes, fell in the fire and was burnt to ashes, now although the room grows chilly, I haven't the heart to poke poor Willy', or 'Father heard his children scream, so he threw them in the stream, saying as he threw the third, children should be seen not heard.' He was fond of reading them the rather gruesome Max and Moritz stories, and Hillaire Belloc's *Cautionary tales*.[89] And there were the family holidays; Lies insisted on her three weeks walking in

Lies and Niko at the wedding of Margaret Bastock and Aubrey Manning. Solihull, 1959. Courtesy Aubrey Manning.

summer, and Niko used to take the entire family to wherever his field camp was, in summer after the birds' breeding season was over. They loved it, and he could combine his family world with the scientific one.

There was little social contact with the 'natives', and Lies and Niko rather kept themselves to themselves, although there were frequent scientific visitors from overseas, and students; also, both Lies and Niko were ardent letter writers. Later they commented that the one person they felt most at ease with in their early Oxford days was a cleaner lady. Their Oxford peers seemed to them superficial, with a sort of clever academic frivolity that was alien to Lies and Niko. They never went out, Niko usually retired early in the evening, often at nine-ish after reading a bit in the *New Yorker* or *Punch*, and the house had to be quiet. His day often started again at five in the morning, when he quietly began to play the keys of his typewriter, or if he was in the field he started his bird-watching. His body started to show signs of stress, which was not surprising under the tasks he set himself, and the pressures that he felt. He suffered from insomnia, he was plagued by ulcers, and at the age of 51 in September 1958, Niko needed major surgery, which removed most of his stomach and duodenum.

During those years Niko was friendly with everyone, but friends with nobody. He never came to be on intimate terms with outside people, there was no talk about personal problems, and he had no really personal relationships with other adults until he was much older. The only person with whom Niko really shared his thoughts was Lies. She knew about his work and about all the people involved, and they were at one over how children should be brought up. They decided to speak English at home as much as possible, to help the children with their communication and getting acclimatized: they took the line that 'we have to fit in, the British did not ask us to come'. They deliberately decided to be frugal, not always because of need, but out of principle: 'we were brought up with the idea that you are not on this earth just to enjoy yourself, you have got to put in as much as you take out'.[90] Yet they contributed to charities, to the Oxford Music Festival and others, anonymously.

The family was unreservedly anti-Church, and they were principled socialists without being politically involved. They were rather old-fashioned over the girls' education: none of the three daughters went to university (they did teacher's training or music), though for the boys this was different: Jack read Physics and Dirk did Biology, both with scholarships. Catrina, the eldest daughter, and Gerry, the youngest, went to university as mature students. Later the children explained this by referring to differences in ability and interest, but they acknowledged that 'our parents did feel that the mother's primary purpose in life was to bring up children – and that this would be very difficult combined with a career.' This was all the more interesting as Lies' mother was the first woman to get a PhD in botany in Holland.

Since their move to England, contact with the rest of their family in Holland was much reduced, especially for Niko, although he religiously wrote to his parents every week when they were still alive. But his dear father died soon after

Niko left Holland, in 1951; his mother came to visit them in Oxford. She died in 1960. The only one of his siblings with whom he had been close was his much younger brother, Luuk, and during the first year of his Oxford life Luuk came to stay, to lecture in the department on his latest ecological work in Groningen. Niko admired him, even felt rather competitive; Luuk, Niko told me, was definitely the clever one in the family.

Luuk's death at 39, in 1955, affected Niko deeply, although he rarely talked about it. He was even more on his own now. He also felt much more vulnerable; he knew that he himself was prone to depression. Oxford had not been the answer to all his hopes, and he had few personal contacts. Restless, he started to think about getting out, about moving again. Just at that time in Germany the death of the famous Gustav Kramer[91] created an opening in the Max-Planck institute as head of bird migration research, and Niko was approached. He was seriously tempted by the possibility, but this time Lies put her foot down firmly: 'You cannot uproot the family again', and that was that.[92] It was the only time that she put the family's interest before that of Niko's career.

Niko then had the idea of starting a new institute of ethology, somewhere in the south of England, and away from the university. Purely by chance, in late 1958 he was visited by a colonel of the US Air Force, which was financing one of his researchers, and Niko 'told him of my misgivings about the future, and of the need I felt there was in Britain for establishing one central centre for advanced ethological research. He was enthusiastic … it was not at all impossible that with American money such an institute could be established.'[93] Niko realized that he would not be able to manage this on his own, so tried to persuade Robert Hinde to join him in the venture, thinking of an institute somewhere between Oxford, Cambridge, and London, also involving a neurophysiologist (David Vowles) and a geneticist (Margaret Bastock), as well as a number of more junior staff.

Niko wrote a detailed memorandum about the plan, but it did not get far and died a death within a couple of months. Robert Hinde was very lukewarm about the idea; without telling Niko he wrote about it in detail to his superior in Cambridge, Bill Thorpe, who poured scorn on it, and who saw it for what it was ('I am very much afraid that this means that Niko is getting fed up with Oxford').[94] The episode ended when Niko wrote a short and rather terse letter to Robert Hinde:

> *After our talk last week I decided that my plans for the future of ethological research should take the shape of a plan for the extension of Oxford. I am therefore going ahead with my own plans … Now my own plans have been worked out a little, and I discussed them with Hardy, and he is sympathetic and even enthusiastic, and is fully determined to push this, along with other plans that exist already.* [95]

Despite Niko's successes in his work and his popularity with colleagues and students, despite his outward good cheer and jolliness, his lack of fulfilment in his more personal life left something sad about him. He felt some guilt about a lack of contact with his family (although they had accepted that entirely), and away from his work his horizons were narrow. In Lies' letters to Holland she showed her nostalgia for the beautiful Dutch skies, and the skating. Niko's solitude at that time, at the end of the 1950s, showed in a BBC radio talk about himself and his family in their adopted country. In *On turning native* he admired England, its education, humour, and tolerance, but he was also critical as a 'happy grumbler', and he referred to 'qualified happiness ... unsatisfactory and unfulfilled ... we have, in a sense, fallen between two stools ... one does not really turn native, yet one loses touch with one's country of origin. Each time I visit my native country, I feel less at home ... This is a sad experience, but it is the penalty one pays for the many advantages of emigration.'[96]

The consequences of that penalty never left him.

What would have been, if Oxford had never happened, if the Tinbergen family had stayed put in Leiden? Quite likely, Niko's and Lies' social life would have been more fulfilled, and the family of the Leiden professor would have remained well-integrated in a familiar society, certainly more so than they were in England. I believe, however, that Niko's ethology would not have flown as high as it did – his mission of spreading the word in an Anglo-Saxon country was greatly assisted by the attractions of Oxford. If he had not moved, he would not have appealed to his fanatical Hard Core, he almost certainly would not have reached people such as Robert Hinde, Desmond Morris, Mike Cullen, and the others (of whom I will say more in chapter 10). As far as his own research was concerned, the Oxford interest in evolution clearly influenced Niko's field of activities, and his later fieldwork, especially on selection pressures and the biological functions of animal behaviour, was deeply affected. Whatever Niko's motivation for moving, whatever the price he paid for it, the resulting development of ethology was what we should be grateful for.

CHAPTER 7

Niko's two worlds: Oxford in the 1960s

Looking back at the 1950s, one gets an impression of Niko's life as hectic, confused, and torn in many directions. But at the beginning of the next decade it gained stability, and he appeared to come to terms with his niche in Britain. At least he seemed to settle down, into two separate existences, related but firmly apart, literally racing from one to the other. One of these worlds was in the field, in his wide-open spaces, in the dunes somewhere in the north of England, or in the Serengeti in Africa. His other world was in the Zoology Department in Oxford.

Dunes, birds, and beasts

For his fieldwork in Britain, Niko's greatest find by far was the peninsula of wind-swept dunes at Ravenglass, along the shores of the Irish Sea below the Lake District in the north of England. They formed a magnificent scenery, one of the most beautiful dune landscapes in Britain, with high tops and huge, bare sands in sensuous curves, with rich little valleys and small lakes, inhabited by natterjacks and lapwings, all part of a long, uninhabited peninsula between a wide, rich river estuary and the sea. It was the home of the largest black-headed gull colony in Europe, its history going back several centuries. Sadly, neither the gulls nor the shifting sands exist any more, and no longer can one follow the tracks of the fox visiting the rabbits, or the hedgehog crossing the steps of a merganser. Vegetation has taken over completely, probably due to nutrients brought by polluted rain. But until the 1970s it was a stunningly beautiful paradise.

Niko loved the Ravenglass dunes, and he was never happier than when following the tracks of animals across the sands, in the very early morning when the wind had not yet disturbed the sands and the light was low. I can still see that small figure, in khaki clothes and gym shoes, a look of concentration on his face, camera around his neck, his finger often pointing at the tracks, massively excited when he could follow in the tracks the animal's actions. A fox had turned sharply upwind (wind direction deduced from the ripples in the sand), walked up to an old boot, lifted its leg (so it was a male) and one could see and smell the urine mark in the sand, then it had continued for a few hundred metres to a rabbit stop (a closed-off hole in the sand where a rabbit kept its young), dug it out, then cached the prey nearby; of the cache one could see how the fox had swept dirt over it with its snout, each whisker marked in the sand. The story was different every time, the sands a rich palette of animal behaviour.

Niko and I walked through these dunes at numerous dawns, he as happy as I ever saw him anywhere. He was not interested in counting birds, or in unusual species, in 'birdwatching' as other people know it, but would be utterly absorbed in the alarm behaviour of a shelduck, or the pecks in the sand left by a snipe. He must have taken thousands of pictures there, as witness to the pure delight he found in the dunes. Some of them were published in his book *Tracks* (jointly with the naturalist/artist Eric Ennion).[1] Years later I realized that Niko was back home there, that the Big Sands of Ravenglass had much in common with the inland dune slopes he had walked in Hulshorst, and the sea dunes near The Hague. In Ravenglass he had found his native habitat, and roaming those sands was part of his *raison d'être*.

Every year a caravan was brought up from Oxford to the Ravenglass peninsula, far from human habitation, and, surrounded by tents, it formed the seasonal headquarters for Niko and his students. Every month of the breeding season he came up for a week or ten days, arriving from Oxford totally exhausted, keen to get back to the birds and the dunes, and to participate in the students' projects.

It all started in a rather low-key way in the late 1950s, with a couple of students at a time. First there were Uli and Rita Weidmann and briefly Mike Cullen, then Colin Beer and Gilbert Manley set out to do PhDs on the black-headed gull: Gilbert to study its displays[2] in much more detail than Martin Moynihan had done, and Colin to analyse incubation behaviour, activities that related to the nest. Both these subjects had been suggested by Niko, but typically, once 'the boys' had started and Niko saw that they could manage, he left them to work things out as they wanted. This, in essence, was Niko's approach to student supervision. 'Niko seemed to have a knack of pointing you in the right direction, give a little shove and then leave you to it.'[3]

Yet he did keep an eye on things, on some projects more than others. When Niko came up from Oxford to Ravenglass, he and Gilbert argued endlessly, in exhausting stand-offs in which Gilbert complained about unwarranted

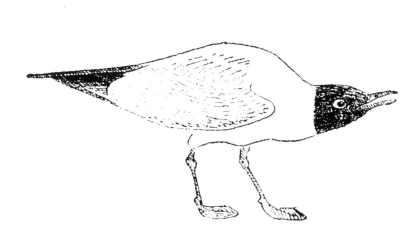

statements by Niko in his 1959 comparative gull paper. Amongst other things, they argued about whether an aggressive display by the gulls during pair-formation really was aggressive or something quite different. The two almost always disagreed completely in their interpretations, with Gilbert becoming quite emotional about it. In the end Gilbert even submitted his PhD thesis without showing it to Niko. More and more Niko came to see the difficulties of using simple observations in the colony to obtain further understanding of the internal causes of the birds' behaviour. Together with the many criticisms that he had received before, in the 1950s, these arguments with Gilbert were one of the reasons for Niko's loss of interest in such questions.

Colin's detailed study of the gulls' behaviour on the nest was quite different; he was interested in the mechanism of nest-building and incubation behaviour, in exactly when the birds did what and why.[4] Niko (by his own confession) did not understand the quantitative aspects of Colin's work, and later he did not even read the entire thesis, but he was highly impressed by the field skills involved, the experiments as well as the observations. One of Colin's activities involved watching incubating gulls from underneath, with Colin in a coffin-shaped, buried observation hide lying underneath a sitting bird that he had enticed to nest on a horizontal glass window. This study of the behaviour patterns affecting egg-laying and incubation was clearly on the boundary between ecology and ethology, one of the beginnings of behavioural ecology.

Colin also experimented with incubation behaviour using various dummies which, when presented on the rim, were rolled into the nest,[5] or were carried away just as the birds did with shells of hatched eggs. Not only eggshells, but also several other types of foreign object were carried away by the bird, but only at the time when there were eggs. When Niko saw this he realized that there was potential for just the sort of field project he needed to do. It became the basis for one of his best-known studies.

Life in the Ravenglass camp was exciting, with a daily routine of watching from observation hides in the colony, and walks along the beach or through the dunes. One volunteer acted as 'slave', to do the cooking and shopping (wading across the wide estuary to the village), and to put people in the hide in the early morning (one always had to be put in a hide, so that birds saw a person walking away and would not be aware that someone was left inside). The slave for Colin and Gilbert was Juan Delius, a German–Argentinian student, who soon started to do his own project alongside: at the suggestion of Colin he began to study the behaviour of skylarks, which sang above the dunes in large numbers. Later he came back to continue this for a PhD, after discussing it with Niko who was not particularly interested in the skylark, but who was persuaded by Juan.

For the students the visits of The Maestro were part of the Ravenglass scene, and Niko felt he belonged there, it was his territory, the students were his people. He got them up early in the morning, he discussed the weather and the birds, the fascinating new things that everybody had seen, and the relations with and between the people in the village. They drank endless cups of instant coffee, he rolled and smoked his cigarettes, they bantered, argued, and teased. One day Gilbert and Colin came back from their early morning stint in the colony to find a note from Niko telling them about a killer whale on the beach, two miles away, asking them to bring their cameras and knives as soon as possible. After a long walk they met Niko in the Land-Rover, who gently pointed out that it was 1 April.

During those first years in Ravenglass Niko once more began to feel the need for his own field research project, something that he had missed out on for more than 10 years. Here he had the opportunity to start one, and there was an ample supply of volunteers to help. Colin Beer's observations provided the last push, and Niko started to experiment with gulls and eggshells. The gulls' eggshell removal was a particularly fortunate find, because in it Niko could investigate combined questions: what made gulls do it (similar to the model experiments he had done in his earlier career), and what was the function or survival value – what are the benefits that the birds gain from it? Function of behaviour had become a major interest to him, and there was something in this particular case that was especially attractive: the very insignificance of the behaviour, an action that did not occupy the birds for more than a few seconds every year, and which was of doubtful importance.

The eggshell-carrying study began in 1959. It was very much Niko's project, lasting three years. Every year there were three volunteers to do the donkey work, with Niko himself taking part whenever he was around. The volunteers were mostly non-Brits, post-docs from South Africa, Poland, and Switzerland, students from Holland who were doing work for their MSc-equivalent degree, or from France, and there was a teacher doing a sabbatical. I was one of the Dutch helpers, arriving in the second year of the project. All of us worked alongside the PhD students who were doing their own projects. We discussed in great detail questions such as whether eggshells could endanger the brood by attracting predators, and how one could test this. First we had to show that the egg's camouflage colour was effective, so out we went with black-headed gulls' eggs. We put them out in the dunes as well as gulls' eggs painted white, and yes, the white eggs were taken in no time by crows and herring gulls, and many of the natural eggs were left alone. Only then could we check whether the presence of eggshells would endanger a gull's egg, in a similar experiment, and yes it did: more of the eggs with eggshells next to them were found first. We did scores of such trials, and in the colony we presented dummies on nests, eggshells, rings, squares, and half ping-pong balls of any colour, and scored the percentage removed by the gulls after half an hour.

The enthusiasm in these early-morning sessions of the field experiments was enormous. We watched the predators and our experimental set-up, and if we came back to the caravan with another 'good' result and lovely observations there would be cheers from the boss. If things went the 'wrong' way, that is if results were unexpected, Niko would find it 'interesting', we would think it maddening. With Mike Cullen's advice the experiments were set up in a

Painting eggs for experiments in Ravenglass, 1961. Courtesy of the Tinbergen family.

thorough and properly quantitative fashion, with randomized presentations. With hindsight one can see that we made mistakes: for instance there were occasions when experiments continued until there was a 'significant' difference in the response to models, until the expectations were confirmed (a cardinal sin in the eyes of statisticians). There was also the possibility of observer bias, at the time when the experiments were laid out in the field, because the observers expected a given result. Standardization of the presentations was difficult and therefore poor, and there were no 'blind' presentations where the observer did not know which model was involved. So the experimenter could unconsciously have 'helped' the results. It was, in fact, a bad way to collect data for statistical treatment. Some mistakes were comparable to those of Bernard Kettlewell's experiments on industrial melanism, mentioned earlier. But at the time nobody realized this, no-one ever objected; Niko was happy and we all were, too.

The results of the eggshell removal study made a lovely story, published in a long and rather chatty joint paper in *Behaviour*[6] and two shorter ones.[7] It showed a survival value in eggshell removal, in that aerial predators are less likely to find the brood, and it also showed its disadvantage (briefly leaving the hatched chick exposed to predation by other gulls), suggesting that this was the evolutionary reason why gulls do not remove an eggshell immediately, but only after some time, when the chick is dry. All kinds and colours of objects are removed from the nest, but the more readily if they are hollow, either white or egg-coloured, have frilly edges, and if they are feather-light. Interestingly, if birds have incubated strange-coloured eggs (for example, black ones) then they are especially ready to remove objects with that colour (though never the eggs themselves). Altogether it was an elegant combination-study of stimuli that elicit behaviour, of the survival function, and of a learning component. It was, and is, generally seen as one of the Tinbergen classics (and never mind the statistics).

One important consequence of the eggshell study was that it gave Niko the confidence he needed for more research on the biological function of behaviour, on what behaviour is for, on its survival value. He had now demonstrated that one can do proper experiments on such questions. From this time onwards, the focus was on function, for himself and for his students, and work on causal aspects of behaviour, so very important in Niko's group until then, was sidelined. I, for one, was clearly affected by it, and my experience in Ravenglass made me want to continue in that direction with a PhD study into the behavioural mechanisms that protect gulls against all kinds of predation, a project that straddled the divide between ecology and ethology. It addressed the function of anti-predator behaviour, and it was clearly inspired by Niko. There was no need for him to tell me what to do: I think I felt what he wanted and what was needed.

I compared the gulls' aggression, fear, curiosity, and some other factors towards each of a large number of enemies such as crows, peregrines, hedgehogs, foxes, people, and stoats. I also quantified the danger to the black-headed gulls from each of those enemies, and by bringing these aspects together one could see the degree of adaptation of behaviour. Hundreds of black-headed gulls were killed by foxes, and hedgehogs and large gulls took masses of chicks. This demonstrated that the gulls' compromise between aggressive behaviour and fear was nowhere near completely successful. Niko was a very enthusiastic supporter throughout; he loved our trips after the fox and the hedgehog, and with my tame crow that I used for experiments. He watched the experiment in which I showed that the closer gulls nested together (which meant the smaller their territories were), the less they were preyed upon by hedgehogs, and we found many other adaptations. Together we followed the animal tracks in the sand, and he very much approved of (but never took part in) my night-long sessions in the observation hide. The study was published as a special supplement of *Behaviour*.[8] Looking back, it was probably the first sign that behavioural ecology had arrived in the Tinbergen camp, although we did not call it that, yet.

Other PhD students with whom I shared the Ravenglass camp in the early 1960s were equally concerned with functional problems; we were all involved in a complete change of direction for the research group. There was Ian Patterson, who ran a study parallel to mine to discover the function of spacing and timing of nests by the gulls: how do they do it, and why do they breed so close together, and in such a synchronized manner?[9] The subject was Ian's idea, and Niko thought it would fit in well. Ian showed first that clustering and

*A student project in
Ravenglass: HK and hedgehog,
1962. Photo Niko Tinbergen.*

synchronization of nests produced higher fledging rates, because predators took more eggs and chicks from outlying and late nests. Then Ian demonstrated that the nest spacing patterns were produced partly by territorial defence, but mostly because of the gulls' being attracted to given areas, whatever the behaviour of the territory owners. It was choice of habitat, and the birds actively selected what was best for them in terms of reproductive output.

A simultaneous but quite different type of study was that of Bob Mash who, at Niko's instigation, tried to discover what the function (survival value) was of the gulls' brown head (black-headed gulls have brown heads in spring and summer, and white heads in winter). Niko was convinced that it had something to do with the gulls' head-flagging display, so Bob used heads of gulls that had been killed by foxes, stuck them on a small machine buried in the sand next to a nest and from his observation hide watched the gulls' reactions when the heads turned away or faced the nest owner. Unfortunately, the gulls were not taken in by the models: they were either scared and fled, or they just pecked them to bits whichever way they faced. Niko had great expectations for this approach, but it simply did not work, interesting as it was.

The camp developed almost a culture of its own. Although The Maestro was there for only a few weeks each year, this culture was firmly rooted in Niko's interests, beliefs, and approach to science and every-day life. The students, of course, did not always regard Niko's influence as a blessing, but his

Niko's students around a bird-hide in the Ravenglass gull colony, 1961. Left to right: Roger Stamm, HK, Madeleine Paillette, and John Houghton. Photo Niko Tinbergen.

style and ideas dominated the camp, even when he was absent. Niko kept us on our toes, and for the 'residents' a visit by Niko meant a considerable upheaval.

Ian Patterson recalled:

> *I have a very clear memory of us feeling at the time that this was all a b. nuisance and we were always grumbling about him, the fact that we'd all be getting on perfectly happily and then he came along and messed it all up. What a relief it was when he went, although looking back you really appreciate what you got from him … these classic visits, where he'd come totally stressed out with committee work and administration and just so happy to be there, and then after a couple of days he'd get conscious of what he had to do back in Oxford and his mind would slowly drift back from Ravenglass to Oxford. He almost always left earlier than he had said he would, a day before or he'd get up one morning and be off quite unexpectedly. He did not sleep very well and was very restless and smoked all the time. He was very highly strung … We all cursed at the time when he could not sleep in the morning and he'd pick a tent at random and come banging on the roof and say 'let's go fox-tracking' and you'd groan 'Oh God'. But out you'd go and on a nice morning it was really marvellous.[10]*

Niko's enthusiasm was incredibly infectious, even at times when he dug us out of our beds in the middle of the night, when we were shattered after long hours in the field, and he was bubbling over from seeing beautiful northern lights.

Early morning walks and hours in the observation hides were followed by joint sessions in the caravan, with a second breakfast and the inevitable instant coffee, when the latest results and observations were chewed over. When we were in Oxford there was rarely a chance of talking about our work with Niko, but here in the camp we had his ear, and somehow he seemed less inhibited about talking to his students about his own approach to science. This involved not only his way of asking questions, but also his focus on the problems and way of cutting through to the essentials of what one had to investigate. It also included that side of him that is now less respectable, his celebration of the instant observation and quick, neat experiment, and his (almost) disdain for quantification. Ian Patterson remarked that Niko's 'untidiness with experiments' was probably largely due to his quickly seeing from the animals' behaviour what was going on, then collecting data really just to substantiate that. 'I can clearly remember him saying that "this is really quite silly and unnecessary but that is the way it is going these days, you've got to have quantitative data before you can get it published", and what he was doing was purely for that purpose rather than a fundamental part of the science.'[11]

Niko, with his spartan lifestyle, did not always appreciate our efforts to make conditions more comfortable. There was no transport when The Maestro was away, so we, the students, bought a clapped-out open jeep, which was not really approved of – Niko felt that young legs should walk. His approach to life also demanded that we all sleep on the ground in the tents, on some marram-grass if we really had to: this edict was also ignored, and we all got mattresses. Later Niko himself (grudgingly) also succumbed to a mattress after his back began to play up. The camp was quite isolated, the fieldwork demanding, and there was often foul weather with rain and howling gales that blew sand everywhere. Nevertheless our (none too frequent) evening visits to the 'Pennington Arms' in the village were not approved of, and we soon learnt not to go when Niko was around.

But everybody put up with everyone else good-naturedly, the camp was full of banter, and there were frequent outpourings of Niko's ample supply of verse and phrase. Practical jokes were common, though I remember Niko himself being far from amused when someone found a pair of very tarty, high-heeled shoes in the tide-line and put them outside his tent. When Niko left again for Oxford, we usually slept it off and settled in again for life without The Maestro. Often there were other scientist visitors, arriving with Niko or under their own steam, ethologists from other countries, or other students of Niko who came to look at our work, people like Cliff Henty who studied thrushes and snails in the dunes, Richard Dawkins, Nick Blurton-Jones, and many others who came just for a few days to see. Ravenglass was a very fruitful experience for many, and a treasured memory.

The end of the studies by Ian and me was also the end of Niko's involvement with black-headed gulls. The main practical reason for this was that the colony had become a large visitor attraction. A warden was appointed, and there was some conflict about who could go where. Yet there were a few more projects

with other birds in Ravenglass. During 1963, my own last full season in Ravenglass, we had a 'slave', Mike Norton-Griffiths, who became obsessed with the
oystercatchers that were breeding along the beach and in the gull colony. He
watched nests from the hide and discovered a fascinating story behind these
birds, and for the next two years he came back to work it out for a PhD. What
he saw was adult birds bringing back mussels from the distant mussel-beds, to
feed their chicks at the nest. They opened the shells and removed the contents
for the chicks to eat, and when the chicks got larger they began to do this
themselves. The interesting bit was that some birds always opened the shells by
hammering them, whereas others always did this by chiselling, and chicks did it
just as their parents did. Mike analysed the behaviour of the parents and chicks
in detail, with Niko watching it all and taking spectacular photographs.

More directly inspired by Niko himself was another PhD study that was
started in Ravenglass about the same time, by an American student. This was
Harvey Croze on crows – he followed up Niko's hunches from the eggshell
experiments, about the way in which crows find camouflaged prey. Harvey and
his wife Nani did experiments with wild and tame crows in the dunes, providing them with food under painted mussel shells, demonstrating in beautiful
detail how these birds applied a 'searching image'.[12] Again, Niko was there in
the background, and he produced a good and acclaimed documentary film,
Crafty predators and cryptic prey.

For a research project for himself, with two post-docs from Germany and
Switzerland (Monica Impekoven and Dierck Franck), Niko put camouflaged

Oystercatcher opening a mussel in front of its chick. Photo Niko Tinbergen.

eggs in the dunes in groups of different density, and demonstrated that eggs at higher density are much more vulnerable, probably because of the 'searching image' that the crows had developed.[13] This, in the mid-1960s, was his last field experiment, and from then on, when he was out in the dunes he would concentrate on either filming, or on the research of his students without being directly involved himself.

Almost every year in the summer Niko brought his family to Ravenglass for the annual holiday, for a few weeks after the gulls and we, the students, had gone. It was his territory, and he could take his children birdwatching along the estuary and tracking across the Big Sand, which they loved. Those dunes were a long way from Holland, but for him, they stirred many memories of Hulshorst.

The four whys

Niko's exploits in Ravenglass in the late 1950s and early 60s, from the eggshell removal work to his incidental field observations, from the early morning tracking trips to the contact with his students, had some far-reaching consequences for him. Apart from giving him tremendous enjoyment, satisfaction, and desperately needed breathing space after being closeted in Oxford, Ravenglass gained or regained him confidence in his field abilities, and especially also in the possibilities of doing proper, scientific observations and experiments on the survival value of behaviour and on selection pressures.

Niko realized that with his approach to the biological function of animal behaviour he was making an important contribution, and the time had come to define this field and the need for it, in a context of the other reaches of ethology. It was this, together perhaps with the realization that he was running out of practical ideas for field research projects, that made him feel he should assert himself again. It was the incentive to write a review of ethology that later would be acknowledged as the best paper of his entire career, his last major one, and one of the few theoretical contributions he made.

'Aims and methods of ethology' was published in 1963,[14] dedicated to Konrad Lorenz for his 60th birthday. Because it was such an important statement I want to discuss it in some detail and recall a few of the most significant points. It defined ethology, and it claimed a niche for this science in the aftermath of the various reservations that had gone before, such as the criticisms from Danny Lehrman, Robert Hinde, and others. Interestingly, and despite the dedication, the paper is not without the odd (good-natured) dig at Konrad, especially at his insistence on the importance of 'innateness'. But Niko finds that 'Lorenz can with justification be said to be the father of modern ethology – even though he has had forerunners; there is nothing amazing about every father having had a father'.

In his paper Niko put Lorenz on a pedestal, without mentioning any of his own contributions, a characteristic piece of Niko modesty. His arguments are not that convincing: he credits Konrad with putting ethology on the map as a biological science: 'he made us look at behaviour through the eyes of biologists, … an achievement of tremendous importance', but although Konrad had interesting ideas (including many wild ones), Niko was much more the strict scientist than Konrad. Lorenz never wrote anything that could touch *The study of instinct* in defining ethology, or even a paper such as 'Aims and methods'. But he showed that one could treat behaviour patterns of animals like their organs, and study their biology in the same way.

Ethology, Niko explained, is

> *the biological study of behaviour. By this I mean that the science is character-ized by an observable phenomenon (behaviour, or movement), and by a type of approach, a method of study (the biological method). The first means that the starting point of our work has been and remains inductive, for which description of observable phenomena is required. The biological method is characterized by the general scientific method, and in addition by the kind of questions we ask, which are the same throughout biology and some of which are peculiar to it. Huxley likes to speak of 'the three major problems of biology: that of causation, that of survival value, and that of evolution' – to which I should like to add a fourth, that of ontogeny.*

Julian Huxley had mentioned his three biological questions half a century earlier,[15] but being a far less persuasive and inspiring writer than Niko was, Huxley did not make anywhere near the same impact.

I have alluded to Niko's 'four whys' in the first chapter, but at the risk of repeating myself, I will discuss them here again: they are that important. Briefly,

Skating on Blenheim Lake, near Oxford, 1962.
Photo Sheila O'Clarey.

in Niko's analysis, the question 'Why does an animal do this?' is asking for one or more of four different kinds of answer. The questioning is fundamentally different in these cases, although the answers may overlap with each other. One type of answer is about *causation*: in that case the question 'Why?' refers to the processes inside and outside the animal that make it behave, and it refers to the organization of behaviour inside the animal. A dog chases a hare 'because' it is hungry, its nervous system is programmed to respond to a running hare, there is the sudden appropriate stimulus, adrenaline is being released, and so on: all this is part of the mechanism of behaviour.

However, 'Why does it?' can also have a second meaning, and refer to the way in which this behaviour has come about in that particular individual: the *ontogeny* of behaviour. Has the dog learnt that chasing a hare brings reward, has the manner of its chase matured in some way, or is there a genetic component? The third 'Why?' refers to the *biological function of behaviour*, to its survival value: the dog chases because the hunt may produce food or for some other ultimate reason. This does not mean that the animal 'thinks' that way, in fact the dog may not think at all. But its behaviour may have evolved because for a dog it has greater survival value than alternatives, and our question intends to address this. The final, fourth 'Why?' refers to the *evolution* of behaviour, for instance: why does a dog chase, and a cat stalk, and how have these behaviour patterns changed over the generations?

With Niko's analysis of behaviour methodology he made a large contribution not only to our approach to animal behaviour, but to biology in general. Seeing this dissection of the way in which our minds question nature was a revelation for me as a student, and for many other people. The statement is so simple, and so important.

Before reviewing each of the four aspects of ethology, Niko also made a long and heartfelt plea for what he saw as yet another duty of behaviour studies, that is, to observe and describe. It was what he himself loved to do in the field, and what he was good at: all his students were always admonished to start with just simple observation, taking a notebook and pencil, and describe. After that should come the questions, and the experiments: but first one should observe, first watch, then wonder. 'Our science needs naturalists and observers as well as experimenters.' But he also saw a problem with the publication of such detailed description, and suggested storage in special archives, a suggestion that was never taken up.

Significantly, 'Aims and methods' included four pages on causation, four on ontogeny, six and a half on biological function or survival value, and two and a half on evolution of animal behaviour. Clearly, biological function was uppermost in his mind. The section on causation did not refer to theoretical models any more: he had lost interest in a hierarchy of behavioural systems and even referred to his own earlier erroneous attempts in that direction. But his focus was on physiology, and he was clearly totally convinced that physiology would provide explanations for all internal behavioural mechanisms. Full of optimism in this direction he wrote that 'The "no-man's land" between ethology and neurophysiology is being invaded from both sides', and he referred to the entire study of causation of animal activities as 'physiology of behaviour'.

He then continued by singing the praises of experiments that investigate biological functions of behaviour, what he called 'survival value'. Niko complained about the lack of interest in this field from people who saw the approach as unscientific, an objection he dealt with in detail, and he stressed the need for simple direct comparative observations to study the effects of behaviour in the field. In this he did not dwell on the many pitfalls associated with observations, and what he called 'correlation' analysis (observing what happens after a behaviour has occurred). However, he did recognize some of the difficulties. Strikingly, he did not mention the obvious and vital role of ecology here. Not long afterwards Niko's behavioural questions of survival value would be studied highly successfully when combined with ecological methods, from which a new branch of science would be born: behavioural ecology.

In his discussion of the ontogeny of behaviour in the individual he dissected the nature–nurture controversy, but shied away from a direct confrontation with his old colleague: 'If I were to elaborate this further I should have to cross swords with my friend Konrad Lorenz himself – both a pleasure and a serious task requiring the most thorough preparation – but this is not the occasion to indulge in swordplay'. Niko's main point was that the simple term 'innate', for behaviour, was not very helpful, but that one should analyse how behaviour arises during development, and in that process one might find that certain aspects would be genetically determined, others not. Until now, he argued, most evidence for 'innate' behaviour was insufficient and negative: merely showing that a male stickleback reared in isolation could go through the appropriate motions is not enough to demonstrate that courtship behaviour is innate. It only demonstrates that certain environmental effects are not important, but not that there are no outside influences.

Then Niko addressed the fourth 'why', which involved the study of the evolution of animal behaviour. He saw this as having two aims: to elucidate the course of evolution (which species did what, and how they were related), and to unravel the dynamics of the evolution of behaviour (exactly how the changes in behaviour evolved).

Finally, with a parting shot, he came back to the label of the entire branch of biology that is Ethology. Without the assertiveness that many people would have liked to see in him, he cautioned his colleagues to modesty: 'in view of the confused public image called up by the term Ethology, it might well be advisable not to overdo the use of the word.' It was the counsel of a visionary. What matters, he said, was that people should be aware of the fundamental unity behind the different questions asked in Biology of Behaviour. 'Aims and methods of ethology' was Niko's own, modest assessment of his science, and today it is still regularly quoted and an important reference point (see Chapter 10).

Walney

In the mid-1960s Niko began a gradual move of his group's activities away from Ravenglass, to another very large gull colony, also along the Irish Sea but a bit further south, at Walney. The reasons were several. As Niko later said, Ian Patterson and I had been the last of his real naturalist-type students, and he missed the company of people who enjoyed the tracks and the dunes as much as he did. Perhaps more importantly, with increasing numbers of visitors the authorities that administered the Ravenglass colony put more restrictions on him and his students as to what they could and could not do in the gullery, and the gullery even got a resident warden. But what I think was the general reason for the move was that Niko had rather run out of ideas for research in Ravenglass. He began to lose the peace of mind that he needed for his 'watching and wondering'. Less and less was he inclined to sit on his own in an observation hide amongst the birds, and more often he needed company. There was a clear waning in his passion for discovery of animal behaviour, and his stream of questions for the Ravenglass black-headed gull colony was drying up.

Ravenglass had given a massive boost to Niko's reputation as an ethologist, and with his field and experimental studies on the survival value of behaviour he had pushed the science in a new direction. It was studies such as the Ravenglass projects that only a few years later would be called 'behavioural ecology'. Looking back, one is struck by the absence of ecology and ecologists in the Ravenglass camp, and if some of David Lack's or Charles Elton's colleagues and students had been involved, perhaps the subsequent decline and demise of the Ravenglass gullery could have been documented and understood. This fell outside the expertise of ethologists. Furthermore, ecologists could also have given behavioural ecology an earlier start. However, all this will always remain speculation.

After his major review of the science, Niko seemed to have few ideas about what to do next on a more practical level. He made up for his lack of research ideas by becoming a film-maker. At that time, more than anything he wanted to film the birds that had started him off on his career, the large gulls, and Walney was the place for that. The sands of Ravenglass would never be far from his mind, though, and he often came back in later years on short visits. After his retirement Niko became friendly with the warden who, during the breeding season, lived in the dunes in his own caravan. Major Jimmy Rose was of similar age, and, like Niko, a totally dedicated naturalist. Throughout the rest of Niko's life they maintained a close relationship, with many a walk in the dunes, and frequent long letters between them.

Walney had a gigantic colony of herring gulls and the very similar lesser black-backed gulls, but it had little of the rich tapestry of Ravenglass. The colony, some 80 000 pairs of gulls, was at the south end of Walney Island, reachable via a bridge in the drab industrial town of Barrow-in-Furness, about

50 kilometres south of Ravenglass. Old gravel pits, derelict cottages, a huge rubbish dump next to the colony (probably the reason why the gulls were there): they were all very unattractive, but the birds, an old castle ruin, and the mudflats provided some compensation. There were some abandoned terraced cottages of former lighthouse-keepers, right on the edge of the colonies, which became the head-quarters for Niko and his group. With the entire set-up came Walter Shepherd, the warden, a delightful old man who loved it all, a friend to Niko and the birds and the students.

There had been an Oxford presence on Walney since the early 1960s. After he finished his PhD on the Ravenglass skylarks in 1961, Juan Delius had been asked by Niko to start a neurophysiological research project in Oxford (see below), and Juan took on another earlier product of the Tinbergen group, Dick Brown (who had previously worked on fruit flies). For a couple of years Dick was to study in the field the species that Juan worked on in the lab: the herring gull. He pioneered Walney research, and frequently we, from Ravenglass, had gone to visit him or vice versa. Niko did not have much in common with Dick and his work: Dick was a highly erudite man, deeply religious, a night-owl, and given to English literature rather than to early-morning natural history.

Not long after the end of Dick's stay on Walney Niko himself took on the gull colony as a field study area, although science was less of an attraction for him there than the possibilities for filming. From 1966 until the early 1970s he maintained a presence in the Walney field station through one or two students and post-docs. Initially he intended to get a group of people going on Walney that would have a deliberate international flavour, and which would represent more disciplines than just straight ethology: it was a strategy to broaden the appeal of ethology into other fields. And true enough, over the next few years he had

Pair of lesser-black-backed gulls, male 'facing away'. Walney, 1967. Photo Niko Tinbergen.

two American anthropologists working there (Barbara and Mike Robertson), as well as a British ethology student (Gill Thomson), and a bit later an American psychology student (Lary Shaffer), another American ethologist (Joe Galusha), and a Dutch undergraduate student (Niko's nephew Joost, son of Luuk).

The Robertsons studied synchronization of laying between gulls in different parts of the colony, there was a study on the exact characteristics of egg camouflage, and several projects investigated the function (effect) of various displays of the gulls. To Lary Shaffer Niko initially suggested a study almost exactly like the one of Bob Mash on the black-headed gull, but this time on the herring gull, using electrical, moving gull models. Lary tried this and turned away from it, as he had no confidence in the Mash models. Instead, Lary ended up with something quite different. Remarkably, of all the Walney projects, the only one in which Niko took a serious interest was that of Lary. This was a study on the interaction between gulls and crabs, especially on the way in which the gulls found the large edible crabs when they were buried in the sand at low tide (Niko and Lies had discovered this when walking along the beach). Niko was full of enthusiasm for the way in which individual gulls, who specialized in this, used minute signs in the sand that betrayed the crabs, and he loved going out with Lary and photographing these things. For the other projects he made some suggestions, he talked to the people who were doing them, but on his part there was little real involvement any more.

Niko was now about 60 years old, and becoming rather frail; and he had problems. Ever since the war he had had depressions, miserable but manageable, but worsening gradually in the Ravenglass days. More or less coinciding with his running out of ideas there, the huge, black periods of misery began to run out of control. When he told me about it in the early 1960s, he worried that he might be prone to the same fate as his younger brother; he experienced these terrible, indescribable, and uncontrollable deep black holes, lasting days on end, later even weeks. He felt mentally blocked up, totally inadequate, there was no way out, and he wanted to see no-one. Depressions run in the Tinbergen family, and some of Niko's children also suffer, although nowadays the affliction can be kept under control with medication.

Lary Shaffer described a typical depression in the Walney days:

> He was there without Lies for a couple of days, and he said to us, 'I just need to withdraw. I just cannot do this, things just are not going well for me. I'll just come and go to suit myself, don't worry about me'. I asked 'Do you want me to bring you food? I'll get you anything.' 'No, no, no, I have everything I need in the caravan.' He had the old Ravenglass caravan up there next to our cottages, and he could heat water so he could make coffee. For those couple of days he lived on coffee and chocolate bars (which he was wont to do a lot of the time anyway). Then Lies came up from Oxford and took care of him, making some food, a sandwich or something and taking it to him. I didn't get a chance to see him, because he was in his caravan, curtains closed, and that was it.[16]

The depressions came back again and again, sometimes month after month. They were ghastly visitations that, because of their severity, affected everyone around him. For Lies these were difficult times, with Niko very dependent on her and gradually getting worse. Strangely, at one stage in the late 1960s, he developed a crush on one of the PhD students, whom subsequently he put in charge of the Walney field station (where she put everyone's back up by being less than efficient, not very tactful, and not very bright). When, inevitably, he confessed to Lies she firmly took charge and made him remove the girl from Walney and Oxford. Characteristically, he told everyone in the group how silly he had been. Walney was not a happy place for Niko.

After he finished filming in Walney in 1968 he only came over occasionally and briefly, although he still supervised one or two students there. One of these was Joe Galusha, with a PhD study on the functions of displays, the same theme as that of Niko's film, *Signals for survival* (see below). There were few new ideas, and the scientific impetus was gone. For the last few years before his retirement in 1974 he left research on Walney to me and my students. We started projects in a different direction, on the learning of anti-predator behaviour by gulls, and on their cannibalism. Niko paid just the odd visit.

Serengeti

Through these 1960s years of dunes and gulls is braided another strand of Niko's life as a naturalist: his exposure to East Africa. Niko came to Africa by a fluke of chance, with no-one better to grab such an opportunity than him. During my own time in Oxford, just after I had finished one of the field seasons in Ravenglass in 1963, a highly inspiring man gave a lecture in the Zoology Department in Oxford. This was John Owen, a former Oxford undergraduate and now the director of the Tanganyika national parks, who came to talk about his country and his ambitions. He needed help: the Tanganyikan government wanted to cull the herds of wildebeest, zebra, and gazelle in the Serengeti for local consumption, and there was no information to predict the impact on the ecosystem. The leopards, lions, and other carnivores that fed on the grazing animals were especially likely to be affected, and they were the main tourist attraction. I went to talk to him afterwards, and we agreed that after I had finished my PhD my wife and I would go to the Serengeti to study the carnivores. John Owen was confident that he would get the money from the Dutch government. Niko sat in on our meeting, smiling and smoking, and the upshot of it all was that a year or so later he came to stay with us, in our small wooden bungalow right in the heart of the Serengeti.

Almost every year from 1964 to 1969, Niko visited for three or four weeks. The immediate threat of culling the game herds had been lifted due to international pressure, and I had narrowed the subject of my study to just spotted hyaenas (which were the most important predators on the Serengeti herds).

Niko joined me, following the hyaenas on my night and dawn trips in the Land-Rover, or I took him up in the small plane, over what must be the most diverse and dramatic wildlife spectacle in the world. Every time he was struck dumb by the animals, and by all the fascinating new behaviour that we saw, things that had never been described before.

The opportunities for observation of animals were fabulous. Typically, he wrote: 'Just yesterday [I saw] a mother cheetah with two almost fully grown cubs. She caught a young antelope, carried it alive to the young, who played with the poor thing, running after it and bringing it down without being able to kill it. Then the mother killed it with one blow, and the family sat down to have their breakfast.'[17] Niko had never had much to do with mammals, and here he was in close contact with large numbers of vastly different individuals, mammals that seemed to behave in much more complicated ways than the birds and insects he had tackled with his ethological studies.

The Serengeti is huge, and we also covered the stunning beauty of the neighbouring Ngorongoro Crater, with the freedom to roam the grassland plains wherever we wanted to go in the Land-Rover. The literally millions of animals, of many species, were all around and largely ignored us. To anyone this would be a staggering experience, and it obviously and profoundly affected Niko. As he said himself, it affected him as deeply as Greenland had done: the Serengeti often brought Greenland days back to him.

Interestingly, Niko was often taken at least as much with the small signs of African life as with the large mammals. He spent hours photographing a large stick-insect, or observing the many different dung beetles, a displaying agama lizard, or the gall-ants in the acacias. He was an incredibly sharp observer, but, just as I had noticed in the Ravenglass days, he was no longer so keenly inclined to question, to wonder why. He was no longer inclined to see research projects everywhere, and never once did he make any suggestions for ethological studies in the Serengeti. The national park called for ecological research rather than behavioural studies, and this was not Niko's forte. Yet his input in the research was as useful and important as ever: he stood behind us, asking what we were doing and why, and he commented on it. He forced us into clarity, and to get our questions straight.

Niko was a very welcome, fatherly guest in our house, and Lies also came once. He was so bubbling with enthusiasm about everything, and he was game for any trip or expedition. His delight was very infectious; it certainly made me realize how incredibly lucky we were to live in such a wonderful place. As a guest he could also have his difficult sides. He always insisted on knowing long beforehand what we were going to do (which in Africa is not easy), he spent most of one bread-and-butter letter on telling me off for driving too fast, and he hated our occasional 'waste of time'. But then all was made up again with his jolliness, and the fun he brought with his marvelling at the birds, or at Solomon (our pet hyaena), or at the wildebeest calves that seemed to tell him 'I've made it, I've made it, I'm three days old', or with his delight when the wild hyaenas had to defaecate when I woke them from their very long slumber.

During one of his visits he was invited to go and see the 'elephant camp' where Iain Douglas Hamilton lived in nearby Manyara, and where Iain took him (on foot) to within almost touching distance of his gentle giants. Again Niko was totally overcome by the individuality of the wild animals, and he felt proud of himself for daring to go so close to possible danger. Iain was doing a fascinating study of the family structure and behaviour of the elephants, and he asked Niko to accept it as a PhD project. Niko gladly took it on, although he left the practical side of the supervision largely to me.

In Africa for the first time, when watching all the large mammals, Niko was confronted with the differences between individuals amongst wild animals. It was something he had known about, of course, but it had never really affected his views: the animal behaviour he had seen was mostly species-specific. I think that he never properly engaged with this experience, and with the implications of individual differences for evolution of behaviour. Perhaps it all came too late for him; it was later to be the domain of behavioural ecology.

Within a few years, the initial presence of three scientists in the Serengeti grew into the Serengeti Research Institute. It acquired substantial buildings, more than 15 scientists, many assistants, and several small planes: all of this was initiated by the German conservationist Bernhard Grzimek, and realized largely by John Owen. Not only was John an excellent naturalist and conservationist

The Serengeti experience, 1964. Photo Niko Tinbergen.

extraordinaire, he was also a formidable fund-raiser and a charmer, and money flowed in from Germany, the United States, Canada, and elsewhere. There was much first-class ecological research carried out there, attracting a great deal of attention to the Serengeti as well as providing a basis for proper management.

After a couple of visits to the Serengeti, Niko was asked by John Owen to become chairman of the international supervisory body for the research institute, the Scientific Council. Despite not being an ecologist, he was obviously very pleased to accept, and for about three years was closely involved in decisions about research policy there. He clearly played an important role in putting the Serengeti research on the map in the late 1960s; amongst others, he arranged for two more of his former Ravenglass students – Mike Norton-Griffiths and Harvey Croze – to join after they had earned their PhDs. They did ecological, management-oriented research rather than studies of animal behaviour. As a neat finishing touch, it was due to Niko's efforts that John Owen was presented with an honorary Doctorate of Science by Oxford University.

The end of Niko's African involvement was rather sad. In 1967 he was persuaded to give a series of lectures in Nairobi, the nearest university to the Serengeti. He stayed in a hotel, he was lonely, and he suffered a serious nervous breakdown, coming near to suicide. One of the lecturers there, Malcolm Coe, took care of him and put him back on the plane to Britain and psychiatric care. After this he came back to the Serengeti once more, in early 1969, but his heart was not in it. He felt he was too much of an observer rather than a participant, he could not just come for what he saw was for him pure enjoyment, and given the pressures of work in his other world, in Oxford, he decided to cut out his Serengeti commitments. These were continued by his first student, Gerard Baerends.

Photography and filming

Walking in the dunes or driving through herds of wildebeest, Niko would always have a camera around his neck. Taking pictures satisfied his hunting instincts, and although he justified it to himself and anyone who would listen that he did it to illustrate science, and to let others share in his experiences, in the end he would admit that he simply followed a rather primitive urge. He was also very good at it. His sketches showed that he was a skilled artist, 'displaying the essence of behaviour with a remarkable economy of line ... and as a boy, he yearned to produce photographs which could accurately capture much more detail than the drawings he was making'.[18]

Following the early years' struggles with bulky plate cameras and primitive lenses, Niko slowly graduated to better equipment. He always had a good state-of-the-art camera (such as a Rolleiflex, later an Alpa-Alnea) but camera quality improved all the time, and after his move to Britain he acquired a Nikon, a standard camera for professionals. Bird behaviour from observation hides, animal tracks in the sand, a moth on a twig, landscapes, scientists at work, children – he took literally thousands of pictures. Until the 1960s these were nearly all in black and white, but thereafter gradually mostly in colour. He always developed and printed his black-and-white photographs himself, and despite the fact that he was not a very practical person in the do-it-yourself sense (he could not hammer a straight nail), he was a master in the darkroom. In the late 1960s he taught darkroom skills to Lary Shaffer, his American student on Walney:

> I remember this like it was yesterday. We went to the darkroom, which was in the front of the old zoo department. It was the department darkroom and it was a mess. Niko was angry about it because somebody had left a bunch of prints washing and they were just dissolving because they'd been there for three days. He threw all that in the waste basket and was spitting and snarling. He said he'd show me with a couple of films that he wanted developed of his own, then

he'd stay and watch me through mine, to help if I had questions. Of course he lit his cigarette and he was leaning over the dishes with this long ash hanging off which never fell in, and he showed me how to develop and print. He showed me everything except his years and years and years of experience. Because he would pull these gorgeous prints off first time really, just having a look at them, and not using a timer under the enlarger, just sticking his hand under the enlarger. Not using print tongs, just sticking his hands in the dishes which he liked to do, one hand for the fix and one hand for the developer, and then wash them in the water that was all over them. I remember he told me that if you get the liquids poured out in the dishes and you forget which was which, if you stick your finger in the fixer it tastes a little salty. That's how you can tell which that is. …too bad if you got a blister. I decided I'd just pay attention as to which was which. Anyway he showed me developing and printing and then he made a few beautiful prints and then left me to my own devices.[19]

Niko's black-and-white prints were splendid, and although he never went in for competitions, he was widely known for his photographs. This was not just because they were technically and aesthetically good, but also because they were interesting. Niko always insisted that a photograph should tell a story, and, dating from his Dutch NJN years, he had the greatest contempt, for instance, for portraits of birds just sitting on nests, the product of the average bird photographer. He saw a story whilst he watched a bird, and that is what he wanted from a print. He often sent his photographs to his friends as Christmas cards, or just at any old time. He was certainly very aware of the fact that part of his success with his publications and lectures was due to his skills with his camera. Photography was an important tool of Niko the communicator.

Photography was also a stepping stone to something in which he could claim even greater success, and for which he would be recognized with one of the greatest prizes in the business. During his first 10 years in Oxford Niko's still photography began to expand into filming. His film-making climaxed in the mid- and late 1960s when, for a while, cinematography took over from his science.

In Holland ever since the war, and later in Oxford, Niko had been content with making short, documentary films about his research and that of his students, first helping other cameramen, and then on his own. Films were useful in his lectures, but they were primitive: silent, mostly black and white, pictures interspersed with text messages, or dependent entirely on a spoken commentary by the lecturer. The equipment was simple, tele-lenses were cumbersome and used sparingly, and zoom lenses were almost unknown, so images of birds were small, and there was little panning and few changes of the angle of photography. These films were often about the results, rather than about the process of research: films about the displays of the black-headed gulls and kittiwakes, about the peppered moth and its melanism, about the life of the eider duck, and about many other subjects. But all of them told a story, despite the fact that Niko himself later used to say rather dismissively that they were no more than animated stills.

Gradually Niko's techniques and equipment improved, and he was determined to keep up the supply of teaching films for his lectures in Oxford, especially when he was doing research in highly photogenic Ravenglass. Then, just at that time in the early 1960s, there were three simultaneous developments that determined the rest of his cinematographic career. Firstly, there was the emergence of television, which greatly widened the scope for nature films. Secondly, Niko began to run out of inspiration and drive to do research himself, and filming became his major interest instead. Thirdly, Hugh Falkus came into his orbit, a man with some resemblance to Konrad Lorenz.

Hugh Falkus lived in a cottage close to the Ravenglass gullery. He was a large man with blond curly hair, a bit younger than Niko. He had a full life of acting, piloting, and shark fishing behind him; he was a great raconteur, a heavy drinker, a man with a tremendous ego, an author and national authority on salmon and trout fishing, and at the time a film director, often working for the BBC. At the time he was doing a series of short TV films on life in Cumberland ('Five minutes with Hugh Falkus'), and in the pub he heard about the Ravenglass goings-on of Oxford students. He waded across the estuary and came to see us, wanting to do a few of his little programmes on our research there. He did four, and we all loved them.

Niko was very taken by Hugh and rather liked the idea of more publicity, so they decided to expand, and do a series of three half-hour films on our research-in-action. We helped him script out research and acted our parts, Niko advised the cameraman with the bird shots and provided some film himself, and Hugh did the commentary. This gave rise to *The gull watchers*, *The sign readers*, and *The beach combers*.[20] According to John Sparks, a BBC professional in natural history films, 'The films were lessons in clear, popular scientific exposition, and full of simple revelation … a breath of fresh air … I have to tell you that the intellectual level of natural history programmes has now sadly dropped well below the standards of those shows!'[21] They were a great success, and even decades later were still used in lectures on animal behaviour.

Apart from the welcome publicity for his research group, what especially impressed Niko was what he learned from Hugh, who was a superb communicator, and who knew how to use the medium of film on television like nobody else. On his own Niko did another one of his educational films in 1965, this time in colour on the research by Harvey Croze: *Crafty predators and cryptic prey*. The result was a tremendous improvement on previous efforts, a fast-moving story, still silent but showing the research in action mixed with good close-ups of crows as predators and spectacular sand landscapes, with research results shown as graphs in sand, or fingers pointing at models. It impressed the viewer with the fascinating detection and learning abilities of crows, and with the ingenious experiments carried out in the field with wild and tame birds.

However, even when he was shooting this, Niko realized his limitations. He

Niko Tinbergen and Hugh Falkus, Ravenglass, 1968. Photo Lary Shaffer.

knew that there were tremendous possibilities beyond what he was doing there, and in 1966 he teamed up with Hugh Falkus to make a major research film, on what Niko himself saw as one of the pinnacles of his scientific achievement. Niko would provide the science and do the camera work, Hugh would write the script and direct the entire story, and he would tell Niko what was needed in order to get the message across. This was the birth of *Signals for survival*.

Signals was about the language of birds, about their displays and what these displays meant, what messages they carried to other birds. It was a prime piece of ethological estate. They decided not to film it on the black-headed gulls in Ravenglass, because the warden there put more and more restrictions on what they could and couldn't do in the colony, and in any case Niko's research there was running out of steam. Niko and his students moved over to Walney, and of the two gulls breeding there in about equal profusion they decided not to select Niko's old love the herring gull, but the very similar and slightly more photogenic lesser black-backed gull.

For two full breeding seasons Niko filmed, while Hugh hectored and admonished and honed the script. 'Niko trooped out to the hides with Hugh's lists of specific shots that would be needed: close up head and shoulders of gulls facing left, medium shot of mated pair with grass background, and so on'.[22] 'Hugh really treated him like a schoolboy during *Signals*'.[23] But Niko loved it, and even now, seeing Lary Shaffer's photographs of him behind his camera in utter concentration is seeing Niko at his very best, as another, different Maestro. The end product was a world away from anything Niko had produced before.

The film opens with Niko talking to camera, obviously slightly nervous. He makes an aggressive face and waves his fist: 'If I do this, you understand immediately what I mean. Birds have a similar kind of language.' This is the last we see of him. He sets the scene with excellent mixes of close-ups of gulls and landscapes, several striking displays without commentary, then a pan through the gull community. Hugh narrates, and explains how this entire social structure depends on communication – demonstrating their point in smooth transfers between individual displays and the large colony, a spectacular fight, a sequence on 'the language of love'. Displays are explained, their function demonstrated as far as one can take it without experiments. The film pursues the story until chicks hatch, and fly off over the mudflats. *Signals* is about a common bird in a common landscape, beautifully shot and presented, a full 50 minutes of fascinating behaviour.

The film was shown on BBC television in 1968, and long afterwards the BBC's John Sparks commented:

> *Once again, Hugh's script was first class – slowly unravelling the language of this gull. There was some doubt as to whether the audience would sit through such a long film – but they did (they might not today – or so we are led to believe) and the programme was considered to be a triumph. ... the BBC selected it as an entry for the Italia Prize – a prestigious TV award – and it won much to everyone's surprise. It is the only time the BBC Natural History Unit has ever won it – even 'Life on Earth' got nowhere. Signals also won a coveted prize in the USA, the 'Blue Ribbon Award'. The filming was all or very nearly all Niko's, and frankly, it was not up to the standard of one of the top wildlife film makers of today. But, when mated with Hugh's story-line – and in this case with BBC sound recorded by John Burton, Signals for Survival must rate as one of the all-time classics.[24]*

The film was followed by a picture book of the same title, mostly still photographs by Niko, a little text by him and Hugh Falkus, and drawings by Eric Ennion.[25]

To receive the Italia Prize in 1969, the top prize for TV documentaries, was a triumph, and Niko sometimes said that he relished it even more than his later Nobel Prize. They were both over the moon with it, and the fact that, at least up to the present, the world-renowned BBC Natural History Unit has not been able to win it again, indicates how outstanding the achievement was of Niko and Hugh Falkus.

It was a climax, followed by a total and permanent cut-off. Fairly soon after these events Niko broke off his friendly relationship with Hugh. He had enough of him. Hugh's ebullient and pompous personality did not really suit Niko at all, and he told Hugh: 'We reached the peak of what we as a team could do, then decided to each follow our own lives. Let's keep it like that. We rub each other the wrong way, or at least you upset me. Let's not try and start anything together again, for that would lead to disaster.'[26] In any case, Niko had learned enough about editing and directing skills to be able to go it alone. But sadly, he would not use this for any further films of his own: almost immediately after *Signals* Niko stopped filming, for good, and he only occasionally touched a film camera again. He was still greatly and very influentially involved with a film that Lary Shaffer was making about sheepdogs, but this was no longer front line, it was looking over Lary's shoulder, murmuring advice.

No-one completely understood why Niko threw in the cinematographic towel just after his enormous success. In a letter he once wrote that he had many good reasons to make *Signals*, such as demonstrating the need for research on the biological function of behaviour, and showing that without displays reproduction would be impossible. He wanted to bring the subject to people other than ethologists, and to show the BBC that providing more scientific content for natural history films is both possible and popular. But then in the end he admitted (trans.): 'this is all rationalization for my filming, which really I do because I enjoy it'.[27] Again, it was Niko the hunter.

If he really did it just for the fun of it, then why give up? Perhaps his success interfered with his enjoyment, perhaps he was concerned about not being able to show again the expertise that he thought was now expected from him, a reaction that would be similar to the one after his Nobel Prize. Perhaps he just felt age creeping up, with increasing problems for the steady hand that was needed. Undoubtedly important was that he had found a film soul-mate in his PhD student Lary Shaffer, whom Niko liked immensely and whom he taught to film – Lary was a good cameraman, much more interested in filming than in his PhD work. Standing behind Lary, Niko could get at least some of the thrills that he experienced when operating the camera himself.

Teaching Lary. Walney, 1969. Photo Beth Shaffer.

He did not quite give up completely on the organizational side of filming. On the heels of the international recognition for *Signals*, Niko was approached by the BBC and Time/Life to do a series of 13 half-hour television programmes, to be called 'Behaviour and survival'. They wanted Niko to supervise the series and make as many programmes as he could. In the end, Niko did almost no filming for this, but he used some of his old material dating back to Ravenglass days. Around 1970 he wrote, directed, and edited the filming of three of the programmes (for example one on oystercatchers, *The mussel specialist*, and one on tracks in the sand and mud, both filmed mostly by Lary Shaffer), and he set up and edited most of the rest (on animals such as the elephant, the impala, and others).

All these activities took place in university time. But the programmes took a lot out of Niko, they involved much effort and acrimony between him, the paymasters, and the scientists and film-makers. He told Desmond Morris: 'The collaboration with all the different experts, script writers and those crazy professional TV people – all wanting something different, all knowing best, and all watering down our stories – has been a nightmare, and although we have some nice films in the series, none of the films is of the type and quality I had been after.'[28] He was always bitter about these films, but they did well on television, and twenty years later they were still being shown and used for educational purposes.[29]

Oxford academia again, Niko's other world

Niko's ground-floor room in the Department of Zoology had a large window, totally overshadowed by a rather gloomy neighbouring building, the Department of Biochemistry. It was a grim view, in a way particularly apposite because that department housed the laboratory of Dorothy Hodgkin, who in 1963, during Niko's time there, was awarded the Nobel Prize for chemistry for her discovery of the structure of insulin. Her biography[30] highlights the fanatical race between her and several others to get the prize, the annual disappointments and dismay when she had been overlooked again, the letters of commiseration and the sense of injustice until, at last, there it was. Such towering ambition for scientific recognition was and is a dominant element in the university, especially Oxford, and it was anathema to Niko. It went entirely against his natural sense of modesty, and it was an affront to his Dutch Calvinistic background. Although he had his aspirations, he despised this particular kind of naked ambition. In consequence, this may have been part of the reason why he himself was rejected by the Oxford establishment (or perceived himself to be).

What made one smile afterwards was the fact that it was Niko, more than any of his colleagues, who carried off the prizes, not only the Nobel Prize at a later date, but also many other awards and medals. Prominent on the list was his appointment as Fellow of the Royal Society, at the age of 55 in 1962, the

*Conferment of Honorary
Doctorate on Ernst Mayr,
Oxford 1966. Left to right:
Niko Tinbergen, Ernst Mayr,
and David Lack, in the garden of
Trinity College.
Courtesy of the Tinbergen family.*

ultimate British accolade in science. At the time he was still a Reader, and Oxford did not even recognize his Dutch degrees. In Oxford it was a plain Mister Tinbergen who gained the highest distinction, and he was not easily for-given. 'FRSes first', said his colleague Arthur Cain slightly sourly when, during a meeting in the Serengeti office, the two arrived at a door simultaneously.

Niko was proud of his FRS, and he asked Baerends to make sure that it would be published in the Dutch *Vakblad* [Bulletin for Professional Biologists]: 'I know that there are colleagues who think that I have been shunted out, others believe fieldwork to be merely play'.[31]

There were numerous other distinctions, and during the 1960s, well before he received the ultimate prize, he became Foreign Member of the Royal Dutch Academy of Science, the American Academy of Arts and Sciences, the German Max-Planck Gesellschaft, the American Society of Zoologists, the German Akademie für Naturforscher Leopoldina, Honorary Member of the Asso-ciation for the Study of Animal Behaviour of the German and the Danish Ornithological Society, Corresponding Fellow of the American Museum of Natural History, the Finnish Society for Flora and Fauna, the American Ornithological Union, the Netherlands Ornithological Union, and the South African Ornithological Union. He received the prestigious Godman-Salvin Medal of the British Ornithological Union, he was Secretary-General of the 14th International Ornithological Congress in 1966 and subsequently its President, he received the Italia Prize for Documentaries, and there were more (and even more to follow later).

Praise was accompanied by requests. The demand from universities for Niko's lecturing and writing skills never let up, to his pride and embarrassment. Here is just a sample of such demands, in chronological order, from the years between 1962 and 1968 and involving either series of lectures or single ones: they came from universities in Oslo, Arkansas, Michigan, Otago (New Zealand), Washington, Newark (USA), New York, Berkeley, Ibadan (Nigeria), Sassari (Italy), Rome, Seewiesen (Germany), Warsaw, Texas, Salamanca (Spain), McGill Toronto, McGill Montreal, Illinois, Massachusetts, Texas, Ohio, San Francisco, Vancouver, Amsterdam, Leiden, Cape Town, Liege (Belgium), Washington, New York, Santa Cruz (USA), Santa Barbara (USA), Dublin – and there may have been more. Virtually all of these invitations were turned down by him. 'Since my Science article [On war and peace in animals and man, see below] I received some twenty new requests [from publishers] for books, and over twenty requests for visiting professorships etc. from the New World.'[32]

Oxford University rather belatedly responded to the flood of distinctions by appointing Niko Professor in Animal Behaviour in 1966, and he was quietly pleased about that ('good for ethology', but there was also the element of being recognized in his own department). And his other connections with the university were put on a more satisfactory footing: in 1966 he resigned from Merton College, and instead Isaiah Berlin, the President of Wolfson College, offered him a Professorial Fellowship in his modern, post-graduate college without the airs and graces and many of the Oxford hang-ups that Niko resented.

In the meantime the head of department, who had attracted and protected Niko there, retired in 1961. Sir Alister Hardy had been one of Niko's kind, a naturalist and a man full of ideas and ventures; Niko was to miss him dearly. They kept in contact, with Hardy keeping up a stream of fascinating suggestions in his letters, such as the idea that mankind evolved in a semi-aquatic environment, or that zebra stripes had evolved to cause miscalculation of distance by an attacking lion, and about his involvement with parapsychology (Hardy had initiated his own unofficial Institute of Parapsychology, and asked Niko to be examiner of theses, which Niko loathed). But within the Zoology Department the scenery changed dramatically, with the appointment of John Pringle as head.

Pringle was an austere and rather charmless man, an insect physiologist, who saw as one of his main missions the replacement of the old zoology building by a new, much larger, and more appropriate one. Just to find a new site was an effort that took years: strings were pulled to be able to build in the green belt around the science area, the all-powerful university Congregation had to vote and rejected it, strings were pulled again, and finally approval was given for a huge concrete building housing both Zoology and Experimental Psychology. The structure must surely count as one of the ugliest in Oxford, although it won a prize from the British Concrete Society.

Niko helped Pringle where he could, with intensive lobbying and in many meetings; he expected advantages for his own group in more space, and better

Staff around the head of department: Zoology, Oxford, 1962. Left to right: secretary Jane Birkbeck (later Kruuk), Sheila O'Clarey (Niko's secretary), David Nichols, Edward Needham, Harold Pusey, John Pringle, Henry Ford, Will Holmes, Arthur Cain, Niko Tinbergen, and Peggy Varley. Photographer unknown.

integration with other groups such as the ecologists (and never mind the infringement of the green belt). His rewards were rather thin. When finally in 1969 and 1970 everybody abandoned the old department and the animal behaviour annexe (in Bevington Road, of which more later), and moved into New Zoology, Niko's group saw a reduction in its space. Perhaps they had more modern comforts, but the work environment had lost much of its old-world and almost inspirational charm.

Another enterprise in which Niko left an important mark on the university was the setting up of a completely new undergraduate course of study, in which ethology played a substantial role. Robert Hinde described it:

> [Niko] joined J. W. S. Pringle and G. A. Harrison, the professor of Anthropology, in promoting and eventually establishing a course in Human Sciences at Oxford. This was an especially remarkable move on his part in that he normally eschewed university politics ... and establishing Human Biology was no small enterprise. The initial steering group met weekly during term time for 18 months, exploring ways of integrating aspects of biological, psychological and social sciences. There was enormous opposition to the establishment of the course from both the university and the colleges, and it was made the subject of the first postal vote in Oxford. Tinbergen played a very active part in the canvassing necessary to win that vote.[33]

The Human Science course became a highly successful addition to the Oxford curriculum.

Afterwards Pringle never had much more time for Niko. He seemed impervious to Niko's successes and personality, possibly rather envious. He even told Niko to pay for his own stamps for his duties as assistant editor of *Behaviour*. After Niko's retirement, Pringle would be instrumental in the dismantling of Niko's ethology in Oxford. But as an ironic twist, more than 30 years after its building and long after both John Pringle and Niko had died, the concrete fortress would be named the Niko Tinbergen Building.

All this was to come, but in the early 1960s Niko himself had his smoke-filled room in the rambling, charming, but inefficient Old Zoology building, where he involved himself and got irritated with university policy, and where he wrote, endlessly. His secretary communicated with him through a hatch, but all of his group, his students, and visitors were elsewhere. Niko had several secretaries in succession: Sheila O'Clarey, Ann Freeman-Taylor, and for a long time, Pat Searle. They mothered him, they mothered his students, and they are warmly remembered. Niko was the type who asked for it; he did not know how to use a secretary, he wanted to type all his letters himself (partly justified by his large correspondence in other languages which only he could manage), he would not dictate, and he always felt highly apologetic if he had to ask her to arrange his large collection of reprints, or organize a meeting. But somehow, his secretary sorted him out, she kept the students out of his hair if needed, she covered up for his long absences from the lab and his highly unusual hours, she knew of his depressions and when there was a tear in his eye, she knew of problems with the children and what he was planting in the garden, and she was a friend of the family. Niko used to write long, personal letters to Sheila, Ann, or Pat when he was away.

The Group, as his PhD students began to refer to themselves, were rather distant from all this. In the late 1950s Alister Hardy had agreed that Niko needed more accommodation, and he came up with the idea of an 'annexe', a building separate from the main department to house the behaviour group, just as the ornithologists (Edward Grey Institute) and the ecologists (Bureau of Animal Populations) were separate. In 1961 this was realized in a typical North Oxford house, in Bevington Road, about five minutes walk from the main department and usually referred to as 'Bevvers'. It was ideal for the job, a free-standing, early 1920s house in its own small garden on a quiet street corner, with 14 rooms spread over four floors and a basement. The Maestro and departmental admin-istration were elsewhere, Mrs Lloyd the cleaner was everybody's best friend, there was a chaotic kitchen where people came with their lunches and cooked and debated and received visitors, in a pleasant messiness with a great atmo-sphere. There were students, like me, who worked there after their months of fieldwork, others who did their entire project in Bevvers, and there was a general coming and going, full of news and full of enthusiasm. We felt that we were doing frontline science.

It was only a few years after the Hard Core, and the Group had developed its own ethos and structure, very much affected by the characters of the time. Mike Cullen was the most important influence, and, of course, there was The Maestro himself. He did not often come to Bevvers, but he pressed everybody there to come every day to the main department for morning coffee, a request that was often ignored. The department was something very distant, and often that included Niko himself – when he was at the department there was little chance of talking seriously to him, or of even a casual conversation. Discussions with him had to be booked through the secretary.

Niko's contact with his crew suffered from his isolation. To be sure, the Group did well. Students were clamouring to join, there were frequently important visitors, theses and papers were being written, conferences attended, there were seminars and parties – everyone who passed through Bevvers is full of memories of the behaviour annexe. The Maestro was felt as a rarely seen presence, though somehow exercising a strong influence. However, immediate contact with his students was minimal, at least there in Oxford – those of us who worked with him in the field were much more fortunate. When I wrote my thesis in Bevvers in 1963, Niko glanced through it rather cursorily, and he came up with only a few small comments; the sessions I had with him in the hide in Ravenglass were much more important. Ian Patterson fared similarly, although Niko added a couple of important paragraphs to his thesis.

Our contemporary, Bryan Nelson, did his field research on gannets, on a small Scottish island, the Bass Rock; Niko visited him several times and they had an intensive contact, with Niko full of ideas about the significance of the gannet's displays. But for Bryan the most important guidance and comments on his thesis came from Mike Cullen. Niko made general comments: from a thesis or a paper he wanted a story, he wanted a clear problem at the start, results, and a clear finish. 'You've got to help the poor reader', he said, even for a highly specialized scientific paper. Mike was the one who delved into the science, who discussed statistics in detail, and who evaluated literature that we used in our writings.

Other students of Niko who passed through Bevvers, apart from the various people who worked on Walney and in Ravenglass, included Mike Robinson, Mike Hansell, Heather Kneale, Richard Dawkins, and Marian Stamp. Mike Hansell and Mike Robinson both started their PhDs in 1963 on insect projects, Mike H. studying the building behaviour of caddis-fly larvae, and Mike R. the rocking movements of stick-insects. As they said:

Niko may have wanted to revisit insect behaviour at a time when most of his interests were in Ravenglass ... he took a fairly hands-off approach to the project ... we used to have periodic and detailed progress meetings in his office, during which he spent more time rolling cigarettes than actually smoking them ... push me to clarify what I now proposed to do and why ... always encouraging me to be more experimental and to ask more important questions.[34]

Marian Stamp (later Marian Dawkins) did her thesis under Niko in years after 1966, on food searching behaviour (searching images) by chicks in captivity. Niko had expected her to follow up Harvey Croze's Ravenglass experiments with crows near Oxford, but Marian wanted to be able to control her animals, so she went a different way. Niko was interested, but it was not quite his cup of tea; it was entirely Marian's project, and she wrote it up not in Oxford, but in Berkeley.

Richard Dawkins' experience of Niko as a supervisor was also somewhat distant. He had been tutored by Niko as an undergraduate at Oxford, when Niko, as work assignments for Richard, would pull a doctoral thesis off his shelf and ask Richard to write an assessment as if he were the external examiner for it. Because of this experience, after graduating Richard abandoned plans to become a biochemist, and in 1962 started his doctorate project with Niko on the development of behaviour in chicks. But within a year he was bored with it and changed to making mathematical models of decision-making in animals. 'Which Niko knew nothing about and didn't understand but was very supportive, and at that point I pretty much in effect shifted to dear old Mike [Cullen], who so often acted as go-between. Mike was superbly equipped to supervise this research that I had moved into and so Niko, without rancour, surrendered me. He remained my official supervisor.'[35]

An important focal point for our science was the weekly seminar, deeply engraved on many a memory. Alas, the original Friday evenings at Niko's house had become too much of a burden on the family, and around 1960 they moved to a more academic venue, in the old Experimental Psychology building, where they were attended jointly by members of Niko's group and those of David Vowles, lecturer in animal behaviour in the Department of Experimental Psychology. Usually some 20-odd people attended, and there was still something homely about them; the most junior students had to organize the inevitable instant coffee (Richard Dawkins and I did it jointly for a few terms).

But there was nothing homely about the science in these seminars. The discussions were fierce, and if you could get your results and conclusions past those seminars, you were pretty safe. Niko always sat fairly far back, smoking, letting the others get on with it unless he felt he was really needed. 'What exactly is your question?' was one of his more predictable interventions. 'Could you please start with that, what do you want to know?' The next day, if one of his own students had given the seminar Niko would often write him or her a long, carefully argued letter about it, never pulling a punch. In the actual discussions, the younger members tended to be much more hard-hitting than Niko himself; they were a merciless, highly intelligent, and very articulate audience. Of course, such discussions were very much for the benefit of the speaker – but several times I saw people in tears after the treatment.

Bevington Road was alive with Niko's students, but Mike Cullen also had his own graduates there in those days, people who later would have prominent positions in academia or public services, such as Felicity Huntingford, John Krebs, and Linda Partridge. Mike really was the central figure in Bevvers; in the kitchen 'he would listen while eating his lunch from an old biscuit tin with a wire handle, one knee up, shoulders highly hunched, rocking back and forth with absorption'[36], dressed in his eternal red sweater. He would spend whole days on a student's problems, designing new methods to solve them and coming up with elegant mathematical solutions. In the face of science his personal life receded into the background, and Mike's entire life revolved around student projects. But he never asked for credit, and rarely even put his name on a paper. He was much more involved in the thesis of almost every single student than Niko ever was, and without him, the scientific activity of Niko's group would not have been anywhere near the level it reached with Mike. What Mike did not have was Niko's command of presentation, nor did he have the vision that we associate with a leader and an innovator of science.

Niko himself was happy with the arrangement for students. It was what he wanted, and he felt successful with his student output. There were jobs aplenty for his PhDs all over the world, and what especially pleased him was that his former students had developed well, each in his or her own niche. In 1968 he wrote (trans.):

> I just drew up a list of all my pupils from my English time and of the positions they have acquired in the world, and I saw that in these almost 20 years I have produced 35 doctors, of which the large majority now produces work that has its own stamp, different for each of them. And that is my pride; they are not His Masters Voice; there are quite a number of them, and all of them do work that is worthwhile ... more and more I am convinced that it is this that our sort of people should find satisfaction in.[37]

By the early 1960s there were several special projects running within Niko's group, apart from the usual student crowd. Central to all its activity was a grant from the British Nature Conservancy, which Niko had secured through the help of the very eminent Max Nicholson. The grant ran from the early 1960s right up to his retirement in 1974, and covered all Niko's fieldwork, the salaries of Mike Cullen and a secretary, a Land-Rover, and various other expenses, with almost no questions asked. It was wonderful support, a sign of the enormous confidence in Niko from outside the university. The second large project, rather surprisingly, came from the US Air Force, and it had an interesting history with a rather sad ending.

The Air Force involvement focussed on the physiology of behaviour, a subject that was expected to open up our understanding of the motivation of animals, and our causal analysis of behaviour. During one of the International Ethological Conferences, in Cambridge in the late 1950s, Niko had been very impressed by the research of Konrad Lorenz's friend Erich von Holst. These were neurophysiological studies of chickens, which demonstrated that several of the birds' behaviour patterns could be activated by electrical stimulation of different regions in the brain. This was the direction in which he wanted his own research group to go, but not with chickens. He wanted to have it done with gulls, the birds about which he knew so much, in the lab as well as in the field. It would be a major link between physiology and field observation, it would show the neurological basis of the birds' motivation of their displays and of other behaviour, a subject that was central to Niko's interest in the 1950s.

After Niko had abandoned his earlier ideas of an inter-university ethology institute with Robert Hinde, funded by the US Air Force, he managed to interest the Air Force in supporting a five-year project on brain stimulation and behaviour, starting in 1961. He appointed his former PhD student Juan Delius to lead it, Dick Brown to do the fieldwork in the gull colony, and some assistants. Just as in the appointment of students, there was no advertising of the positions; things were not done that way in those days. Niko knew a person whom he thought suitable or likeable, and took him or her on. Large aviaries were erected in the garden of Bevington Road with a population of 50 young herring gulls; experiments aimed to stimulate given parts of their brains with micro-electrodes and to measure their behaviour, and to provide a comparison of this with behaviour in the field.

The project was beset by problems from the beginning.[38] The neighbours complained about the very noisy and smelly gulls (not surprisingly, in suburban Oxford), the university had no planning permission to erect cages (but it was granted later), and the adult gulls were too wild and kept on bashing themselves against the sides of the cages. So the researchers had to work with juvenile gulls only, and these did not show any of the displays that one sees in the colony. Even the young birds often shook the electrodes off their heads. Dick went his own way in the fieldwork, and there was no collaboration with Juan. Niko lost interest fairly soon after the project had started, leaving it all to his juniors to sort out.

Even more dispiriting for Niko was that the few results of the electrical brain stimulation were totally unexpected, and bore no relationship to his theoretical framework for behaviour. For instance, the classical, *The study of instinct* hypothesis about threat behaviour was that it was a conflict, a mixture of aggression and fear. Niko expected that there would be a 'fear centre' in the brain, and an 'aggression centre': stimulate either of them with electrodes and the bird would attack or flee, stimulate both of them simultaneously and one expected threat behaviour. What happened was that Juan with his electrodes could elicit clear threat behaviour, also clear fear behaviour, but no aggression. When stimulation elicited threat, if the bird then saw something that usually produced a slight fright, the result was all-out aggression.[39] It was all quite inexplicable and this, together with the theoretical problems of behaviour motivation (see previous chapter) was, for Niko, another nail in the coffin of causation studies. After four years of brain stimulation Juan had enough, and the project was abandoned.

None of this detracted from the lively science scene in the group, which revolved around Mike but was established by Niko. There was still a lot happening, but then gradually, in the second half of the 1960s, things began to peter out somewhat. Just as in the study areas in Ravenglass and Walney, Niko's fund of ideas began to run out: his preoccupation with filming took him somewhat away from science, and he was plagued by health problems. Several years later, around 1968 when Niko was over 60 years old, Oxford ethology really went through the doldrums, as Niko himself remarked. He was aware that there was a lack of guiding spirit. It showed in the nature of student projects, which had little of the originality that marked his earlier studies: they tended to expand on previous ones.

A fundamental weakness in Niko's establishment in Oxford was the lack of an appropriate number two and successor. Mike was an excellent complement to Niko, and a better scientist in some ways. But Lies knew that, ultimately, Niko was disappointed in him,[40] in his lack of vision and imagination. He felt that Mike went off on tangents (such as details of colour vision, or the mathematics of fish-schooling) and had lost contact with ethology.[41] There was no doubt that Niko appreciated the absolutely vital role Mike had played in his group of students; for Mike's and Esther's farewell he wrote to them: 'it is not possible to do justice to what you both have meant to us and so many members of our happy little community',[42] and he clearly meant that. But another aspect of their relationship showed elsewhere in the same letter: 'I know that I have not always been an easy "boss". Although I hope that on the whole I did not interfere too much in what you did, I do remember Mike's – very friendly – protests against my insistence that he take part in the teaching. "I am after all a research officer" he said more than once.' It illustrates Niko's veiled frustration at the absence of any leading role by Mike (who was just interested in his science), and at no time would such a role have been more welcome than in the late 1960s, when Niko himself began to fade.

But there were other, supporting developments. In 1967 the Zoology

Department decided to give Niko an additional lectureship for ethology, because of the large interest from undergraduate students. The first appointment in this lectureship was Colin Beer, who after his PhD work in Ravenglass had moved to Rutgers University in New York, but felt restless there. Colin stayed for only a year in Oxford before moving back to a position with Danny Lehrman in Rutgers, and in 1968 Niko again asked several of his graduates to apply for the lectureship. Fortunately Richard Dawkins, who after finishing his doctorate had left Oxford for Berkeley, had had enough of the New World, and he became the lecturer. Richard was a welcome permanent addition, although in his first few years in the post Niko hardly realized the importance of the contribution Richard had to make. That came gradually after Richard's first book, *The selfish gene*, in the mid-1970s.

At the time Niko was riding high with his filming, with *Signals for survival* well on the way and heading for the big prize. But many of his former closest students were abroad, people such as Bryan Nelson in Galapagos, and Mike Norton-Griffiths, Harvey Croze, and myself in East Africa. He had health problems, suffered severe depressions, and there were problems with a student. More and more also he was becoming concerned about the state of the human race (see later). Then, just when life in some ways appeared to be at an all-time low, he rediscovered his former student, Desmond Morris.

Desmond had moved a long way since he did his doctorate with Niko on sticklebacks in the 1950s. In 1967 he published his 'Zoologist's study of the human animal', *The naked ape*,[43] which was a runaway success, simultaneously praised as good human ethology and denounced as scientific pornography. It made Desmond a millionaire, and he retired to a villa on Malta where Niko came to visit him in January 1969, on his return to England after staying with us in the Serengeti. Niko was welcomed with open arms, and he and Desmond had the most stimulating discussions, scheming and planning.

Niko had been extremely impressed by the book.

> *I have now read practically the whole of* The Naked Ape, *and as I went on, my pride and admiration grew ... both contents and style of communication – absolutely masterful. I really mean it: it is in its kind a masterpiece ... an approach that is very much the logical continuation of the Lorenz–Tinbergen approaches combined – I really congratulate you – the fools who criticize don't know what they are talking about.*[44]

Niko now felt that, through Desmond, he had seen the light again, and that what he himself needed to do, and wanted to do with his science, was to apply ethology to the human race. He was through with animal studies, there were more important considerations than the displays of gulls. It was almost as if he had a crush on Desmond, and he certainly sounds rather off-balance in the spate of letters to his former pupil:

I am making the most spectacular come-back, and it is clearly permanent. I have now the best of two worlds: my old enthusiasm and drive, and my acquired maturity. I am busy giving new impetus to my group, and all echelons are already responding. That will remain my main task in the sense of: I must never fail to do my utmost to produce good, independently working ethologists. But far beyond that I am now engaged in a grand scheme, which I know exactly how to tackle. Building on what you and Konrad have done for the promotion of Ethology of Man, I am going to join this effort in my way: by emphasising ... the urgent need for an all-out intensive study of Man's behaviour, by applying the methods of ethology. That is where I can put on the pressure. ... I suddenly see my 'niche', and my chance. You have, both in writing The Naked Ape *and by coming and seeing us, done something wonderful for me: I suddenly see my new job.*[45]

In his bread-and-butter letter after Malta he sent Desmond a photocopy of the title page of *The study of instinct*, annotated with the words 'Now bury' above the title, and 'Forgive, but don't forget' below it.[46] In Malta, Niko and Desmond had cooked up a scheme for the return of Desmond to Oxford, to join Niko's group again, with a fellowship in Wolfson College. Niko wanted to republish his own papers in an edited volume, with a long foreword by Desmond. He wanted Desmond to breathe new life into the group, and his attempts to charm Desmond into this sound almost desperate. Although he

The new Department of Zoology and Experimental Psychology in Oxford, now named the 'Niko Tinbergen Building'. Photo HK, 2000.

never says so explicitly, Niko clearly wanted Desmond to become his number two and successor. But unfortunately, great scientists rarely have a number two.

Desmond played along with it for quite some time. He came back from Malta, but the Oxford scheming came to nothing. He had the use of a room in the department for a few years, but never again did he take an active part in the Oxford group. He had his own agenda as a tremendously successful popular science writer and film-maker, and he had done his stint with ethology. There was no break between the two men: the initiative of Desmond moving back into Niko's orbit gradually petered out, but they would always remain friends.

Writing, lecturing, and conferences

If Niko had had an active interest in any of the student projects in his group in the last decade of his working life, his name could have been on many important papers from that period, had he been that way inclined. However, after 1965 he advised, he discussed when he was needed, he gave the young scientists a free rein, but he did not get involved. Nowadays this would have been different, and even at that time there were many academics who, as supervisors of students, were directly participating in the research in some way or other, and who would be one of the authors on all resulting publications of their students. Niko was rarely a joint author, and in consequence, his output of scientific papers after the mid-1960s was far less substantial than it could have been.

There still was a steady trickle of popular natural history articles from his hand for the Dutch *De Levende Natuur*, about one or two per year, about the Ravenglass foxes or the research in the Serengeti, the elephants in Manyara, or the gannets of the Bass Rock. There were also a few similar ones for English magazines such as *Animals* or the American *Natural History*, articles in which he mostly wrote about the work of others. There were also his lectures and review papers, especially on subjects such as evolution and behaviour, and on what was to become Niko's last big passion, the relevance of ethology to mankind. His last actual research papers were the ones that resulted from his Ravenglass field experiments in the early 1960s.

Niko's review papers at that time were rarely submitted to the regular, peer-reviewed scientific journals, but instead were written mostly by invitation for edited volumes on evolution, social behaviour, sex and behaviour, ornithology, zoology, and other subjects.[47] They summarized the by then somewhat dated ethological views on the evolution of displays from conflicts between the basic 'drives' of aggression, fear, and sex. They were still based on the general idea of unitary 'drives' (despite the criticism of Hinde and others that we saw earlier). Repeatedly, Niko discussed the conclusions one could draw about the evolution of behaviour from comparisons between related species, drawing on his own observations on gulls and on the research of others. Much of it went over the same ground again and again, over the same stories from the work of his

students such as the change in courtship behaviour of fruit flies after artificial selection (Stella Crossley), and the adaptive behaviour of the kittiwake (Esther Cullen). One sees much of *The study of instinct* and his later comparative paper on gull behaviour repeated, as well as a great deal of emphasis on the biological function of behaviour. The implications of the eggshell removal study were frequently brought back. Overall, one is left with the strong impression from that time that Niko was writing because it was expected of him, and he did not want to disappoint. One could say he was chewing the cud.

Ever since Niko had published *The study of instinct* he had had the intention of updating, editing, and then rewriting it. But only seven or eight years after it had come out, he began to feel that on his own he could not do it any more, that the subject had developed beyond his grasp. He worried about it for years, then approached Robert Hinde about the possibility of a collaborative effort to rewrite it, as a new handbook of ethology.

> *I would only be too delighted if we two could have a go at it together. My only hesitation comes from doubt whether I will be up to it; I am determined not to tie you to an enterprise which I might not be able to bring to a good end, and so cause you to waste time and energy. But on the other hand: you would be the only person with whom I feel I could collaborate.*[48]

Robert and he decided to have a go. They drew up the plans, outlines and work schedules, but in the end it did not work out, at least the collaboration did not. Two and a half years later Niko wrote to Robert:

> *It would be awful if this blasted book would in any way impair our friendship, which is to me more important than the fact that we are colleagues ... I am sorry that you feel guilty about having bullied me. Don't forget that I can kick as well as the next man if I feel I am being unfairly treated ... I did feel very*

unhappy about first having asked you to join in this enterprise and then not having lived up to expectations ... There is just too much other work, I am absolutely swamped.[49]

Niko's 'being swamped' was a matter of priorities, of course. Very soon after, Niko signed a contract with the American Time/Life Book publishers for a popular book on animal behaviour. Robert Hinde finished the handbook on his own: *Animal behaviour* was published in 1966.[50] It was a landmark in the science, extremely scholarly, hard to read even for experts, but a reference point for many years to come. Niko was full of respect for it, although he regretted its lack of interest in the evolution and the biological function of behaviour (as Niko said, this lack was 'in typical Cambridge tradition'), and he felt there was too much emphasis on environmental influences on behaviour rather than genetic ones.[51]

A year before Robert's book, Niko's own *Animal behavior* had been published.[52] It was a popular volume in every sense of the word, and it brought him large financial reward. It was a big, successful, commercial approach to science which was reprinted several times. Coffee-table sized, 200 pages, dominated by spectacular photographs and colour graphics, it laid a great deal of emphasis on the researchers themselves (with full page photographs of the greats of ethology in action) as well as on their animals and results. It covered many of the same topics as *The study of instinct*, and its obvious aim was to bring ethology to the masses. It was written not just by Niko but by him jointly with the Time/Life editors, and that came at a price: the presentation was Niko's, but heavily edited and Americanized by non-scientists, throwing much of the usual scientific caution to the winds. Niko never felt completely happy about the book. Nevertheless, this is what he had chosen to do instead of writing a scientific handbook, and this happened at about the same time as his big film-making success, *Signals for survival*. It was the appeal of the mass audience.

As he was no longer in the flush of youth, it is not surprising that Niko's ethological review papers and university lectures in the 1960s were getting somewhat out of step with what was happening in his science. He was asked to produce, and he wrote and talked about what he and his students had done in the past, but at the same time he was seriously losing touch with what was happening elsewhere. He had problems in keeping up with the literature, and he was fully aware of this (trans.): 'in confidence something that I should only whisper: I, too, find many modern behaviour studies very difficult to read. This is partly because really difficult issues are being researched, which I simply do not understand. But partly also there is undoubtedly bad writing involved, without consideration for the reader.'[53]

Niko's own science had grown beyond him. Where in younger years he relied on his intuition ('Funny how one intuitively does a great number of things in research for which one cannot really provide the logic and justification until later'[54]), when he reached his mid-sixties this was nowhere near enough:

having to lecture about a field that now baffles me … there is almost no generalization you can make any more. I try desperately to concentrate on how to go about it and all the time starting with commonplace observations and step-by-step analysing both the adaptedness and the causation, development and evolution aspects. Oddly enough, the more I try to read and understand what all those clever people are on about, the less certain I feel about what I have to tell, and every lecture is agony beforehand – I am just scared stiff. And at the same time one has the reaction 'do these youngsters know absolutely nothing about animals? Have they never looked? Are they having clever thoughts about nothing?' [55]

Gradually also in his writing, Niko began to consciously hark back to his earlier work; prompted by Desmond Morris, he felt that he could still make an impact by repeating what he had said a long time ago.

I have further kept thinking about your plan to edit a number of my papers. The more I think about it, the more I realize that you are dead right, and together we could use this for putting right, with little editorials, correcting a number of misconceptions. I can (putting all modesty aside) see an exciting, coherent story. … [I found, thirty years after its publication] my old snow bunting paper and glanced through it, and you know, I found it not bad at all, in fact pretty exciting reading; I had completely forgotten what was in it, and thought: 'that was really a jolly good piece of work.' [56]

In the end Niko went ahead with the project on his own, without Desmond, and he re-published 18 of what he thought were his best papers, in two volumes that came out in 1972, *The animal in its world*.[57] His friend, the famous biologist Sir Peter Medawar, wrote the foreword for a collection of papers that was an excellent representation of Niko's output, several of them appearing in English for the first time. It included his first 'bee-wolf' paper (1932) and his latest ones on childhood autism (1971; see later) and the importance of ethology for human behaviour (1972), with, in between, many of the most important ones that I have already discussed in this and previous chapters. There were also some curious omissions, such as the 1940 paper on 'displacement activities', and his best-known 'Aims and methods of ethology' (1963). The first of these two was left out because Niko thought he had presented the message rather too often[58] (and he had had endless disagreeable debates on this topic with Adriaan Kortlandt, who wanted recognition). In his collected papers he presented the ground covered in 'Aims and methods' by another, later paper along the same lines, entitled 'Ethology' (1969), which he liked better but which had appeared in a rather obscure edited volume of general science papers.[59]

Leafing through *The animal in its world* now, some thirty years later, one is still fascinated by the breadth of the field that Niko covered, and by the simplicity. The easy presentation of these papers made them accessible to everyone, not just the highly specialized ethologist. Yet it was good hard science. Crucially, these two volumes confirmed Niko as an enormous authority covering a fascinating field: crucially, because this happened just at the time that the next Nobel Prizes were being considered in Stockholm.

Starting in the 1960s, Niko had become more and more reluctant to go to conferences or on lecturing trips. He found them far too exhausting, the demands on his attention overwhelming, and especially during conferences he found it depressing to realize that his knowledge was so limited. The biennial International Ethological Conferences had started during the 1950s, as 10-day events held in a different country each time, with some one or two hundred participants, by invitation only. They provided a wonderful meeting point, a marvellous atmosphere, and a breeding ground of excellent science. In 1961 the IEC was held close to Konrad's Seewiesen; students and grand old men mixed, and new ethological concepts and ideas were discussed during midnight swims. Niko was exhausted afterwards, partly also because he and Konrad were frequently used as instantaneous translators during the conference (only few scientists spoke more than one language, and talks were in English, German, or French).

In 1963 Niko went to the next IEC, in The Hague, with some reluctance; he could not very well not go, as it was in the backyard of his youth. But that was his last ethological conference. Decades later, all older ethologists still remember exactly which IEC was when, who went there, and what happened. But Niko could not take them any more. He still did some lecturing trips abroad, but they were fewer, and especially after the breakdown during his lecturing trip in Kenya in 1967, he used to take Lies along with him whenever possible, as he said 'on doctor's orders'.

Niko's conference attendances did not just peter out, though: he left the conference circuit with a bang. In 1966 he was conference secretary for the

Self-portrait in wood: Niko's handicraft on Walney.
Photo Lary Shaffer.

enormous International Ornithological Conference in Oxford, which was a highly prestigious, gigantic effort in organization at a time when conferences were still organized by the scientists themselves, rather than by a firm of professionals. There were over a thousand participants, several parallel sessions of lectures in different buildings, and opening and closing speeches to be given. He made Mike Cullen walk between buildings to time exactly how long people would need between lectures, and a secretarial staff to organize the lecture halls, parties, receptions, and excursions. It took several months of his time, and a massive amount of energy from his people, too, but it was a calculated expenditure: this conference put him and his group in a bright ornithological spotlight. Fame was the reward, but he was never seen again as a full conference attendee.

Ethology and humanity

Popularizing his science was one aspect of Niko's career that became ever more prominent during the 1960s. Increasingly this became not just popularizing ethology, but finding a role for ethology in helping our own species, in saving humanity from the social and environmental disaster that Niko saw looming. He had always been a crusader, right from his teenage years onwards and brimming with missionary zeal. But until now he had been advocating an interest, a science, a new approach. This became proselytizing for what he saw as the good of mankind. He saw the human population explosion and its behavioural consequences as a great threat, never mind that he had five children himself. Persuading others of the need for understanding our own behaviour in this new context was all-important to him.

In *The study of instinct* (1951) and several of his other books there were already references to the usefulness of ethology in understanding human behaviour, at the time severely criticized by Danny Lehrman. In 1964 Niko gave a lecture on 'Animal roots of human behaviour' as one in a series of lectures to his Oxford students, later published as one of his collected papers.[60] Part of this lecture was clearly inspired by Konrad Lorenz' (1963) book *Das sogenannte Böse*, in 1966 translated as *On aggression*.[61] This book related phenomena such as human aggression, warfare, and even criminality to population densities and numbers, and put them firmly in the territory of ethology. The increase in technology also caused behavioural concerns. Niko wrote, for example:

> Man's aggression has become so dangerous because inhibition by fear is deliberately reduced by whipping-up group aggression and by various training methods. ... Man, by developing long-range weapons, has rendered the appeasement behaviour of his fellow-men ineffective because long-range appeasement has not kept track with long-range aggression. It is easier to drop an atom-bomb from a plane, or to send off a rocket, than to strangle a man or a child with one's own hands – one does not actually see the misery one causes.

... The problem concerns us vitally. Yet what are we really doing about its study? Why are we not putting more intensive effort in a large-scale scientific study of aggression? ... Our ignorance is really appalling. It has for instance been suggested by Lorenz, that even if we would succeed in making non-aggressive men, we might not improve matters at all. Aggression, especially group aggression, has in the animal kingdom a correlate of very positive value: true friendship seems to develop particularly between members of a group who are aggressive to an outside group. To what extent are aggression and the inclination to form such social ties linked? We have no idea – but the problem is open to investigation. My own guess is that Lorenz is rashly jumping from an aspect of genetic evolution to one of phenotypic control. ... If we want to understand our animal heritage – which must be there because we have descended from animals – we shall have to apply the same methods in human ethology as are beginning to be applied with success in animal ethology.

Lorenz' book described human aggression as being just like that of animals, as an innate behaviour. Aggression has many of our more pleasant attributes tied up with it, such as friendship, laughter, inventiveness, exploration, and he suggested that, therefore, there would be no point in attempting to get rid of our aggressive 'drive'. But as an alternative, he suggested one should aim to re-direct aggression, in the same way as animal aggression can be re-directed into a harmless channel. Human aggression could be redirected into sports (for example football matches – such re-direction, Lorenz stated, is the principal function of sport), or into attacking environmental hazards (for example land reclamation) or other endeavours. It was such statements of mere ideas as hard fact, as well as the recognition of animal roots in human behaviour by the ethologists, that later attracted so much opprobrium from campaigners, and that would develop into the highly vitriolic 'sociobiology debate'.

In those years when Niko's own, specialized science went rather stale on him, he took up the cause of ethology as a remedy for ills of humanity, again prompted by a Lorenz initiative just as he had been in the 1930s. This time there was no adulation of Lorenz. In fact Niko was somewhat critical of Konrad's writing, which generated a distinct coldness in their relationship. Niko reviewed *On aggression* for the BBC magazine, *The Listener*,[62] and sang its praises. But in his inaugural lecture (see below) he noted:

I am apprehensive because these books [including Morris' The naked ape], each admirable in their own way, are being misread. Very few readers give the authors the benefit of the doubt. Far too many either accept uncritically all that the authors say, or (equally uncritically) reject it all. I believe that this is because both Lorenz and Morris emphasize our knowledge rather than our ignorance ... present as knowledge a set of statements which are, after all, no more than likely guesses ... what we need is a sense of doubt and wonder, and an urge to investigate, to inquire.[63]

Primate behaviour: Niko, Konrad Lorenz, and Otto Koehler during the International Ethological Conference in Starnberg, 1961.
Photographer unknown.

To his friend Gerard Baerends he announced (trans.):

I now consider it my task to present the material in a more scientific form, because I always gave so much attention to aggression, and because more than the others I am focussed on testing, experimentally if possible, and on a critical examination of our methods. I want to write a book about this. As a first step I have decided, after all, to give an inaugural lecture on it [N. had been appointed to a chair in Oxford two years before, in 1966], ... then elaborate it into a book, and I am now working hard on this. ... I have to see to it that, at least in England, ethology will be recognized as an essential part of medical research, and be financed as medical research just like physiological research on animals ... For that I have to make it clear in a wider audience, but also in the highest scientific policy-making circles, what it is that ethology can contribute.[64]

Niko's inaugural lecture made quite a splash, but his book never saw the light; he stopped writing it after a few chapters. The lecture, 'War and peace in animals and man', was presented in February 1968, published in *Science*,[65] and immediately translated into German.[66] In it, he draws parallels between fighting people and animals, moving between the attacks of sticklebacks and gulls and those of armies, with frequent reference to Konrad's book. Territoriality is a common theme, and he 'examined the hypothesis that man still carries with him the animal heritage of group territoriality'. Niko compared the simple territories of birds with the group territories of hyaenas and mankind. Niko's thesis was that we need more research, especially on issues such as the 'innateness' of aggression, on the potential for education to reduce or redirect it, on the role of 'culture' versus 'genes' in our behaviour, and on the importance of fear in balancing aggression. Most importantly, he stressed that one should not simply use the results of animal studies to understand human behaviour (as a short-cut, in the way Konrad did), but that one should use the methodology of ethology and apply that directly to people (this admonishment by Niko has frequently been forgotten by later critics). Niko, in contrast to Konrad and Desmond, underlined our ignorance, rather than our knowledge.

The reaction of his Oxford colleagues to the inaugural lecture was not particularly favourable, and perhaps somewhat bemused. David Lack wrote to Niko saying that wars were started after ripe consideration of gains and profit, not because of some aggressive instinct: 'there has been confusion between means and ends'.[67] The head of the Zoology Department, John Pringle, disagreed with numerous statements, and Niko made appeasement noises in return: 'I am only too aware of the shortcomings of my lecture and know that I still have a lot of catching-up to do.'[68]

'Cobbler, stick to your last' is a popular saying in Holland. The slight unease amongst colleagues about Niko's move into the problems of humanity and away from his own experience did not pass him by; but he could not stop, the concern with human behaviour had overwhelmed him. He had always had some doubts about what he had been doing, about whether it was really justified that he should spend his life out amongst nature doing what he felt like. Consequently, throughout his entire scientific life he had produced justifications for his birdwatching. In fact he argued for its rights so often that a hidden sense of guilt was unmistakable:

> It is, I think, only natural for a man to have occasional doubts about the value of what he is doing; at any rate, such doubts have often occurred to me. ... once in a while the embarrassing question comes up: 'So what?' A little devil seems to look over one's shoulder and to take great pleasure in kindling this little spark of doubt ... I usually beat my little devil into retreat with the following arguments. It seems to me that no man need to be ashamed of being curious about nature. It could even be argued that this is what he got his brains for and that no greater insult to nature and to oneself is possible than to be indifferent to nature.[69]

But 10 years later, in 1968, I believe that he felt his abilities as a scientist/naturalist to be on the wane, whereas his concern about the fate of mankind was on the increase, and his guilt was coming to the surface. He had to do something that he could justify in terms of immediate benefits for mankind. His missionary zeal had found another purpose.

What he had not expected was the tremendous backlash, from students, other academics, and the general public, against the involvement of an animal science in the organization of our own society. Almost right at the beginning, of what Niko felt was a crusade to establish ethology as the right approach to at least some aspects of human behaviour, he was hit by people's disapproval in a way he had never experienced before. Interestingly, it was also the time of violent student unrest in many Western countries.

In December 1969 Niko gave a rare lecture abroad, in Simon Fraser University, Vancouver. Some days previously he had spoken in McGill, and somehow the Vancouver students knew what to expect. They distributed a leaflet beforehand, and a bulletin afterwards, and Niko's lecture became a riot. As the students saw it, the lecture was presented by

> *Professor N. Tinbergen, a notorious biologist who has been presenting the theories of innate aggressiveness, instinctive urges for territory, need for 'living space', etc. which have been popularized in the writings of Konrad Lorenz, Robert Ardrey, Desmond Morris and other so-called scientists. During the discussion period it was pointed out to Tinbergen how his ideas were fascist, the same ideas the Nazis encouraged and developed and that they had no scientific base whatsoever ... When his flimsy rhetoric failed to divert the discussion, the chairman of the meeting broke up the meeting and protected this Nazi from being fully exposed to the people.[70]*

> *During his talk on sticklebacks and seagulls he emphasized all the fascist ideas such as innate aggression, instinctive urge for territory (private property), need for living space (lebensraum) etc., the same ideas which can be found in Hitler's* Mein Kampf. *Despite the fact that Tinbergen repeatedly cautioned against extrapolating the results of animal experiments to man, he ignored his warning and proceeded to do just that.[71]*

Not surprisingly, Niko was bemused and quite upset to be called a Nazi, especially given his experiences during the war, and only later could he see the irony of it all. To the Master of Wolfson College he wrote:

My wife and I tried hard, in the short time available, to understand these youngsters because we shared so much of their hostility against American commercialism and greed, but we too came to the conclusion that they had completely closed minds, and that the only people of our acquaintance we could compare them with were the very strict Dutch Reformed Protestants.[72]

Sir Isaiah Berlin's reaction was 'I am only too happy to think that the College contains such out and out Nazis as yourself and Desmond Morris'.[73]

It was a baptism of fire for Niko, exposed to the highly emotional rhetoric of rebels, where rational arguments count for little and false impressions for much. The Vancouver incident must have been one of the first salvos in the acrimonious 'sociobiology debate' (see later) of the following decades, which was to spread far beyond these initial arguments. Niko was not an ideal speaker for such occasions, because he easily became flustered. A few years after Vancouver another incident occurred, covering part of the same ground but this time on paper rather than in a lecture theatre, and in Holland.

In 1973 the Dutch journalist Rudy Kousbroek published a public lecture in Holland, 'Ethology and culture-philosophy' (trans.),[74] in which he lambasted the ethologists, especially Lorenz, with many of the same reservations that Niko himself had about Konrad's and Desmond's books, but expressed with much greater force and vitriol. The main Dutch quality broadsheet *NRC-Handelsblad* asked Niko to reply, which he did with a vengeance, pointing out many misrepresentations and misconceptions.[75] As an example, he wrote that ethologists do not pronounce on whether a behaviour is inherited or learned, but they do ask to what extent inheritance and environmental factors are involved; they do not just state that aggression is innate and cannot be changed. Kousbroek answered, others interfered, and it developed into a newspaper brawl, with Kousbroek having the last word. Other scientists, including Gerard Baerends and Niko's old mentor, Jan Verwey, clearly felt that Niko should not have dirtied his hands this way. And with benefit of hindsight, this is what Niko felt himself: he was no good at brawling, and should have kept out of it.

The Vancouver row occurred well before 1975, the year when Edward Wilson climbed on to the human biology bandwagon with his voluminous *Sociobiology*,[76] and sparked fierce discussions in America that became known as 'The sociobiology debate' (see Chapter 10). In the subsequent writing of the history of this controversy,[77] Vancouver has been quietly forgotten, giving Wilson the dubious honour of starting it all.

The black dog, at home, at work, everywhere

One ever-recurring theme in Niko's life was his depressions, which hit him not just during his fieldwork but at any time, and probably even more often when he was in Oxford. They had begun after the war, very low-key but noticeable.

Since about 1960 his down moods had become progressively worse and more frequent, and he never tried to hide them. Everybody seemed to know about it: colleagues, students, even people who did not see him that often. Clearly the depressions very much affected his enjoyment of life, his relations with people, and his work; when the black misery overtook him again, he could be out of action for weeks at a time, doing nothing, or sleeping, or perhaps reading a bit. Always he had to take his misery home with him.

Later in the 1960s, when yet another bad turn would overtake him, Niko sometimes became almost suicidal. He would be paranoid about little things and difficult, and people around him often also felt miserable because of Niko's suffering. Both Niko and Lies tried to shield the children from it, and did so quite effectively: Gerry, the youngest, remembers mostly the happy times. To see Niko in a depressed mood was immensely sad, and for outsiders it was difficult to understand the huge contrast between the jolly, brilliant, and famous scientist, and the miserable little man in that same body.

His student Lary Shaffer told me:

> *Pat [Niko's secretary] had warned me that he was bad ... just as I was leaving her office, he came out of his room and we sort of fell into step. The corridor zigzagged a couple of times before we got into the entrance hall – and he backed himself into a corner and took a deep breath and just pinned himself against the wall. 'I just saw so-and-so go by – she's a terrible busybody and she won't leave me alone, I'll just hide here until she's gone'. There he was, flattened against the wall, hiding from her.*[78]

He sought psychiatric help, on several occasions spending time in hospital, but the actual cause of his depressions was never properly identified. He had developed a deep contempt for psychiatrists, which was to become even worse

when he and Lies started their study of the behaviour of children (see next chapter). Time and again Niko was convinced that he had beaten his disease, and many of his letters referred to the endless struggle. But it only became worse, especially after his retirement in 1974.

For a long time he had been overtly concerned about his health, and it was a favourite topic in conversation and letters. Lies took it up with great vigour, and she often sent pages-long letters to friends, Niko's students, or later her own children, with advice about health, vitamins, and new treatments. Niko had many ailments; there had been the gastrectomy as treatment for ulcers, which removed two-thirds of his stomach; he frequently had debilitating back problems and influenza attacks; and he was a heavy smoker. Lies, who felt all this as her responsibility, was not in good health either: she had angina, a hysterectomy, and several times broke bones; Niko often referred to her problems in his letters (in 1963 he told Baerends in cyclist slang that (trans.) 'Lies is in bed with a "punctured inner tube"').[79] But his own depressions were a topic that recurred in his letters more frequently than any other.

'It is wonderful to feel better at last; I got rather fed up with being a tottering, nervous wreck'.[80] In 1965 he wrote to his former PhD student Bryan Nelson:

> It is now almost four months since I got that neurological trouble of which the arm business is only the less important side. Ever since my return from Africa I have been either confined to bed, or have worked for part of the day only. And what work I did was of poor quality. I got a relapse a fortnight ago ... I have never in my life flopped so completely. Naturally I hate to cause such inconvenience to so many people, but I just cannot continue ... But there is a gradual, though slow improvement, and I hope to recover completely.[81]

It is sad to read such rather self-centred involvement from someone who was just 57, and who not so many years earlier had been athletic, a man full of initiatives, a number one on many fronts, with not a hint of hypochondria.

In 1968 Niko told Gerard Baerends about his trouble (trans.):

> I must briefly and precisely tell you what has really been wrong with me. Now I am cured, thoroughly investigated and treated, it is clear that I had a progressive, exponentially increasing phenobarbitone poisoning of the central nervous system, caused by ten years of phenobarbitones on doctor's advice, and this has strongly affected my brain. During the last years I have gradually gone downhill, so since about 1964 I got more or less used to it and had accepted that apparently I was ageing early and (what worried me most) was losing my scientific interest. It was a blessing in disguise that I also got a virus infection of the c.n.s., which jointly with the poisoning led to my acute illness in Nairobi. It is only now that I notice how ill I have been. It is like waking up from a years-long nightmare. My interest has returned, my brain is working again

and with pleasure, and I have lots of energy. Only my rhythm has gone haywire, so often I am wide awake at three in the morning, I work from 3–7 hard and intensively, and then work a normal day. I have to be especially careful that this explosion of energy does not affect people around me too much. But I finally have the will to live and work – I was so far in Nairobi that four times I awoke at night and found myself with enough poison in my hand and a glass of water, to finish myself off completely. Then I suddenly decided: 'that, never', and I went to a doctor who immediately sent me to England. ... I am now possessed by a 'sense of urgency', I have to make up for so many years, for example by reading the literature, that I am working like mad. You cannot imagine what relief it is to want to read again, and not to consider it a ghastly duty. But I also have to prepare myself that I may be taken by lung-cancer.[82]

He wrote similar letters to others, and so did Lies. When Niko was due to stay with us in the Serengeti in late 1968, his visit was preceded by a long letter from her:

He should on doctor's advice no longer go on travels by himself. He ought to have a watchdog (who stands between him and too strenuous a life) with him.

Black-headed gull killed on its nest by a fox. Ravenglass, 1962.
Photo Niko Tinbergen.

However, we could not afford my fare to the Serengeti … Niko gave me permission to write … directives as to ways and means of keeping him healthy. … Since Niko's illness now nearly four years ago and the crisis in Nairobi last year we have found that one sure way of getting a relapse is physical over-exertion. The whole syndrome … will return with all the nasty side effects. He will be unable to sleep, he will feel absolutely exhausted, have great difficulty in understanding what he hears or reads, not be able to communicate clearly, not remember what he has read or said or done even a short while ago and, as if this mental fog (as he calls it) which will descend on him within 24 hours of the over-exertion were not enough, after 36 hours a fit of deep depression will settle on him. … one hour of leisurely walk is about the measure of the amount he can carry without after effects. … at least 9 or 10 hours rest in bed every day … Do not be taken in by a cheerful face or talk, rather judge him by his colour … If he looks grey or yellow, if he gets cramps in his right arm … then those are signs that he is overtired.

And so on, for two closely typed pages.[83]

The physical and mental decline in Niko in the 1960s coincided with a slow-down in his work output. This was not just in the numbers of his papers and books, but across the board in his ideas for new projects, in his grasp of new developments in ethology, and in his filming and photography. What he clearly found maddening was the fact that there was no simple explanation, in fact there were different explanations every time. Niko and people around him used to talk about 'the bug' that struck him again, as if it helped to be able to refer to something extraneous, rather than a genetic factor in the family. But no single 'bug' was ever identified.

The debilitating affliction hurt him especially because he felt he had to keep up appearances. People needed to be convinced that he could not help it. The lengths he used to go to were illustrated in an incident a few years later, when he suffered back problems again: on a trip to Holland Lies had to carry their two suitcases. 'Partly at her advice all the time I limped a bit more, so I need not feel so embarrassed' (trans.).[84] At times he persuaded himself that his misery was due to his exalted position. To one acquaintance he wrote 'the man at the top is a little mad, or, if sane, is now and then *very* lonely and either hallucinating, or God, or is desperately unhappy'[85].

Niko was not depressed all the time during the 1960s, but certainly quite often. It could put a miserable damper on family life, apart from the conse-quences for the interactions with his academic environment, for his fieldwork, writing, and lecturing. Lies saw the maintenance of Niko's achievements as her own responsibility, and to see him collapse as he did was torture for her as well as for him. Otherwise, the family had everything going for them, living in the quiet Lonsdale Road in North Oxford, surrounded by a pleasant garden and fields, the river and trees behind; one could not wish for better. Niko's struggle with himself threw a large shadow over all this.

Part of the Tinbergen brood had fledged by then. The eldest, Jack, had gone to Cambridge to read physics, then spent two years in Antarctica before returning to Birmingham University for an MSc, then went to Holland in the early 1960s. He continued for a PhD in astronomy in Leiden (the only Tinbergen offspring to become an academic), and married a Dutch girl, Ineke. Catrina, the second child, emigrated to Canada in 1960 after going to teacher training college, and she taught French there, as well as becoming a professional potter. She married a Dutch expatriate, Gus Loman. Number three, Dirk, did a year in a music conservatoire in Devon, then started biology at Cambridge in 1960, but, as he said: 'not out of great conviction'. After he finished he became a teacher and married an English girl, Faith.

The two youngest girls, Janet and Gerry, were still at home in the early 60s; later they studied music in Glasgow, Janet from 1964 to 1968, and Gerry for two years after that. Niko's affliction probably impacted more on Janet and Gerry than on the others, as it caught them in their teenage years and when still at home. Yet they remember mainly the good times with him, his attentiveness. He was 'Father', drawing posters for them, swimming in the river behind the house, writing poems; there were the Sunday-trips to the Wytham woods, watching the badgers there, and collecting blackberries. 'A loving childhood, and enormous security', commented one. The family was remarkably self-contained, happy in many ways, but with a sad element that never completely disappeared.

The children look back on their youth with warmth and satisfaction. One of them commented about their parents: 'Any couple who have brought up five children to be happy, get on with each other, to be useful and worthy citizens and have plenty of laughs on the way, must have done a pretty good job.'[86]

Looking at it from the outside, Niko's personal life in the 1960s had taken on a rather humdrum quality. Evenings had to be quiet at home, without noise, with Niko normally in bed well before nine. Often he watched TV, with crime programmes such as *Z-cars* being favourites, and the news. He took a passive interest in politics, had a thorough dislike for the Conservative government (he hated 'you've-never-had-it-so-good' Harold Macmillan), and began to take seriously to gardening (eulogizing over his Jerusalem artichokes). There was no social life to speak of; apart from some students, and behaviour friends and colleagues from abroad coming to stay, Lies and Niko saw few other people at home. They did not go out much (except Lies with her daughters to occasional concerts), and they had little interest in other subjects, despite the fantastic opportunities that Oxford threw their way. Niko blamed the job at least partly: 'It is one of the very real problems to scientists that too much pressure is exerted by the administrative and organizational frills of their job, which defeats all but the very ablest and very strongest; the time for real thinking is increasingly difficult to find, let alone for social contacts.'[87]

Janet, who in later years saw more of her parents than the other children did, commented: 'You probably don't appreciate that if somebody is teetering on the edge of a depression, the sheer effort of struggling to keep out of the abyss is absolutely exhausting. This leaves very little extra energy for following up what might otherwise be a great opportunity.'[88]

As an example of a missed opportunity, Niko met Sir Ernst Gombrich, purely by chance during some university gathering in Oxford. Gombrich was by then a world-renowned art historian with several professorates, at the time director of the Warburg Institute in London, and an almost exact contemporary of Niko. He was famous for his book, *The story of art*,[89] but his interest overlapped with that of Niko especially in his book *Art and illusion*.[90] In this he quoted Niko's results on 'sign-stimuli', such as the stickleback's response to red, and generally Gombrich was keenly interested in ethology. He was an active participant in a Royal Society committee on communication; Niko had taken part in this, too, but soon excused himself. There was an extensive correspondence between the two[91] (and Gombrich's very elderly mother taught the youngest Tinbergen girls piano,[92] whilst his sister translated Niko's German for his collected papers). But there was hardly any social contact. Between Gombrich and Niko the interest in common ground was very one-sided: it came from Gombrich, who was keenly interested in ethology and in the science of art. Niko showed no interest in Gombrich's approach to art; he was delighted that Gombrich was keen, but just left it at that, and they saw very little of each other.

Contact with relatives in Holland was fairly sporadic. Luuk was long gone and Niko's parents were no longer there. In 1969 Jan received the Nobel Prize for Economics (see next chapter) – it caused a stir worldwide, but not much in Lonsdale Road, nor did Niko feel inclined to revamp the dormant relationships with his brother Dik and sister Mien. A year later Luuk's son Joost came to stay, to do a masters project with his uncle for his Dutch university course in biology. He was sent to Walney and had a great time – it could have been a warm family connection, but it was all rather low key. They hardly talked about Joost's late father, who had been so close to Niko. 'The Tinbergens just are like that,' Joost commented, 'very bottled up.'[93] He was to be the only one in the next generation of the family to become a professional researcher of animal behaviour, in Holland.

Niko and Lies became more inward looking than they had been. Because of his health, Niko spent increasingly more time at home rather than in the office or in the field, and he saw far fewer people, with Lies often keeping callers away at Niko's request. It meant a greater dependence on Lies, and gradually she also became more involved in Niko's science. By the end of the 1960s all the children except Janet had left home, and Janet lived her own life, playing and teaching cello; Lies had time on her hands. This gave her an opportunity; Lies had always been an intensely observant child-watcher, keenly interested in whatever children did and how adults responded. This interest, together with Niko's urge to make his science more applicable to mankind, developed into a serious project. In about 1970 they started a systematic study together, of the behaviour of healthy and abnormal children: the ethology of childhood autism, Niko's last great project that totally absorbed him.

The autism study gave him a much-needed boost, as well as a justification for spending time away from the department and his students, and he felt that, after all these years, he was giving Lies a chance to become involved and to do something creative away from the family. From other directions he was getting welcome good news: the two volumes of his collected papers were about to be published, to his tremendous gratification. And a final boost for his ego was the request from the Royal Society to deliver the prestigious Croonian Lecture in 1972.

The subject that Niko chose for the Croonian Lecture was somewhat similar to that for his inaugural lecture four years earlier, and as he acknowledged without apology, went well beyond his own field of expertise. In 'Functional ethology and the human sciences'[94] he first described to his non-specialist audience what functional ethology is: the study of adaptiveness of behaviour, of the way in which natural selection has moulded that part of the behaviour of animals that is genetically determined. He talked about his eggshell removal experiments, about the way foxes cache their prey, about anti-predator and camouflage behaviour, about the relationship between such functional studies and the causation of behaviour, and about comparisons between species. Instead of going over the old nature–nurture controversy again, he stressed the plasticity of behaviour of individuals, the extent to which animals can adjust to their environment, for instance by learning. Then he arrived at our own species, at our own genetic and cultural evolution, and he stressed the need for science to understand to what extent our behaviour can be modified and adjusted to our environment, or alternatively, to what extent it is genetically determined.

He suggested some examples where present-day demands on 'human nature' exceed the limits of adjustability of people: for example, mother–child bonding being disrupted by increased absence of mothers, the increased occurrence of childhood autism as a consequence of social maladjustment, and the demands on children from educational systems. And there is the environment: 'It is the comparison of the adaptedness of animals with that of Man which reveals that our conquest of the environment is causing habitat changes at a pace that genetic evolution cannot possibly match – not even if directed and speeded up by the, morally and practically doubtful, genetic engineering that some have proposed.' In each of these fields, he suggested, the methods used by ethology had an important role to play in understanding what is happening. 'The main purpose of my paper is therefore to urge all sciences concerned with the biology of Man to work for an integration of their many and diverse approaches, and to step up the pace of building of a coherent, comprehensive science of Man. In this effort towards integration animal ethology cannot stand aside.'

It was a grand and passionate statement, dealing with both animal and human behaviour, in sweeping comparisons. There were no new scientific insights; people listened because of Niko's authority in animal studies, and because many shared his feeling of unease about the human condition. Niko was pleased with the lecture himself, pleased especially because he had shown that he could still deliver. But he had no ready medicine for what he saw as the weaknesses of society and science. Before long, much of it was forgotten again.

After the Croonian Lecture Niko was coasting along to retirement. His physical and mental health were shaky, he was no great light in the department, with one or two exceptions his students did not see very much of him, his animal studies had come to a close, and former pupils were holding the fort. Life at home was rather empty. He had a productive career to look back on, but little promise ahead, like many people in retirement.

Then came the call from Stockholm.

CHAPTER 8

The Nobel Prize, and human behaviour

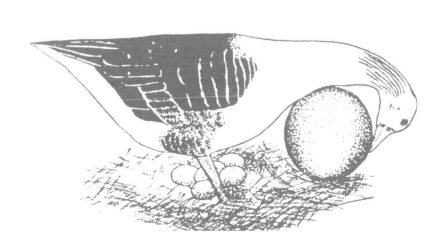

Nobel laureate

Thursday, 12 October 1973 started as just an ordinary, rather dull morning in Niko's life. He had been somewhere in the department, walking through the uninspiring, clinical corridors back to his room, and he called in on Pat, his secretary. 'You just missed a personal call from Stockholm.' She realized what was happening, he did not. Back in his own room, the call came again, and Niko responded with disbelief. The Nobel Prize for Physiology or Medicine, jointly with Konrad Lorenz and Karl von Frisch.

It took a while for it to sink in. Before he was hit by the explosion of interest from the media and colleagues, Niko was rather dismissive; he did not quite realize the meteoric impact. Another prize? It would mean publicity, what on earth was he going to do with the money, he would have to ring Lies and Pringle and start telling his friends, and he was busy. But within hours all hell broke loose, and his life had changed forever.

The Nobel Prize is still the most prestigious of all international awards. Since 1901 it has been given out annually in six different fields. However, there is no award for biology: that falls within the bracket of 'Physiology or Medicine'. In any one field, an award is given to one person or a maximum of three people at a time, and this year it was the study of animal behaviour that triumphed. It was given to the three scientists '*for their discoveries concerning organization and elicitation of individual and social behaviour patterns*'.

We were all stunned by it: none of the people involved with Niko had expected it, and none of us had seen ethology as competing in that league. A Nobel award for such a wide theme was unusual; scientists habitually get it for a single discovery, such as Dorothy Hodgkin for the unravelling of the structure of insulin in 1964. As another example, Peter Medawar became a Nobel laureate in 1960 for his 'discovery of acquired immunological tolerance' (related to the body's rejection of tissue transplants); in fact, he was probably the main protagonist recommending the honour for the three ethologists. Sir Peter had been a friend and admirer of Niko for many years, a mentor who had helped his research on several important occasions.

In the animal behaviour trio Karl von Frisch had, indeed, made a single and most important discovery. His scientific contribution in understanding the fascinating communication between honeybees was widely acknowledged. He was the odd one out and had little contact with the wider scene of animal behaviour studies, whereas Konrad and Niko were central. But all three recipients had been active in a field that stirred the imagination of the general public, in a science that was close to people's hearts. It was Konrad and Niko who had established the biological study of animal behaviour; their contribution was not so much their own discoveries of organization and elicitation of behaviour, but their approach to the subject, their methodology. The press went into overdrive, the tabloids as well as the serious papers and magazines, with headlines screaming from every front page. The three had become public property.

After the first bout of disbelief and pooh-poohing, Niko loved it all. Even before the press had tracked him down, he got on his bike and called on Desmond Morris, who now lived in a large villa not far from Niko in north Oxford. He rang the bell, and when Desmond opened the door Niko stood on one leg, and shouted 'Cockadoodledoo!'[1]

Then, and in the weeks to follow, came the onslaught of a mad publicity circus. A sample of newspaper headlines captures the spirit: 'Nobel prize for good behaviour', 'Nobel recognition for ethology', 'Nobel prize for sex trio', 'Film-maker − writer − scientist Tinbergen rightly receives Nobel prize for medicine', 'Nobel-brothers: genes? Definitely not', 'Nobel-prize winner: I love animals more than children'. Niko was exhausted by the scores of interviews, and at times furious because of the many distortions, disappointed because of the press' emphasis on what he thought were the wrong points.

Two issues that the papers were repeatedly interested in, and which Niko judged irrelevant, were the 1969 Nobel Prize (for economics) of his brother Jan, and Niko's relationship with Konrad, especially after the war. Two brothers receiving the big prize had never happened before, and the public wanted analyses, and pictures of the two together. Niko said that a recent photograph of the two brothers was out of the question (neither of them was going to travel for it), and in his many interviews he dismissed the idea that he and Jan would be sharing some special genes: they had just been fortunate in their upbringing. It certainly did not look as if Jan and Niko took a great deal of interest in each other's achievement − yet, in the years to follow there would be a rapprochement, initiated mostly by Jan (Chapter 9).

Niko found it more difficult to deal with questions about Konrad now that their names were mentioned in the same breath, and Lorenz himself received a barrage of inquiries about his Nazi past. Lorenz had, indeed, been a Nazi Party member and very much in favour of the *Anschluss*, the annexation of Austria by Germany. Niko was asked if he agreed that Konrad had expressed Nazi sympathies and racialist statements, and why he protected Konrad. Niko had written to Konrad, asking him specifically to include in his autobiographical note for the Nobel committee an explicit regret about his Nazi past. Lorenz said that he would do anything that Niko asked him to, but he never did this, never expressed any reservations about what he had done before and during the war. Niko, nevertheless, continued to protect Konrad, 'seriously disappointed' that Konrad did not recant things he had said in his political naïvety, but he stood by him as a friend.[2]

The Nobel Prize-winning brothers, Jan and Niko Tinbergen, December 1973. Courtesy of the Tinbergen family.

In early December 1973 Lies and Niko set off on their trip to Stockholm, for Niko to receive the prize, and to give an acceptance lecture. They went via Holland: as if the Nobel Prize was not sufficient, Niko had also received, announced a few months before the Nobel Prize, the greatest scientific accolade that Holland has to offer, the Swammerdam Medal. Highly prestigious in the Netherlands and administered by the Society for Natural Sciences and Medicine, it is handed out once every 10 years to a Dutch-born scientist, and it was to be conferred on him in Amsterdam, a few days before the ceremony in Stockholm.

The Amsterdam meeting was for Niko a moving occasion, with many of his old friends, colleagues, and teachers in the audience. Niko lectured, as well as Gerard Baerends, and there was a warm reception. It was an occasion that would have been a climax in Niko's career if everybody had not been very much aware of the events that were scheduled to come three days later. Niko talked about his walking in the footsteps of the great Dutch naturalist Jacques Thijsse; as an afterthought, he said he was glad that Thijsse was not present (he had died almost 30 years earlier), because he would have been very upset by what had happened to Holland, a country now dominated by industry instead of beautiful nature.

The celebrations in Stockholm, around the actual award ceremony on 12 December 1973, were a grandiose whirlwind, a scenery and ambience totally alien to Niko's way of life and principles, and that he would never have approved before. Now, he was bowled over by it. In a letter to Sir Peter Medawar he described:

Three days before the official prize-giving in Stockholm I had to receive the Swammerdam medal in Amsterdam, and take part in a one-day symposium … We met scores of our former students (but also my old professor Boschma), as well as of course relatives. Next day straight on to Stockholm, arrival in fine, very cold weather with snow on the ground … very jolly reception … then in the Grand Hotel 20 minutes before the next reception. The receptions were often fun, but many of the same people turned up; we could have done with half of them. The Grand Hotel was of course marvellously comfortable, and our attendant and the driver of the Nobelbil were very pleasant and helpful people … You were quite right – it is a grandiose occasion. We enjoyed the prize-giving ceremony itself very much – the young king, poor boy is very shy. The banquet in the Golden Hall-cum-Blue Room was great fun, fantastically noisy – super-sherryparty syndrome … I was placed next to an 80 years old 'Boss of the ladies-in-waiting' a Mrs Rudebeck, and we had a whale of a time – I could even teach her that a tot of brandy in your coffee is not a bad idea. The smaller dinner party in the palace was very charming; by mistake the King took Lies as his right-hand lady, which was a stroke of luck for her … now she had Prince Bertil on her right, and flirted unashamedly with him (the old rogue as she called him – once he had a little wine in him he was great fun). My Nobel lecture went in my opinion well, although I had to cut part – it was made for 40 minutes but I was last and had to economize; the king came and the naughty boy was 20 minutes late. Lorenz's talk will probably in writing be interesting, but because he tried to speak freely and get cheap laughs from the audience he messed it up, a pity. The interest was embarrassing: there were two overflow halls, packed full … we sailed through pressures that I would not have weathered on previous occasions, and that was not just 'euphoria', for the striking improvement began three weeks before … as a result we stand so differently, that on photographs I look disgustingly like a crowing cock, very embarrassing … as you predicted, we have greatly enjoyed it.[3]

Soon after their return the Tinbergens withdrew to their small country cottage in Cumbria (which I will mention later), exhausted, counting their blessings, and writing thank-you letters. The Nobel Prize money was £50 000, to be divided between the three laureates; Niko received almost £17 000. He decided to divide it up mostly between people working close to him, and Lary Shaffer, Margaret Manning (née Bastock), and I received almost a quarter of it each, to spend on equipment. The rest went to various libraries and small projects, and he only kept £2000 for books and equipment for himself. Niko was strange about money; in this case he was very concerned that everybody would now think him rich and request favours, and he went out of his way to warn several people off before they had even thought to ask.

He sent about 700 printed letters to all his well-wishers (instead of Christmas cards), headed 'Advance, Ethologia', thanking everyone for their friendship and telling them how flattered he was.

Receiving the Nobel Prize for Physiology or Medicine from the king of Sweden. December 1973, Stockholm. Courtesy of the Tinbergen family.

> *But I want to assure you that I am aware of the great responsibilities this distinction carries. I shall, to the best of my ability, try to direct my future effort towards joining forces with all those who are working so hard to find remedies for the predicament in which our species has managed to get itself entangled. May our scientific offspring be given the opportunity to continue what I am cocky enough to consider 'the good work!*

The group was euphoric, and threw a great, boozy jollification. But the official Oxford response to the achievement was lukewarm; Pringle organized a drinks party.

Niko's high of the 'Nobel months' was not to last very long. There were scores of invitations to speak at prestigious lectures and conferences, invitations to become involved in committees, and requests for his opinion about policies and rights and wrongs of the world. This flood of begging letters was to continue for years, and almost all of them received a negative answer. He emphasized in the thank-you round-robin how much he felt the responsibility of the distinction weighing on his shoulders. This weight dragged him down, into more of the old depressions. He was deeply worried that students and other people would now expect knowledge and insights that he could not provide. He felt this especially over behavioural and natural history issues, and it was this feeling of inadequacy that made him avoid contact with academia, and decline invitations. Many a student or young colleague was keen just to talk to Niko, to share something of his glory, or just to get the feel of what he was like – but Niko saw this as a responsibility that he could not carry, and he felt people were expecting things from him that he could not deliver. There were long periods when he just closed himself off completely, guarded by Lies.

The Nobel Prize for von Frisch, Lorenz, and Tinbergen may have been cause for general celebration, but there were critics, too. Few questioned the distinction of Karl von Frisch, but Lorenz was haunted in the press for his former Nazi sympathies. Niko's animal ethology and political past were largely beyond reproof, but where he became involved in research and advice on human behaviour he drew a great deal of fire. One specific target was his Nobel Prize acceptance lecture during the ceremony.

Even more than in his inaugural in 1968 and in his Royal Society Croonian Lecture in 1972, Niko dwelled on what he saw as ethology's mission to help humankind. He did not talk about his animal studies. The title was 'Ethology and stress diseases'[4], and he focussed on childhood autism, and on a therapy for postural improvement, the Alexander technique (see below). These were Niko's almost exclusive, recent interests then, reflecting a gradually increasing concern with the subjects that went back several years. His critics found him way beyond his expertise.

Visiting Konrad Lorenz, back again where it all started, in Altenberg, 1978.
Photo I. Eibl-Eibesfeldt.

Childhood autism

The part of Niko's Nobel lecture that dealt with autism summarized an earlier paper by Lies and him. It aptly described his passionate involvement in the study of the disease, which was to last for a decade. The magazine *Psychology Today* wrote about Niko:

> *Tinbergen remains torn between enthusiasm about ethology and despair over its possible value. He is troubled by the guilt that comes to a man who grew up in post-Victorian times when every person did his duty. That duty was, by definition, unpleasant, and Tinbergen's joy in observing gulls and other creatures convinced him that he was a shirker. The guilt has gnawed at him for years, making him physically ill and leaving him with only a third of his stomach. Finally, after a lifetime of doing what he loves best, he has turned to autistic children.*[5]

The subject of childhood autism had begun to take Niko's and Lies' interest in the late 1960s, only a few years before the Nobel award. Their first paper on the subject, in 1972, was rather strident, long, and largely ignored, but following his outspoken Nobel lecture in 1973 Niko was thrown right into the centre of the field. It generated withering criticisms as well as some enthusiastic praise from many corners of the globe. In 1976 he referred rather disparagingly to his autism work: 'the little study made by Lies and myself of the problem of autistic children was an isolated excursion … we were prevented from following it up';[6] nevertheless, in 1983 the couple's work culminated in their substantial book on the subject, *'Autistic children': new hope for a cure*,[7] which was reprinted two years later. In general, the paper, Nobel lecture, and book caused much shaking of heads, but here and there a recognition that ethology had done some good.

Childhood autism, or Kanner's syndrome, afflicts thousands of children. It is described as a condition in which, from early age onwards, children are unable to form relationships with people, not even with their parents, and they show serious mental retardation, though with isolated and sometimes exceptional abilities (for example musical, artistic, or mathematical). Other symptoms are abnormal reactions to sounds and other stimuli, an abnormally strong resistance to change, and a strong attachment to objects. The children show obsessive repetitive behaviours, and they are prone to very severe fear or anger. Autism causes horrible misery to individuals and families, and it is hardly surprising that many scientists have become totally involved and dedicated to finding an explanation and a remedy.

One of the first problems they meet is that the condition has so many different faces. No two cases are the same, there is huge variability in severity and in symptoms; in fact, what is described as one syndrome may be a range of mental conditions with different causes. It is this that was at the bottom of many of the severest criticisms the Tinbergens had to answer, especially because they (or rather Niko, because he wrote it all) were so stridently categorical in their statements. They claimed a cure, but their detractors maintained that they did not know what they were talking about, and that the Tinbergens' subjects were not really autistic.

The Tinbergens, enlarging on earlier work by Corinne and John Hutt,[8] made the important point that almost all the symptoms of autism could also be met, separately, in 'normal' children. They admired and closely followed the work of the American psychiatrist Martha Welch, whom they invited to write a long appendix to their later book. Significantly, Welch's contribution started with: 'Autism is caused by faulty bonding between mother and child'. She argued that curing autism has to be based on a repair of this bonding; the Tinbergens state again and again that almost all cases can be traced back to early failures of the contact between parent and offspring. Implying, of course, a failure in parenting. Their cure consisted in repairing the bond between mother and child.

To start with, Niko argued that ethology could make a large contribution to understanding and curing autism, firstly because autistic behaviour patterns also occur in normal children and can be described and put into context, and secondly because much of the behaviour of autistic children is non-verbal (their speech develops little or it regresses), and it demands the type of observation that ethologists use to describe the behaviour of animals. So they (especially Lies) set out to study mother–child relationships, watching in shops and on buses, often falling back, for reference, on their relationships with their own children. Most of the photographs of children's behaviour in their publications on autism are of the Tinbergen's own children and grandchildren.

They observed, rather than talked to and interfered with, their subjects, a method pioneered for children's behaviour years earlier by Niko's former student Nick Blurton-Jones[9] and much applied since then by researchers such as the Oxford psychologist John Richer. Unashamedly comparing with animal studies, especially with the displays of gulls and other birds, Niko concluded that the child's behaviour towards its mother and other adults involved a conflict between timidity (fear) and sociability. Similarly, behavioural conflict is at the root of many animal relationships; for example a female gull shows fear and attraction in her displays during pair formation. Niko argued that in children there is nothing new here, except that it appears to go wrong in the autistic child.

The Tinbergen husband–wife team made a very attractive combination, with Niko as the experienced behaviourist and Lies as the fanatic children-watcher. Niko himself felt pleased that, after a life-long pursuit of his own interests, now Lies could have a crack of the whip. Lies' influence was very strong; the study was a joint one, but it was largely Niko lending his abilities to what Lies wanted to do, doing it the way she wanted. Several people commented to me on how, at the time, Lies 'kept Niko under control', even 'kept people away from him', in order to protect him from the outside world, to prevent his exhaustion and fend off his horrible depressions. An interview for *New Scientist* in 1972 comments on Niko's reticence, and his wife's nipping in with 'quite surprising insistence' on a rather irrelevant point. 'There is a moment's silence for the whole pleasantly quiet interview has been changed. She apologises in a kind of way for her intensity. So does he ... he is a tolerant man who doesn't want to dominate – a rare enough thing.'[10]

The Tinbergen style of writing about autism is often rather strident and somewhat ranting, and in their last book they themselves even admit to the 'fairly aggressive tone of our 1972 publication'.[11] Although this 'aggressive tone' was absent in the Nobel lecture, in their book the Tinbergens did not improve much on the earlier paper. They were emphatic, often using italics to make their point, with the old Niko-expressions such as 'time and again', 'there is no doubt', 'of course', and statements such 'We submit that ... objections are founded on shallow thinking', 'our evidence ... is hard, whereas evidence on correlations ... are scientifically useless', and many more. They decried research into structural problems of autism, advocating instead a focus on the symptoms of the disease. But at the same time they themselves never produced actual hard data relevant to their own study, only examples from their immediate acquaintance and highly selective references to literature.

The Tinbergen lack of proper data in their publications did not help; for instance, it is difficult to get any impression of how many autistic or normal children they actually looked at. They described behaviour of normal children in contacts with adults, they referred to 'many cases' and discussed six selected individuals in their book, children who showed symptoms and who were more or less successfully treated. There were 'many discussions with parents, therapists and teachers'. One feels a great lack of objectivity, and the proselytizing style detracts from the impact. Hard science it was not.

The autism book is doom-laden, with several references to a 'sick society', the pollution of our habitat, over-exploitation of resources, and to the '*psycho-*

logical forms of pollution which form a serious threat to our well-being and to that of our children' (their italics).

> *We are damaging the human breeding stock of tomorrow. Quite apart from, for example, the effects of starvation, of lead poisoning etc. on children's brains, we cause by breaking up the social context of groups of extended families and even of family life itself, very serious long-term damage: we breed and raise women and men who have not had the chance to develop fully their potential for optimal parental behaviour.*

Niko and Lies noted that autism is more common in the professional classes, and 'it seems that working-class and peasant mothers are, intuitively or of necessity, better mothers than many intellectuals and over-affluent mothers with few children'.[12] They suggested that, for a mother, holding down a job and rearing children properly is almost incompatible, and 'we consider it axiomatic that the children's interests come first'. One may note that in their own lives the Tinbergens were consistent; up to then Lies had spent her entire married life rearing their children, and while both sons went on to university after completing their secondary education, none of the three daughters did (although two of them did attend university later, as adults).

The core of Niko and Lies' suggestions was that there is a large range of severity in conditions of autism, and that most, if not all, are caused by environmental effects (especially deficient bonding with the mother) at a very early age. In an interview in 1974 Niko states categorically that 'A number of these children are damaged by their parents, even though the parents may have acted with the best of intentions. But they shouldn't feel guilty about it. Many psychiatrists have said that the parents of autistic children are odd in some way – either strained or apprehensive or overserious.'[13]

The Tinbergens were convinced that these environmental effects can be identified through ethological analysis of observations, and can usually be undone by the right treatment (that is, repair of bonding): such treatment is achieved by teaching the mother. In the 1972 paper and the Nobel lecture Niko advocated that 'anything must be done to avoid over-intimidation' of the autistic child, 'watching all the time but acting only when the baby demands it', acting lovingly to regain the child's confidence. But some years later their advice on how the mother should be taught was radically altered, and the Tinbergens' preferred approach became that advocated by Martha Welch,[14] 'forced holding' of the (often struggling) patient, in a tight, intimate, and enforced embrace by the mother daily, for half an hour or longer. It was this last treatment that appeared to be often amazingly successful, but it was curiously irrelevant to the Tinbergen's theory of behavioural conflict. Their recommendations had little to do with their ethological study and hypotheses.

Criticisms of their approach[15] were especially that the Tinbergens were not dealing with really autistic children (who, it was suggested, are organically different before birth or from a very early age), that Niko and Lies were merely treating one of the symptoms of autism (social relationships), that it was unfair to blame parents, and that their observations on 'normal' children were irrelevant ('how much can one learn about polio by observing the patients, or by observing colleagues on crutches after a ski-ing weekend?'). Leading the attack against Lies and Niko was Dr Lorna Wing from London, who herself had an autistic child.

Dr John Richer, a London psychologist who has worked extensively on autism, tried to put the differences into perspective. He commented:

> *Coming from the sanity of the science of ethology, Niko did not perhaps allow sufficiently for the pseudo-scientific and political thinking of psychiatry and psychology, … equal status of physiological and environmental causes, genetic influence, the objectivity of direct observation … was not taken for granted. So the fact that Niko did not spell it out led to more misunderstanding and some pretty unpleasant stuff … [some] people seemed to agree with him about the need to change the pompous pseudo-science of psychiatry and psychology. Perhaps too the Dutch straight talking clashed with British difficulty with that! Certainly it all got very emotional. There was a TV programme by the late Desmond Wilcox on Holding Therapy in which Lorna Wing appeared, and as Desmond said, shot herself in the foot. She and the National Autistic Society which she helped found … lodged a complaint against the BBC but then withdrew it at the last minute.*[16]

The Tinbergens also had their defenders; for example the *Economist* in 1988 refers to scientists at the meeting of the British Association for the Advancement of Science, who 'praised not only his work on animals but also his controversial study of autistic children, which brought an avalanche of criticism upon him in the 1970s. … But some more conventional psychologists attacked Dr Tinbergen for raising false hopes and putting too much blame for the condition on the child's family. … His detractors, like sticklebacks, are just defending their territory.'[17]

Niko's response to the 'après-Nobel' criticisms was typical: 'When a scientist ventures into a neighbouring field, he is likely to express unconventional views: and if he utters unkind criticism as well, he has to expect counter-criticism.'[18] He did not expect to be applauded for his efforts, especially since he himself held psychiatrists in contempt. On the face of it he took all criticisms on the chin, but I have little doubt that they did affect him personally; he was wounded, and they aggravated his depressions.

In the long run his excursion into autism science did his reputation little good. Even many years later it is referred to somewhat condescendingly; as an example, one 2002 account of Oxford zoologists sneers that 'Tinbergen also believed that childhood autism was caused by "refrigerator mothers", and in his 1983 book *'Autistic children': new hope for a cure* floated the theory that autistic children could be cured by a flurry of maternal hugging.'[19] Some psychiatrists are of the opinion that Niko's views will just fade away.[20]

What does shine through and will remain, though, after all these years and despite all the reservations one may have, is the Tinbergens' deep love of children, and their urgent desire to help in what is a horrible affliction. This was probably the Tinbergens' great driving force, not the science itself. Recently it has been demonstrated that autism is, indeed, an organic problem: it is biochemically detectable as a physical abnormality at birth,[21] not just an affliction environmentally induced by, for example, lack of parental bonding. Evidence has emerged recently that autism may be an autoimmune disease.[22] So there is little doubt that the Tinbergens, and Martha Welch with her holding therapy, were addressing only one of the symptoms of the syndrome, not the roots of the disease. But that symptom of social incompatibility, the lack of emotional contact between autistic children and their parents and friends, is one of the most distressing aspects of the disease, and if Lies and Niko contributed to its relief (which almost certainly they did), they achieved what they wanted.

The use of ethological methods in psychiatry, that is, the routine of detailed observation without in any way interfering with the patient, was acknowledged as a 'potentially very useful approach',[23] especially the comparison of observations of autistic and normal children. The method may not have been properly applied by the Tinbergens themselves, their work may have been lacking in quantification and objectivity of selection, but they did support the principle and greatly publicized it. Apart from ethological methods, the theoretical framework of ethology also has its uses in psychiatry now. John Richer, after referring to the criticism that the Tinbergens blamed parents, writes: 'The second misunderstanding was of the nature of motivational conflict behaviour. Many critics were simply not aware of the power of direct observation, of how motivations are inferred, and particularly of the diversity of motivational conflict behaviour.'[24] Indeed, from the Tinbergens' circle, experts such as Nick Blurton-Jones and John Richer have been highly successful applicants of ethological, observational methods in their studies of child behaviour.

The Tinbergen autism episode, at the end of Niko's career and brought into sharp focus by his Nobel lecture, was not a happy one. The science was not beyond reproach, the criticisms were emotional and unpleasant, and the effects on Niko's personal life went deep. But autistic children probably benefited, even if it was for the wrong reason, and in the end the Tinbergens' intervention also moved science forward.

The Alexander technique

The first part of Niko's Nobel acceptance lecture had caused surprise, because the autism subject was rather new ground for him, it was controversial, and there was not much relevance to the subject for which the Nobel Prize had

Niko making a point, around the time of the Nobel award. Photo Lary Shaffer.

been awarded. But the second half of his lecture drew even more criticism: it dealt with the Alexander technique. Afterwards, one can only say that this entire section was a silly mistake on Niko's part, bad judgement at a time when obviously he had lost some of his grip. For an animal behaviour expert to devote almost half of a Nobel lecture, when the world's finest were listening, to some very minimal experience with an 'alternative', non-scientific technique to improve human body posture and movement, was totally out of order. Afterwards, he was made to realize this in no uncertain manner.

The Alexander technique has not been properly defined, but a great deal has been written about it. In essence, trained teachers help people to properly use their body, by first explaining what is 'proper use', then persuading them to anticipate and guide every movement and posture, to rationalize muscle movement, and in that way to promote natural use, especially of the back and neck. The idea is simple, but unsustainable claims have been made about the effects of the technique on one's overall physical and psychological health (including heart and lung diseases, cancer, depressions, etc.). Niko took it, hook, line, and sinker.

What had happened was that, in the same year as the Nobel Prize, his daughter Janet, 27 years old and a professional cello player, had been prompted to go to an Alexander teacher in Oxford, as she was having repetitive strain, back, and neck problems; many musicians use the Alexander method to help with this. She felt that she benefited, and Niko read a small book about the technique by Wilfred Barlow,[25] son-in-law of the eponymous Frederick Alexander, and main proponent of the technique in Britain. He wrote to Barlow:

your book was so convincing that because my wife had such a high blood pressure I said: we must try this. And if I ferry her along, I could just as well ask for treatment myself. And then I was truly staggered and delighted to see that my deep depressions, which I have had for years and years, disappeared as if by magic. And with it clarity of thought, overall interest, and resilience against the miserable world news also came back. ... I have become firmly convinced of the enormous value of the Alexander therapy – for therapy it is – and I have become a missionary too.[26]

Niko and Lies had become 'patients' and friends of a well-known couple of Alexander teachers, Dick and Elizabeth Walker.

Alexander was an Australian, born in 1869, a professional public speaker who sorted out his voice problems by improving his stance and movements, then proceeded to write about this to teach others. In his Nobel lecture Niko gushed: 'This story, of perceptiveness, of intelligence, and of persistence, shown by a man without medical training, is one of the true epics of medical research and practice.' Alexander had followers who became teachers themselves, a movement was born. During Alexander sessions, a teacher manipulates a student, and with careful hand movements and pressures on various parts of the body focuses attention on individual muscle systems, during normal, everyday-type movements and attitudes. Slouch, hypertension of muscles, over-correction of postures, all such are immediate problems that are addressed, and psychological benefits are said to follow.

The Alexander technique has become something of a cult, hero-worshipping the memory of the man himself, with much fuzzy writing around it. In Barlow's book about the 'Alexander principle' the main thesis is: 'Use Affects Functioning' (sic), upon which he builds a large set of arguments. His physiological explanations are often ignorant and wrong, and the claims he makes for the benefits of the 'principle' are unsupported by the simple case histories that he quotes. The Alexander treatment appears to be just one of many alternative medicine approaches to physical health that make similar claims to smoothing life's difficulties.

Niko used some of Barlow's illustrations for his Nobel lecture, and he enumerated many of the benefits of the 'therapy', which he said

consists in essence of no more than a very gentle, first exploratory, and then corrective manipulation of the entire muscular system ... we can already confirm some of the seemingly fantastic claims made by Alexander and his followers ... their long list includes first of all what Barlow calls the 'rag bag' of rheumatism, including various forms of arthritis; but also respiratory troubles, even potentially lethal asthma; following in their wake, circulation defects ... gastro-intestinal disorders of many types; various gynaecological conditions; sexual failures; migraines and depressive states that often lead to suicide – in short a very wide spectrum of diseases, both somatic and mental, that are not caused by identifiable parasites.

The Nobel lecture then provided the only piece of scientific respectability to the Alexander technique by referring to 'some recent discoveries in the borderline field between neurophysiology and ethology', especially the 'key-concept' of reafference (Niko quoted a paper from 1950).[27] This is the idea that the brain compares feedback about posture and movement to a blueprint of what the posture or movement should be, and it is this blueprint that has gone wrong in present-day human society.

The references in Niko's lecture to the Alexander technique attracted a spate of protests, especially in letters to the editors of the American and British general science magazines *Science* and *New Scientist*, most of them pouring scorn. A full-page letter in *Science*[28] mentions earlier references to the Alexander technique as 'dangerous quacking', and it castigates Niko for his use of terms such as 'extra-ordinary', 'seemingly fantastic', 'surprising', and 'astonishing' when taking seriously Alexander's and Barlow's claims of wide-ranging benefits. It notes that Alexander's work was concerned not with postures, but instead with what he called 'use' and 'misuse'. It draws attention to the fact that no-one ever discussed 'placebo effects', it calls Niko's illustrations of skeletons (borrowed from Barlow) 'anatomical science fiction', and finds 'Tinbergen's photographic exhibit of slump, slouch, and postural vice – no different from what most of us have encountered in elementary physical education – of no special relevance to the Alexander technique'. Niko's reply was non-committal, ending with: 'Alexandering may be good for you – why not give it a try?'[29]

A *New Scientist* article[30] was somewhat more gentle, yet equally critical. It made the point that Niko refers to an Alexander 'treatment', a word avoided by Alexander teachers themselves; the process has nothing to do with corrective manipulation as implied by Niko, but 'it is more a kinaesthetic education', a learning how the body should move. 'Professor Tinbergen's description of what

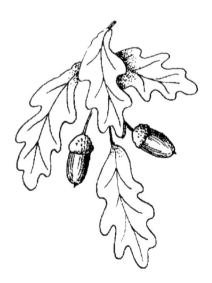

appears to be some form of osteopathic treatment has very little to do with the Alexander technique.' Several weeks of *New Scientist* correspondence followed, until the editor closed it; writers of letters referred to 'Professor Tinbergen's ludicrous description in his Nobel address', and there were statements in defence of Niko, including one from Wilfred Barlow who mentioned that he had vetted Niko's Nobel lecture, and that Niko referred comments and queries on it back to him.

In the years after, Niko gave one more lecture about the Alexander technique,[31] about animal adaptations and his views on the evolution of 'good' and 'bad' body posture, with the evil influence of modern Western ways of life. Slowly, his interest in Alexander petered out; his depressions, headaches, and pains had started again soon after the Nobel celebrations were over, and after a couple of years it was conceded that the Alexander technique did not do a great deal for him. In his autobiographical sketch 'Watching and wondering' some 10 years later,[32] there is no mention of Alexander: his brush with it was past. But to this day, pamphlets and books on the Alexander technique refer to the Nobel Prize winner's scientific justification of its claims, and he has been adopted as a hero of the technique.

Some two months after his Nobel acceptance speech and considering all the reactions, Niko commented (trans.): 'I feel that as far as autism is concerned and stress in general, I have to shut up for a bit. In my Nobel lecture in Stockholm I have stuck out my neck rather too far, and really I have very little to say about cancer patients.'[33]

All in all, perhaps the Nobel lecture would be best forgotten.

CHAPTER 9

Winding down

Retirement

Somehow it seemed an incongruous and irrelevant deflation, that Niko should retire within months of his glory. But university rules dictated abdication at 67, and in fact Niko was more than ready to leave the Oxford department on the appointed date: 30 September 1974. Earlier that year he told Baerends (trans.): 'I am more or less preparing myself to withdraw, and I am still very much in doubt about what best to do after my retirement. ... I will continue to contribute a bit in the lab, but I do feel very outdated (a well-known after-Nobel phenomenon!).'[1] He had felt for a long time that it was necessary for someone like him to fade away, and earlier he had told Konrad Lorenz 'The greater the man, the more necessary for his successor for him to fade out – and even at my modest level I have decided to make myself scarce when I retire.'[2]

Three of Niko's senior pupils, Gerard Baerends, Colin Beer, and Aubrey Manning, edited *Function and evolution in behaviour*, a volume of 17 essays in Niko's honour at his retirement, written by his former students and colleagues, with an introduction about The Maestro himself.[3] It gave an overview of studies that were immediate follow-ups from Niko's own work and mostly by his 'own people', ranging from theory to field studies, with subjects from digger wasps to hyaenas, gannets and rooks to spiders. It was a splendid representation of the current ethology of Niko's school, and Niko himself took great pleasure from it. He was most impressed by the contribution of Gerard Baerends, on the 'conflict hypothesis' as an explanation for the evolution of displays, and he sent Gerard an extensive critique[4] whilst in hospital with depression.

When the date of retirement arrived, the Zoology Department let Niko go without ceremony, but his research group, students, and friends arranged an excellent party in Niko's college, Wolfson. There were about 60 friends and pupils from the old days in Oxford and recent ones, old friends from Holland, and Niko was deeply touched and quite emotional. For the occasion I had arranged a large scrapbook[5] with photographs, and written and artistic contributions from people covering Niko's entire career, which, I think, pleased him immensely. The style of the contributions, photographs, and drawings bore testimony to Niko's pervasive influence on all of us, a long way beyond the science that he imparted.

Niko certainly was not sorry to leave the Zoology Department. In the last years he had spent less and less time there; he preferred to work at home as he could not relax in the clinical atmosphere of the new, concrete building with its large windows, and he felt out of his depth amongst the new developments of behavioural science. Computers, rigorous quantification, talk of models, all of this was anathema to him. In what used to be 'his' group there were several friends who shared his passion for animals, fieldwork, and natural history, but somehow they, too, became less visible. Niko's successor David McFarland (see Chapter 10) had been in place for a few months; he was friendly, but his and Niko's interests had little in common. The congenial atmosphere of the old days had gone.

Desmond Morris had a room in the animal behaviour section, organized for him by Niko a few years earlier and, when it was agreed that Niko was to have a desk in the department after his retirement, he suggested that he move in with Desmond, on a time-share basis.[6] He thought that he would use the room in the morning, Desmond in the afternoon. His way was paved with good intentions, but three years later a note from Niko to Desmond read: 'you may have noticed that I have at last been in our room in the lab'.[7] Another two years later, 1980, the department sent him a bill for some minor photography charges; Niko, offended, wrote a long letter to the new head (and successor to John Pringle), Sir Richard Southwood,[8] who reacted gallantly and told Niko he was welcome to whatever services he wanted. But Niko cleared his desk, never to set foot in the room again.

His plans for retirement were ambitious, they varied with time, and they were all largely overtaken by events. He intended to continue the autism work with Lies, but also he hankered back to his old ethology. He even thought of doing some fieldwork again, and he was keen to start a study on food-fighting between starlings, in his own garden in Oxford, for which he took on a girl student. She was not the right type, however; she could not take the early rising that Niko always requested of his field people, a fact that could not be hidden from Niko in his own garden. After some months she left. He was all ready to write more books, first of all 'a new, methodological introduction to ethology, not much larger than *The study of instinct*, and with just a little more Man in it.'[9] Then 'I have decided, spurred on by Konrad Lorenz's (in my opinion very bad) little book on the Eight Deadly Sins, to write an equally short, but I hope better account of the human predicament.'[10] It was to be called 'Man – guinea pig of evolution', but it never got any further than drafts for the first four chapters.[11] Then he thought of 'a generally understandable book about the origin and consequences of the cultural evolution'.[12] With his friend Major Jimmy Rose, the voluntary warden of the Ravenglass dunes, he went some way towards a popular coffee-table book of photographs and essays on the dunes, to be called 'Sandy Acres'. None of these ideas ever came to fruition, and only the book that he wrote together with Lies, on autism, saw the light of day.

Niko still did the odd lecture, on the autism work and on the Alexander technique, and he wrote some more popular papers, including several for his old Dutch love, *De Levende Natuur*. There was a long paper in 1981 on human aggression, 'On the history of war',[13] covering earlier ground from the Croonian lecture, and a popular contribution 'The importance of being playful'.[14] The titles were gripping, and the subjects of general concern; for example, in the play article Niko argued that in recent years we have seriously altered our social environment: it has become more complicated, so personal adaptation for individuals – learning – is that much more important now. Children and animals play a lot, and they demonstrably learn and acquire skills that way, from which Niko concluded that play is essential. However, he argued, institutionalized education is taking its place, which may be harmful and it turns children off (one remembers that Niko himself was a truant who hated school). The problem with Niko's argument was that children may well learn just as much without playing, but it is very difficult to experiment with this kind of issue.

Niko wrote some more brief articles about the history of ethology, and he helped other historians of science. What took a considerable amount of his time, some seven or eight years later, was a long autobiographical article, which I will discuss below. So Niko continued doing some of the same things he had done before, but in many ways his retirement left him somewhat confused, and bereft of purpose. A year later, a letter to his old Dutch friend Kees Hana started: 'now I am sitting at home, like a rather useless little chap, I just wanted to write to you'.[15] Even his interest in autism had ups and downs at that time; he had reservations about its relevance, and he was 'feeling more attracted to pure animal work'.[16]

When Niko answered Bill Thorpe, the Cambridge behaviourist who was writing a history of ethology,[17] he wrote that 'the little study made by Lies and

The Tinbergen house at 88 Lonsdale Road, Oxford. Photo HK, 2000.

myself of the problem of autistic children was an isolated excursion .... [which we were] prevented from following up ... attracted vigorous criticism from experts on the subject.'[18] This, *nota bene*, on a subject on which, two years earlier, he had given his Nobel lecture. The next year he told his German friend Renki Eibl-Eibesfeldt that he had stopped all autism work during the last two years. 'I am suddenly an old man, and I have not yet recovered from the blow.'[19] Yet he did return to the autism work soon after he wrote this, and five years later the Tinbergens' book was published.

Sadly, many of Niko's best-laid plans, schemes, and commitments for his retirement never left the drawing board, because soon after the dazzling events of the Nobel Prize were past, his body and spirit gave way again, badly. Poor physical and mental health were to dog him for the rest of his years. For one thing, Niko had been an increasingly heavy smoker ever since the war. It used to be a running joke, his rolling of a cigarette at any time of day, letting you roll one of your own with his tobacco if you were a friend, or rolling one for you (and you had to lick it yourself) if you were a very good friend. In later years, when he became more and more stressed and his cigarette consumption rocketed, he smoked them ready-made, with Lies stacking up his supplies. At the time of his retirement he went through 500–600 per week,[20] four packets per day, in contempt of himself for being an addict. Yet, after feeling the effects of a few more years of this, he managed to rid himself of the poisonous habit and in 1976 he stopped it altogether, quite proud that he could do it.

Smoking was only a minor part of his troubles, though, and at the time it was probably a consequence more than a cause. He had become a hypochondriac, often concerned with his symptoms, and Lies probably exacerbated this with her worries, and with her almost fanatic preoccupation with nutrition and vitamins. Between them they spent a great deal of time considering their ailments and dosages. Letters from his retirement years frequently referred to his health, especially to his depressions, and almost every friend received long accounts, usually with an up-beat twist to them ('we now know what was wrong, I am over it thank god, but what happened was ...'), and at times Lies added her version of events. Then the next year there would be another, different crisis: 'but this is now all behind us, I am a changed person ...'. Niko's depressions were ghastly, some almost suicidal, and they were getting worse. The fate of his brother Luuk was always in the back of his mind.

Hardly half a year had passed since his retirement when things had become so bad and potentially dangerous that Lies felt she could not cope any more. The consultant psychiatrist who had treated Niko several years earlier, Dr Irvin Kraeger, advised admission to hospital, and against Niko's strong opposition he was taken to Kings College Hospital in London, with 'severe agitated depression with suicidal tendencies'.[21] He was there for several weeks and came out in an 'up mood', but before long the depression was there again.

This was the pattern for the next few years, with deep, black downs without any activity, and jubilant up-swings. For example, he wrote in December 1977:

After three-plus years of that damn 'morbid depression' I have at last really emerged, and I am more alert, more widely interested, harder working than I have been in the last 15 years or so! Over the last two months my body has been throwing out the last remnants of the various nasty drugs I have had (lithium among them), and we are convinced that my total stop on smoking, dating from 18 months ago, is also having beneficial effects! ... Am now writing like mad on our revised autism work, and I am going to resume outside commitments: late April to USA, late June to Konrad, then to a meeting of Nobel laureates in Lindau on Lake Constanz.[22]

The cause of the depressions was variously identified by GPs, psychiatrists, or by Lies and Niko themselves, as a genetic factor involving under- or over-active thyroid or lack of blood sugar (hypoglycaemia), then it was the treatment itself (lithium), a virus, then diet, lack of vitamins, or something generally termed the 'bloody bug'. Niko could never accept his problems as a mental disease, it had to be something physical. Each time he was convinced that this was it, he had overcome the problem, and each time the depressions came back again. He passionately hated and loathed his stays in hospital, combined with a deep dislike and mistrust of the medical profession, especially of psychiatry. I believe that this must have been an important factor in the pronounced aggressive anti-medical establishment stance he took in the autism writings.

The depressions came to a sudden end in late March 1983, when Niko had a couple of bad strokes, just at the time of the publication of the autism book. Lies and he were staying in their holiday cottage in the north of England (see below), and one morning Lies woke up and realized that Niko was unconscious. An ambulance took him to the hospital in Carlisle, and he was then transferred to a large specialist unit in Newcastle upon Tyne, where he was in a coma for several weeks. Lies was with him all the time, totally committed and deeply worried; initially, the prognosis was bad.[23] When he came round he could not move or speak, and his memory of people had gone.

Recovery was slow, but after several weeks he could be moved to Oxford. In the John Radcliffe Hospital he was operated upon, and lymph fluid drained from his brain; this brought immediate improvement. He was wheelchair-bound, had difficulties in moving and speaking, but gradually, month after month, he improved. There were setbacks, but his sense of humour came back; he was frail, but often jolly. They were difficult times for Lies, because she had to look after his every need, and she had her own problems with high blood pressure and angina. April 1984 found both of them in hospital, Lies because of her heart, Niko because nobody else could look after him. Health was an almost full-time occupation, and they fussed even over little things (like having the amalgam fillings in their teeth replaced because of potential mercury poisoning).

An old Dutch friend, visiting in 1985, reported that Niko was (trans.):

much, much better than I could have hoped. As soon as I was inside he shook
me firmly by the hand. For walking he uses a stick, and undoubtedly he finds
it difficult, but he does it; also he gets up from his wheelchair by himself. … His
conversation was totally OK. He does not speak loudly, but I had no problems
in understanding him. We talked about all sorts of things, old and new, politics,
psychology, you name it. He was full of enthusiasm … humour and good cheer.[24]

One of Niko's own comments was 'creaking carts go furthest', and 'the grim
reaper has not got me yet'. He realized that his memory often failed him, but it
did not worry him much; he enjoyed his garden, watching television, and the
contacts with the people around him, with his children and especially with his
grandchildren. He wrote many letters to friends and family, but now all by
hand, first rather shakily but soon again in almost his old, firm writing. He could
never use a typewriter again. Despite his infirmity in these years of the mid-
1980s, he had a contentedness in his late seventies that had not been there for
many years. He was still a difficult patient, but there were no more depressions,
and he enjoyed watching the birds and the fox in his garden, the natural history
around him and on television for which he had not found the time before.

In his later years, until his stroke, the joys of birds, plants, and insects around
him had rather eluded Niko. After he finished with his student projects in
Ravenglass his wonderful dunes had more or less disappeared below his
horizon, and he had concentrated on filming in Walney and on studies with
children. Although he still supervised students in the field, he could not relax;
birds and bees, 'watching and wondering' seemed far from his mind, even in the
early years of his retirement. But it did come back, as did his interest in his 'old'
ethology rather than what was developing out of it.

Letters written by Niko during the last years before retirement rarely show
him as the marvellous naturalist that he was; he seemed to have no time for
natural history. Then, in 1974, when he started a correspondence with an old
Dutch NJN soul-mate, Kees Hana, it was full of descriptions of the recent
changes that Niko saw in the Ravenglass dunes. He wrote about the willow
herbs, brambles and creeping willow that were invading, with the hawk-moth
caterpillars he found on them, and about observations of plants and insects in his
own garden in Oxford and around Slakes, the holiday cottage in the north. He
was watching the spotted flycatchers catching insects, the sheep and their lambs
around the cottage, and the fox between his cabbages, just delightful stories of
what had always absorbed him.

The one thing that was different from the Niko of younger years was that
there was no 'wondering' aspect any more. He still was a nature watcher with
few equals, but the sharp questions that made him stand out thirty years earlier
were missing. Right through all his remaining years Niko delighted himself and
his friends with his fascination in all aspects of life around him, even in his
suburbia, but he did not find science in it any more. He recognized this; once,
after a long letter with lovely observations on sheep he wrote:

Natural history during retirement: tracks of adder, natterjack, shelduck, and rabbit crossing.
Photo Niko Tinbergen.

> *And so on and so on. But I do not find anything new, nor do I really care*
> *whether I do or not. ... My reaction to seeing some nice bit of behaviour in my*
> *garden or around our cottage in Westmorland is often 'Thank God that I need*
> *not do research about that; I can just look at it, wonder a little about it, draw*
> *a few simple conclusions, and for the rest enjoy it'.*[25]

Once Niko had more time on his hands he visited the Ravenglass dunes
again, the scene of so much natural history fun in earlier years. Major Jimmy
Rose, the voluntary warden, was someone to whom he became close. He was

about the same age, they had a rapport, and they were bound together by their passion for wildlife. There was a plan to do a book together about the dunes, which never materialized, but they had a great time in their joint walks over the sands, along the pools with the natterjack toads, and in the gull colony. Niko noted the changes in vegetation in the dunes, but not being an ecologist it never really worried him, he just watched in fascination the sudden increase in numbers of species of plants and insects. Then, within a few years in the 1980s the entire gull colony, once the largest in Europe and which had been there for many centuries, the colony where Niko and his students had done such pioneering research, vanished. The cause was never established, but most likely it was the large increase in nutrients in the rainfall, an aerial pollution that caused those beautiful bare, shifting sands to disappear under thick vegetation. Niko was not very sentimental about it: '... the former gullery. What a shame!', and no more than that, in a letter to Jimmy Rose.[26]

Even in the last few years before his retirement Niko had barely kept up with developments in ethology. In the years following the Nobel Prize, the little that he saw of his science did not please him much, although he tried to be sympathetic. The person with whom he discussed science, more than with anyone else, was his old friend and very first PhD student, Gerard Baerends, professor in Groningen. From the 1950s on there was a steady stream of letters between the two. Typically, three years into his retirement Niko wrote (trans.): 'Ethology is in a phase in which animals are forgotten, and abstract problems take their place. Yet I have to admit that work like that of McFarland [his successor in Oxford] and Richard Dawkins is magnificent and sharp.'[27] But then a couple of years later (trans.): 'I cannot follow McFarland's stuff (and I have my doubts)', [28] and in 1980 he stated that (trans.): 'the more abstract thinking of Maynard Smith, Hamilton, Trivers, and Dawkins I do not completely understand, and moreover, I suspect that they know too few animals, and know too little about the multitude of phenomena and aspects.'[29] It was an expression of the old worry in our kind of science, about the gap between theory and field studies, when theory appears to be disconnected from practical knowledge of animals.

But Niko was still keenly interested in the problems and methods of old, 'classical' ethology, in the arena where he had earned his spurs, and in which people like Gerard Baerends were still very active. Baerends and his group continued with field studies on gulls, trying to understand behaviour in terms of conflicts in motivation, and producing models of a hierarchy in the organization of behaviour, treating the animal as a 'black box' where one only knows input and output. In many other centres ethology developed in different directions, such as behavioural ecology, cognitive ethology, neurophysiology of behaviour, etc. (see Chapter 10), but Baerends argued that there was much left unsaid in their old field, and he found a keen listener and reader in his old teacher. Niko was highly impressed with Baerends' work, and their exchange of letters contained many discussions of it, Niko even contributing his arguments and observations when he was staying in hospital in London.

In the correspondence between the two there are many pages with thoughts such as the following, when Niko, from his bed, responded to Baerends' contribution to the volume in Niko's honour, *Function and evolution in behaviour*.

> *Your ideas about the different levels of interaction in the balance between sex, aggression, escape, staying put in different species and different sexes and ages seem well founded ... one will have to ask why, in terms of adaptedness to niche, each species, sex, age has the type of balance that it has. I am a little unhappy about saying that a species is overall aggressive or overall shy. Ten-spined sticklebacks are 'shy' with respect to predators, very aggressive in intra-specific encounters. Kittiwakes are aggressive amongst themselves, are tame to us on the cliff, but are shy when collecting nest material.*[30]

Other discussions cover Baerends' recent publications on herring gulls and their relevance to Niko's old Ravenglass interests. This especially concerned the camouflage of gulls' eggs and the behavioural repertoire connected with it,[31] and other subjects.

Right in the middle of some scientific argument in a letter, Gerard Baerends wrote that a hobby flew past his window, before presenting a lengthy diatribe against a recent 'Introduction to animal behaviour', which rejected some important aspect of the 'Lorenz/Tinbergen paradigm' (that is, the conflict of different motivations of behaviour).[32] These were Niko's old scientific interests in his retirement; newer developments of ethology passed him by. He was quite open about this; he acknowledged that 'my work consists mostly of writing new prefaces or re-editing old books.'[33] He certainly spent a great deal of time on the various reprints of his old books, and he was quite keen on giving semi-popular interviews about his own, scientific contribution. He was inordinately proud of the long interview in *Psychology Today* in 1974, 12 pages of 'A conversation with Nobel Prize winner Niko Tinbergen', and he ordered 1200 reprints, to be sent to almost everyone he knew.

A few years after the stir caused by his Nobel acceptance speech, he worked up enough enthusiasm again for the autism work, 'bracing myself for the unbelievable, hostile (not merely critical) attacks that will continue to come'.[34] This did not involve further observations, but it meant finishing the various drafts for their book, collecting more 'examples' to prove their point. 'I only just managed to get a readable text written before I became senile.'[35] What both he and Lies saw as especially important was proselytizing, convincing people that 'their' method, the forced holding method, was the way to go about curing autistic children, and in between Niko's bouts of depression they wrote to many practising psychologists. 'This has been a very, very difficult struggle against prejudice and indifference, but we can see the ultimate success coming. It is a happy final chapter of our lives, and I personally feel that it justifies the Nobel Prize (for 'Medicine'!) that I got, somewhat prematurely, in 1973!'[36]

In 1986 the Tinbergens and their method twice had an airing on BBC news, and they were delighted by that. Niko told his friend Jimmy Rose 'As non-medics we are not used to this kind of thing and we felt very excited about this outcome of a long, uphill struggle. Even the old-fashioned British psychiatric "Establishment" has now got to take notice. From my "Watching and Wondering" paper you will have understood that we had not really hoped to live to see this.'[37]

The battle that the Tinbergens fought against the medics was a battle on behalf of autistic children. But in this, all the resentment emerged which Niko had built up during his own struggle against depression, which he also saw as a fight against psychiatrists. He thoroughly disliked the medical establishment, and even before his depression problems started he had an antipathy towards doctors. It was all the more ironic that he was the recipient of the Nobel Prize for Medicine.

Most of the attention that followed Niko's Nobel award was felt by him as a an oppressive obligation. However, some of the aftershocks of the prize were rather pleasant ones. For instance, there were the awards of two honorary doctorates, from the University of Edinburgh in 1973, organized by Aubrey Manning, and from the University of Leicester in 1974, organized by Uli Weidmann. There was an Emeritus Fellowship from Wolfson College in Oxford, also in 1974, and various other honorary positions from professional

societies (see Chapter 10). But although he quite liked all that, Niko's deep-seated modesty was always cynically in conflict with such distinctions. For example, to Robert Hinde he wrote:

> That whole matter of 'distinctions' is an odd corollary of our competitive society. There is no doubt that some of them do give one a boost – and so I am glad to be able to congratulate you on your election as a foreign associate to the National Academy of Science; in your case this both means something and will help your institute along; in my case it was one of those almost meaningless post-Nobel gestures.[38]

And in the *Psychology Today* interview he said: 'I agree with what my brother Jan said when he received the Nobel Prize in economics, "Such distinctions ought to be given to fields of research, rather than to individuals."'[39]

What did strike many of Niko's friends as remarkable, and rather sad, was that he never received any civil honour. Having achieved what he did, one could have expected a knighthood, but that never came his way. Perhaps his foreign background did not help, although other naturalized scientists (for example Hans Krebs) did become 'Sir'. More likely the reason was that Niko was never 'one of the boys', never one of the Oxford establishment, and never a great committee member or chair. In any case, if he had been offered a civil honour I am not sure that he would have accepted.

Right through into the 1980s Niko received a mass of requests for lectures and attendances at conferences, and applications for help and support for science, peace and human rights, and other issues. Most of them he hardly read; 'I have my hands full with saying "no"' (trans.), he told Baerends.[40] But some he did follow up, a seemingly random sample of the requests that he received, and, if he did get involved, he knew that his voice counted. Amongst the many opportunities that came his way, he did not want to attend the grand occasion of the Lord Mayor's dinner in London, he did not sign requests from Amnesty International for the release of particular prisoners of conscience (argument: no favouritism, and he had been one himself), but on his own initiative he did write to his local MP in support of bringing back the death penalty.[41]

He did sign a letter to Reagan and Brezhnev calling for a stop to the arms race, and attended a large rally in Trafalgar Square for the same cause;[42] he did support two scientists in Connecticut who were about to be sacked for initiating a study on race and intelligence;[43] and he did attend several meetings of the Nobel laureates in medicine in Lindau on Lake Constanz. But he did not attend a 1988 meeting in his honour of the British Association for the Advancement of Science, and he declined an invitation from a Dutch TV company for a programme on his life's work (argument: there was not much modern relevance, he was not a leading personality any more, the old field work could not be reproduced, and he did not want to take part in a programme of just interviews). A 1987 invitation from the French president François Mitterrand for Niko to attend a wide-ranging discussion, on the state of the world, on underdevelopment, pollution, ecological equilibrium, and new biology,[44] fell on equally stony ground. He had strong opinions on many of the issues involved, however far they may have been from his own field of expertise, but fears that he might overstretch himself and undermine his own mental and physical health made him steer clear.

Ever since Niko withdrew from active field research in the 1960s, which was also when his depressions took serious hold of him, his views on the state of the planet and the future of humanity became more and more gloomy. Visiting Holland did not help – burgeoning population, industry and wealth had destroyed much of the natural beauty Niko had seen in his youth. From personal experience I know the effect this has on an expatriate Dutch naturalist: a feeling of pain and anger, and total detachment from one's roots.

Niko's concerns were often with the fate of humanity rather than with conservation of the natural world, but not everyone was sympathetic to his doom-laden letters. To Ernst Gombrich he complained about a 'typical' TV programme: 'Its restlessness (contrived by a variety of tricks) strikes me as pathological and (I am convinced) in the long run harmful because of "over-input" … many children not only tolerate this restlessness, but like it. … I begin to believe more and more that our civilisation exerts a growing stress on its members by a process of "information input overloading".[45] He was concerned about 'the amount and quality of inputs that modern society forces upon us … Sheer volume of noise … the sheer quantity of information that we get from the mass media is simply too much for many people … children lap it up, adjust surprisingly well to the tempo, but may well become addicted and as a consequence restless as adults.'[46]

Gombrich took a much more sanguine view:

> *I am afraid that I am never easily convinced when the past is praised in contrast to the present. As a historian I believe that most ages were and are pretty horrible (or rather unpretty and horrible) ... But the point I wanted to make is whether the people in the past did not sometimes suffer from under-stimulation ... The fantasies about Hell ... in lots of sermons may suggest something of the kind, and so do the paranoid pre-occupations with witches and demons. For vast numbers life must have been very void and dreary.*[47]

But Niko was not easily convinced that things were not as miserable as all that. He tried to persuade Desmond Morris to do a television series entitled 'The Predicament of Man', sending him pages full of suggestions.[48] A planned book on the origin and consequences of cultural evolution was abandoned, as (trans.): 'I am kept from doing this because, if I'd really do it well, I'd make the younger generation desperate.'[49]

In his *Psychology Today* interview, Niko said:

The human predicament is not just a question of behavior, but of the relationship between behavior and environment. By progressively changing our environment faster and faster, we outpace genetic evolution by at least a thousandfold. Adaptedness is a certain relationship between the environment and what the organism must do to meet it, and man is faced with a loss of that adaptedness, and so has to adjust individually. The amounts of strain now imposed on the individual may well overstretch man's capacities to adjust. ... Excessive strain shows up in man in stress diseases, in increased admissions to mental hospitals. To mention one example about which my wife and I know something, stress appears to have led to a sharp increase of autism in industrialized societies.[50]

A few years later he wrote to his old friend Ernst Mayr: 'At the moment we must be concerned with the sanity and health of the whole of humanity ... I simply cannot see our species survive much longer.'[51]

In his autobiographical article Niko warned about the increasing human population, the insufficiency of world food production, the use of non-renewable resources, pollution, and armament, and finds that

the inescapable conclusion is that the outlook for the survival of the human species is very gloomy indeed. ... if we do not change our life-style and reverse the trends I have listed, Homo sapiens, and with him many other higher forms of life on Earth, will soon, at best experience an unprecedented population crash, or, at worst and in my opinion more likely, become extinct ... this crunch seems to approach with frightening inevitability ... we shall have to reverse the trends ... there is no choice, and time is running out.[52]

In his gloomy assessment of the state of humanity, Niko paralleled his old friend and colleague, Konrad Lorenz, but there was a different quality to their forebodings. Konrad focussed on 'innate', deleterious characteristics of human behaviour, whilst Niko addressed the entire human ecology as well as social behaviour. Not entirely unexpectedly, Niko was quite critical of Konrad's pronouncements on the subject. He objected particularly to Konrad's pronouncement (in his book *On aggression*[53] and later) that aggression is 'innate' in people, with the implication that nothing can be done about it apart from channelling it in the right direction.

Old friends

Niko's reservations about Konrad's writing were symptomatic of a changing relationship. In the 1930s Konrad and Niko had been very close friends, in a warm personal relationship that extended over their scientific partnership. They shared a deep love of animals, and a sense of humour that often spilled over into the riotous laughter of two 'Lausbuben' (street urchins). Together they campaigned against what they saw as, in science, a hostile outside world. But within this friendship there always had been a large contrast between the two, with Konrad in the role of the egocentric extrovert, using big words on wide philosophical pronouncements, the eternal story teller with ideas that were rarely thought through, a large man smoking a pipe, surrounded by people and dogs. Niko was the modest scientist, a step-by-step thinker coming out with flashes of insight or jokes, the small, quiet, and deferential birdwatching scientist who mastered language whilst rolling his cigarette.

It was this unlikely combination of Konrad and Niko that developed a science, but in the eyes of the world, Konrad always came first. On the surface, Niko had always swum along with this tide; 'Lorenz', he said, 'is *the* great pioneer of Ethology … with truly unrivalled power of observation'.[54] But deeper down something rankled in him, and more and more as time passed. The personal differences, which once were ignored or even seen as a strength in their partnership, came to be objectionable. 'We are often a little annoyed by Lorenz's over-assertiveness and vanity',[55] he wrote, and he referred to 'our dear Konrad, whose views on the history of Ethology become more and more Lorenzian!'[56] 'He and his wife live with a pack of dogs – I find it rather sickening, but then I'm not an animal lover.'[57] When a sycophantic biography of Konrad appeared in 1983[58], Niko commented:

> Such a book makes me uneasy, with its uncritical obsessive adulation and the implication that his life has been planned like this from the beginning. A really great man does not need this kind of propaganda. I hate saying this because I do like and admire so much in Konrad. But humility and modesty are not amongst his most striking assets. Who wants to live surrounded by an adoring clique? And to add to the acclaim oneself?[59]

Konrad and Niko had gone through a coldness in their relationship that reached its greatest depth in the 1960s, when Konrad became more assertive, and Niko more critical of Konrad's ego and especially of his science. Niko profoundly disapproved of Konrad's dichotomy of innate versus learned behaviour, arguing that one should see the organization of behaviour as a scale of intensity in many kinds of environmental influences on the genes (including learning). He also objected to Konrad's uncritical, authoritative statements, which were always pronouncing mere suggestive hints in his observations as proven facts. Lorenz interpreted Niko's stance as hostile to him and to their old ideals, ranking Niko with 'the other English speaking ethologists' ranged against him.

However, Niko was not hostile, he was critical.

> It is to me sad to see how Konrad, who in 1937 cleared the way to almost all that is being done now in Ethology, and who then stressed: 'these are

hypotheses — we must test them', has, in his recent utterances, betrayed himself, and cannot now stand any disagreement any more; he thinks in a 'closed system'. This has assumed such pathological proportions that he has taken deep offence at my saying that I agree with [the American animal psychologist] Schneirla that we must look at the entire developmental process; Konrad writes to me that it would have been more honest if I had said that I agree with S. that 'everything is learned'. This reading an entirely different meaning into my words is what disturbs me; I must conclude that either he is ageing terribly, or that he is at the moment for some reason deeply disturbed. This, in combination with a very German authoritarian father-attitude (which was always there but which, already three years ago, had become too strong) may well mean that he is going to continue to wreck his own life's work, and will become very unhappy in the process.[60]

Niko's, on the whole gentle, disapproval of Konrad continued for the rest of his life, although on the rare occasions that they met they appeared to be the best of friends, with back-slapping, roars of laughter, and sharp-witted, teasing exchanges. Criticism emerged in public during interviews at the time of the Nobel award, when Niko openly urged Konrad to come clean over his Nazi record: (trans.): 'The best advice I can give you is that you should say in Stockholm, where the world will be listening: I admit that I have done that and it was wrong, but it was because of political naïvety.'[61] Konrad never admitted anything. It cannot have done their friendship much good, but it did not show.

Together with Niko's more critical attitude towards Konrad came several attempts to set the record straight about his own contribution to ethology. Despite his natural modesty and his recognition in the joint Nobel award, Niko did feel that he was depicted too often as Konrad's aide-de-camp, with Konrad having the ideas and Niko performing some experimental checks. Every so often his annoyance about this came out into the open, and he was at pains to correct people. To one historian of science, the American Richard Burkhardt, Niko wrote:

The greatness of Lorenz has in my opinion (and that of many others) been due to his uncanny but fairly intuitive ability to use and reject selectively what he heard from others in the world of ideas and facts, and to combine that with what he, again fairly intuitively, derived from his truly unrivalled power of observation. But in his theorising he has not only been vague, but has also ... taken a stand, stubbornly and eloquently advocated ... sometimes correct but fairly often wrong and research-stifling ... He has often changed his mind, never said so clearly but has done it in a seemingly flowing way, and hardly ever acknowledged the source. Mind you, knowing how gifted he was in 'appropriating' for example jokes from others ... As soon as he was taken by an idea, it became his, and I think one could not say that this was anything dishonest — it was part of his (very egocentric) personality.[62]

Lies, Niko, and Konrad after a meeting of Nobel laureates in Germany. Söcking, 1981.
Photo I. Eibl-Eibesfeldt.

Niko then continued to show that it was he who had demonstrated that ethology is the biological study of behaviour, whilst Konrad Lorenz had used some rather silly definition such as 'the branch of research started by Oskar Heinroth'. In his letter, Niko upbraids Burkhardt:

> *In my opinion, [in your manuscript] you really reverse our roles, because as I said, it has taken me years and years to make Konrad accept that it was important to spell out this idea of 'biological study'. ... Admittedly this is a rather personal point, but it is in my view fairly typical of our collaboration. Something similar applies to his and my comparative studies. I have acknowledged in print that I started comparative studies on the prompting of Lorenz, but our comparative studies went beyond 'mere homologising' [that is, comparing like with like in different species], whereas Lorenz, however detailed his Anatinae [ducks] work was, neglected the functional, ecological angle, and only because of this could come to the wrong view that signal movements were moulded by one selection pressure only: the requirements of the signalling function. ... we could point out that the evolution of signalling, and in fact social behaviour in general, could only be understood by recognising that the requirements of habitat, food etc. had a say in shaping such behaviour. ... he had, like many of his colleagues in Germany and Austria, rather a blank spot with regard to modern ecology.*

Other problems that Niko pointed out in Lorenz' contribution were that

> *his psycho-hydraulics model has hampered rather than furthered research …*
> *my idea about the hierarchical organisation was a step forward, and especially*
> *valuable since I linked the higher levels with the lower levels of integration …*
> *Lorenz has never really given up thinking in terms of the dichotomy innate*
> *versus acquired behaviour … Konrad's most serious research-blocking term*
> *was 'innate drive' … The continued use of this dual term shows that Konrad*
> *has not really seen what we mean by the four questions.*

Despite Niko's unease about his personal and scientific relationship with Konrad, in their last years the two men were very affectionate. Niko felt desperately sad for Konrad when the latter lost his only son, and they kept frequently writing to each other. Konrad sent a telegram for Niko's birthday: 'Welcome to the 70th decade' – typical Konrad, was Niko's comment, 'a bright idea and he gets it wrong.'[63] There was much nostalgia, especially on Konrad's part: 'that summer in Altenberg, where we together rolled the eggs of the greylag geese and dig ponds, was probably the most beautiful in my life'.[64] After Niko's first stroke: 'Thank god you're getting better. Already once before I thought you were dead, when people told me in Groningen of the suicide of your brother and I thought it was you.'[65] The letters are full of warmth, and one feels the vulnerability of the two old people, both in their eighties. The long pages of friendship were scribbled by Niko, and dictated by Konrad, who was unable to write any more. Konrad's last letter to Niko, typical in several ways and three weeks before Niko's death, ends: 'Dear Niko, that you are still here and that you participate in me, is more or less the most beautiful thing in my old age, and I thank you for that.'[66]

Many other comrades-in-arms kept writing to Niko throughout his retirement, and Niko responded volubly. Often, in the many, many pages of letters that he wrote, one senses the real Niko, where he unburdened himself and showed his feelings on paper with much greater ease than when talking to people, except perhaps to Lies. With his best and oldest friend, Gerard Baerends, Niko exchanged more letters than with anyone else, but there were also reams of correspondence with Desmond Morris, Jimmy Rose, and a host of others, colleagues and former students, and with new and unknown people, almost all from the world of science. Leafing through these letters one senses Niko's concerns in life, his feelings of guilt, his enjoyment of living things around him, the misery that he saw in the changing world of society and the environment, his absorption with his physical and mental well-being, and after retirement one notices the ebbing away of his fascination with science.

With Gerard Baerends, often addressed by Niko as Baerendje, Niko talked animals, they gossiped about other ethologists and the quality of their work, about biopolitics and day-to-day occurrences, about vitamins and depressions, about families and staying with each other. Sometimes Niko wrote the same things twice within a few days, but what did it matter – the two were friends. Baerends was a solid, painstaking, and very well-organized scientist, who kept and filed every letter that he ever received, as well as copies of his own.[67] He was a soul-mate with the same interests, though without Niko's exuberance, enterprise, and naturalist's flair, and without Niko's skills of communication. Baerends was always a solid support, personal or scientific, on all levels.

One thing that the two discussed in detail was a successor for Konrad Lorenz, who had to retire from the Max-Planck institute in Seewiesen at about the same time as Niko in Oxford.[68] Niko was asked for his advice by the Max-Planck Gesellschaft: he wanted Baerends to succeed Konrad, and Konrad very much liked the idea. Gerard Baerends initially reacted positively, especially because his own position of authority, as head of department in the University of Groningen, was made very difficult by a stifling process of democratization. His hands were tied by endless committees of staff and students, and he wanted to leave. But when the university, and the Dutch Royal Academy, realized that they were about to lose a top scientist, they offered Baerends a personal chair with assistants and no other obligations, and he decided to stay in Groningen. In the meantime, he and Niko had persuaded the Max-Planck authorities that Konrad should not stay on as an emeritus in Seewiesen when a new head was appointed there, and Niko, not wanting to do things secretly, explained this to Konrad, whose ego was understandably wounded. In the end, Konrad received a new institute with staff and expenses back in his home country, Austria, and one of Konrad's disciples, Wolfgang Wickler, became his main successor in Seewiesen. Niko was keenly involved in such science politics and power machinations.

Desmond Morris was another dear friend, living nearby in Oxford, and he and Niko saw each other as well as maintaining a long correspondence.[69] Desmond had become a very popular authority on the biology of human behaviour, and his books had attained cult status. The two often talked about their books; Niko admired Desmond's easy, popular writing with which he was so successful, and especially because Desmond's work dealt with human behaviour – his was an ethological advance into human psychology territory. But Niko also gently chided him.

About Desmond's autobiographical *Animal days*, Niko wrote:

> *Congratulations on a delightful book – a touch too hammy here and there to my taste, but nevertheless a fine mixture of scientific integrity and that special brand of irreverent, almost puerile wit that Konrad and I too have so often indulged in. … My main reaction was: what a terrible shame that, when you worked in our lab as a graduate and postdoctoral worker, we mutually missed so much about the other's life: I was too preoccupied with making a success of our group … to have given sufficient attention to your personal life and your many activities in other fields (although I remember seeing one of your surrealist films, but not clicking with it at all). And since your work was so*

lab-bound I never developed those 'comrade-in-arms' ties that I could not help developing with my fellow field workers. If you had worked in the field, say in Ravenglass, we would mutually have discovered many of the more lighthearted, emotional and irreverent sides of each other's characters. ... About von Frisch: since you don't speak or understand German, it has escaped your attention that, when he gave a popular or elementary lecture, he expressed himself so beautifully, lucidly, and not at all pompously. He was a rather serious and in some ways a dull man, but he was a master of communication, with a lyrical touch in much of what he said too.[70]

Of a totally different calibre was Niko's relationship with Major Jimmy Rose, warden of the Ravenglass dunes for some years during Niko's retirement. He lived close to the Tinbergens' holiday cottage in northern England. The long, frequent letters[71] between them were full of details of what is happening in the country, the swallows returning, fly-catchers fledging, the weather, the vicissitudes of common acquaintances in the village, always returning to Niko's and Lies' health, and events around the Nobel Prize and the autism struggle. They are two old men sitting on a bench, chatting.

Between Niko and his old American friend, the animal behaviourist and endocrinologist Frank Beach, there was another series of affectionate, old-gentlemen-together letters, some of them five pages long. Frank and Niko were close in many ways, not geographically (he lived in California), but as people

Naturalists in the dunes: Niko and Jimmy Rose in Ravenglass, 1980s. Photo Lary Shaffer.

and scientists. In his last letter, only a few months before Niko's death, Frank commented on parts of the science scene, with 'E. O. Wilson a sloppy thinker', and Ernst Mayr 'only interested in ultimate causes'. He made points that were equally valid for both Niko and Frank:

> It is a continuing surprise to me to realize how much of my professional work has become the central part of my life. My entire ego structure, the feeling of who and what I am, is intimately bound up with my perception of myself as a scientist. ... The facts are that you and I probably will never see one another again. That doesn't make me sad but one has to face one's own mortality. And one can be thankful for modern methods of communication.[72]

An interesting exchange in these retirement years occurred between Niko and the epistemologist Sir Karl Popper, generally regarded as one of the greatest philosophers of science of the twentieth century. He had an enormous influence on the structure of scientific thinking, on the nature of experiments, and on the kind of questions one asks in science. In 1974 Niko had responded to Popper's Herbert Spencer lecture with a critique on Popper's distinction between genetic and environmental programming of the individual, and in his letter he said 'observation is a process of interaction between the individual and the environment, in which the internally given potential cannot be realized (cannot lead to programming) without the environment ... It seems to me that in saying that 'the instructions come from within' you repeat, at a new level, the mistake we ethologists made so often ... when we called certain behaviour mechanisms 'innate'.[73] Popper basically agreed: 'every perception is a rapid process of exploratory learning; that is, of matching expectations (hypotheses) against the external world by way of trial and error (= selection).'[74]

The warmth of Niko's relationships with other people in the last years of his life comes through in scores of his letters, to old colleagues like Ernst Mayr, Peter Scott, Lars von Haartman, Friedrich Goethe, and Renki Eibl-Eibesfeldt, and to former students such as Aubrey Manning, Bryan Nelson, Harvey Croze, Lary Shaffer, me, and others. But parts of his previous work scenery just disappeared – he abandoned them. There was little contact with Leiden; once in the late 1970s he went back to Hulshorst with Jan van Iersel and Leen de Ruiter. But letters were few. Similarly, there was not much exchange with people like Robert Hinde or the Oxford behaviourists; they were too much into modern behaviour studies and Niko had lost interest in that. He went out of his way, however, to respond in detail to students who wrote to him with questions.[75]

Rather pathetically, Adriaan Kortlandt, his sparring partner of long-gone days, was cut off without ceremony. In the early 1980s Kortlandt had retired from his post in Amsterdam and moved to Oxford, in order to be close to the ethology action. But in the behaviour group there few people took notice of him, and he was left in the cold. From his home Niko wrote to Kortlandt that he did not think his move to Oxford was a good one, that he did not want to get involved again in ethological debate with Kortlandt, and that he did not feel that there were personal reasons for seeing him.[76] They never met again, though Adriaan lived within walking distance of Lonsdale Road.

One, totally unexpected tie that emerged again after Niko's Nobel Prize was with his brother Jan: they began to write to each other, after a lifetime of mutual neglect. As boys they were poles apart, with a wide divergence in character and interests, and later they and their wives were not very close. But as old men the two brothers met again. Jan was a giant; his Nobel Prize, preceding Niko's by four years, was given for contributions in the field of econometrics, of measurement of economic forces. He had also been awarded 10 honorary doctorates and a good handful of civil honours. Like Niko, but in his own way and coming from a different field of expertise, Jan was committed to the social and environmental problems of the world. Together, the two brothers were potentially a large force for betterment.

Their letters in the 1970s and 1980s[77] were fairly short and to the point; there was some affection (but not much); mostly, one feels, it was Jan exploring Niko's scientific contribution and not vice versa. The two did remain enormously different in outlook. As Niko told a Dutch friend (trans.): 'My brother Jan wants to make everything measurable, but I keep asking him: "You want to help making people happier, but how do you measure happiness?" His standard reply is always: "By measuring you get somewhat closer to what you want to understand." I doubt it.'[78] One could hardly find a view of science further removed from that of Niko, the adventurer. But they did have some common interests, such as the world's over-population, and expectations of over-exploitation of resources.

Despite his friendly overtures, Jan was clearly critical of Niko, although he did not say so outright in his letters. He used hidden barbs such as (trans.): 'Of course I read your exposition with interest. Previously you had also presented me with a number of similar facts and opinions, and they are full of valuable qualitative knowledge, next to conjecture and (enormous) gaps.'[79] Or, in Niko's last year of life, Jan wrote (trans.): 'your contribution is mostly qualitative, less in quantitative work, and yours is at least as important as measuring and counting. The measurement of feelings remains a controversial business.'[80] However, underneath Jan's critical jabs there was an envy of his brother. He once said (trans.): 'In science there are accurate and exact little people, and there are the wild men who come with ideas to be tested by the exact little people. I belong to the wild men.'[81] But whatever Jan's genius, a wild man he was not – what he admired in Niko was that which he wanted to be himself.

The one time in their lives that the two brothers were together on a podium, and both contributed to a conference, was in 1974 in Holland, when a symposium was held on the future of the Wadden Sea, for a large audience. The Wadden Sea is a large area of tidal flats, between the Friesian islands and mainland Holland, Germany, and Denmark, with masses of birds and fabulous landscapes, threatened by drainage, industry, and pollution. Jan talked about the comparison of economic and environmental values, and the mechanism of government and management;[82] Niko gave a presentation on many of the ills of humanity, the cultural evolution, environmental and social pollution, and the need for reorganization of society along non-capitalist lines.[83] Niko's talk was rather more vague than that of his brother, neither of them dealt specifically with the Wadden Sea problems, and there was not much common ground. Nevertheless, they found an interested and sympathetic audience.

Despite their renewed contact, the gap between the two Nobel-awarded brothers was never bridged. Mostly this was, I believe, because Niko was just not interested. Jan, in his letters and lectures, sometimes referred to his position and his achievements with a degree of pride that did not sit easily with Niko's sense of modesty, and Niko must have felt some inadequacy whenever Jan sang his quantification refrain. Niko could not be bothered any more. Unlike Jan, who even in retirement kept his work interest with his eyes on the far horizon, Niko in his last two decades lived in a much smaller world.

A family, a cottage, a life

One important part of that world of Niko was in the north of England. In the late 1970s his former PhD student, Lary Shaffer, showed a delightful film on television, *Man bites dog*. It is set in the hills of the north, in Westmorland (now part of Cumbria), a landscape of green pastures, fells, and sheep, with few people, and rain as raison d'être for many trees and flowers.

A small, white-haired man sits against one of the many stone walls between the fields, looking old and vulnerable, and he talks to camera, narrating the story of sheepdogs. Niko, relaxed, sometimes with a cigarette, talks about their behaviour, derived from that of hunting wolves, and one sees the fabulous cooperation between shepherd, dog, and sheep when a flock is taken across the fells; there is wonderful scenery, light, and snow. The shepherd is a friend, Edwin Dargue, whose dogs are part of his life (his most severe punishment of a puppy being a bite in its ear).

All this had started several years earlier.[84] Niko was still filming in Walney, and Lary was with him, doing his study on gulls and crabs but becoming totally absorbed by filming. Lary was almost like a son to Niko, they were always doing things together and Lary, a man with many highly practical skills, was there to help Niko with anything he needed. Niko wrote numerous notes to Lary about exactly what needed filming and from what angle, and which nail needed hammering.

One day, as on many other occasions, they had left Walney at night in the Land-Rover, to spend an early morning in Ravenglass. It was a couple of hours' drive away, and they wanted to film the sands and the birds at dawn, together with Jimmy Rose who stayed there in his caravan. On the way back across

'Slakes', Niko and Lies' second home near Dufton, Westmorland. Photo Niko Tinbergen.

the high hills and moorlands, they stopped to eat their lunch. As they sat on the tail-gate and looked across the magnificent fells, they could see a large flock of sheep, driven fast by two collies, the sheep swerving, tightly packed, moving exactly as ordered. Sheepdog working is always an awe-inspiring sight, and Niko, pulling on his cigarette was thinking of a study, and a film. 'There must be something in it', he said several times – he had one of his hunches. Next time he was in Ravenglass he mentioned it to Jimmy – who countered almost immediately: 'I've got just the thing'.

In his village, Dufton in Westmorland, Jimmy introduced Lary and Niko to Edwin Dargue, and Niko was totally taken by the farmers and the animals, who had a way of life in the country that he had never experienced himself. Within months Jimmy had drummed up a local farmer who would not mind selling a little cottage, way off the road, and in 1972 Lies and Niko bought 'High Slakes'. Slakes was a simple house, dark, damp, with stone floors, with wood fires and without electricity, surrounded by stone-walled pasture land, a small stream behind it with huge, tall trees. It was idyllic, and Niko just loved it. Lary and his wife Beth could base themselves at Slakes (making many repairs and modernizations in the process), and they filmed Edwin and his dogs. A couple of years later Lary bought his own place nearby. For the next 14 years, in spring and summer, Niko and Lies came up from Oxford every few months for a couple of weeks at a time. Often one or more of their children joined them, with or without family, and friends from the south or abroad were invited. I also stayed a few times at Slakes with my family, sometimes when Lies and Niko were there, sometimes on our own. Slakes had a little life of its own.

Niko had obtained a substantial grant for Lary from the Nuffield Foundation. The sheepdog film took several years to make, and in the process Lary
studied the way young dogs were trained by the shepherd (sadly, this was never
published). Niko was intensely interested in the project and full of advice and
comments. After his own success with *Signals for survival* it was almost as if he
handed over this part of his estate to Lary.

When most of the filming had been done, Lary wanted to get Niko into the
film, at least for an introduction and comments. That was 1976, a time of Niko's
deep depressions, when he was in Oxford and did not want to travel. But he
did agree to an exciting solution: the company who was accepting the film,
Yorkshire Television, offered to fly him out to Dufton from Oxford, in the
company helicopter, with Lies. It was this trip that resulted in the old, white-
haired man holding forth, sitting against the stone field-wall. It was a great
success, and Niko talked and wrote about the low flight across the country for
months. A few days after Lary's film was screened on television, Janet was told
by Niko's dentist: 'Tell your dad I enjoyed his film, but if he ever goes on TV
again without his teeth, I'll kill him.'[85]

Slakes was an ideal diversion for Niko, a reminder that one could get away
from it all, and live a life as he felt one should, primitive and well removed from
urban pressures. But it was at Slakes that he had his first stroke in 1983. He left
it on a stretcher, and a few years later the cottage was sold again. Lary had
disappeared from Niko's life somewhat earlier. Despite the acclaim for his sheepdog film, after he finished it Lary decided that the world of film-makers was not
for him, and he wanted to go back to America. In 1976 he and his wife departed,
and contacts with Niko and Lies were reduced to the exchange of letters. In the
late 1970s Niko and Lies went to stay with Lary in America, one last time.

It was a rare occasion, because by then Niko travelled seldom – he was
worried about over-exertion, and he did not much want to lecture. There were
a few trips to see his daughter and grandchildren in Calgary, in Canada, one or
two more to the United States, to meetings in Holland and Germany, once to
Israel, all of which were rather low-key events. By his own design, his world
contracted sharply; in his last ten years it may have contained some writing
and patching up of former output, but mostly it was a world of domesticity,
gardening and family, letters, and memories.

Family involved many people, and was enjoyed immensely by Niko. 'We
now have nine grandchildren, (and that's the lot, for our children have been
wiser than we and have small families)', he wrote to Aubrey Manning.[86] He
must have been thinking of his own pronouncements on overpopulation, but
regardless, of course, he doted on them. When he retired four of his children
were happily married, some with their own children since the mid-Sixties, and
around retirement several more grandchildren arrived. In the end Niko and Lies
had three granddaughters and six grandsons.

In those first years, especially, when he had more time and energy, the three
Canadian grandsons (Catrina's, then 8 to 16 years old) received lovely long

letters: the young boys being addressed as 'Gentlemen!', with pages of exciting drawings and enthusiastic descriptions of kayaking ('what to do, when upside down in your canoe', a complete guide for kids),[87] a balloon trip ('Bye, brats, large and small, and keep looking out for us high in the air. White and red stripes and a mauve top, that's us'),[88] a helicopter ride, animals, and whatever took his fancy. The other grandchildren, too, received long letters from 'Opa', with dried flowers from the garden, stamps, drawings, or whatever interested the lucky recipient. One sensed the little boy in Niko himself, who so thoroughly enjoyed these things. With his grandchildren he was often the father that his own children had partly missed out on.

It is a picture of a different Niko, yet with some of the same constraints. In one letter he described looking after the young child of an acquaintance:

> there she is, bored stiff of course, and here we are, not exactly bored stiff, but very much tied by [her]. This is of course mainly Mother's [that is, Lies'] job, though Janet and I help as much as we can. But the other day I took her out in her push-chair, and although she was not too unhappy, she did, for more than half an hour, just sit folded forward, looking at the pavement, and not enjoying the ride. I did get a charming smile when I stopped and talked to her, but for the rest of the time she sat or rather hang dumb (I felt embarrassed that people might think I was walking with an idiot).[89]

Behind all this normality of family life was the old observer, the birdwatcher who used his skills on children, and who discussed the significance of even the smallest move of his grandchildren with Lies. Five years before his death their

Retirement: Niko playing with grandchildren, 1980s. Courtesy of the Tinbergen family.

autism book included scores of observations and photographs of 'normal' children, almost all made of their own offspring. It was no surprise to Niko's children themselves, who saw it happen and who had been exposed to this in their own youth: 'you always knew that you were being observed', said one.

As before, the Tinbergens hardly went out, and they saw few friends or strangers; Desmond Morris and old Sir Alister Hardy called in sometimes. Their daughter Janet, who lived nearby, did most of their shopping. She had left the parental home in 1979, remained single, and was a great support for Lies during Niko's more difficult periods in the last ten years. He was totally dependent, and jointly, the two women looked after him and his whims. For all their unstinting support of Niko, neither Lies nor Janet had much sympathy for, or a great deal of interest in, his natural history or scientific concerns apart from autism. Niko once described his daughter's interest in these later years as 'rather allergic to natural history films and "those bloody gulls"'.[90] They led an existence of gardening, watching the television (Niko just had to see the six o'clock news, and he was an addict of *Z-Cars*, Morecombe and Wise shows, children's programmes, and others), and Niko consuming paperback detectives at a great rate and with remarkable recollection of detail; rarely read 'good' books, however. There was a weekly supply of magazines, the *New Yorker* (first thing to look at: the cartoon by Chas Adams), *New Statesman*, *The Listener*, and *New Scientist*.

Retirement reflections: photographing Lies and granddaughter. Photo Niko Tinbergen.

The Tinbergens were generous, especially to their children and grand-children, but lived very frugally themselves, with the magazines (and books, many of them) being one of the few luxuries they allowed themselves. Soon after the Nobel Prize the occasional visitor to the house would be offered a drink, proudly 'with ice!', because for the first time they had acquired a fridge. A drink, a gin-and-tonic, was indeed another of Niko's delights; in his later years Niko became quite partial to his daily tipple, where earlier he had felt himself something of a devil when he drank the very occasional small bottle of beer in the dunes. Lies could not take alcohol. Their house remained spartan; it was not that Lies and Niko could not afford the odd spot of luxury, but rather that Dutch Calvinism retained its hold over them right to the end. In fact, Niko left quite a sum of money when he died, in an estate (including their house) of over £300 000,[91] which was a decent amount in those days.

There was little doubt that self-denial was also at the root of Niko's profound sense of modesty, one of the characteristics that contributed such a great deal to his charm. Immodesty was something he deplored in others, in Konrad, even in students. Once, only a short time before his death, he wrote to me about an Oxford student who had just published a book: 'however much I admired the book, I do feel that it is very self-centred, very much "I, I, I".'[92] Niko's deprecating, and at the same time realistic, appraisal of self-worth is best expressed in the autobiographical contribution he wrote in the early 1980s for a volume of 'Autobiographies of the Founders', *Studying animal behavior*.[93] It is a piece in remarkable contrast with almost all the other 19 contributors, which included nearly all the great names in ethology; in Niko's auto-assessment there is no boasting, no pomposity, no sense of greatness. I will quote here part of the epilogue in his very aptly titled 'Watching and wondering'.

> *Looking back over all these years that have, after all, passed so quickly, I often find myself asking whether I have done the right things, and done enough. Of course there are a lot one regrets — missed opportunities, wrong handling of problems and people, neglect of duties, and if one insists on finding fault with oneself, many more things that annoy one or make one blush. But I would be a hypocrite if I dismissed what I have done as insignificant, and I would also be ungrateful if I did not acknowledge that I have been extremely fortunate in having been born a healthy and reasonably bright boy, and in having been given such fine opportunities, provided first of all by my quite exceptional parents, second by the naturalist's paradise in which I grew up, and third, to no small degree, by having been exposed to the influence of such men as Jac. P. Thijsse, Jan Verwey, Julian Huxley, Erwin Stresemann, Ernst Mayr, Karl von Frisch, and Konrad Lorenz, to mention only a few of the many persons who have affected my interests and my work.*
>
> *Admittedly, I have been, compared with them, rather like a butterfly flitting cheerfully from one flower to the next, rather than like a steadily working, 'flower-constant' worker honey bee. But such has always been my*

nature, and if, as in the words of Dick Hillenius, I have 'always been a boy with a talent for playing truant' and as a consequence I have missed much and gained much, I have at least been true to my nature.

My most 'creative' work was done before I was forty; my achievements in communication, my writing, speaking, photography and filming, peaked somewhat later; and I was lucky in finding, toward the end of my life, an intellectually less-demanding but socially extremely rewarding task in the study, done jointly with my wife, of childhood autism, a study that taught me, amongst other things, to appreciate at its true value her exceptional gifts as a childwatcher and childminder.

Finally, I am sure that I share with many of my colleagues the awareness of having, so far, left too many tasks undone, most of which I will never complete. Apart from fields from which I have either shied away (for instance, cybernetics and philosophy) or that I have been at times keen on but unable to enter (such as skin diving and sky diving), … the literature is simply gaining on me, and the problem of 'information input overload', real enough for people in their thirties, is now insurmountable for me. Ironically, this overload is in part the outcome of what we ourselves set in motion, and hoped for, when we began to develop and teach ethology! But what men in my position can truly say is that they have been privileged to have lived in such an interesting time and to have witnessed and assisted in both the birth, or rather the rebirth, and the coming-of-age of a fascinating new branch of biology.

If I were to characterize what my scientific life has been about, I would quote the lighthouse keeper of Goethe's Faust II:

> *Ihr glücklichen Augen!*
> *Was je ihr gesehn,*
> *Es sey wie as wolle,*
> *As war doch so schön!'*

[You fortunate eyes! What ever you have seen, Be it as may be, Oh, it was so beautiful!]

In those last years, small, thin, and often in a wheelchair, there was a smile and a contentedness about Niko that had rarely been there before. The depressions had gone, and slowly also he improved physically; he had his extended family, and he was happy with his life, and about what he had achieved. 'I've had a good run for my money.'

Five and a half years after that first stroke at Slakes, the announcement came in the *Oxford Times*.

Tinbergen, Nikolaas (Niko), on 21 December 1988, peacefully at his home in Oxford, aged 81. He requested that his body be given to medical research. Please do not send flowers; donations in his memory would be gratefully received by Childline, etc., Oxford.

Clowning to the camera, 1976. Photo Lary Shaffer.

Lies described to Lary Shaffer what had happened.

> *Niko was quite well in his last months although he had the occasional day of suddenly walking much less well, but then that would pass off. Then, in the afternoon of the 21ˢᵗ, he was quite chatty and quite cheerful, but suddenly thought he was going to be sick and made some odd noises. He went [out of the room] and I did not immediately understand that he was really ill, but saw it when I went out to have a look. He died some five minutes later, slumped ... and I could not feel a pulse any more.[94]*

There were no memorial services or other gatherings to mourn Niko's passing, on his own specific instructions. But Oxford behaviour people felt that some kind of science meeting was required, and a year later 'The Tinbergen Legacy' conference took place. It was attended by several of his children and 120 of his former students, colleagues, and admirers, with the talks later published as a book.[95]

Lies lived for another year, and died just before the Legacy conference. Two weeks after Niko died she fell down the stairs, broke one ankle and sprained the other, but with Janet looking after her she managed to keep going. She arranged for Niko's papers to be taken into the Bodleian Library in Oxford (after she and the children shredded everything they thought should not be kept for posterity, including all correspondence with Lies herself), and asked Niko's nephew Joost, the son of Luuk, to sort out his photographs and find a suitable destination: they ended up in the Dutch State Archives in The Hague. Her work was done.

She sold the house and moved to a small bungalow in Leicester, near her son and his wife, Dirk and Faith. In March 1990 she died in hospital in Leicester, of angina; she, too, willed her body to science.

Konrad Lorenz had died two months after Niko.

CHAPTER 10

Niko's legacy

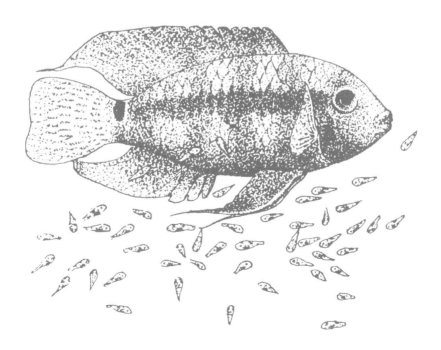

An evaluation

Niko Tinbergen was, indeed, the birdwatcher who received the Nobel Prize. How was he different? He was brilliant, yes, with ambition, persistence, and presentation, as well as a dose of good fortune. He had unusual powers of observation and, with that, he had the ability to see a biological question when watching an animal. In the questions he asked, he was an innovator.

However, there was also something else, something simple and obviously highly significant. A recent book on seven modern scientific superheroes[1] (astronomers, geneticists, a physiologist, an immunologist) argued that apart from many other personal characteristics, what these giants had in common, above all, was that they were nice. As a reviewer put it, it helps to be a daring fighter, but the ability to win cooperation from absolutely anyone who can help you is what really counts. Niko had exactly that. He was the most charming person you could wish to meet, and whether you were a chairman or a charwoman, he was immensely considerate with a lovely sense of fun and humour, and utterly without guile. People loved him even before being exposed to his remarkable talents as a communicator, lecturer, writer, photographer, or film-maker. There was also something glamorous about Niko, there was an aura of the white hunter about the great man who spent so many patient hours in bird hides, who came back from the cold and mud with his theories, stories, and photographs, and at the same time could move in exalted circles, talking so eloquently about his field craft.

Good fortune played a big part. Niko was extremely lucky in his family background, with his tolerant and intelligent parents – his father a masterly communicator with a broad interest – and his siblings a collection of clever and ambitious people, including one brother at least as good a naturalist–ecologist as he was himself. There was, just by chance and at the right time, NJN, the Dutch youth organization that grafted onto Niko its ethos of nature-watching and roughing it close to the wild plants and birds, and in Holland he had the opportunity to be at close quarters with an uniquely rich wildlife. Another stroke of luck was his partner in life: not many people would have been so self-effacing in supporting Niko in his aims as was Lies, herself a clever and critical observer of animals and people. Finally, within his animal science he came of age in Greenland, where an enormous nature was impressed upon him and where, from being what we would now call a 'green', he became a hunter. Affected by Inuit shamanism he came to see animals as mechanisms, a key secret of his outlook in ethology.

Amongst the other ingredients of the successful Niko, communicating skills were a peripheral, yet absolutely essential characteristic. 'Inspiring' was the word that people used again and again about him, and his lectures were fascinating to watch and to listen to. His written articles are still fun to read. It was not just his enthusiasm, which was enormous without being emotional, but also the expression of it: his exposés were put in clear and simple language, directly to the point; he hated jargon and long words. 'If you cannot tell a story clearly and simply, then you do not understand it yourself.' His modesty helped; he did not want to use blown-up sentences, and his personality required him to be brief and exact. His simple, no-frills, no-luxury ethic gave him the directness that people admired.

There was also his command of languages. Apart from speaking Dutch and English he was fluent in German, and spoke tolerable French. He already had this mastery of language in Dutch, almost certainly acquired directly from his father, and in the process of transferring his communication to another language, English, he was forced to think about word use, which clarified his expression. It was not just language, either: he had a similar approach to photography; he often said that a picture or a film had to express a simple story, and clearly. Next to photographs he also used his drawing skills to tremendous effect, on the blackboard, in his papers and books, and in his letters.

I believe that Niko would never have come as far as he did without his charm and his communication skills, despite his intellect and scientific insights,

Niko's delight: the lesser black-backed gulls he filmed on Walney.
Photo Niko Tinbergen, about 1967.

driving ambition, and tenacity. His fame also spread widely because he cared, he bothered to address people other than his scientific colleagues, and he was a scientific popularizer in the best tradition. Of course, we recognize him as a scientist, for the contribution he made as a thinker and fieldworker. But without those 'peripheral' attributes he would probably have gone unnoticed. He was also fortunate that he worked in a science that was appealing to a general public, and in a science where he, as a rather private person, could develop animal behaviour studies on his own as well as in conjunction with Konrad, and with his many co-workers.

Niko himself, at the end of his life, did not boast about his contribution. If anything, he was rather apologetic about it:

> I have not made any 'major discovery'. What I have been acknowledged for is a method of approach, which could be briefly characterized by saying that I have applied to the phenomenon 'behaviour' all the questions that are (or ought to be) asked in Biology with reference to other life processes; in other words that I have tried to understand the functioning of mechanisms responsible for behaviour in the same way as Biology tries to understand the functioning of other organ systems. My approach has been 'objectivistic' and my interests were cause-effect relationships ... I worked initially rather on my own, driven by some non-rational urge which I identify with that of the born hunter who wants to understand and outwit his prey animals ... Very little in my work has been 'thought out' rationally from the start; my recognition of a problem and my flashes of insight towards a solution have always come intuitively, i.e. I cannot find fully rational origins.[2]

As always, Niko was unduly modest. He is known for his 'four whys' of animal behaviour, a distinction into these four lines of inquiry that was very clearly and simply enunciated in *The study of instinct* (1951) and 'On aims and methods of ethology' (1963). He separated the 'Why?' of causation, of ontogeny, of survival value, and of evolution. In addition, and very importantly, Niko stressed the inter-fertility of the four questions: when following one of them, the others should always be kept in the back of one's mind. The impact of these 'four whys' on our thinking about animal behaviour has stood the test of time, and they are still frequently referred to. His modesty also hid the fact that he was the author of several successful books and many articles, giving insight and pleasure to a multitude of people.

Many years have passed since it all happened, and we should now be in a position to dissect and compare the influence of the two main players in the youth of ethology. Yet this is difficult. Niko's name is often mentioned in the same breath as that of Konrad Lorenz, and one glibly says that they complemented each other, that Konrad was the man with the ideas, whereas Niko was the experimenter who tested. But I hope that from the foregoing pages a more complicated picture has emerged, rooted in the very different characters of the two. There was Konrad the extrovert who spouted ideas or took them from others, who brought animals in, watched them carefully, and pontificated. And there was Niko the naturalist, who observed behaviour where it had evolved, who asked careful questions, who experimented with beautiful simplicity, and who sorted Konrad's chaff from the corn.

As well as his outdoor skills, it was Niko's clear and simple reasoning that set him apart from Konrad Lorenz's approach: Konrad had the bright flashes of inspiration, but it was Niko who saw them through scientifically, developing the right ideas and throwing out the dross. It was not a case of Niko merely filling in the gaps that Konrad had left open, but of Niko turning ideas into science. Niko's stressing of the need to study the biological function of animal behaviour was quite outside Konrad's ken.

One colleague of Niko with whom a comparison almost forces itself upon us is Robert Hinde, a grand authority, author of handbooks on animal behaviour and of many scientific papers. Colin Beer, professor at Rutgers University and a former student of Niko, commented:

> I used to think of Niko and Lorenz as constructors, as continental philosophers who are the proposers of ideas. Traditionally, British philosophers are the disposers, they cut ideas to bits. I see Robert Hinde in an analogous position. He was the arch-critic of the constructs of classical ethology; … by and large, his was the cold hand of the analyst, who would pick things apart.[3]

In his own research Niko contributed substantially to all four of his 'whys', and in each case this led to a major advance – either directly, or indirectly by others who responded and criticized. Niko approached by induction – he did things as a naturalist would, watching animals in their own world, then wondering why. Never did he start with an explicit hypothesis, and then select his subject to test it, as is normal procedure nowadays.

The principle of Niko's field experiments was innovative: where laboratory workers would experiment by keeping all the conditions around an animal constant, and then change whatever factor was to be investigated, Niko did things differently. His approach was to leave the animal in its natural environment and let nature have its way, then experiment by changing only the one aspect he was interested in and judge the impact of the change. Since then, this approach has become much more commonplace. Niko's achievement was to start the ball rolling. Niko and Konrad together were instrumental in establishing animal behaviour studies as part of biology; it was one of Niko's many contributions to take ethology into the natural environment of animals, as a rigorous, experimental discipline.

The study of causation, of the mechanisms underlying animal behaviour, was historically Niko's starting point in ethology. His demonstration of the environmental factors that hunting wasps used for orientation drew attention. This was followed by the analysis of stickleback courtship into separate elements, each in response to different stimuli from environment or partner. Konrad's idea of the 'innate releasing mechanism' or IRM made simple sense of all this. The concept that animals are structured to respond to different stimuli at different times opened up the field for biological analysis. For instance, Niko drew attention to 'displacement activities', that is, behaviour that appeared to occur out of context, and he suggested that this was the result of simultaneous activation ('conflict') of different 'drives' (such as escape and staying put).

With these ideas he activated a vast number of studies on 'conflict behaviour', including displays.[4] There was no doubt that in all these developments it was Niko who was at the forefront, although others working at the same time, or alongside him, sometimes published similar ideas simultaneously (for example, see Chapter 6 re Adriaan Kortlandt). Yet, somehow it was always Niko who was at the centre of the action, and he articulated developments in a way that appealed to science. Niko suggested the internal hierarchical organization of behaviour, again a large and fertile concept for further theorizing by others. Niko's own model of behavioural hierarchy was soon overtaken, especially because he neglected to take any feedback mechanisms into account. His pupils, Gerard Baerends, and later Richard Dawkins, picked up that particular ball and ran with it, splendidly.[5]

Whilst contributions from Niko to the study of causation of behaviour were many and diverse, his involvement with behaviour development or ontogeny was less prominent, yet still significant. His early insect-orientation studies demonstrated the wasps' learning of landmarks after one exposure, but he himself never took the theory underlying this discovery any further. More important was Niko's contribution to the seemingly endless 'nature–nurture' debate, about the way in which behaviour changes in the individual's lifetime. Niko created order in a raging discussion, mostly between American psychologists (Theodor Schneirla, Danny Lehrman) on the one hand, and Konrad Lorenz on the other, about whether the behaviour studied by the ethologists

was 'innate' or 'acquired'. Niko's intervention, admission of mistakes and friend-ship with Danny Lehrman created an atmosphere of cooperation between the Americans and the (mostly) British and Dutch ethologists. He saw the heuristic value of recognizing that there is no clear boundary between innate and learned, but that every behaviour pattern is affected by a large set of environmental and genetic values. Lorenz dug in his heels with his extreme position of either-or, and did not do the cause of ethology much good, especially later when he insisted on the innateness of human aggression.

Where perhaps Niko scored most fruitfully was in the initiation of field studies on 'function', on adaptiveness, or what he called the survival value of behaviour. This work addressed the effectiveness of behaviour, as well as the costs or disadvantages. His eggshell removal studies, and the work of his students like Ian Patterson and myself on gulls, revealed behaviour that protected against predation, but there were also penalties, and one talked in terms of compromises or trade-offs. It was the beginning of considerations of optimal performance, the line of questioning that developed into behavioural ecology, even though the cradle of that new science stood only partly in Niko's school.

The fourth and final 'why', the course of evolution of behaviour, saw another large contribution by Niko, in his comparative study on the behaviour of gulls. Here was a major advance on similar work by Lorenz on ducks: Niko recognized that mere homologies of patterns in related species do not get one very far. He emphasized that it is the environment that exercises selection pressure, not social needs. Therefore the entire ecology of each species has to be taken into account for a proper understanding. His stroke of luck was the study by Esther Cullen on a very aberrant, cliff-breeding gull, the kittiwake, which showed that its pelagic feeding (hence cliff-breeding) was at the bottom of a large host of unlikely behavioural adaptations, and this put the behaviour of many other species of gull into perspective. Comparing the kittiwakes and all his own gull studies, Niko provided 'new insights into how signalling behaviour originates in the course of evolution'.[6] Again, we see a link with later develop-ments in evolution studies and behavioural ecology.

On closer inspection many of Niko's studies had failings, and they would not have passed a present-day reviewer. Conclusions on the red belly of male sticklebacks serving as sign-stimulus to another male were unwarranted and results could not be repeated; other 'classical' studies were similarly defective, such as the response of geese to an over-flying predator model, the pecking of herring gull chicks at the red spots on their parents' bills, the experiments on eggshells and camouflage, and others. Usually none of his research was quantified in any way. It was often the celebrated simplicity of Niko's field experiments that caused the flaws, such as the absence of blind tests and the subjective influence of the experimenter on the results. It hardly mattered: the presentation was convincing, the arguments made sense, and even now I feel that I am quibbling over detail when I criticize the data on which all the magic ethological developments were based.

He made a crucial contribution to a new degree course in Oxford in Human Science, and Niko's final contribution in that direction of science was the application of ethology to studies of human behaviour, which was also the aspect of his work for which he was most reviled (with comments along the line of 'children aren't gulls!'). His hypothesis on the cause of childhood autism was based on internal conflict between approach and avoidance, similar to his hypothesis on the cause of animal displays. An evaluation of Niko after his Nobel Prize, in *Science*, mentioned that 'this award might be taken ... as an appreciation of the need to review the picture that we often seem to have of human behavior as something quite outside nature, hardly subject to the principles that mould the biology, adaptability, and survival of other organisms'.[7]

His lifetime scientific success was, by any standards, enormous. Inevitably it came at what I see as a huge cost. There was the cost to his family: his children loved him deeply and he them, but he always remained somewhat aloof, he had no time, his main interest had to be elsewhere. There was the cost to Lies, who dedicated her entire life to providing for Niko, with no reward for herself except her children and her fulfilment in easing Niko's path. There was the cost to his own enjoyment of life: if he was not working, guilt was never far away, and rarely did he allow himself luxury of any kind. His work thrived on his need to justify himself to the world, on the heavy weight of a responsibility for letting the world benefit from his existence. Throughout his career he kept on 'morally' justifying his birdwatching and larking around with insects, until finally the urge to provide immediate returns for what he had been given proved too strong, and he switched to seeking relief for children from the scourge of autism. The tight, Dutch background was a harness, with all the benefits and constraints that it brought. There was no doubt that Niko loved his life with the birds. But always, always, there was that background of obligation and guilt.

Output: publications and impact

Strictly speaking, success cannot be measured, and it is unclear even what we mean by the word. But we may have an idea of the influence someone had on those who came after them, and on a more basic level we can quantify 'output'. In recent years 'impact assessments' have also become available, summarizing the numbers of times books or papers have been quoted by other scientists. By these measures, Niko's output was prolific and his impact long-lasting. With his large productivity of scientific and popular papers and books, I found it tempting to look for some general trends, and how this related to other parts of his life and development.

Altogether, Niko published 352 books and scientific and popular articles, a remarkable number by any standards. Of these, 16 were books, several of which were translated into many languages. A few books were written jointly with others, but in all cases Niko was the dominant author and each had Niko's stamp all over it. Some were serious science (1946, *Inleiding tot de diersociologie* [in Dutch, trans.: Introduction to animal sociology]; 1951, *The study of instinct*; 1953, *Social behaviour in animals*), some were more popular science (1953, *The herring gull's world*; 1954, *Bird life*; 1958, *Curious naturalists*; 1965, *Animal behavior*; 1983, *Autistic children*), two volumes contained what he judged to be his most important scientific papers (1972, *The animal in its world, 1 and 2*). There were also several popular, as well as two children's, books (1930, *Het vogeleiland* [in Dutch, trans.: Bird island, jointly with several others]; 1934, *Eskimoland* [in Dutch]; 1947, *Klieuw/Kleew* [Dutch and English]; 1954, *The tale of John Stickle*; 1967, *Tracks* [jointly with Eric Ennion]; 1970, *Signals for survival* [jointly with Hugh Falkus and Eric Ennion]).

Of his books, *The study of instinct* was the most famous, although Niko himself became quite critical of it only a few years after writing it. After several requests from publishers he allowed a final reprint (without any alterations from the original, but with a very modest preface in which Niko considered it 'of merely historical interest'). It came out just after he died.[8] One young reviewer in 1989 was not impressed: 'much of the material is out of date, and sometimes this leads not just to omissions but to serious errors ... Some cases of grave, factual and theoretical misconceptions ...'[9]. *Sic transit gloria mundi.*

Yet the book is still widely quoted, now more than 50 years after it first saw the light of day. The Web of Science citation index shows that, since 1974, *The study of instinct* has been quoted, in the journals covered by the Web, between 16 and 48 times per year. In the years since 1995 it is quoted on average 33 times per year, and since 1974 this has been fairly steady. There is no downward trend.

Of Niko's articles in journals almost twice as many (66%) fall into the 'popular' as the 'scientific' category (34%). Most of this 'popular' effort was in Dutch: taking all his publications, 30% were in English, 61% in Dutch, and 9%

in German. Compared with present-day scientists he was a loner when publishing, the sole author of 89% of his papers.

In the course of his life there was one peak in Niko's scientific output (in
terms of numbers of papers) in his early thirties, and an even larger one in his
early fifties. His popular writing peaked in his early twenties and in his early
forties. Undoubtedly these trends were affected by the war and the move to
Oxford soon after, which happened when he was in his mid-thirties and early
forties. Other, obvious lifetime trends were an increase in the proportion of
articles that he wrote in English, and a corresponding decrease in Dutch, with
German publications mostly restricted to before the war.

Niko's single most important paper is probably his 'On aims and methods in
ethology' in 1963.[10] Nowadays it is quoted even more often than *The study of
instinct*: since 1974 between 20 and 48 times per year, since 1995 on average 34
times per year. Curiously, Niko himself did not think enough of it to include it
in his collection of most important papers, *The animal in its world*. What he did
include were his early papers on the homing of *Philanthus* (bee-wolf), the gulls'
eggshell removal story, a paper on food hoarding by foxes, his comparative
study of the behaviour of gulls, the studies on 'gaping' young blackbirds, the
protective function of stickleback spines, human behaviour, and autism; as
theoretical papers he included his contributions on behaviour and natural selection, appeasement, and ethology in general. His theoretical contribution in terms
of numbers of papers is small, and obviously he did not think much of it himself.

The output in number of films was not very substantial. But what he
produced left a stirring memory, and his international prize-winning *Signals for
survival*, the last one he made, became a wildlife classic. He was immensely
proud of it, probably even more than of his Nobel award. Nowadays equipment
and camera-work are much better than what Niko could come up with, but

*The Maestro at his peak, filming in the
1960s.*
Photo Lary Shaffer.

Signals had a very strong science content as well as excellent imagery, and that made it. Earlier he had made at least six other films (silent, mostly black and white), almost all for educational and demonstration purposes, and he supervised more than a dozen which were filmed by other cameramen.

Rewards

If honours and prizes are criteria of 'success', Niko did pretty well in life. High above any other accolade was the Nobel Prize for Physiology and Medicine. He had a professorial chair in Leiden before he left there, he had a chair in Oxford and numerous visiting professorships in universities in many countries, and he had honorary doctorates in Edinburgh and Leicester. He was FRS, Fellow of the Royal Society in Britain, the highest scientific honour in the country, and in Oxford he was initially Fellow of Merton College (from which he resigned), later Fellow, then Emeritus Fellow of Wolfson College. He became Foreign Member of the Royal Netherlands Academy of Sciences and Arts and of the U.S. National Academy of Sciences, Member of the German Academy of Natural Sciences and Honorary Member of the German Ornithological Society, Honorary Fellow of the Royal College of Psychiatry and of the American Academy of Arts and Sciences, and he received distinguished awards from the American Psychological Association, the Argentinian Society for the Protection of Animals, and there were many others. For his film *Signals for survival* on television he received the coveted Italia Prize. Niko particularly esteemed the Swammerdam Medal from the Dutch Academy of Sciences and Arts, which is given to a natural scientist only once every 10 years, but there was also the Godman Salvin Medal of the British Ornithological Union, and so on. All this to a man who professed to dislike prizes, and whose Calvinistic Dutch disdain for any honour that lifted a person above the common denominator was deeply engrained in his day-to-day life. No wonder it caused him anxieties.

Niko's name will also live on in other, some more, some less ostentatious ways. Deservedly but somewhat ironically, the concrete building of Oxford University that houses the departments of Zoology and Experimental Psychology is now named the 'Niko Tinbergen Building', despite the somewhat chequered history of its relationship with Niko. The Tinbergen children commissioned a flight of steps through Grizedale Wood, not far from Slakes, 'Dedicated to the memory of Niko Tinbergen (1907–1989) and his wife Lies Tinbergen (1911–1990)'. The Association for the Study of Animal Behaviour now has an annual 'Niko Tinbergen Lecture' as the highlight of its meetings, and the German Ethological Society awards an annual Niko Tinbergen Prize for the best scientific contribution. Several books have been dedicated to him (including one of my own), a volume of animal behaviour science, *Function and evolution in behaviour*,[11] was written specially for him by his former students, and *The Tinbergen legacy*[12] was produced by disciples after his death.

Very endearingly, several children of admiring parents were named after him (although he was a godfather only once), including the son of the evolutionary anthropologist, Sarah Hrdy.

Science that followed

When Niko retired from his chair in Oxford, John Pringle, the head of the Zoology Department, decided to appoint a successor to teach animal behaviour, but at the level of reader, not professor. It was rather a pity, given the honours that had been bestowed on Niko and his science only a year earlier, and it was indicative of the competition and jealousies in the department at the time. As expected, there was considerable interest in the post when it was advertised, and the final short-list of six for the readership contained the names of several of Niko's scientific offspring. People considered were John Crook, Desmond Morris, Nick Blurton-Jones, David McFarland, Mike Cullen, and me. Most observers expected Mike Cullen to get the post. But Pringle made it clear that he was not interested in continuing Niko's line of work, he just wanted to add the brightest brain to his department. He discussed this with Niko, and Niko agreed; he told Pringle that on that measure, his advice was McFarland. After some gruelling interviews, with Robert Hinde and John Pringle on the panel, David McFarland became Niko's successor.

One could hardly have found anyone more unlike Niko. David's initial experimental studies were carried out on pigeons that made choices between food and water in boxes. He introduced models of animal behaviour in which feedback played a major role, unlike anything Niko had ever considered, and decision theory became prominent. Mostly, McFarland was a highly quantitative theoretician in animal behaviour, and as the ethologist Felicity Huntingford summarized it: 'His aim is articulated most clearly when he asks "How are animals so organized that they are motivated to do what they ought to do at that particular time?"'[13] He published a string of rather difficult books (for example *Feedback mechanisms in animal behaviour*, *Motivational control systems analysis*, *Problems of animal behaviour*, *Quantitative ethology*),[14] admired by experts but not really understood by others. He had several bright students but did not build a group around him, and later on was seldom in the department, and rarely lectured. Niko told Lies that he was disappointed.[15]

From Niko's group at the time of his retirement, both Mike Cullen and I left Oxford. Several stayed on, however, such as Richard Dawkins and Marian Dawkins. One of Mike Cullen's students, John Krebs, who was soon to make a large name for himself in behaviour studies, was appointed lecturer in the ecology/ornithology section of the department, and was later promoted to a Royal Society professorship. About 25 years after Niko's departure, Marian Dawkins was awarded a personal chair in animal behaviour, and Richard Dawkins one in communication of science.

Whilst on Niko's home-patch ethology was losing its connection with its roots, elsewhere the science he had left behind was also changing direction fast, or was under attack, or was merging with other disciplines.

> *Ethology is dead, or at least senescent. That is, if you think of ethology in the narrow sense – the study of animal behavior as elaborated by Konrad Lorenz, Nikolaas Tinbergen, and Karl von Frisch. It has been quiescent for some time. No exciting ideas have been emerging, and data gathering on key issues has lost its direction, despite the fact that many of the central precepts of ethology remain poorly tested. The pioneers of ethology would probably agree.*[16]

This was written at the time of Niko's death by George Barlow, himself an eminent ethologist in America. And in a sense he was right; now, in the twenty-first century, the word ethology is rarely heard, and even amongst biologists a majority does not know its meaning. But Barlow also argued that, in fact, ethology in its modern form continued its existence in a different guise, absorbed in 'sociobiology'.

At the end of his career Niko had seen this coming and, much to his credit, had approved and encouraged the absorption of his science into others. In 1978 he wrote:

> *But one can already see that a more or less integrated Biology of Behaviour would be far too wide a complex of science for Ethology to parade as a name for it. In other words, I feel that 'Ethology' is the name for a phase in the evolution of the behavioural sciences … The more I think about this, the more I feel that the idea of a phase is helpful, provided it is linked to the idea of the ethological fashion not having passed or disappeared, but incorporated into the behavioural sciences.*[17]

Others who are prominent today do not agree with George Barlow's obituary of ethology. Colin Beer sees that 'ethology today is as alive and strong as ever',[18] and Marian Dawkins says 'there is more of ethology today than there was before … if you actually look at behaviour studies now, I think they are much more like ethology was in the 1960s than in the 1970s or 1980s when people were off being completely obsessed with selfish genes and adaptive explanations, and ignoring all but one of the four questions.[19]

One of the sciences involved in a post-Tinbergen merger with ethology was ecology. As we have seen, Niko himself did not see or follow up the advantages that an interdisciplinary approach between ethology and ecology could bring, despite the many opportunities he had, despite quoting the presence of ecologists as one of the reasons for moving to Oxford, and despite having a brother close to him and friends who were ecologists. But some of his Ravenglass students did involve ecology in their work, our theses being in the border region between the two disciplines. Niko himself, in his emphasis on 'function'

A long, dry journey: natterjack on the sands. Photo Niko Tinbergen.

and 'selection pressures', asked questions that could properly be answered only by an ecological approach, and when he discussed functional advantages and disadvantages of behaviour such as eggshell removal by birds, he was looking at problems of optimality. Already in the 1960s these problems were intensively discussed in Niko's group in Oxford, and the first foundations were being laid for the later development of ideas such as 'optimal foraging'.

Thus, at the time of Niko's retirement, *behavioural ecology* was born. On the other side of the Atlantic it is usually called 'sociobiology' (although that term has somewhat different connotations, the subject matter is very similar). Behavioural ecology has probably become the most important offspring of ethology, although in its conception the contribution of ethology itself was limited. In 1974, from Niko's group in Oxford, I organized the first behavioural ecology conference in Britain, and internationally such conferences were to become almost annual events. In the first years of the new science the role of John Krebs, one of Mike Cullen's most prolific students, was pivotal, and there were many relevant new developments, in Britain and America, well away from the old ethology, that were vitally important.

All of a sudden, after ethology had become somewhat stuck in the doldrums, the new science boomed. In *The Tinbergen legacy* one of the contributors pointed out that in the three main ethology journals (*Behaviour, Animal Behaviour*, and *Ethology*, formerly *Zeitschrift für Tierpsychologie*) the proportion of papers dealing with the biological function of behaviour was less than 10% throughout the 1950s and 1960s, but increased to 45% in the 1970s and to over 70% in the 1980s[20]). Behavioural ecology moved away from the old ethological concepts at great speed, and ten years later its ideas were unrecognizably different from those of Niko and Konrad. The new talk was of game theory, kin-selection, and behavioural strategies. The new heroes were people such as Bill Hamilton, John Maynard Smith, Robert Trivers, and Edward Wilson.

Behavioural ecology varies from 'classical' (for example population-) ecology in that it targets the behavioural mechanisms underlying an animal's relationships with its environment. It differs from ethology in that it is not interested in the analysis of behaviour itself, but in its ecological, social, and evolutionary consequences. It does overlap with the old 'functional ethology', but the differences are huge. Konrad and Niko worked with 'sign-stimuli' and single action patterns, whereas behavioural ecologists talk about behavioural strategies, that is, large complex sequences of behaviour with different options and feedbacks, taking in many more aspects of the environment at all stages of the behaviour. Animals need to evolve 'evolutionarily stable strategies' (John Maynard Smith), which cannot be upset by the evolution of an alternative, more successful one.

Where the old ethology talked about simple selection pressures and animals pursuing their own advantages, the idea of kin-selection has now taken hold (the name coined, incidentally, in 1964 in an informal chat between Niko Tinbergen, John Maynard Smith, David Lack, and Arthur Cain in Oxford).[21] This idea suggests that a particular behaviour may be selected for in evolution because it is advantageous, not for the animal which is performing it, but for relatives with some of the same genes, for example its offspring or siblings. The idea has enormous repercussions for our understanding of the functionality of behaviour, and of sociality. Optimal foraging theory (a concept developed by John Krebs) addresses the costs and benefits of different foraging strategies, where old ethology talked about the function of feeding behaviour patterns. A large difference with old ethology is the absence of interest in what causes behaviour, in its more physiological aspects and the internal organization within the animal as a 'black box'.

Studies of animal 'life history' have produced fascinating insights into the interdependence of many characteristics of an animal, aspects that would never have been considered by either the old ethology or ecology. One relates rates of reproduction and mortality to body size, food, and habitat selection, and to how they affect entire social organizations, courtship patterns, communication, and anti-predator strategies. In Niko's group the kittiwake study of Esther Cullen was a forerunner, showing the impact of cliff-breeding on a huge range of behaviours, but at the time it was not followed up. In summary, there is a very large range of problems being addressed by behavioural ecology in a way of which the old functional ethologists would have said 'if only we had thought of it'.

In 1980 Bill Hamilton gave the annual 'Niko Tinbergen Lecture' for the Association of the Study of Animal Behaviour, and he wrote about this to Niko, who replied:

> *I have often 'kicked myself' for not having cottoned on at the time to the*
> *importance of the work you, Trivers, Maynard Smith, did when you did it,*
> *and that it took Richard Dawkins' book to make me see the importance of the*
> *direction you three symbolise for me. ... The study of individually known*
> *animals has of course been of tremendous importance. ... The 'system view' of*
> *a species' characteristics, structural, behavioural, ... emerged during the*
> *'fifties, but we never got beyond that.*[22]

In the context of the new developments in behavioural ecology, our understanding of evolution has made huge progress, in subjects that ethology (in one of Niko's 'four whys') could only nibble at. Much of this was made possible by the progress of genetics, where DNA analyses have opened new worlds, but also through fresh, clear reasoning. It is difficult to trace such progress back and assess the contribution made by Niko's earlier questions. But the contribution is there, direct or indirect, amongst others through the large influence of Niko's student Richard Dawkins in his many books, starting with the hugely successful *The selfish gene.*[23]

Throughout the 1970s and 1980s there was one, very strident fallout of the new knowledge of animal behaviour. It is now referred to as 'the sociobiology debate'.[24] When Niko had been heckled by student hotheads in Vancouver in 1969, he had been confronted by the vanguard of a strong, anti-science movement which was to dominate many discussions over the next twenty years. It came to a head in 1975 with the publication of Edward O. Wilson's *Sociobiology,*[25] a large volume on social behaviour and organization of animals, very pleasantly written and illustrated. However, one chapter was devoted to the behaviour and organization of humanity, and its morals, intelligence, and conscience, and it was this that caused the uproar. In the following years numerous articles were written on the subject, lecturers were shouted down, eggs thrown, and buckets of water emptied on the stage, mostly in America. It was not just emotion, there was also a strong scientific contingent that provided a base for it.

The question at the centre of all this was whether human behaviour could be studied in the same way as that of animals.[26] Objectors were concerned about the implications of research: they argued that if one allowed the analysis of genetical or acquired mechanisms of behaviour, of measures of intelligence, of abilities, then the door would be open for, amongst other things, racial or gender assessment. Such science could be the basis for Nazi or Marxist policies. Scientists such as Edward Wilson and Richard Dawkins favoured a non-

political position of science, taking the position of 'Defenders of the truth',[27] and leaving the political implications of their research to the politicians. Niko would have been way out of his depth in the debate. Only in the late 1990s did the furore die down again.

A different post-Tinbergen offshoot of ethology is the science that calls itself *cognitive ethology*. 'Cognition, broadly defined, includes all ways in which animals take in information through the senses, process, retain and decide to act on it.'[28] Obviously, this new development would have fallen well within the remit of the previous ethology. But cognitive ethology recognizes a much larger complexity of information that animals take into account, and of their information processing, compared to classical ethology. It also considers concepts such as animal awareness and consciousness, issues of subjectivity that were carefully avoided by Niko and Konrad. It was started in 1976 with the publication of a book on 'animal awareness' by the American Donald Griffin,[29] and Niko's former pupil Colin Beer became one of the protagonists.[30]

Within cognitive ethology many of the studies are remarkably similar in design to those of earlier ethologists, with sharply defined questions and experimental procedures.[31] But others (including Griffin and Beer) are seriously involved in subjective aspects, and they consider it necessary to leave concepts such as 'consciousness' deliberately vague. Colin Beer argued that one more question should be added to Niko's original four, about a conscious 'intentionality' in animals, and that 'the study of intentionality and its consequences justifies cognitive ethology as a distinct undertaking'. He noted somewhat wryly that 'Niko would not have approved'.[32] No, indeed not.

Other cognitive ethologists (with whom Niko would probably have agreed) refer to such concepts as 'theoretically vacuous terms that belong only in folk psychology', and that 'one of the biggest challenges for research on non-verbal species is determining how to formulate clear behavioural criteria for processes that are usually accessed verbally in adult humans.'[33] There is a rich variety of research going on, including work, for instance, on goal-directed behaviour, formerly spurned by Niko and his followers as 'un-scientific'. But there are also new approaches to spatial memory (with clear connections to Niko's *Philanthus* work sixty years earlier),[34] and here, as in a great deal of other research, one sees the study of animal behaviour going back to the roots of the 'four whys' of ethology.[35]

One question in the 'four whys', which so much excited classical ethology, receives much less attention than any of others now, in the post-Tinbergen era. It is that of causation, the problem of the internal mechanisms that make animals perform a particular behaviour. Perhaps the lack of ubiquitous principles in causation has put people off: there almost appears to be one different mechanism for every behaviour for every species studied. Perhaps it is just the attraction of the other questions which decides research priorities. Whatever the reason, one recognizes a gap here. As Marian Dawkins pointed out, it means that there is no smooth link-in between behaviour studies and neurophysiology, which, incidentally, is the same need that was highlighted by Niko in *The study of instinct* fifty years earlier. It also means that questions asked by *applied ethology* are more difficult to answer, for example questions about animal welfare related to farming. Marian said: 'Nobody can answer these questions, because we are no longer working on causation questions, and I think that behavioural ecology has now realized that you have to think about causation as well, that you can't just go on talking about the adaptive significance of a choice without knowing about underlying mechanisms.'[36]

There is no doubt that the study of animal behaviour, nursed into being by Niko, is very much alive today, and kicking strongly. Perhaps some of the passion, some of the bubbling enthusiasm of the 1950s and 1960s has disappeared, and perhaps fewer totally new and original ideas and theories are spawned in these later years. But then, that is only to be expected. Science moves in leaps and bounds, with new revolutionary ideas setting a trend for some time. Then people follow. One can live secure in the knowledge that at some stage more new leaps will be made.[37]

Torch-bearers

The greatest source of satisfaction for Niko in his declining years was the output of his many former students. Amongst them were the people who continued where he left off, but many also followed their own path in different sciences. Niko glowed, as I mentioned previously (trans.): 'The large majority now produces work that has its own, for each of them different stamp. And *that* is my pride; they are not His Master's Voice.'[38]

The Tinbergen Legacy meeting in Oxford 1990, one year after Niko's death. Some of those present: 1. Alec Kacelnik, 2. John Kennedy, 3. Adriaan Kortlandt, 4. Gerard Baerends, 5. Robert Hinde, 6. Nicky Clayton, 7. Ab Perdeck, 8–9. Uli and Rita Weidmann, 10. Aubrey Manning, 11. Desmond Morris, 14. Nick Davies, 16. Tim Guilford, 20. Marion Petrie, 22. Sean O'Neill, 23. Colin Beer, 24. Gilbert Manley, 25. Fae Hall, 26. John Philipson, 27. Richard Dawkins, 28. Mike Robinson, 29. Mrs Robertson, 38. Jos Baerends, 39. Donald Broom, 40. Robin McCleery, 41. Fritz Vollrath, 43. Joost Tinbergen, 45. Marian Dawkins, 46. Sheila O'Clarey, 47. Bryan Nelson, 48. Felicity Huntingford, 49. Ian Patterson, 50. Morris Gosling, 52. Cliff Henty, 54. Juan Delius, 55. Cliff Davies, 57. Robert Mash, 58. Peter Slater, 60. John Krebs, 63. Lary Shaffer, 64. Jane Kruuk, 66. David Macdonald, 67. Hans Kruuk, 73. Linda Partridge, 74. Jonathan Kingdon, 80. Tim Roper, 81. Steven Carlston, 85. Janet Tinbergen, 86. Mike Hansell, 87. Gerry Carlston (née Tinbergen), 88. Faith Tinbergen, 89. Heather McLannahan, 90. Tim Halliday, 91. Dirk Tinbergen, 93. David McFarland.

This is not the place to follow the careers of all Niko's scientific offspring, but surely, an outline of his legacy in terms of human endeavour is not out of place. Although Niko himself may not have heard The Maestro's voice in the music of his former pupils, we all felt throughout much of our further lives that he had set us on our path. Just as he had nursed ethology, he also guided the first steps of the students who had used his ethology as a launch pad. The later performances of these people, to whom Niko had given so much, are part of the portrait of the man, and without going into too much detail, some notes on a rather arbitrarily selected score of them will complement the picture, if only to show the extent of the avalanche that he started.

Although he lived most of his life in the Netherlands, Niko had not had the opportunity to raise many PhD students there. This was partly because of the intervention of the war, and partly because he left just at the beginning of his most productive period. **Gerard Baerends** was his outstanding Dutch pupil, his first PhD student, who also married another of Niko's students, and the person who made more of a contribution to classical ethology than any of the other disciples who came after.

Gerard did his PhD about eight years before Niko left Holland. During and immediately after the war he was employed in something quite different from his digger wasps, in fisheries research, and especially on problems of overfishing. Niko worked hard for Gerard to be put forward as his successor in Leiden in the late 1940s, but by then Gerard had already agreed to a chair in Groningen, and declined the Leiden vacancy.[39] In the following years ethology in the Leiden that Niko left would be dominated by Jan van Iersel and Piet Sevenster (both trained by Niko although he was not their actual PhD supervisor). Leiden became the stickleback centre of the world, ethology *sensu stricto*, and a clear legacy of Niko that continued in the direction in which it had begun.

Gerard Baerends built his own empire; he became head of department in Groningen, and later had a personal chair. He was a highly methodical man, with a slow, solid, and always very well thought-out delivery. Although he was not particularly charismatic, he achieved great academic authority, and for several decades was the voice of ethology in Holland. Gerard made a large contribution to 'classical' ethology, particularly with his very careful analyses of the hierarchical organization of animal behaviour. At the same time he encouraged ecological work in his group, and almost half of his students were ecologists. He was an imaginative researcher, and with his wife Jos and with his students he produced several excellent projects on the incubation behaviour of herring gulls, the behaviour of herons, the reproductive behaviour of cichlid fish, and others. He continued the studies on the causation of behaviour long after they had gone out of fashion elsewhere. Gerard also became, at my suggestion, the successor of Niko in his involvement in the Serengeti Research Institute. The Max-Planck Institute in Germany invited Baerends to succeed Konrad Lorenz, when Konrad retired, but Groningen held the greater attraction.

Baerends had a large number of productive students (including 43 PhDs), amongst them Jaap Kruyt and Rudi Drent who, one after the other, became his successors in the University of Groningen. Piet Wiepkema became a professor in Wageningen, and several were appointed as directors of important biological institutes in Holland, to mention but a few. They themselves have spawned many PhD students since. Generally speaking, the scientific apples that fell from Niko's tree in Holland fell close to the stem; his pupils in his native country stuck fairly closely to animal behaviour studies.

Leen de Ruiter was trained by Niko, initially in Hulshorst but mostly later in Oxford, in the early 1950s. He took his PhD in Groningen on the work he had done with Niko, on the effects of camouflage of caterpillars. He then set up a research unit in the field covering the relationships between physiology and behaviour, especially of feeding. He became professor of comparative physiology and developed himself as a neurophysiologist cum ethologist. But he maintained a wide interest: for instance, it was Leen who finished the writing up of Luuk Tinbergen's work (after Luuk's sudden death) on the population dynamics of woodland insects. He also had many PhD students, and his research group made excellent contributions to the understanding of physiological mechanisms underlying feeding behaviour, in the process moving a long way from the simple ethological paradigms. Leen himself withdrew relatively early from the academic research scene, and, before retiring, he was prominent in the Dutch science research council where he could influence government research policies.

Margaret Bastock and **Aubrey Manning** made another one of the couples to emerge from Niko's following. They moved to Edinburgh, where Margaret, between caring for her children, wrote a book on courtship behaviour;[40] she started research on aggression, and on the strength of that was appointed as lecturer in the psychology department. While still in Oxford Margaret had had a PhD student, Stella Crossley (née Pearce), who later became professor of psychology in Monash University, in Melbourne. Aubrey, with his huge enthusiasm and fascination for anything that moved, became the professor of zoology in Edinburgh. Aubrey was a superlative communicator, like Niko; at the same time as Margaret wrote her book, he wrote an excellent and very well used *Introduction to animal behaviour*;[41] later he was to cooperate with Marian Dawkins to produce many successive editions of it. Aubrey continued with his research in genetics of behaviour, especially of mice, and he had about a dozen PhD students on behaviour of insects, birds, primates, and anything that took their interest; some of these pupils are themselves now appointed to professorial chairs and fame (for example Peter Slater in St Andrews). In ethology circles he will always be remembered for his flamboyant chairmanship of many of the ethological conferences in the 1970s and 1980s, where he created an atmosphere of tremendous enthusiasm. Now retired, in the outside world Aubrey is a highly popular director and presenter of television series on biology and geology.

Bill Russell was one of the very early Oxford pupils of Niko, and although not formally registered with Niko he was one of the Hard Core. He used his grounding in ethology to become one of the foremost fighters aiming at reducing the use of animals in laboratory experiments. He was co-author of *The principles of humane experimental technique*[42] ('replacement, reduction, refinement'). Later he became professor in the Department of Sociology in Reading. In *Human behaviour* (1961) and in the later *Violence, monkeys and man*,[43] he, jointly with his wife, described human behaviour in ethological terms. He never attracted the following of people like Konrad Lorenz or Desmond Morris, who approached the same topic similarly, nor was he the butt of so many criticisms as they were. His influence is probably felt mostly in the field of animal welfare.

A more flamboyant character from the same time in Oxford (early 1950s) was **Martin Moynihan**, Niko's first American student. When he died, he was known as the man who built the Smithsonian Tropical Research Institute in Panama, from almost nothing into a world-class centre with a large scientific staff. He travelled widely, especially in Central and South America, and was a keen scuba-diver. He produced several books on animal behaviour (amongst others, *The New World primates*[44] and *Communication and non-communication among cephalopods*[45]), and a large number of papers on theoretical issues as well as on research in many different birds, primates, and other animals. Just as of Niko, people said of Moynihan 'his greatest strength as a scientific administrator was his ability to select good people and to give them the freedom to pursue their interests'.[46] But he was also an able author, he wrote well, with the hallmark of his writings his excellent drawings of animals. Obviously he had much in common with Niko, but their differences in temperament and worldly interests were even greater, and they soon lost contact in the years after Martin left Oxford. Moynihan had few students and died rather young, at 68; his legacy was in his publications and the Institute.

Desmond Morris is a larger-than-life character from Niko's 1950s Hard Core, and at one time his was a household name, after he published *The naked ape*.[47] The book had five impressions within a few months, was published in 24 languages, and made him a millionaire. Scientist, painter, film-maker and presenter: Desmond is the ultimate communicator, with great flamboyance, deep insights, funny jokes, and many pronouncements that have to be taken with large grains of salt. He seemed involved in several almost separate lives. First of all, his numerous books, soundly based in Tinbergen's ethology, have been decidedly influential in shaping people's ideas of mankind as an animal species. He wrote several books before *The naked ape*, which was then incredibly successful, then there came a string of others, including *The human zoo*,[48] *Man-watching*,[49] *Gestures*,[50] *The soccer tribe*,[51] *The human sexes*,[52] and several others about human behaviour. He also wrote many others about the relationships between people and various animals (snakes, pandas, dogs, cats) – he has a remarkable feeling for the market. In a second line of existence Desmond produced many films and television programmes, initially on animals, later on human behaviour and art, including two surrealist films in his very young years.

But a third interest is probably for him the most important: his life as a painter, also remarkably successful. Desmond developed a style of his own, initially influenced by Joan Miró; his many paintings have been exhibited all over the world, and are much sought after by collectors. There is an animal presence in his work, and his 'biomorphs' could only have come from someone with a deep understanding of nature, although the abstract visions in his paintings seem miles away from his life as a scientist. Where the artist and scientist in him did make contact was in his excellent book, *The biology of art*,[53] in which Desmond the ethologist experimented with captive chimpanzees, and as an artist compared their painting abilities with those of children. On a different tack again, the art historian in him wrote an authoritative book on ancient Cypriot pottery.[54]

After leaving Niko's group in Oxford he went to the London Zoo, where he became head of a film unit making animal programmes for television. Several years later he was appointed curator of mammals, and he developed a prolific research unit with several PhD students (including Malcolm Lyall-Watson, who was to become a well-known writer about the supernatural). However, Desmond suddenly gave it all up and followed his other inclination, becoming the director of the Institute of Contemporary Art in London. Several years into that he gave up paid employment altogether, living off *The naked ape* in the tax haven of Malta, before settling permanently in Oxford. He was one of Niko's closest friends, and Niko had a tremendous admiration for Desmond's presentational skills. I believe that, through Desmond, much of Niko's legacy was distributed over a very wide field, often without anyone being aware of it.

In 1950 **Robert Hinde** was, officially, a student of David Lack, but in practice Robert was Niko's pupil, and it was Niko who supervised his PhD. Now Robert is a grand old man of animal behaviour studies, a professor in Cambridge, Fellow of the Royal Society and of the British Academy, formerly master of St John's College in Cambridge, honoured with a CBE, author of many books, and intellectual father to many students – he has gone a very long way since Niko hauled him up about his stuffy writing. Following Bill Thorpe, Hinde developed animal behaviour research in Cambridge. He was put in charge of the Sub-Department of Animal Behaviour in Madingley, which since then has produced an enormous output of research, and he himself had numerous students who reached dizzy scientific heights, including Pat Bateson (his future successor), Peter Marler, Jane Goodall, and Dian Fossey. His first and very influential book was *Animal behaviour*,[55] originally planned jointly with Niko, which was the handbook of ethology and animal psychology for many years. In Cambridge his research soon abandoned birds for monkeys, and later Hinde 'came to find more satisfaction in the study of humans than in that of animals'.[56] Amongst his many books were *Biological bases of human social behavior*,[57] *Towards understanding relationships*,[58] *Primate social relationships*,[59] *Relationships*,[60] *Why gods persist*,[61] and *Why good is good*.[62] He also produced a vast number of papers and edited volumes.

From Robert Hinde came brilliant analyses rather than great new sparks of insight, and his undoubtedly very powerful appeal was mostly to specialist

science. In theoretical development, and in studies of animal and human relationships, Hinde continued far beyond where Niko had left off.

Throughout the 1950s and 1960s **Mike Cullen** had been Niko's right hand
in Oxford, and his wife Esther's kittiwake story had become a paradigm of
Tinbergen ethology. After the kittiwakes Esther more or less withdrew from
research, and she never again wrote a scientific paper. Mike had been the
analytical and quantitative backbone of Niko's group, and when Niko retired
Mike decided to leave Oxford, taking an appointment to a chair in Monash
University, in Melbourne. Much as he liked Australia, he never again found the
vibrant atmosphere that had characterized Oxford: Mike's heyday was under
Niko, who steered him, and when The Maestro was gone, so was the inspiration. Esther and he separated. In Australia, as in Oxford, Mike lived for his
research (mostly on penguins) and his students. He produced only a few papers,
and did not care to put his name on the output of his students.

Throughout his career it was Mike's PhD students who distinguished him;
he had about 20 in all, and they revered him as 'a much-loved mentor who
taught us how teaching should be'.[63] Mike had that genius that, somehow,
enhances other people's abilities. Several of his students rose to very prestigious
positions, amongst them John Krebs (knighted, Royal Society professor in
Oxford, FRS, one of the leading lights in the development of behavioural eco-
-logy, and for many years directing, first, British environmental research in the
Natural Environment Research Council, then the Food Standards Agency).
Others were Felicity Huntingford (professor in animal behaviour in Glasgow,
author of a well-known textbook on animal behaviour[64] and many papers), and
Linda Partridge FRS (professor of evolutionary genetics in University College,
London).

Colin Beer, who did his D. Phil. work on gull incubation behaviour in the
1950s, returned to his native New Zealand, but only for a few years, then came
back to Oxford in 1968 as a lecturer in Niko's group for one year. He moved on
to the States, to Rutgers University in Newark, where he settled to work with
Danny Lehrman, whom he soon succeeded as professor. Colin always retained
what he called 'a Tinbergen eye and ear', staying involved in fieldwork on gulls,
especially on their calls, and in some ways getting closer to Niko's way of doing
science by 'becoming decreasingly obsessed with quantification'.[65] He, too, had
many students in America. He was much more of a philosopher than Niko ever
was, in fact Niko thoroughly disliked philosophy, but Colin published several
papers in the area where ethology and philosophy meet. He became strongly
involved in cognitive ethology, and 'animal intentionality' became a main focus.

Juan Delius, the Argentinian who had studied skylarks under Niko and
then headed his brain-stimulation programme in Oxford, continued to lecture
in behaviour and physiology in Durham, England before becoming professor
first in Bochum, then in Konstanz, Germany. He was Niko's main disciple in
Germany, and delivered several PhD students: he stayed in academia. But in his
interest he moved well away from classical ethology, publishing widely on the

'This is my reward' – some of Niko's students in Ravenglass, 1959. Left to right: Uli Weidmann, Colin Beer, Gilbert Manley, and Juan Delius. Photo Niko Tinbergen.

role of neurophysiology in learning, working mostly with pigeons in boxes rather than with skylarks in the wide blue sky. He also became involved with cognitive ethology, especially with spatial learning.

A contemporary of Colin and Juan at Oxford was **Nick Blurton-Jones**, who ended up with professorships in psychology and anthropology in Los Angeles, UCLA. Like Niko, Nick is a self-effacing man, an observer, and some-one who is responsible for a large part of the Tinbergen legacy with his studies on children in the West, and on hunter-gatherer societies in Africa. He did not publish a vast amount, but what he did made a large impact, and he had many PhD students, who are now making names for themselves. Nick's best-known work is probably the edited volume *Ethological studies of child behaviour* (1972).[66] He started with Niko studying birds (titmice and geese), but soon he 'saw that the ethological techniques used on animals were far superior to those used on people, and wanted to know if they could be applied to humans'.[67] In the Institute of Child Health in London he followed this up, and his methods found wide application; Nick quickly became one of the recognized authorities in child behaviour.

Nick's move to Los Angeles enabled him to start a long-term programme of studies on the Hadza people in northern Tanzania, a very small tribe of hunter-gatherer people with a lifestyle now on the brink of extinction. His study was anthropology, and his questions became more ecological, such as what deter-mines birth intervals, and what contribution do children make to foraging. But one can trace his Tinbergen background in the strict operational terms and rigorous questioning in his research. In his anthropological field as well as in child psychology Nick has a wide following, and Niko was proud of him.

I myself was one of Niko's students who moved away from academia, but continued with wildlife research in conservation-related subjects. I moved to Africa and was involved in setting up the Serengeti Research Institute, then came back to Oxford for a few years to be in charge of Niko's field research group. When Niko retired I moved to the Institute of Terrestrial Ecology in the Scottish Highlands, and eventually a personal chair in Aberdeen University. My field of interest stayed mostly with mammals, but moved into behavioural ecology, especially social organization and foraging of carnivores. I think that my career was built on my PhD project with Niko, and it resulted in, amongst other things, several books[68] and a score of PhD students (some of whom now have professorships, several books to their name, and many PhD students themselves, people such as David Macdonald and Gus Mills).

Several others from Niko's PhD ranks moved high into non-academic circles. **Michael Robinson**, of tropical insect and spider behaviour fame, became director of the Smithsonian Zoo in Washington; **Iain Douglas Hamilton** stuck to elephants and Africa, and became the world's foremost campaigner for the conservation of elephants, with several best-selling books to his name.[69] **John Mackinnon**, who did his PhD on orang-utans under Niko in the early 1970s, became director of the Asian Bureau for Conservation in Hong Kong, and a high-profile campaigner for conservation problems in South-east Asia, especially for primates. Another student of primates, **Bob Martin**, stayed more in university life, moving into anthropology as had several others of Niko's students. He became professor of physical anthropology in London's University College, later professor and director at the Anthropological Institute in Zurich, before moving to the Field Museum in Chicago.

Without contest, the two staunchest pillars of support for Niko's ethology in Oxford after his retirement have been **Marian Dawkins** and **Richard Dawkins**. They had married as students with Niko, and after a postdoctoral

period in Berkeley returned to Oxford, where Richard took up general science writing, and Marian focused on behavioural science involved in animal welfare problems such as battery farming. They separated, and each became highly successful in their own field, both confirmed Tinbergians in their clear questioning and pragmatic approach to science. Marian was given a personal chair in animal behaviour in the Zoology Department; she had a large influence on animal welfare science with her many papers and books,[70] and her considerable number of PhD students. Together with Aubrey Manning she wrote the successful and now standard *An introduction to animal behaviour*,[71] with many highly acclaimed further editions. Even before David McFarland's retirement Marian really was Niko's successor in Oxford, and in 2002 she gave the annual Tinbergen lecture to the Association for the Study of Animal Behaviour as Richard had done previously.

Richard Dawkins has become a household name in Britain, since his 1976 book, *The selfish gene*. He has a remarkable ability for clear and imaginative thinking and writing, and Niko was full of praise for him, although Richard is in no way a naturalist. Niko's insistence on clarity and his 'four whys' provided guidelines for Richard's thinking, and with his books[72] he has had a tremendous influence on the public appreciation of biology. He had few students, but he wrote a number of important theoretical papers on the mechanisms of animal behaviour and of evolution, some of them jointly with John Krebs, and then became seriously involved in semi-popular writing on evolution. He was installed with a privately endowed professorship in Oxford, in 'the Public Understanding of Science', and also became FRS. In Britain he is the best-known contemporary proponent of Darwinism, although to the general public he is at least as well known for his fervently anti-religious stance.

One of Niko's last PhD students was **Lary Shaffer**, field man and film-maker, and closer to Niko than most. When Niko retired and Lary had finished his PhD on herring gulls and crabs, and his major TV film on sheepdogs, Lary returned to America. He wanted a change, he wanted to work with students, to teach, and he decided to give up research as well as filming. He started to lecture in psychology in the State University of New York in Plattsburgh, became a professor, and he was so effective that students elected him the most popular prof on the campus. Lary was joint author of an introductory psychology textbook[73] but otherwise published little, and he had no PhD students. But the hundreds of undergraduates who went through his hands carried him on their shoulders. In his own way, he spread Niko's ethology message to a large and receptive audience.

The assembled collection of graduates from Niko's school may not have numbered more than 40 people, and for the sake of brevity I have only been able to mention some points of the histories of a few, including some of the most prominent ones. But between them these people cover a large area of society, several have become giants in their field, and they had and have an enormous effect: one feels Niko's teaching reverberating through scores of books from the

Memories: birdwatching in Ravenglass, with Caracho, the tame crow.
Courtesy of the Tinbergen family.

hands of his students, through films on television, and through the courses in animal behaviour, psychology, behavioural ecology, sociobiology, anthropology, and others in universities throughout the world. At least as important is that several of Niko's former pupils, or pupils of pupils, have high profiles in conservation and conservation research. It is not surprising that Niko was more proud of his legacy in people than of anything else that he was leaving behind.

One would like to know what was behind the general success of Niko's former students. Did they achieve because he instilled them with the necessary wisdom and abilities? Was it the group and the Oxford atmosphere that did it? Or did he merely select the right people? Most likely it was a fortunate mixture of all three causes, with the last one being the least important. Niko rarely selected students, and rarely solicited grants for which students could apply so he could take the best one; on the contrary, students used to seek him out, and we sometimes thought that Niko would take anyone who had the inclination and whom he liked, as long as he or she was 'a good observer'. However, with the group he created he provided a wonderful base for the development of critical abilities. Whatever the way in which they arrived on his doorstep, each single one of his students, for the rest of his or her life, remembers Niko with deep admiration, affection, and gratitude.

Memories

Supporting his skills as a naturalist and in teaching was that warm smile, his enthusiasm, and the indomitable sense of humour allied to a rich fund of stories and jokes. There was also the humanity of his small vulnerability, the black depressions, his Dutchness, with the pleasant, slight accent, and his Calvinistic judgements. One remembers the discussions, with Niko's total dedication to the rooting out of obfuscation. That was the social Niko, the teacher.

But when I think of him, I see that small, khaki-clad, bespectacled, and grey-haired man with his camera, following the track of a fox on some sandy slope, a curious naturalist whistling to himself.

Notes

Sources of documents mentioned in the notes

G. P. Baerends archive, Department of Zoology, University of Groningen, Haren, the Netherlands.

Bodleian Library (Tinbergen collection), University of Oxford, UK.

J. Bretchka, Vienna, Austria, private archive.

British Film Institute, London, UK.

University of Chicago Library, USA.

Irenaeus Eibl-Eibesfeldt, Andechs, Germany, private archive.

Richard Gombrich, Oxford, UK, private archive.

Harvard University Library, Cambridge, Mass., USA.

Heimans en Thijsse Stichting (Heimans and Thijsse Foundation), Plantage Middenlaan, Amsterdam, the Netherlands.

Robert Hinde, Cambridge, UK, private archive.

Adriaan Kortlandt, Oxford, UK, private archive.

Hans Kruuk, Aberdeen, UK, private archive.

Mrs Catrina Loman, Calgary, Canada, private archive.

Aubrey Manning, Edinburgh, UK, private archive.

John Maynard-Smith, Brighton, UK, private archive.

E. Mayr papers, Harvard University Archives, Cambridge, Mass., USA.

Desmond Morris, Oxford, UK, private archive.

'Naturalis' Institute, University of Leiden, Leiden, the Netherlands.

Bryan Nelson, Castle Douglas, UK, private archive.

M. Nice, archive W. C. Allee, University of Chicago Library, USA.

Jim Rose, Kirkby-in-Furness, UK, private archive.

Leen de Ruiter, Groningen, the Netherlands, private archive.

Bill Russell, Reading, UK, private archive.

Lary Shaffer, Plattsburgh, NY, USA, private archive.

Dirk Tinbergen, Leicester, UK, private archive.

Jaap Tinbergen, Groningen, the Netherlands, private archive.

Miss Jacomien Tinbergen, Delft, the Netherlands, private archive.

Janet Tinbergen, Oxford, UK, private archive.

Wolfson College, Oxford, UK.

A. W. Yerkes, private archive (quoted by R. Burkhardt, unpublished MS.).

Zoologisch Laboratorium, Leiden, the Netherlands. Archives are deposited in 'Naturalis' Institute

Chapter 1

1. N. Tinbergen, 1951. *The study of instinct.* Clarendon Press, Oxford.
2. C. Darwin, 1872. *The expression of the emotions in man and the animals.* John Murray, London.
3. W. H. Thorpe, 1979. *The origins and rise of ethology.* Heinemann, London.

Chapter 2

1. N. Tinbergen, 1985. Watching and wondering. In: *Studying animal behavior* (ed. D. A. Dewsbury), pp. 431–63. Chicago University Press.
2. I., J., and C. Tinbergen, 1996. Tinbergens door de eeuwen heen. [Tinbergens through the centuries]. Magazine *Oud Nieuws.* Privately published, The Hague.
3. N. Tinbergen and H. Kruuk, 1960. Van den Vos Reynaerde [Of the fox Reynard]. *De Levende Natuur.* **63**, 193–203.
4. Mrs R. Pul, pers. com.
5. Tinbergen, Watching and wondering.
6. Tinbergen, Watching and wondering.
7. Interview with Mrs T. Tinbergen-Frensdorf (widow of Luuk), December 1999.
8. N. Tinbergen 1973. Autobiography of Nikolaas Tinbergen. Website of Nobel Foundation: <http://www.nobel.se/medicine/laureates/1973/tinbergen-autobio.html>
9. Miss Jacomien Tinbergen, pers. com., 8 September 2000.
10. Miss J. Tinbergen, pers. com., 8 September 2000.
11. Interview with F. Makkink, May 2000.
12. S. Schama, 1987. *The embarrassment of riches: an interpretation of Dutch culture in the Golden Age.* Collins, London.
13. Miss J. Tinbergen, pers. com., 8 September 2000.
14. J. M. M. Duyf, 1993. *Een wereld van verschil: het leven en werk van Jan Tinbergen* [A world of difference: life and work of Jan Tinbergen]. Tinbergen Institute, Rotterdam.
15. Interview with Mrs T. Tinbergen-Frensdorf, December 1999.
16. Tinbergen, Watching and wondering.
17. L. Tinbergen, 1934. *Veldkenmerken van steltlopers, zwanen, ganzen en eenden* [Field recognition of waders, swans, geese and ducks]. NJN, The Hague.
18. J. Verwey, 1955. In memoriam Luuk Tinbergen. *Ardea*, **43**: 293–308.
19. E. Hall, 1974. A conversation with Nobel Prize winner Niko Tinbergen. *Psychology Today*, March.
20. Tinbergen, Watching and wondering.
21. N. Tinbergen, 1949. Jac P. Thijsse en de biologische wetenschap [JPT and biological science]. In *Het voetspoor van Thijsse* [On the tracks of Thijsse] (ed. A. F. M. Besemer, K. Hana, N. Tinbergen, and J. Wilcke), pp. 15–17. H. Veenman and Zonen, Wageningen.
22. Tinbergen, Jac P. Thijsse.
23. Tinbergen, Watching and wondering.
24. For example: G. Harmsen, 1961. *Blauwe en rode jeugd* [Blue and red youth]. Van Gorcum, Assen. M. Coesel, 1988. *Van klunzen, vaklui en oude sokken* [untranslatable; approximately 'Of freshers, experts and old socks']. Jeugdbondsuitgeverij, Amsterdam. M. Coesel, 1997. *The NJN, een gemeenschap van individualisten* [NJN, a community of individualists]. Opulus Press, Leiden.
25. N. Tinbergen, 1926, Een woord tot de leiders [A word to our leaders]. *Amoeba*, **6**: 41–3.
26. N. Tinbergen, 1929. Voorjaar [Spring]. *De Meidoorn*, **1**: 56–8.
27. N. Tinbergen, 1928. Een strandwandeling [A walk on the beach]. *Amoeba*, **7**: 82–4.

28. N. Tinbergen, 1926. De taak der vogelfotografie [The task of bird photography]. *Amoeba*, **6**: 30–3.

29. N. Tinbergen, 1923. Levende Venusschelp [Live Venus shell]. *Amoeba*, **3**, December, p. 47.

30. N. Tinbergen, 1923. Gevaarlijke kastanjeknoppen [Dangerous chestnut buds]. *Amoeba*, **3** (December): 47–8.

31. N. Tinbergen, 1924. Vogelwaarnemingen bij Den Haag [Bird observations near The Hague]. *Amoeba*, **3**: 40–1.

32. N. Tinbergen, 1924. Strandvondsten Kerstcongres District IV [Beach findings during Christmas congress]. *Amoeba*, **4**: 71.

33. N. Tinbergen, 1924. Zeevogels en de storm [Sea birds and the gales]. *Het Vaderland*, 28 February 1924; and Ontmoetingen met eekhoorns [Meeting squirrels]. *Het Vaderland*, 13 April 1924.

34. G. van Beusekom, 9 January 1974, letter to G. Baerends, Baerends archive.

35. Tinbergen, Watching and wondering.

36. N. Tinbergen, set of letters home, August–September 1925. Bodleian Library, Oxford.

37. N. Tinbergen, 1926. Twee maanden op de Kurische Nehrung [Two months in the Kurische Nehrung]. *De Levende Natuur*, **31**: 129–35, 161–7.

38. N. Tinbergen, 1925. De trek der nachtzwaluwen [The migration of nightjars]. *Amoeba*, **4**: 33–4.

Chapter 3

1. N. Tinbergen, 1985. Watching and wondering. In *Studying animal behavior* (ed. D. A. Dewsbury), pp. 431–63. Chicago University Press.

2. N. Tinbergen, 1929. Een merkwaardige schipbreukeling [Strange flotsam]. *De Levende Natuur*, **33**: 45–8.

3. K. H. Voous, 1995. *In de ban van vogels: ornithologisch biografisch woordenboek van Nederland* [Enthralled by birds: ornithological biographical dictionary of the Netherlands]. Scheffers, Utrecht.

4. J. Verwey, 1929. Die Paarungsbiologie des Fischreihers [Reproductive biology of the grey heron]. *Verhandl. d. 6e Int. Ornithol. Kongr. Kopenhagen*, 1926, 390–413. 1930. *Zoologische Jahrbücher*, **48**: 1–120.

5. Voous, *In de ban van vogels.*

6. N. Tinbergen, 1946. G. J. Tijmstra. *Ardea*, **34**: 400–1.

7. P. Sevenster, 1991. Ethologisch onderzoek in het verleden; Niko Tinbergen [Ethological research in the past; Niko Tinbergen]. In *Meeuwen* (ed. T. W. M. Bakker and D. A. G. Buizer), pp. 44–52. Stichting Uitgeverij KNNV, The Hague.

8. N. Tinbergen, 1932. Waarnemingen aan zilvermeeuwen in de broedkolonie te Wassenaar [Observations on herring gulls in the colony in Wassenaar]. *De Levende Natuur*, **37**: 213–19, 248–52.

9. A. F. J. Portielje, 1928. Zur Ethologie bezw. Psychologie der Silbermöwe *Larus argentatus argentatus* Pont. [The ethology and psychology of the herring gull, *L. a. a.*]. *Ardea*, **17**: 112–49.

10. Tinbergen, Waarnemingen aan zilvermeeuwen in de broedkolonie te Wassenaar.

11. Sevenster, Ethologisch onderzoek in het verleden; Niko Tinbergen.

12. N. Tinbergen, 1927. Meijendel-onderzoek. Stuifduinen [Meyendel research, wind dunes]. *De Levende Natuur*, **31**: 355–60.

13. G. van Beusekom, F. P. J. Kooymans, M. G. Rutten, and N. Tinbergen. *Het Vogeleiland* [Bird Island]. Schoonderbeek, Laren.

14. L. Shaffer, 1991. The Tinbergen legacy in photography and film. In

The Tinbergen legacy (ed. M. S. Dawkins, T. R. Halliday, and R. Dawkins), pp. 129–38. Chapman & Hall, London.

15. Interview with F. Makkink, May 2000.

16. Interview with F. Makkink, May 2000.

17. See list of Tinbergen publications.

18. N. Tinbergen, 1930. Een vogelwinter [A bird winter]. *De Levende Natuur*, **36**: 6–14, 53–9.

19. Letter by NT, 6/8/1929, Bodleian Library archives.

20. N. Tinbergen, 1931. Zur Paarungsbiologie der Flussseeschwalbe (*Sterna hirundo hirundo* L.) [About reproductive biology of the common tern, *S. h. h.*]. *Ardea*, **20**: 1–18.

21. J. M. Cullen, 1960. The aerial display of the arctic tern and other species. *Ardea*, **48**: 1–37.

22. G. F. Makking, 1931. Die Kopulation der Brandente (*Tadorna tadorna* (L) [The copulation of the shellduck]. *Ardea*, **20**: 18–22.

23. For example, J. P. Thijsse, 1901. De graafwespen, wespen en bijen van Nederland [Digger wasps, wasps and bees of the Netherlands]. *De Levende Natuur*, **5**: 224–6, 248–52.

24. J. H. Fabre (translated 1919). *The hunting wasps*. Hodder and Stoughton, London.

25. Interview with W. H. van Dobben, 1989. In D. R. Röell, 1996, *De wereld van instinct* [The world of instinct]. Erasmus, Rotterdam.

26. Translated from L. and N. Tinbergen, 1931. Waarnemingen aan roofvogels en uilen [Observations on raptors and owls]. *De Levende Natuur*, **36**: 98–104.

27. N. Tinbergen, 1958. *Curious naturalists*. Country Life, London.

28. O. Uttendörfer, 1930. Studien zur Ernährung unserer Tagraubvögel und Eulen [Studies on the food of our raptors and owls]. *Abh. der Naturf. Ges. Görlitz*, **31**: 1–180.

29. N. Tinbergen, 1933. Die Ernährungsökologischen Beziehungen zwischen *Asio otus otus* L. und ihren Beutetieren, insbesondre den *Microtus*-arten [Food–ecological relations between *Asio otus* and its prey, especially *Microtus* species]. *Ecol. Monogr.*, **3**: 443–92.

30. N. Tinbergen, 1932. Waarnemingen aan roofvogels en uilen [Observations on raptors and owls]. *De Levende Natuur*, **36**: 334–5. 1932. Über die Ernährung einer Waldohreulenbrut (*Asio otus otus* (L.)) [About the food of a brood of tawny owls]. *Beitr. Z. Fortpflanzbiologie d. Vögel*, **8**: 54–5.

31. N. Tinbergen, 1930. Entomologie. *Amoeba*, **7**: 109–12.

32. K. von Frisch, 1923. Das Problem des tierischen Farbensinnes [The problem of colour vision in animals]. *Naturwiss.*, **24**: 470–6. E. Wolf, 1926. Ueber das Heimkehrvermogens der Bienen [About homing abilities of bees]. *Z. f. vergl. Physiol.*, **3**: 615–91.

33. Tinbergen, *Curious naturalists*.

34. N. Tinbergen, 1932. Über die Orientierung des Bienenwolfes (*Philanthus triangulum* Fabr.) [About the orientation of the bee-wolf]. *Z. f. vergl. Physiol.*, **16**: 305–34.

35. Tinbergen, *Curious naturalists*.

36. J. Loeb, 1918. *Forced movements, tropisms and animal conduct*. Philadelphia, London. A. Kühn, 1919. *Die Orientierung der Tiere im Raum* [Spatial orientation of animals]. Fischer, Jena.

37. Bodleian Library archives.

38. N. Tinbergen, 1935. Field observations of East Greenland birds I. The behaviour of the red-necked phalarope (*Phalaropus lobatus* L.) in spring. *Ardea*, **24**: 1–42. 1939. Field observations of East Greenland birds II. The behavior of the snow bunting (*Plectrophonax nivalis subnivalis*

(Brehm)) in spring. *Trans. Linn. Soc. New York*, **5**: 1–94.

39. N. Tinbergen, 1933 and 1934. Torssukátaq I, II, III. *De Levende Natuur*, **38**: 344–53; **39**: 1–14, 41–52.

40. N. Tinbergen, 1934. *Eskimoland*. Van Sijn and Zonen, Rotterdam.

41. I. Geertsen, 1990. *Karale Andreassen, en østgrønlandsk kunstner* [K. A., an east Greenland artist]. Atuakkiorfik, Nuuk.

42. N. Tinbergen, 1934. Kajakduikelen [Kayak toppling], 17–23, journal unknown.

43. J. J. ter Pelkwijk, 1933. *Diary of my journey to Denmark, Greenland and Iceland in August and September, 1933, together with F. P. J. Kooymans* [in Dutch]. Coll. A. J. Gorter-ter Pelkwijk, Naarden.

44. H. E. Howard, 1920. *Territory in bird life*. John Murray, London.

45. Howard, *Territory in bird life*.

46. E. M. Nicholson, 1930. Field notes on Greenland birds. *Ibis*, **12**: 280–314, 395–429.

47. Tinbergen, Field observations of East Greenland birds II.

48. Tinbergen, Torssukátaq II.

49. Tinbergen, Field observations of East Greenland birds II.

50. Tinbergen, Field observations of East Greenland birds II, p. 72.

51. Tinbergen, Field observations of East Greenland birds I. Tinbergen, Torssukátaq III.

52. N. Tinbergen, 1934. Enkele proeven over het ei als broedobject [Some experiments on the egg as object of incubation]. *Ardea*, **23**: 82–9.

53. P. Bettenhausen and R. Kerkhoven, 1999. *Eskimoland: Verleden, heden en toekomst van de Groenlandse Inuit* [Eskimo land: past, present and future of the Greenland Inuit]. Uniepers Abcoude, Museon, The Hague.

54. N. Tinbergen, 1955. Autobiographical sketch. In *Group*

processes (ed. B. Schaffner), pp. 311–12. Josiah Macy Jr. Foundation, New York.

55. J. J. ter Pelkwijk, *Diary of my journey*.

Chapter 4

1. N. Tinbergen, 1933. Torssukátaq I. *De Levende Natuur*, **38**: 344–53. 1934. Torssukátaq II, III. *De Levende Natuur*, **39**: 1–14, 41–52.

2. C. J. van der Klaauw, 1934. Uitwendige doelmatigheid en einddoel bij Kant en in de moderne biologie [External effectiveness and purpose of Kant and in modern biology]. Public lecture, Leiden. 1934. Ökologische Studien und Kritiken I. Die Bedeutung der Teleologie Kants für die Logik der Ökologie [Ecological studies and critiques I. The significance of Kant's teleology for the logic of ecology]. *Sudhoffs Archiv für Geschichte der Medizin und der Naturwissenschaften*, **27**: 516–88.

3. W. McDougall, 1923. *An outline of psychology*. Methuen, London.

4. N. Tinbergen 1935. Over de betekenis van 'territorium' in het leven der vogels [On the meaning of 'territory' in the life of birds]. *Vakblad voor Biologen*, **16**: 95–106.

5. N. Tinbergen, 1936. The function of sexual fighting in birds; and the problem of the origin of 'territory'. *Bird Banding*, **7**: 1–8.

6. Tinbergen, Over de betekenis van 'territorium' in het leven der vogels.

7. Letter to A. Kortlandt, 25/6/1939, Kortlandt archive.

8. A. Kortlandt, 1989. Dr. A. F. J. Portielje. De apostel der dieren. *Dieren*, **5**: 18–25.

9. A. F. J. Portielje, 1928. Zur Ethologie bzw. Psychologie der Silbermöwe, *Larus argentatus argentatus* Pont. *Ardea*, **17**: 112–49.

10. P. Sevenster, 1991. Ethologisch onderzoek in het verleden; Niko Tinbergen. In *Meeuwen* (ed. T. W. M. Bakker and

D. A. G. Buizer), pp. 44–52. Koninklijke Nederlandse Natuurhistorische Vereniging, The Hague.

11. A. F. J. Portielje, 1938. *Dieren zien en leren kennen* [Seeing animals and getting to know them]. Nederlandse Keurboekerij, Amsterdam.

12. W. H. Thorpe, 1979. *The origins and rise of ethology.* Heinemann Educational, London.

13. N. Tinbergen, 1939. Review of A. F. J. Portielje, *Dieren Zien en Leeren Kennen* [Seeing animals and getting to know them], in *Ardea*, **28**: 111–13.

14. D. R. Röell, 1992. F. J. J. Buytendijks (1887–1974) ontwerp van een Christelijke dierpsychologie [F. J. J. B's design for a Christian animal psychology]. *Gewina*, **15**: 34–50.

15. Tinbergen collection, Bodleian Library archives; Heimans en Thijsse Stichting archives.

16. J. A. Bierens de Haan, 1940. *Die tierische Instinkte und ihre Umbau durch Erfahrung* [Animal instincts and their alteration through experience]. Brill, Leiden. 1945. *Instinct en intelligentie bij dieren* [Instinct and intelligence in animals]. Noorduijn, Gorinchem.

17. Letter by NT to Bierens de Haan, 9/11/1937. Heimans en Thijsse Stichting archives.

18. N. Tinbergen, 1951. *The study of instinct.* Clarendon Press, Oxford.

19. J. A. Bierens de Haan, 1937. *Labyrinth und Umweg: ein Kapitel aus der Tierpsychologie* [Maze and detour: a chapter from animal psychology]. Brill, Leiden.

20. Letter by NT to Bierens de Haan, 13/5/1937, Heimans en Thijsse Stichting archives.

21. McDougall, *Outline of psychology.*

22. D. R. Röell, 1996. *De wereld van instinct.* Erasmus, Rotterdam, p. 151.

23. J. B. Watson, 1914. *Behavior: an introduction to comparative psychology.* Holt, New York.

24. J. B. Watson, 1924. *Behaviorism.* Chicago University Press.

25. N. Tinbergen, 1985. Watching and wondering. In *Studying animal behavior* (ed. D. A. Dewsbury), pp. 431–63. Chicago University Press.

26. E. S. Russell, 1934. *The behaviour of animals.* London.

27. Tinbergen, *Study of instinct.*

28. Tinbergen, Watching and wondering.

29. C. L. Morgan, 1894. *An introduction to comparative psychology.* Walter Scott, London.

30. Thorpe, *Origins and rise of ethology.*

31. J. S. Huxley, 1914. The courtship habits of the great crested grebe (*Podiceps cristatus*); with an addition to the theory of sexual selection. *Proc. Zool. Soc. Lond.*, **84**: 491–562. 1923. Courtship activities in the red-throated diver (*Colymbus stellatus* Pont.); together with a discussion on the evolution of courtship in birds. *J. linn. Soc.*, **35**: 253–91.

32. R. W. Burkhardt Jr., 1992. Huxley and the rise of ethology. In *Julian Huxley: biologist and statesman of science* (ed. C. K. Waters and A. van Helden), pp. 127–49. Rice University Press, Houston.

33. Tinbergen, Watching and wondering.

34. N. Tinbergen, 1936. Waarnemingen en proeven over de sociologie van een zilvermeeuwenkolonie. [Observations and experiments on the sociology of a herring gull colony]. *De Levende Natuur*, **40**: 262–80, 304–8.

35. N. Tinbergen, 1958. *Curious naturalists.* Country Life, London.

36. In the years before the war Hulshorst students included Gerard Baerends and Jos van Roon, who later married; others included Niko's brother Luuk, G. Schuyl,

D. Kuenen, A. Besemer, W. Kruyt,
R. van der Linde, A. Quispel,
A. Meeuse, J. Rooth, and
W. W. Varossieau.

37. Interview with F. Makkink,
May 2000.

38. N. Tinbergen, 1935. Über die
Orientierung des Bienenwolfes
(*Philanthus triangulum* Fabr.)
[On the orientation of the bee-
wolf]. II. Die Bienenjagd [Bee
hunting]. *Z. f. Vergl. Physiol.*,
21: 699–716. N. Tinbergen and
W. Kruyt, 1938. Über die
Orientierung des Bienenwolfes
(*Philanthus triangulum* Fabr.) III. Die
Bevorzügung bestimmter
Wegmarken [Preference for certain
road signs]. *Z. f. Vergl. Physiol.*,
25: 292–334. N. Tinbergen and
R. J. van der Linde, 1938. Über die
Orientierung des Bienenwolfes
(*Philanthus triangulum* Fabr.). IV.
Heimflug aus unbekannter Gebiet
[Return from unknown areas].
Biol. Zentralbl., **58**: 425–35.

39. Tinbergen, *Curious naturalists*.

40. G. Schuyl, L. Tinbergen, and
N. Tinbergen, 1936. Ethologische
Beobachtungen am Baumfalken
(*Falco s. subbuteo* L.) [Ethological
observations on hobbies].
J. f. Ornithol., **84**: 387–433.

41. R. W. Burkhardt, 1981. On the
emergence of ethology as a
scientific discipline. *Conspectus of
History*, **1**: 62–81.

42. Tinbergen, Watching and
wondering.

43. Tinbergen, Watching and
wondering.

44. In the 1930s, undergraduate
students of Tinbergen included
T. Alberda, G. P. Baerends,
M. Boeseman, D. Caudri,
A. F. H. Besemer, L. K. Boerema,
J. van der Drift, E. Elton,
D. Gooszen, B. Kok, D. Kreger,
D. J. Kuenen, R. J. v. d. Linden,
B. J. D. Meeuse, P. J. Nieuwdorp,
B. Oving, J. J. ter Pelkwijk,
A. Quispel, J. v. Roon,
L. Tinbergen, W. Varossieau,
P. van Veen, F. v. d. Weerd,
C. Weurman, and others.

45. G. P. Baerends, 1991. Early
ethology: growing from Dutch
roots. In *The Tinbergen legacy*
(ed. M. S. Dawkins, T. R.
Halliday, and R. Dawkins), pp.
1–17. Chapman & Hall, London.

46. N. Tinbergen, 1936. Eenvoudige
proeven over de zintuigfuncties van
larve en imago van de geelgerande
watertor [Simple experiments on
the function of sense organs of
larval and adult robber beetles]. *De
Levende Natuur*, **41**: 225–36.

47. J. J. ter Pelkwijk and N. Tinbergen,
1936. Roodkaakjes ['Red-jaws'].
De Levende Natuur, **40**: 129–37.
J. J. ter Pelkwijk and N. Tinbergen,
1937. Eine Reizbiologische
Analyse einiger Verhaltensweisen
von *Gasterosteus aculeatus* L [Analysis
of stimuli in some behaviour
patterns of G. a.].
Z. f. Tierpsychol., **1**: 193–204.

48. J. P. Strijbos, 1976. *Vogelvrij*.
Schuyt, Haarlem, p.119.

49. R. J. Rowland and P. Sevenster,
1985. Sign stimuli in the three-
spined stickleback (*Gasterosteus
aculeatus*): a reexamination and
extension of some classic
experiments. *Behaviour*, **93**: 241–57.

50. W. J. Rowland, 1982. Mate choice
by male sticklebacks, *Gasterosteus
aculeatus*. *Anim. Behav.*, **30**: 1093–8.

51. K. J. Bolyard and W. J. Rowland,
1996. Context-dependent response
to red coloration in stickleback.
Anim. Behav., **52**: 923–7.

52. M. Milinski and T. C. M. Bakker,
1990. Female sticklebacks use male
coloration in mate choice and
hence avoid parasitized males.
Nature, **344**: 330–3. T. C. M.
Bakker and M. Milinski, 1993. The
advantages of being red – sexual
selection in the stickleback.
Mar. Behav. Physiol., **23**: 287–300.

53. J. M. M. Duyf, 1993. *Een wereld van
verschil: het leven en werk van de
econoom Jan Tinbergen* [A world of

difference: life and work of the economist Jan Tinbergen]. University Publishers, Rotterdam.

54. Interview with Mrs. T. Tinbergen-Frensdorf (widow of Luuk), November 1999.

55. K. H. Voous, 1995. *In de ban van de vogels: ornithologisch biografisch woordenboek van Nederland* [In the grip of birds: ornithological biographical dictionary of the Netherlands]. Scheffers, Utrecht. J. Verwey, 1955. In memoriam Luuk Tinbergen. *Ardea*, **43**: 293–308.

56. D. Morris, 1979. *Animal days.* Jonathan Cape, London.

57. Tinbergen, Watching and wondering.

58. K. Lorenz, 1985. My family and other animals. In *Leaders in the study of animal behavior: autobiographical perspectives* (ed. D. A. Dewsbury), pp. 259–87. Chicago University Press.

59. K. Z. Lorenz, 1927. Beobachtungen an Dohlen [Observations on jackdaws]. *J. Ornithol.*, **75**: 511–19. 1931. Beiträge zur Ethologie sozialer Corviden [Contributions to the ethology of social corvids]. *J. Ornithol.*, **79**: 67–127. 1932. Betrachtungen über das Erkennen der arteigene Triebhandlungen der Vögel [Considerations about recognition of species-specific instincts in birds]. *J. Ornithol.*, **80**: 50–98.

60. K. Z. Lorenz, 1935. Der Kumpan in der Umwelt des Vogels. *J. Ornithol.*, **83**: 137–215; **83**: 289–413.

61. K. Z. Lorenz, 1937. The companion in the bird's world. *Auk*, **54**: 245–73.

62. O. Heinroth, 1911. Beiträge zur Biologie, namentlich Ethologie und Psychologie der Anatiden [Contributions to the biology, especially. Ethology and Psychology, of the Anatids]. *Verhandl. d. V. intenat. Ornithologen-Kongressses Berlin*, **1910**, 589–702.

63. J. J. von Uexküll, 1909. *Umwelt und Innenwelt der Tiere* [Outer and inner world of animals]. Springer, Berlin.

64. Tinbergen, Watching and wondering.

65. Lorenz, My family and other animals.

66. K. Lorenz, 1937. Über die Bildung des Instinktbegriffes [On the construction of the instinct concept]. *Naturwiss.*, **25**: 289–300, 307–31.

67. Letter of 13/05/37, Heimans en Thijsse Stichting archives.

68. K. Lorenz and N. Tinbergen, 1938. Taxis und Instinkthandlung in der Eirollbewegung der Graugans. *Z. f. Tierpsychol.*, **2**: 1–29.

69. Letter from Ernst Mayr to NT, 26/1/1982, Bodleian Library archives.

70. N. Tinbergen, 1948. Social releasers and the experimental method required for their study. *Wilson Bulletin*, **60**: 6–51.

71. References in N. Tinbergen, 1958. On anti-predator responses in certain birds – a reply. *J. comp. Physiol. Psychol.*, **50**: 412–14.

72. W. M. Schleidt, 1961. Reaktionen von Truthühnern auf fliegende Raubvögel und Versuche zur Analyse ihrer AAM's [Reactions by turkeys to flying raptors and experiments to analyse their IRMs]. *Z. f. Tierpsychol.*, **18**: 534–60.

73. N. Tinbergen, 1965. *Animal behavior.* Time Inc., New York, p. 130.

74. N. Tinbergen and D. J. Kuenen, 1939. Über die auslösenden und die richtunggebenden Reizsituationen der Sperrbewegung von jungen Drosseln (*Turdus m. merula* L. und *T. e. ericetorum* Turton) [About the releasing and the directing stimulus situations of the gaping movement of young thrushes]. *Z. f. Tierpsychol.*, **3**: 37–60.

75. N. Tinbergen, 1973. Autobiography of Nikolaas Tinbergen. Website of Nobel Foundation:

<http://www.nobel.se/medicine/la ureates/1973/tinbergen-autobio.html>

76. Letter by NT, 19/12/1939, to the Committee of the Dutch Zoological Society, Zoology Laboratory archives.

77. For example, letters by NT to J. Bierens de Haan (Heimans en Thijsse Stichting archives) and H. Boschma ('Naturalis' Institute archives).

78. Letter by NT, 20/9/1938 to H. Boschma ('Naturalis' Institute archives), and 22 September 1938 to J. Bierens de Haan (Heimans en Thijsse Stichting archives).

79. Letter by NT, 20/9/1938 to H. Boschma, 'Naturalis' Institute archives.

80. Letter by NT to R. W. Burkhardt, 5/5/1979, Bodleian Library archives.

81. N. Tinbergen, 1939. On the analysis of social organization among vertebrates, with special reference to birds. *Amer. Midl. Naturalist*, **21**: 210–34.

82. Letter by NT, 22/9/1938 to J. Bierens de Haan, Heimans en Thijsse Stichting archives.

83. Letters by NT to H. Boschma, 20/9/1938 and 11/10/1938, 'Naturalis' Institute archives.

84. M. Boeseman, J. van der Drift, J. M. van Roon, N. Tinbergen, and J. J. ter Pelkwijk, 1938. De bittervoorns en hun mossels [Bitterlings and their mussels]. *De Levende Natuur*, **42**: 129–36.

85. N. Tinbergen and J. J. ter Pelkwijk, 1939. De kleine watersalamander [The smooth newt]. *De Levende Natuur*, **43**: 232–7.

86. N. Tinbergen, 1940. De schutkleur der takspanners [Camouflage of stick caterpillars]. *De Levende Natuur*, **44**: 230–4.

87. N. Tinbergen, 1938. De Noordveluwe [The north Veluwe]. *De Levende Natuur*, **42**: 330–7.

88. N. Tinbergen, B. J. D. Meeuse, L. K. Boerema, and W. W. Varossieau,

1942. Die Balz des Samtfalters, *Eumenis semele* [Courtship of the grayling butterfly]. *Z. f. Tierpsychol.*, **5**: 182–226.

89. N. Tinbergen, 1941. Over de 'taal' der dieren [About the 'language' of animals]. *De Levende Natuur*, **46**: 81–8, 107–12, 125–9.

90. N. Tinbergen, 1941. Een hommel die de weg wist [A bumblebee that knew the way]. *De Levende Natuur*, **46**: 119.

91. N. Tinbergen, 1941. Wat brengt een zilvermeeuw ertoe zijn prooi te laten vallen? [What causes a herring gull to drop its prey?]. *De Levende Natuur*, **46**: 119.

92. N. Tinbergen, 1942. De staartmees als bouwkunstenaar [Longtailed tits as building masters]. *De Levende Natuur*, **46**: 215–18.

93. N. Tinbergen, 1939. Review of M. M. Nice, *The watcher at the nest*, in *Ardea*, **28**: 51–2.

94. Tinbergen, review of *Dieren Zien en Leeren Kennen*.

95. N. Tinbergen, 1941. Over de waarde van het populariseren van de biologie [On the value of popularizing biology]. *Vakblad voor Biologen*, **22**: 106–9.

96. Tinbergen, *Curious naturalists*, p. 102.

97. G. P. Baerends, 1941. Fortpflanzungsverhalten und Orientierung der Grabwespe *Ammophila campestris* Jur [Reproductive behaviour and orientation of the digger wasp *Ammophila*]. *Tijdschr. Entomol.*, **84**: 68–275.

98. G. P. Baerends, 1985. Two pillars of wisdom. In *Studying animal behavior* (ed. D. A. Dewsbury), pp. 13–42. University of Chicago Press.

99. N. Tinbergen, 1942. An objectivistic study of the innate behaviour of animals. *Bibliotheca Biotheoretica D*, **1**: 39–98.

100. Tinbergen, Objectivistic study, p. 93.

101. R. Dawkins, 1976. Hierarchical organisation: a candidate principle

for ethology. In *Growing points in
ethology* (ed. P. P. G. Bateson and
R. A. Hinde), pp. 7–54.
Cambridge University Press.

102. Baerends, Two pillars of wisdom,
pp. 13–40.

103. Tinbergen, Objectivistic study,
p. 62.

104. Tinbergen, Objectivistic study.

105. N. Tinbergen, 1940. Die
Übersprungbewegung
[Displacement activity].
Z. f. Tierpsychol., **4**: 1–40.

106. A. Kortlant, 1940. Wechselwirkung
zwischen Instinkten [Interactions
between instincts]. *Arch. Neerl.
Zool.*, **4**: 443–520.

107. Röell, *De wereld van instinct*.

108. Letter by NT to J. Huxley,
published by Huxley in 'Scientific
affairs in Europe' (10 November
1945). *Nature*, **156**: 576–9.

109. Letter by NT to A. Kortlandt,
14/11/1940. Kortlandt archive.

110. N. Tinbergen, 1940. Elk vogeltje
zingt zoals het gebekt is [Every bird
sings to the shape of its beak].
University Lecture, Leiden. Luctor et
Emergo, Leiden.

111. D. C. Tinbergen, 1940. *Dit is dat
boecskijn here Nikolaas* [This is the
booklet about mr. Nikolaas].
Private published, The Hague.

Chapter 5

1. Letter by NT to Margaret Nice,
23/6/1945, Allee archive.

2. M. de Keizer, 1979. *De gijzelaars van
Sint Michielsgestel* [The hostages of St
Michielsgestel]. Sijthoff, Alphen.

3. P. Geyl *et al.* (ed.), 1946. *Beekvliet:
gedenkboek gijzelaarskamp St.
Michielsgestel* [Beekvliet: memorial
volume to the hostage camp St
Michielsgestel]. Roelants,
Schiedam.

4. For example: Geyl *et al.*, *Beekvliet*.
R. Peereboom, 1945. *Gijzelaar in
Gestel*. Tijl, Zwolle. De Keizer, *De
gijzelaars van Sint Michielsgestel* (and
references therein).

5. Letter by NT to his parents,
23/9/1942, Bodleian Library
archives.

6. Letter by NT to his sister Jacomien
Tinbergen, 23/9/1942,
J. Tinbergen archive.

7. M. F. F. A. de Neree tot Babberich,
1946. Cursussen. In *Beekvliet*
(ed. P. Geyl *et al.*), pp. 153–74.

8. L. J. C. Boucher, 1945. *The Spark
papers*. Boucher, The Hague.

9. N. Tinbergen, 1946. De
schoenpoetsers [The shoeshines]. In
Beekvliet (ed. P. Geyl *et al.*),
pp. 231–2.

10. Letter by NT to his parents,
19/9/1942, Bodleian Library
archives, Oxford. The 'Dutch East
Indian group' were mostly residents
of Dutch East India on leave in
Holland, who had been taken
hostage in response, after the
colonial government in the Dutch
East Indies (later Indonesia)
interned all German citizens in
1940 and treated them rather badly.

11. N. Tinbergen, 1946. *Inleiding tot de
diersociologie* [Introduction to animal
sociology]. Noorduijn, Gorinchem.

12. J. A. Bierens de Haan, 1945. *Instinct
en intelligentie bij dieren* [Instinct and
intelligence in animals]. Noorduijn,
Gorinchem.

13. Tinbergen, *Inleiding*, p. 7.

14. Tinbergen, *Inleiding*, p. 122.

15. R. Dawkins, 1976. *The selfish gene*.
Oxford University Press.

16. N. Tinbergen, 1948 *Klieuw* (in
Dutch). Boucher, The Hague;
1947, *Kleew* (in English), Oxford
University Press, New York. 1943.
'De geschiedenis van de
dauwdruppel' [The history of the
dew drop], unpublished, J.
Tinbergen archive. 1943. 'De oude
eikenbalk' [The old oak beam],
unpublished, D. Tinbergen
archive. 1944. 'Het zandboek' [The
sand book], unpublished, Catrina
Loman (née Tinbergen) archive.

17. N. Tinbergen, 1952. *The tale of John
Stickle*. Methuen, London.

18. Interviews with Mrs T. Tinbergen-Frensdorf, November 1999, and Catrina Loman, November 2000.

19. Letter by NT to R. Yerkes, 18/10/1946, Yerkes archive.

20. J. J. ter Pelkwijk, 1948. *Deze mooie wereld* [This beautiful world]. Ploegsma, Amsterdam.

21. U. Deichmann, 1996. *Biologists under Hitler*. Harvard University Press, Cambridge, Mass.

22. K. Lorenz, 1940. Durch Domestikation verursachte Störungen arteigenen Verhaltens [Disturbed species-specific behaviour caused by domestication]. *Z. f. angewandte Psychol. u. Charakterkunde*, **59**: 1–81. See also Deichmann, *Biologists under Hitler*.

23. Letter by O. Koehler to O. Antonius, 10/10/1942, Bretchka archive.

24. Letter by O. Antonius to O. Koehler, 16/10/1942, Bretchka archive.

25. Letter destroyed. Pers. comm., Agnes von Cranach (daughter of K. Lorenz) to B. O. Foeger.

26. R. Burkhardt, MS., in preparation.

27. Letter by NT to Margaret Nice, 23/06/1945, Nice archive.

28. Letter by NT to J. Bierens de Haan 7/6/1945, Heimans en Thijsse Stichting archives.

29. K. Lorenz, 1985. My family and other animals. In *Studying animal behavior* (ed. D. A. Dewsbury), pp. 259–87. Chicago University Press.

30. See accounts in W. H. Thorpe, 1979. *The origins and rise of ethology*. Heinemann, London.

31. R. A. Hinde, 1990. Nikolaas Tinbergen. *Biographical Memoirs of the Royal Society*, **36**: 547–65.

32. Lorenz, My family and other animals.

33. Letter by NT to R. Yerkes, 18/10/1946, Yerkes archive.

34. Letter by NT to E. Mayr, 11/11/1945, Mayr archives.

35. Interview with E. Cullen, November 2000.

36. Interview with Mrs T. Tinbergen-Frensdorf, November 1999.

37. Interview with Mrs T. Tinbergen-Frensdorf, November 1999.

38. Letter by NT to J. Bierens de Haan, 7/6/1945, Heimans en Thijsse Stichting archives.

39. J. R. Durant, 1986. The making of ethology: the Association for the Study of Animal Behaviour, 1936–1986. *Anim. Behav.*, **34**: 1601–16.

40. Letter by NT to G. Baerends, 10/10/1946, Baerends archive.

41. N. Tinbergen, 1947. De natuur is sterker dan de leer [Nature is stronger than teaching]. Inaugural Lecture, University of Leiden, Leiden.

42. N. Tinbergen, letter to all Leiden biology professors, 29/9/1947, 'Naturalis' Institute archives.

43. Letter by NT to E. Mayr, 9 March 1949, Mayr archive.

44. Letter by NT to J. Huxley, 1945, in *Nature*, **156**: 576–7.

45. N. Tinbergen, 1958. *Curious naturalists*. Country Life, London.

46. Circular by NT to Hulshorst participants, June 1946, de Ruiter archive.

47. Interview with P. Sevenster, September 2000.

48. N. Tinbergen, 1948. Wat prikkelt een scholekster tot broeden? [What stimulates an oystercatcher to incubate?]. *De Levende Natuur*, **51**: 65–9.

49. N. Tinbergen, 1947. Orientatie en orientatievlucht bij *Bembex rostrata* L. [Orientation and orientation flight in *Bembex*]. *Tijdschr. v. Entomol.*, **88**: 435–8.

50. L. de Ruiter, 1952. Some experiments on the camouflage of stick caterpillars. *Behaviour*, **4**: 222–32.

51. L. de Ruiter, 1956. Countershading in caterpillars. An analysis of its

adaptive significance. *Arch. Neerl. Zool.*, **11**: 285–342.

52. Tinbergen, *Curious naturalists*.

53. In Dutch universities students graduated with a degree called 'doctoraal', approximately equivalent to a British or American masters degree. It entailed three small research projects, as well as several years of lectures and practicals.

54. N. Tinbergen, 1949. De functie van de rode vlek op de snavel van de zilvermeeuw (*Larus a. argentatus* Pontopp) [The function of the red spot on the bill of the herring gull]. *Bijdragen tot de Dierkunde*, **28**: 453–65.

55. N. Tinbergen and A. C. Perdeck, 1950. On the stimulus situation releasing the begging response in the newly hatched herring gull chick (*Larus argentatus argentatus* Pont). *Behaviour*, **3**: 1–39.

56. F. Goethe, 1937. Beobachtungen und Untersuchungen zur Biologie der Silbermöwe auf der Vogelinsel Memmertsand [Observations and research on the biology of the herring gull on the bird island Memmertsand]. *J. Ornithol.*, **85**: 1–119.

57. N. Tinbergen and J. van Iersel, 1947. 'Displacement reactions' in the three-spined stickleback. *Behaviour*, **1**: 56–63.

58. Interview with P. Sevenster, September 2000.

59. Letter by NT to E. Mayr, 11/11/1945, Mayr archive.

60. Published paper somewhat extended from the talk: N. Tinbergen 1948. Social releasers and the experimental method required for their study. *Wilson Bulletin*, **60**: 6–51.

61. Letter by NT to H. Boschma, 5/7/1946, 'Naturalis' Institute archives.

62. Letter by NT to E. Mayr, 2/22/48, Mayr archive.

63. Letter by NT to Bierens de Haan, 16/12/48, Heimans en Thijsse Stichting archives.

64. Letter by NT to E. Mayr, 9/3/1949, Mayr archive.

65. Tinbergen, Social releasers and the experimental method required for their study. 1948. Physiologische Instinktforschung [Physiological study of instinct]. *Experientia*, **4**: 121–33. 1950. The hierarchical organization of nervous mechanisms underlying instinctive behaviour. *Symp. Soc. Exp. Biol.*, **4**: 305–12.

66. Letter by NT to J. Bierens de Haan, 22/8/1946, Heimans en Thijsse Stichting archives.

67. Tinbergen, The Hierarchical organization of nervous mechanisms.

68. W. Craig, 1918. Appetites and aversions as constituents of instincts. *Biol. Bull. Woods Hole*, **34**: 91–107.

69. Tinbergen, The Hierarchical organization of nervous mechanisms.

70. E. von Holst, 1937. Vom Wesen der Ordnung im Zentralnervensystem [The nature of organization of the central nervous system]. *Naturwiss.*, **25**: 625–31, 641–7. P. Weiss, 1940. Self-differentiation of the basic patterns of coordination. *Comp. Psychol. Monogr.*, **17**: 1–96.

71. Tinbergen, Social releasers and the experimental method required for their study.

72. Tinbergen, Physiologische Instinktforschung.

73. Weiss, Self-differentiation of the basic patterns of coordination.

74. K. Lorenz, 1950. The comparative method in studying innate behaviour patterns. *Symp. Soc. Exp. Biol.*, **4**: 221–68.

75. N. Tinbergen, 1985. Watching and wondering. In *Studying animal behavior* (ed. D. A. Dewsbury), pp. 431–63. University of Chicago Press.

76. Interview with Janet Tinbergen, October 2000.

77. De Keizer, *De gijzelaars van Sint Michielsgestel.*

78. Letter by D. Lack to A. Hardy, 28/4/58, Hardy archive.

79. Interview with P. Sevenster, September 2000.

80. Interview with Mrs T. Tinbergen-Frensdorf, November 1999.

81. Letter by NT to E. Mayr, 5/9/1945, Mayr archive.

82. Letter by NT to J. Bierens de Haan, 7/3/1947, Heimans en Thijsse Stichting archives.

83. Letter by NT to E. Mayr, 26/8/1947, Mayr archive.

84. Letter by NT to E. Mayr, 22/2/1948, Mayr archive.

85. Letter by NT to E. Mayr, 22/9/1948, Mayr archive.

86. Letter by NT to E. Mayr, undated (around January 1949), Mayr archive.

87. Interview with C. Loman, November 2000.

88. Interview with R. Hinde, October 2000.

89. Tinbergen, Watching and wondering.

90. Letter by NT to J. van Iersel, 1/10/1948, 'Naturalis' Institute archives.

91. Letter by NT to J. van Iersel, 1/10/1948, 'Naturalis' Institute archives.

92. Letter by NT to colleagues in Faculty of Mathematics and Sciences, undated (probably March 1949), 'Naturalis' Institute archives.

93. Letter by NT to G. Junge, November 1949, Zoology Laboratory archives.

94. Interview with P. Sevenster, September 2000.

Chapter 6

1. A. Sampson, 1962. *Anatomy of Britain.* Hodder and Stoughton, London.

2. Maynard Smith archive.

3. Interview with P. Sevenster, September 2000.

4. Letter by NT to G. Junge, January 1950, Zoology Laboratory archives.

5. Interview with R. Hinde, October 2000.

6. Letter by NT to H. Boschma, November 1951, Zoology Laboratory archives.

7. Letter by NT to H. Boschma, November 1951, Zoology Laboratory archives.

8. Fay Hall, pers. comm., November 2000.

9. J. Krebs and R. Dawkins, 2001. John Michael (Mike) Cullen (1927–2001). *Ibis*, **143**: 704–5.

10. Letter by NT to A. Manning, March 1976, Manning archive.

11. Interview with D. Morris, June 2000.

12. A. Manning, 1985. The ontogeny of an ethologist. In *Studying animal behavior* (ed. D. A. Dewsbury), pp. 289–313. University of Chicago Press.

13. D. Morris, 1979. *Animal days.* Jonathan Cape, London.

14. N. Tinbergen, 1951. De feilbaarheid van het instinct [The fallibility of instinct]. *De Levende Natuur*, **54**: 181–90. 1952. When instinct fails. *Country Life*, 15 February: 412–14.

15. E. Cullen, 1957. Adaptations in the kittiwake to cliff-nesting. *Ibis*, **99**: 275–302.

16. Interview with Esther Cullen, November 2000.

17. L. Shaffer, 1991. The Tinbergen legacy in photography and film. In *The Tinbergen legacy* (ed. M. S. Dawkins, T. R. Halliday, and R. Dawkins), pp. 129–38. Chapman & Hall, London.

18. Films now in the British Film Institute archives.

19. B. D. Kettlewell, 1955. Selection experiments in industrial melanism in the Lepidoptera. *Heredity*, **9**: 323–42.

20. British Film Institute archives. N. Tinbergen, 1958. *Curious naturalists*. Country Life, London.

21. J. Hooper, 2002. *Of moths and men: an evolutionary tale*. Fourth Estate, London.

22. Morris, *Animal days*.

23. Interview with D. Morris, June 2000.

24. Manning, Ontogeny of an ethologist.

25. M. Bastock and A. Manning, 1955. The courtship of *Drosophila melanogaster*. *Behaviour*, **8**: 85–111.

26. N. Tinbergen, 1953. *The herring gull's world*. Collins, London.

27. N. Tinbergen, 1951. *The study of instinct*. Clarendon Press, Oxford.

28. B. Greenberg, 1952. Review of N. Tinbergen, *The study of instinct*, in *Physiol. Zool.*, **25**: 381–3.

29. L. Carmichael, 1952. Review of N. Tinbergen, *The study of instinct*, in *Science*, **115**: 438–9.

30. Greenberg, review of *The study of instinct*.

31. Carmichael, review of *The study of instinct*.

32. T. J. Roper, 1989. Tinbergen's legacy: *The study of Instinct* (reissue). *Trends Ecol. Evol.*, **4**: 318–19.

33. N. Tinbergen, 1952. 'Derived' activities: their causation, biological significance, origin and emancipation during evolution. *Quart. Rev. Biol.*, **27**: 1–32.

34. N. Tinbergen, 1953. *Social behaviour in animals*. Methuen, London.

35. N. Tinbergen, 1952. *The tale of John Stickle*. Methuen, London.

36. N. Tinbergen, 1954. *Bird life*. Oxford University Press, London.

37. N. Tinbergen, 1958. *Curious naturalists*. Country Life, London. Revised 1974, Penguin Books, Harmondsworth, UK.

38. N. Tinbergen, 1951. Recent advances in the study of bird behaviour. In *Proceedings of the 10*[th] *International Ornithol. Congress, Uppsala* (ed. L. von Haaften),

pp. 360–74. 1952. A note on the origin and evolution of threat display. *Ibis*, **94**: 160–2.

39. N. Tinbergen, 1952. The curious behavior of the stickleback. *Scientific American*, December, 22–6.

40. D. Lehrman, 1953. A critique of Konrad Lorenz's theory of instinctive behavior. *Quart. Rev. Biol.*, **28**: 337–63.

41. N. Tinbergen, 1942. An objectivistic study of the innate behaviour of animals. *Bibliotheca Biotheoretica D*, **1**: 39–98.

42. K. Lorenz, 1940. Durch Domestikation verursachte Störungen arteigenen Verhaltens. *Z. angew. Psychol. Charakterkunde*, **59**: 2–81.

43. N. Tinbergen and D. J. Kuenen, 1939. Über die auslösenden und die richtunggebenden Reizsituationen der Sperrbewegung von jungen Drosseln (*Turdus m. merula* L. und *T. e. ericetorum* Turton). *Z. f. Tierpsychol.*, **3**: 37–60.

44. Letter by NT to G. Baerends, 24/5/1954, Baerends archive.

45. Manning, Ontogeny of an ethologist.

46. B. Schaffner (ed.), 1955. *Group processes*. Transactions of the First Conference. Josiah Macy Jr. Foundation, New York.

47. N. Tinbergen and A. C. Perdeck, 1950. On the stimulus situation releasing the begging response in the newly hatched herring gull chick (*Larus argentatus argentatus* Pont). *Behaviour*, **3**: 1–39.

48. E. Mayr, pers. comm., 18 August 2001.

49. Letter by NT to R. Hinde, 14/10/1954, Hinde archive.

50. J. Hirsch, R. H. Lindley, and E. C. Tolman, 1955. An experimental test of an alleged innate sign stimulus. *J. Comp. Physiol. Psychol.*, **48**: 278–80.

51. N. Tinbergen, 1958. On anti-predator responses in certain birds –

a reply. *J. Comp. Physiol. Psychol.*, **50**: 412–14.

52. W. M. Schleidt, 1961. Reaktionen von Truthühnern auf fliegende Raubvögel und Versuche zur Analyse ihrer AAM's [Reactions by turkeys to flying raptors and experiments to analyse their IRMs]. *Z. f. Tierpsychol.*, **18**: 534–60.

53. A. Kortlandt, 1940. Wechselwirkung zwischen Instinkten [Interaction between instincts]. *Arch. Neerl. Zool.*, **4**: 443–520.

54. A. Kortlandt, 1955. Aspects and prospects of the concept of instinct. *Arch. Neerl. Zool.*, **11**: 155–284.

55. R. Dawkins, 1976. Hierarchical organisation: a candidate principle for ethology. In *Growing points in ethology* (ed. P. P. G. Bateson and R. A. Hinde), pp. 7–54. Cambridge University Press.

56. Interview with A. Kortlandt, October 2000.

57. M. Bastock, D. Morris, and M. Moynihan, 1953. Some comments on conflict and thwarting in animals. *Behaviour*, **6**: 66–84.

58. A. D. Blest, 1961. The concept of ritualisation. In *Current problems in animal behaviour* (ed. W. H. Thorpe and O. L. Zangwill), pp. 102–24. Cambridge University Press.

59. Letter by NT to R. Hinde, 1/11/1953, Hinde archive.

60. Letter by NT to R. Hinde, 15/1/1959, Hinde archive.

61. Interview with R. Hinde, October 2000.

62. For example, R. A. Hinde, 1956. Ethological models and the concept of 'drive'. *Brit. J. Philos. Sc.*, **6**: 321–31. R. A. Hinde, 1959. Unitary drives. *Anim. Behav.*, **7**: 130–41.

63. Letter by NT to R. Hinde, 26/8/1959, Hinde archive.

64. Letter by NT to R. Hinde, 31/3/57, Hinde archive.

65. R. Hoogland, D. Morris, and N. Tinbergen, 1957. The spines of sticklebacks (*Gasterosteus* and *Pygosteus*) as a defence against predators (*Perca* and *Esox*). *Behaviour*, **10**: 205–36.

66. N. Tinbergen, 1959. Einige Gedanken über 'Beschwichtigungsgebärden' [Some thoughts about appeasement gestures]. *Z. f. Tierpsychol.*, **16**: 651–65.

67. N. Tinbergen, 1958. Bauplan-ethologische Beobachtungen an Möwen [Blue-print ethological observations on gulls]. *Arch. Neerl. Zool.*, **13**: 369–82. N. Tinbergen, 1959. Behaviour, systematics and natural selection. *Ibis*, **101**: 318–30.

68. R. A. Hinde and N. Tinbergen, 1958. The comparative study of species-specific behavior. In *Behavior and evolution* (ed. A. Roe and G. G. Simpson), pp. 251–68. Yale University Press, New Haven.

69. N. Tinbergen, 1959. Comparative studies of the behaviour of gulls (*Laridae*): a progress report. *Behaviour*, **15**: 1–70.

70. Interview with Piet Sevenster, September 2000.

71. Interview with Janet Tinbergen, October 2000.

72. David Lack (1910–73), director Edward Grey Institute of Field Ornithology. Ex-schoolmaster who became an FRS, author of many books, and who dominated ornithology for many years. He emphasized the importance of food availability to explain almost all population phenomena. Ruled his group with a firm hand; 'had tea' instead of seminars. A religious and somewhat formal person.

73. Charles Elton (1900–91), founder and director of the Bureau of Animal Populations, a separate unit within the Oxford University Department of Zoology. One of the founding fathers of the science of ecology; research emphasis was on population cycles; author of

many books; retired 1967. I remember him as a diffident and friendly small man, bald and bespectacled, a gentle, intensely private person, religious and very widely read.

74. Interview with R. Hinde, October 2000.

75. D. Lack, 1954. *The natural regulation of animal numbers*. Clarendon Press, Oxford.

76. Letter by NT to R. Hinde, 9 Nov 1955, Hind archive.

77. *Ibis*, 1956, Vol. 98, no. 3.

78. N. Tinbergen, 1957. The functions of territory. *Bird Study*, **4**: 14–27.

79. N. Tinbergen, 1956. On the functions of territory in gulls. *Ibis*, **98**: 401–11.

80. Letter by NT to R. Hinde, 9 Nov 1955 and 14 Nov 1955, Hind archive.

81. Interview with R. Hinde, October 2000.

82. K. Lorenz, 1952. *King Solomon's ring*. Methuen, London. 1954. *Man meets dog*. Methuen, London.

83. N. Tinbergen and G. J. Broekhuysen, 1954. On the threat and courtship behaviour of Hartlaub's gull (*Hydrocoloeus novae-hollandiae hartlaubi*). *Ostrich*, **25**: 50–62. N. Tinbergen, 1954. Van 'Leeus' en 'Bobbejanen' [About lions and baboons]. *De Levende Natuur*, **57**: 12–14. N. Tinbergen, 1954. Een meeuwenkolonie tussen de aronskelken [A gull colony between the arum lillies]. *De Levende Natuur*, **57**: 41–6. N. Tinbergen, 1954. Een week in het Krugerpark [A week in the Kruger Park]. *De Levende Natuur*, **57**: 181–7, 201–8.

84. Interview with F. Makkink, May 2000.

85. Interview with Dirk Tinbergen, March 2001.

86. Interview with Rita Weidmann, March 2001.

87. Interviews with Catrina Loman, November 2000; Janet Tinbergen, October 2000; Gerry Carleston, October 2000; Dirk Tinbergen, March 2001; Jack Tinbergen, November 1999 and April 2001.

88. Lies Tinbergen, pers. comm., 1965.

89. Interview with Catrina Loman, November 2000.

90. Interview with Janet Tinbergen, October 2000.

91. N. Tinbergen, 1959. Obituary: Gustav Kramer (1910–1959). *British Birds*, **52**: 306–8.

92. Interview with Catrina Loman, November 2000.

93. Letter by NT to Robert Hinde, 8/10/1958, Hind archive.

94. Letter by W. H. Thorpe to Robert Hinde, 30/11/1958, Hind archive.

95. Letter by NT to Robert Hinde, 14/2/1959, Hind archive.

96. N. Tinbergen, February 1961. BBC radio talk: *On turning native*.

Chapter 7

1. E. A. R. Ennion and N. Tinbergen, 1967. *Tracks*. Clarendon Press, Oxford.

2. G. H. Manley, 1960. The swoop and soar performance of the black-headed gull, *Larus ridibundus*. *Ardea*, **48**: 37–51.

3. Interview with C. G. Beer, August 2000.

4. C. G. Beer, 1961. Incubation and nest building behaviour of black-headed gulls. *Behaviour*, **18**: 62–106; **19**: 283–304; **21**: 13–77.

5. C. G. Beer, 1962. The egg-rolling behaviour of black-headed gulls *Larus ridibundus*. *Ibis*, **194**: 388–98.

6. N. Tinbergen, G. J. Broekhuysen, F. Feekes, J. C. W. Houghton, H. Kruuk, and E. Szulc, 1962. Egg shell removal by the black-headed gull, *Larus ridibundus* L.; a behaviour component of camouflage. *Behaviour*, **19**: 74–117.

7. N. Tinbergen, H. Kruuk, and M. Paillette, 1962. Egg-shell

removal by the black-headed gull (*Larus r. ridibundus* L). II. The effects of experience on the response to colour. *Bird Study*, **9**: 123–31. N. Tinbergen, H. Kruuk, M. Paillette, and R. Stamm, 1962. How do black-headed gulls distinguish between eggs and egg-shells? *Brit. Birds*, **55**: 120–9.

8. H. Kruuk, 1964. Predators and anti-predator behaviour of the black-headed gull, *Larus ridibundus* L. *Behaviour* (Suppl.), **11**: 1–129.

9. I. J. Patterson, 1965. Timing and spacing of broods in the black-headed gull *Larus ridibundus*. *Ibis*, **107**: 433–59.

10. Interview with I. Patterson, January 2001.

11. Interview with I. Patterson, January 2001.

12. H. Croze, 1970. Searching image in carrion crows. *Z. f. Tierpsychol.* (Suppl.), **2**: 1–86.

13. N. Tinbergen, M. Impekoven, and D. Franck, 1967. An experiment on spacing-out as a defence against predation. *Behaviour*, **28**: 307–21.

14. N. Tinbergen, 1963. On aims and methods of ethology. *Z. f. Tierpsychol.*, **20**: 410–33.

15. J. S. Huxley, 1914. The courtship habits of the Great Crested Grebe (*Podiceps cristatus*); with an addition to the theory of sexual selection. *Proc. Zool. Soc. Lond.*, 1914: 491–562.

16. Interview with L. Shaffer, August 2000.

17. Letter by NT to his secretary Ann Freeman-Taylor, 2 Dec 1965.

18. L. Shaffer, 1991. The Tinbergen legacy in photography and film. In *The Tinbergen legacy* (ed. M. S. Dawkins, T. R. Halliday, and R. Dawkins), pp. 129–38. Chapman & Hall, London.

19. Interview with L. Shaffer, August 2000.

20. Shaffer, The Tinbergen legacy in photography and film.

21. An email from J. Sparks, 14/3/2001.

22. Shaffer, The Tinbergen legacy in photography and film.

23. Interview with L. Shaffer, August 2000.

24. An email from J. Sparks, 14/3/2001.

25. N. Tinbergen, H. Falkus and E. Ennion, 1970. *Signals for survival*. Clarendon Press, Oxford.

26. Letter by NT to Hugh Falkus, Sept. 1976. Bodleian Library archives.

27. Letter by NT to G. Baerends 4/5/67, Baerends archive.

28. Letter by NT to D. Morris, 1/10/1972, Morris archive.

29. Shaffer, The Tinbergen legacy in photography and film.

30. G. Ferry, 1998. *Dorothy Hodgkin: a life*. Granta, London.

31. Letter by NT to G. Baerends, 27/3/1962, Baerends archive.

32. Letter by NT to Danny Lehrman, 3 Sept 1968, Bodleian Library archives.

33. R. A. Hinde, 1990. Nikolaas Tinbergen 15 April 1907 – 21 December 1988. *Biographical Memoirs of Fellows of the Royal Society*, **36**: 549–65.

34. M. Hansell, pers. comm., 7 December 2000.

35. Interview with R. Dawkins, October 2000.

36. J. Krebs and R. Dawkins 2001. Obituary of Mike Cullen. *The Guardian*, 10 April.

37. Letter by NT to G Baerends, 1968 undated, Baerends archive.

38. Interview with J. Delius, October 2000.

39. J. D. Delius, 1973. Agonistic behaviour of juvenile gulls, a neuroethological study. *Animal Behaviour*, **21**: 236–46.

40. Letter by Lies Tinbergen to G. Baerends, 28/7/1989, Baerends archive.

41. Interview with Mike Cullen, November 2000.

42. Letter by NT to Mike and Esther Cullen, February 1976, Kruuk archive.

43. D. Morris, 1967. *The naked ape.* Jonathan Cape, London.

44. Letter by NT to Desmond Morris, 16/12/1967, Morris archive.

45. Letter by NT to Desmond Morris, 7/12/1967, Morris archive.

46. Letter by NT to Desmond Morris, 16/01/1969, Morris archive.

47. N. Tinbergen, 1963. On adaptive radiation in gulls (tribe *Larini*). In *Feestbundel* (ed. H. Boschma), pp. 209–23. Zool. Mededelingen 39, Rijksmuseum van Natuurlijke Historie, Leiden. 1964. The evolution of signalling devices. In *Social behavior and organization among vertebrates* (ed. W. Etkin), pp. 206–31. University of Chicago Press. 1964. Aggression and fear in the normal sexual behaviour of some animals. In *Pathology and treatment of sexual deviation* (ed. I. Rosen), pp. 3–23. Clarendon Press, Oxford. 1965. Some recent studies of the evolution of sexual behavior. In *Sex and behavior* (ed. F. A. Beach), pp. 1–34. Wiley, New York. 1965. Behavior and natural selection. In *Ideas in modern biology* (ed. J. A. Moore), pp. 521–42. Proc. 16th Zool. Congr., Washington, DC. Doubleday, New York. 1967. Adaptive features of the black-headed gull *Larus ridibundus* L. In *Proc. XIVth Int. Ornithol. Congr.* (ed. D. W. Snow), pp. 43–59. Blackwell Scientific, Oxford. 1969. Ethology. In *Scientific thought 1900–1960* (ed. R. Harré), pp. 238–68. Clarendon Press, Oxford.

48. Letter by NT to Robert Hinde, 26/4/1960, Hind archive.

49. Letter by NT to Robert Hinde, 1/10/1962, Hind archive.

50. R. A. Hinde, 1966. *Animal behaviour.* McGraw-Hill, New York.

51. Letter by NT to G. Baerends, undated, probably late 1967, Baerends archive.

52. N. Tinbergen, 1965. *Animal behavior.* Time Inc., New York.

53. Letter by NT to H. Boschma, 19/11/1962, 'Naturalis' Institute archives.

54. Letter by NT to D. Morris, 20/8/1968, Morris archive.

55. Letter by NT to D. Morris, 4/11/1972, Morris archive.

56. Letter by NT to D. Morris, 22/1/1969, Morris archive.

57. N. Tinbergen, 1972. *The animal in its world: explorations of an ethologist 1932–1972.* i: *Field studies.* ii: *Laboratory experiments and general papers.* Allen & Unwin, London.

58. Tinbergen, *The animal and its world,* ii, p. 88.

59. Tinbergen, Ethology.

60. N. Tinbergen, 1964. The search for animal roots of human behaviour. Lecture to Oxford undergraduates. Published in *The animal and its world,* ii, pp. 161–74.

61. K. Lorenz, 1963. *Das sogenannte Böse.* Borotha-Schoeler, Vienna. 1966. *On aggression.* Methuen, London.

62. N. Tinbergen, 1966. Instinct parliament. Review of K. Lorenz, *On aggression,* in *The Listener,* **76**: 736–7.

63. N. Tinbergen, 1968. On war and peace in animals and man. *Science, New York,* **160**: 1411–18.

64. Letter by NT to G. Baerends, undated, probably late 1967, Baerends archive.

65. Tinbergen, On war and peace in animals and man.

66. N. Tinbergen, 1969. Von Krieg und Frieden bei Tier und Mensch. In *Kreatur Mensch* (ed. G. Altner), pp. 163–78. Heinz Moos, Munich.

67. Letter by D. Lack to NT, 14/10/1968, Bodleian Library archives.

68. Letter by NT to John Pringle, 30/4/1968, Bodleian Library archives.

69. N. Tinbergen, 1958. *Curious naturalists*. Country Life, London, p. 267.

70. Mimeographed Bulletin of the Natural Science Study Group, Vancouver, December 1969, Wolfson College Archives, Oxford.

71. *Science News*, Vol. 1, no. 2. Progressive Natural Sciences Study Group, Vancouver, December 1969, Wolfson College archives.

72. Letter by NT to Sir Isaiah Berlin, 25/2/1970, Wolfson College archives.

73. Letter by Sir Isaiah Berlin to NT, 20/2/1970, Wolfson College archives.

74. R. Kousbroek, 1973. *Ethologie en cultuurfilosofie* [Ethology and culture-philosophy]. Johan Huizinga Lecture, 1972. Harmonie, Amsterdam.

75. N. Tinbergen in *NRC Handelsblad*, 2/3/1973. Kousbroek heeft de klok horen luiden [Kousbroek heard something, but doesn't know the rights of it].

76. E. O. Wilson, 1975. *Sociobiology: the new synthesis*. Belknap Press, Cambridge, Mass.

77. U. Segerstråle, 2000. *Defenders of the truth: the battle for science in the sociobiology debate and beyond*. Oxford University Press.

78. Interview with L. Shaffer, August 2000.

79. Letter by NT to G. Baerends, 4/2/1963, Baerends archive.

80. Letter by NT to D. Morris, 11/10/1965, Morris archive.

81. Letter by NT to Bryan Nelson, 4/5/1965, Nelson archive.

82. Letter by NT to G. Baerends, undated, early 1968, Baerends archive.

83. Letter by Lies Tinbergen to H. Kruuk, 12/12/1968, Kruuk archive.

84. Letter by NT to G. Baerends, 10/1974, Baerends archive.

85. Letter by NT to Sir Ernst Gombrich, undated, probably 1968, Gombrich archive.

86. Janet Tinbergen, pers. comm., 7 October 2002.

87. Letter by NT to Sir Ernst Gombrich, 17/10/1962, Gombrich archive.

88. Janet Tinbergen, pers. comm., 7 October 2002.

89. E. Gombrich, 1950. *The story of art*. Phaidon, London.

90. E. Gombrich, 1960. *Art and illusion: a study in the psychology of pictorial presentation*. Phaidon, London.

91. Letter between NT and Sir Ernst Gombrich, 1962–75, Gombrich archive.

92. Prof. Leonie Gombrich was a famous music teacher. She had been taught by Bruckner, had played with Schoenberg, and knew Brahms and Mahler, so for the Tinbergen girls she was a godsend.

93. Interview with Joost Tinbergen, November 1999.

94. N. Tinbergen, 1972. Functional ethology and the human sciences. Croonian Lecture, 1972. *Proc. R. Soc. Lond. B.*, **182**: 385–410.

Chapter 8

1. Interview with D. Morris, June 2000.

2. Radio interview, on Radio Hilversum in Dutch, with NT and Konrad Lorenz, 'Hier and nu', 26 November 1973, and a letter by NT to Sir Peter Medawar, 18 January 1974, Bodleian Library archives.

3. Letter by NT to Sir Peter Medawar, 18 January 1974, Bodleian Library archives.

4. N. Tinbergen, 1974. Ethology and stress diseases. In *Les Prix Nobel en 1973*, pp. 196–218. Norstedt, Stockholm.

5. E. Hall, 1974. A conversation with Nobel Prize winner Niko Tinbergen. *Psychology Today*, March 1974.

6. Letter by NT to W. Thorpe, 8/9/1976, Bodleian Library archives.

7. N. and E. A. Tinbergen, 1983. *'Autistic children': new hope for a cure*. Allen & Unwin, London.

8. C. and S. J. Hutt, 1968. Stereotypy, arousal and autism. *Psychol. Forschung*, **33**: 1–8.

9. N. Blurton-Jones, 1972. Characteristics of ethological studies of human behaviour. In *Ethological studies of child behaviour* (ed. N. Blurton-Jones), pp. 3–33. Cambridge University Press.

10. D. Cohen, 1972. Observing animals. *New Scientist*, 13 July: 92–4.

11. N. and E. A. Tinbergen, *'Autistic children'*, p. 211.

12. N. and E. A. Tinbergen, *'Autistic children'*, p. 37.

13. Hall, Conversation with Nobel prize winner Niko Tinbergen.

14. R. Welch, 1983. Retrieval from autism through mother-child holding therapy. In *'Autistic children'* (N. and E. A. Tinbergen), pp. 322–36.

15. For example, L. Wing and D. M. Ricks, 1976. The aetiology of childhood autism: a criticism of the Tinbergens' ethological theory. *Psychol. Medicine*, **6**: 533–43. B. Rimland, 1975. Autism, stress, and ethology. *Science*, **188**: 401–2. D. L. and B. Bridgeman, 1975. Letters. *Science*, **188**: 402–3.

16. Letter by J. Richer, 16 March 2001.

17. Look, listen, learn. Editorial in *The Economist*, 17 September 1988: 135–6.

18. N. Tinbergen, 1975. Letters. *Science*, **188**: 405–6.

19. J. Hooper 2002. *Of moths and men: an evolutionary tale*. Fourth Estate, London.

20. M. Rutter, 1999. Autism: two way interplay of research and clinical work. *J. Child Psychol. Psychiat.*, **40**: 169–88.

21. K. B. Nelson, J. K. Grether, L. A. Croen, J. M. Dambrosia, B. F. Dickens, L. L. Jelliffe, *et al.*, 2001. Neuropeptides and neurotrophins in neonatal blood of children with autism or mental retardation. *Annals of Neurol.*, **49**: 597–606.

22. F. Torrente, P. Ashwood, R. Day, N. Machado, R. I. Furlano, A. Anthony, *et al.*, 2002. Small intestinal enteropathy with epithelial IgG and complement deposition in children with regressive autism. *Molecular Psychiatry*, **7**: 375–82.

23. D. L. and B. Bridgeman, Letters. Interview with N. Blurton-Jones, November 2000. Letter by J. Richer, 19/3/2001, Kruuk archive.

24. J. Richer, 1988. The Tinbergens' work on early infantile autism. Unpublished lecture, British Association for the Advancement of Science, 150th Annual Meeting, Oxford, September 1988.

25. W. Barlow, 1973. *The Alexander Principle*. Victor Gollancz, London.

26. Letter by NT to Wilfred Barlow, 5/12/1973, Bodleian Library archives.

27. E. von Holst and H. Mittelstaedt, 1950. Das Reafferenzprincip. *Naturwiss.*, **37**: 464–76.

28. E. Maisel, 1975. Letter. *Science*, **188**: 404–5.

29. N. Tinbergen, 1975. Letter. *Science*, **188**: 405–6.

30. R. Lewin, 1974. Did Nobelist go too far in advocating Alexander Technique? *New Scientist*, October 1974, p. 344.

31. N. Tinbergen, 1976. Use and misuse in evolutionary perspective. Alexander Memorial Lecture November 1976. In *More talk of Alexander* (ed. W. Barlow), pp. 218–36. Victor Gollancz, London.

32. N. Tinbergen, 1985. Watching and wondering. In *Studying animal behavior* (ed. D. A. Dewsbury), pp. 431–63. University of Chicago Press.

33. Letter by NT to G. Baerends, 15/2/1974, Baerends archive.

Chapter 9

1. Letter by NT to G. Baerends, 15/2/1974, Baerends archive.

2. Letter by NT to G. Baerends, 2/5/1973, Baerends archive.

3. G. Baerends, C. Beer, and A. Manning (ed.), 1975. *Function and evolution in behaviour.* Clarendon Press, Oxford.

4. Letter by NT to G. Baerends, 19/3/1076, Baerends archive.

5. Janet Tinbergen archives.

6. Letter by NT to D. Morris, 13/1/1974, Morris archive.

7. Letter by NT to D. Morris, 9/10/1977, Morris archive.

8. Letter by NT to R. Southwood, 28/4/1980, Bodleian Library archives.

9. Letter by NT to Sir Peter Medawar, 13/1/1974, Bodleian Library archives.

10. Letter by NT to Bill Russell, 8/1/1975, Russell archive.

11. Man – guinea pig of evolution, four chapters, Bodleian Library archives.

12. Letter by NT to G. Baerends, 11/12/1979, Baerends archive.

13. N. Tinbergen, 1981. On the history of war. In *Aggression and violence: a psychobiological and clinical approach* (ed. L. Valzelli and L. Morgese), pp. 31–8. Edizioni St Vincent, Milan.

14. N. Tinbergen, 1975. The importance of being playful. *Times Educational Supplement,* 10 January: 19–22.

15. Letter by NT to K. Hana, 29/10/1974, Bodleian Library archives.

16. Letter by NT to G. Baerends, 10/1974, Baerends archive.

17. W. H. Thorpe, 1979. *The origins and rise of ethology.* Heinemann, London.

18. Letter by NT to W. Thorpe, 8/9/1976, Bodleian Library archives.

19. Letter by NT to I. Eibl-Eibesfeldt, 15/6/1977, Eibl-Eibesfeldt archive.

20. Letter by Lies Tinbergen to G. Baerends 21/1/1978, Baerends archive.

21. Letter by Lies Tinbergen to Bill Russell, 1/10/1975, Russell archive.

22. Letter by NT to D. Morris, 3/12/1977, Morris archive.

23. Letter by Lies Tinbergen to D. Morris, 11/4/1983, Morris archive.

24. Letter by Bas Meeuse to G. Baerends, 25/8/1985, Baerends archive.

25. Letter by NT to Aubrey Manning, 14/3/1980, Manning archive.

26. Letter by NT to Major J. Rose, 8/9/1986, Rose archive.

27. Letter by NT to G. Baerends, 19/5/1977, Baerends archive.

28. Letter by NT to G. Baerends, 11/12/1979, Baerends archive.

29. Letter by NT to G. Baerends, 27/1/1980, Baerends archive.

30. Letter by NT to G. Baerends, 19/3/1976, Baerends archive.

31. Letter by NT to G. Baerends, 25/1/1983, Baerends archive.

32. Letter by G. Baerends to NT, 11/10/1986 (about M. S. Dawkins, 1986, *Unravelling animal behaviour,* Longman, Harlow). Baerends archive.

33. Letter by NT to G. Baerends, 4/9/1974, Baerends archive.

34. Letter by NT to Major J. Rose, 1/10/1978, Rose archive.

35. Letter by NT to E. Mayr, 4/2/1982, Bodleian Library archives.

36. Letter by NT to B. Nelson, 9/3/1987, Nelson archive.

37. Letter by NT to Major J. Rose, 6/6/1986, Rose archive.

38. Letter by NT to R. Hinde 26/5/1978, Hinde archive.

39. E. Hall. A conversation with Nobel Prize winner Niko Tinbergen. *Psychology Today*, March 1974.

40. Letter by NT to G. Baerends, 25/4/1974, Baerends archive.

41. Letter by NT to John Patten, 17/3/1982, Bodleian Library archives.

42. Letter by NT to Major J. Rose, 8/7/1982, Rose archive.

43. Letter by NT to the Principal of the University of Connecticut, 28/7/1974, Bodleian Library archives.

44. Invitation to NT, 15/7/1987, Bodleian Library archives.

45. Letter by NT to Ernst Gombrich, 4/6/1975, Gombrich archive.

46. Letter by NT to Ernst Gombrich, 19/6/1975, Gombrich archive.

47. Letter by E. Gombrich to NT, 3/7/1975, Gombrich archive.

48. Letter by NT to D. Morris, Oct. 1985, Morris archive.

49. Letter by NT to G. Baerends, 11/12/1979, Baerends archive.

50. Hall, Conversation with Nobel Prize winner Niko Tinbergen.

51. Letter by NT to E. Mayr, 4/2/1982, Bodleian Library archives.

52. N. Tinbergen, 1985. Watching and wondering. In *Studying animal behavior* (ed. D. A. Dewsbury), pp. 431–63. University of Chicago Press.

53. K. Lorenz, 1966. *On aggression*. Methuen, London.

54. Letter by NT to R. Burkhardt, 16/6/1982, Bodleian Library archives.

55. Letter by NT to Dr I. Kraeger, 1/6/1978, Bodleian Library archives.

56. Letter by NT to A. Manning, 6/7/1985, Manning archive.

57. Letter by NT to D. Morris, Oct. 1985, Morris archive.

58. A. Festetics, 1983. *Konrad Lorenz. Aus der Welt des grossen Naturforschers*. Orac, Vienna.

59. Letter by NT to D. Morris, 21/4/1984, Morris archive.

60. Letter by NT to Dr Anthony Storr, 8/4/1968, Bodleian Library archives.

61. Interview with NT on Dutch radio programme 'Hier en Nu', 26/11/1973.

62. Letter by NT to R. Burkhardt, 16/6/1982, Bodleian Library archives.

63. Interview with Gerry Carleston (née Tinbergen), October 2000.

64. Letter by K. Lorenz to NT, 27/6/1979, Bodleian Library archives.

65. Letter by K. Lorenz to NT, 7/9/1983, Bodleian Library archives.

66. Letter by K. Lorenz to NT, 1/12/1988, Bodleian Library archives.

67. Baerends archive.

68. Letter by NT to G. Baerends and vice versa, April and May 1973, Baerends archive.

69. Letter by NT to D. Morris, Morris archive.

70. Letter by NT to D. Morris, 4/7/1979, Morris archive, about D. Morris, 1979, *Animal days*, Jonathan Cape, London.

71. Correspondence by NT to Jimmy Rose, Rose archive.

72. Letter by Frank Beach to NT, 5/3/1988, Bodleian Library archives.

73. Letter by NT to Sir Karl Popper, 28/7/1974, Bodleian Library archives.

74. Letter by Sir Karl Popper to NT, 12/8/1974, Bodleian Library archives.

75. For example, a four-page letter to two Dutch students, Oost *et al.*, 25/1/1981, about innate/learned,

E. O. Wilson's *Sociobiology*, human adaptation and society, the role of women, etc. Bodleian Library archives.

76. Interview with A. Kortlandt, October 2000.

77. Correspondence in Bodleian Library archives.

78. Letter by NT to Mrs Balk, 19/12/1982, Bodleian Library archives.

79. Letter by Jan Tinbergen to NT, 2/12/1977, Bodleian Library archives.

80. Letter by Jan Tinbergen to NT, 29/1/1988, Bodleian Library archives.

81. J. M. M. Duyf, 1993. *Een wereld van verschil. Leven en werk van de econoom Jan Tinbergen* [A world of difference. Life and work of the economist Jan T.]. University of Rotterdam.

82. J. Tinbergen, 1974. Natuur en milieu vanuit economisch gezichtspunt [Nature and environment from an economic perspective]. *Waddenbulletin*, **4**: 116–18.

83. N. Tinbergen, 1974. Een bioloog-etholoog over vragen van welvaart en welzijn [A biologist-ethologist on questions of prosperity and well-being]. *Waddenbulletin*, **4**: 119–25.

84. Interview with Lary Shaffer, August 2000.

85. Janet Tinbergen, pers. comm., 7 October 2002.

86. Letter by NT to A. Manning 14/3/1980, Manning archive.

87. Letter by NT to the Loman boys, 28/1/1976, Loman archive.

88. Letter by NT to the Loman boys, 4/2/1974, Loman archive.

89. Letter by NT to C. and G. Loman, 14/12/1976, Loman archive.

90. Letter by NT to D. Morris, 4/7/1979, Morris archive.

91. *The Independent*, 10/5/1989: Professor Nikolaas Tinbergen, FRS, left estate valued at £303 683.

92. Letter by NT to H. Kruuk, 30/1/1988, Kruuk archive.

93. Tinbergen, Watching and wondering.

94. Letter by Lies Tinbergen to L. Shaffer, 4/5/1989, Shaffer archive.

95. M. S. Dawkins, T. R. Halliday, and R. Dawkins (ed.), 1991. *The Tinbergen legacy*. Chapman & Hall, London.

Chapter 10

1. T. Anton, 2000. *Bold science*. W. H. Freeman, London.

2. Unpublished notes: 'Summary of N. Tinbergen's views (1982 as seen by himself) on his contribution to the study of behavior'. Bodleian Library archives.

3. Interview with C. Beer, August 2000.

4. G. P. Baerends, 1975. An evaluation of the conflict hypothesis as an explanatory principle for the evolution of displays. In *Function and evolution in behaviour* (ed. G. Baerends, C. Beer, and A. Manning), pp. 187–227. Clarendon Press, Oxford.

5. Baerends, An evaluation of the conflict hypothesis; R. Dawkins, 1976. Hierarchical organisation: a candidate principle for ethology. In *Growing points in ethology* (ed. P. P. G. Bateson and R. A. Hinde), pp. 7–54. Cambridge University Press.

6. P. Marler and D. R. Griffin, 1973. The 1973 Nobel Prize for Physiology and Medicine. *Science*, **182**: 464–6.

7. Marler and Griffin, The 1973 Nobel Prize for Physiology and Medicine.

8. 1989, Oxford University Press.

9. T. J. Roper, 1989. Tinbergen's legacy: *The study of instinct* (Reissue). *TREE*, **4**: 318–19.

10. *Z. f. Tierpsychol.*, **20**: 410–33.

11. Ed. G. Baerends, C. Beer, and A. Manning, 1975. Clarendon Press, Oxford.

12. Ed. M. S. Dawkins, T. R. Halliday, and R. Dawkins, 1991. Chapman & Hall, London.

13. F. A. Huntingford, 1991. War and peace revisited. In *The Tinbergen legacy* (ed. M. S. Dawkins, T. R. Halliday, and R. Dawkins), pp. 40–59. Chapman & Hall, London.

14. D. J. McFarland, 1971. *Feedback mechanisms in animal behaviour.* Academic Press, London. 1974. *Motivational control systems analysis.* Academic Press, London. 1989. *Problems of animal behaviour.* Longman Scientific, Harlow (with A. I. Houston), 1981. *Quantitative ethology.* Pitman, London.

15. Letter by Lies Tinbergen to G. Baerends, 28/7/1989, Baerends archive.

16. G. W. Barlow, 1989. Has sociobiology killed ethology or revitalized it? *Perspectives in ethology*, **8**: 1–45.

17. Letter by NT to R. Hinde, 1978, quoted in R. A. Hinde 1990. Nikolaas Tinbergen. *Biographical Memoirs of Fellows of the Royal Society*, **36**: 549–65.

18. Interview with C. Beer, August 2000.

19. Interview with M. Dawkins, June 2000.

20. Huntingford, War and peace revisited.

21. J. Maynard Smith, pers. comm., 17/01/2002.

22. Letter by NT to Bill Hamilton, 29/10/1980, British Library, London.

23. R. Dawkins, 1976. *The selfish gene.* Oxford University Press.

24. U. Segerstråle, 2000. *Defenders of the truth: the battle for science in the sociobiology debate and beyond.* Oxford University Press.

25. E. O. Wilson, 1975. *Sociobiology: the new synthesis.* Belknap Press, Cambridge, Mass.

26. J. Alcock, 2001. *The triumph of sociobiology.* Oxford University Press.

27. Segerstråle, *Defenders of the truth.*

28. S. J. Shettleworth, 2001. Animal cognition and animal behaviour. *Animal Behaviour*, **61**: 277–86.

29. D. R. Griffin, 1976. *The question of animal awareness.* Rockefeller University Press, New York.

30. C. G. Beer, 1992. Conceptual issues in cognitive ethology. *Advances in the Study of Animal Behaviour*, **21**: 69–109. 1996. Trial and error in the evolution of cognition. *Behavioural Processes*, **35**: 215–24.

31. See review by Shettleworth, Animal cognition and animal behaviour.

32. Interview with C. Beer, August 2000.

33. Shettleworth, Animal cognition and animal behaviour.

34. C. R. Gallistel, 1990. *The organization of learning.* MIT Press, Cambridge, Mass.

35. M. S. Dawkins, 1989. The future of ethology: how many legs are we standing on? *Perspectives in Ethology*, **8**: 47–54.

36. Interview with Marian Dawkins, June 2000.

37. T. Kuhn, 1962. *The structure of scientific revolutions.* University of Chicago Press.

38. Letter by NT to G. Baerends, undated 1968, Baerends archive.

39. R. H. Drent, 2000. Dropping the pilot: Gerard Baerends 1916–1999. *Ardea*, **88**: 113–18.

40. M. Bastock, 1967. *Courtship: an ethological study.* Aldine, Chicago.

41. A. Manning, 1967. *Introduction to animal behaviour.* Edward Arnold, London.

42. W. M. S. Russell and R. L. Burch, 1959. *The principles of humane experimental technique.* Methuen, London.

43. C. Russell and W. M. S. Russell, 1961. *Human behaviour*. Deutsch, London. 1968. *Violence, Monkeys and Man*. Macmillan, London.

44. M. Moynihan, 1976. *The New World primates*. Princeton University Press.

45. M. Moynihan, 1985. *Communication and non-communication among cephalopods*. Indiana University Press, Bloomington.

46. I. Rubinoff, 1994. Reflections on the Moynihan era. *Smithsonian Tropical Research Institute Newsletter*, **13**: 25–6.

47. D. Morris, 1967. *The naked ape*. Jonathan Cape, London.

48. D. Morris, 1969. *The human zoo*. Jonathan Cape, London.

49. D. Morris, 1977. *Man-watching*. Jonathan Cape, London.

50. D. Morris, 1979. *Gestures*. Jonathan Cape, London.

51. D. Morris, 1981. *The soccer tribe*. Jonathan Cape, London.

52. D. Morris, 1997. *The human sexes: a natural history of man and woman*. Network Books, London.

53. D. Morris, 1962. *The biology of art*. Methuen, London.

54. D. Morris, 1985. *The art of ancient Cyprus*. Phaidon, Oxford.

55. R. A. Hinde, 1966. *Animal behavior: a synthesis of ethology and comparative psychology*. McGraw-Hill, New York.

56. R. A. Hinde, 1985. Ethology in relation to other disciplines. In *Studying animal behavior* (ed. D. A. Dewsbury), pp. 193–203. University of Chicago Press.

57. R. A. Hinde, 1974. *Biological bases of human social behavior*. McGraw-Hill, New York.

58. R. A. Hinde, 1980. *Towards understanding relationships*. Academic Press, London.

59. R. A. Hinde, 1983. *Primate social relationships*. Blackwell Scientific, Oxford.

60. R. A. Hinde, 1997. *Relationships: a dialectic perspective*. Psychology Press, London and New York.

61. R. A. Hinde, 1999. *Why gods persist: a scientific approach to religion*. Routledge, London.

62. R. A. Hinde 2002. *Why good is good: the sources of morality*. Routledge, London.

63. J. Krebs and R. Dawkins, 2001. Obituary of Mike Cullen. *The Guardian*, 10 April.

64. F. A. Huntingford, 1984. *The study of animal behaviour*. Chapman & Hall, London.

65. Interview with Colin Beer, August 2000.

66. N. Blurton-Jones (ed.), 1972. *Ethological studies of child behaviour*. Cambridge University Press.

67. Interview with Nick Blurton-Jones, November 2000.

68. 1972, *The spotted hyena*, University of Chicago Press. 1975, *Hyaena*, Oxford University Press. 1989, *The social badger*, Oxford University Press. 1995, *Wild otters*, Oxford University Press. 2002, *Hunter and hunted*, Cambridge University Press.

69. I. and O. Douglas Hamilton, 1975. *Among the elephants*. Collins, London. 1992. *Battle for the elephants*. Doubleday Transworld, London.

70. M. S. Dawkins, 1980. *Animal suffering: the science of animal welfare*. Chapman & Hall, London. 1986. *Unravelling animal behaviour*. Longman, Harlow. 1993. *Through our eyes only?* W. H. Freeman, Oxford.

71. A. Manning and M. S. Dawkins, 1998. *An introduction to animal behaviour*. Cambridge University Press.

72. R. Dawkins, 1976. *The selfish gene*. Oxford University Press. 1982. *The extended phenotype*. W. H. Freeman, Oxford. 1986. *The blind watchmaker*. Longman, Harlow. 1995. *River out of Eden*. Weidenfeld & Nicholson, London. 1996. *Climbing Mount Improbable*.Penguin, London. 1998. *Unweaving the rainbow*. Penguin, London.

73. L. Shaffer and M. R. Merrens, 2001. *Research stories for introductory psychology*. Allyn & Bacon, Boston.

Niko Tinbergen's publications

1923
—Levende Venusschelp. Amoeba, 3: 47.
—Gevaarlijke kastanjeknoppen. *Amoeba*, **3**: 47–8.

1924
—Strandvondsten Kerstcongres District IV. *Amoeba*, **4**: 71.
—Vogelwaarnemingen bij Den Haag. *Amoeba*, **3**: 40–1.
—Zeevogels en de storm. *Het Vaderland*, 28 February.
—Ontmoetingen met eekhoorns. *Het Vaderland*, 13 April.
—N. Tinbergen and H. J. Brouwer. Eenige vogelwaarnemingen over October, November, December te Schevingen. *Amoeba*, **3**: 80–2.

1925
—De trek der nachtzwaluwen. *Amoeba*, **4**: 33–4.

1926
—Twee maanden op de Kurische Nehrung. I. Rossiten en de Vogelwarte. *De Levende Natuur*, **31**: 129–35, 161–7.
—De taak der vogelfotografie. *Amoeba*, **6**: 30–3.

1927
—Meijendel-onderzoek. Stuifduinen. *De Levende Natuur*, **31**: 355–60.
—De duinen van de Hoek van Holland. *De Levende Natuur*, **32**: 226–30.
—Meijendel. *Het Vaderland*, 30 September 1927.
—Een woord tot de leiders. *Amoeba*, **6**: 41–3.
—Bespreking van J. P. Bouma: Het Haagsche vogelboek. *Amoeba*, **6**: 57.
—Het geheim van den smid. *Amoeba*, **6**: 83–5.

—Wind en weer. *Amoeba*, **7**: 18–20.
—Ornithologies verslag van het N.J.N.-Kamp De Koog (Texel), 18–29 August.

1928
—Een strandwandeling. *Amoeba*, **7**: 82–4.
—De Herfsttrek in 1927. *Amoeba*, **7**: 96–9, 107–11.

1929
—Een merkwaardige schipbreukeling. (*Ommastrephes sagittarius* d'Orb.). *De Levende Natuur*, **33**: 45–8.
—In de schuilhut. *De Levende Natuur*, **33**: 279–84.
—Na de Novemberstormen. *De Levende Natuur*, **33**: 319–27.
—Een waardig en ijzig besluit van de Kerst-reunie, naar Lekkerkerk. *Amoeba*, **8**: 70–2.
—Stadsvogels. *Amoeba*, **8**: 74–7.
—Een vogelparadijs in de stad. *Amoeba*, **8**: 91–4.
—Boekbespreking van A. Schierbeek: *De wonderwereld van het microscoop*. *Amoeba*, **8**: 125–6.
—Ockenburg 1. Bij de tapuiten. *Amoeba*, **9**: 19–23.
—De vogels bij Denekamp. *Amoeba*, **9**: 53–5.
—Voorjaarsvreugde in de Vogeltuin. *Het Haagsche Volk*, 11 June 1929.
—Wilde vogels in de stad. *De Meidoorn*, **1**: 42–4.
—Voorjaar. *De Meidoorn*, **1**: 56–8.
—Visdieven. *De Meidoorn*, **1**: 68–71.
—Ooievaars. *De Meidoorn*, **1**: 98–100.
—Onze roofvogels (I) Valken, (II) Buizerden en Kiekendieven, (III) Sperwer en Havik, (IV) Hun Verhouding tot de Mensen. *De*

Meidoorn, **1**: 149–52, 161–4, 178–9;
2: 5–7.

—A breeding pair of herring-gull x
lesser black-backed gull. *Ardea*,
18: 40–1.

—Twee kapmeeuwen met afwijkend
kleed. *Ardea*, **18**: 92–3.

1930

—Een vogelwinter (wat de Haagse
Trekwaarnemers zagen). *De Levende
Natuur*, **34**: 6–14, 53–9.

—Onze stadsreigers. *Het Vaderland*,
4 April 1930.

—Ockenburg I. Bij de tapuiten.
Amoeba, **9**: 19–23.

—De vogels bij Denekamp. *Amoeba*,
9: 53–5.

—Entomologie. *Amoeba*, **7**: 109–12.

—Boekbespreking van J. P. Strijbos:
Waar de stilte spreekt. Amoeba,
9: 212.

—De kieviten in de lente. *De Meidoorn*,
2: 37–8.

—Nog eens over het territorium. *De
Meidoorn*, **2**: 55–7.

—Ransuilen. *De Meidoorn*, **2**: 130–1.

—Over het voedsel van de Blauwe
Reiger (*Ardea, cinerea cinerea* L.).
Ardea, **19**: 89–93.

—N. Tinbergen, G. van Beusekom,
F. P. J. Kooymans, and M. G.
Rutten. *Het Vogeleiland*. A. G.
Schoonderbeek, Laren.

1931

—Uit het dagboek van de Beer (Hoek
van Holland). *De Levende Natuur*,
35: 125–34.

—Havik in de duinen. *De Levende
Natuur*, **35**: 139–41.

—Strandvogels in de winter.
De Meidoorn, **3**: 17–19.

—Storm aan het strand. *De Meidoorn*,
3: 24–6.

—Stuifduinen. *De Meidoorn*, **3**: 35–7.

—Zur Paarungsbiologie der
Flussseeschwalbe (*Sterna hirundo
hirundo* L.). *Ardea*, **20**: 1–18.

—Eine Beobachtung über die
Ernährung der Steinkauzes (*Athene

noctua vidalii* A. E. Brehm). *Ardea*, **20**:
74–5.

—Verzoek om medewerking bij een
onderzoek naar de voedingsoecologie
van de Ransuil (*Asio o. otus* L.). *Ardea*,
20: 128–9.

—L. Tinbergen and N. Tinbergen.
Waarnemingen aan roofvogels en
uilen. I, II, and III. *De Levende Natuur*,
36: 69–80, 98–104, 131–7.

1932

—Waarnemingen aan roofvogels en
uilen. IV. Boomvalken. *De Levende
Natuur*, **36**: 33–41, 75–80, 105–9.

—Waarnemingen aan roofvogels en
uilen. V. Ransuil (*Asio otus otus* (L.)).
De Levende Natuur, **36**: 334–5.

—Waarnemingen aan zilvermeeuwen in
de broedkolonie te Wassenaar. *De
Levende Natuur*, **37**: 213–19,
248–52.

—Over ransuilen. *De Meidoorn*,
4: 108–10.

—Beobachtungen am Baumfalken (*Falco
s. subbuteo* L.) *Journal für Ornithologie*,
80: 40–50.

—Über die Ernährung einer
Waldohreulenbrut (*Asio otus otus*
(L.)). *Beiträge zur Fortpflanzungsbiologie
der Vögel*, **8**: 54–5.

—Über die Orientierung des
Bienenwolfes (*Philanthus triangulum
Fabr). *Zeitschrift für vergleichende
Physiologie*, **16**: 305–34.

—Vergelijkende waarnemingen aan
enkele meeuwen en sterns. *Ardea*,
21: 1–13.

—N. Tinbergen and L. Tinbergen. Over
het voedsel van de sperwer (*Accipiter
nisus* (L.)) in de Nederlandsche
duinstreek. *Ardea*, **21**: 77–89.

1933

—Die ernährungsökologische
Beziehungen zwischen *Asio otus otus*
L. und ihren Beutetieren, insbesondre
den Microtus-Arten. *Ecological
Monographs*, **3**: 443–92.

—Uit het leven van de Bijenwolf
(*Philanthus triangulum* Fabr.). I and II.
De Levende Natuur, **38**: 1–6, 39–45.

—Slechtvalk en Spreeuw. *De Levende Natuur*, **38**: 326–7.

—Torssukátaq I. *De Levende Natuur*, **38**: 344–53.

1934

—Torssukátaq II and III. *De Levende Natuur*, **39**: 1–14, 41–52.

—Kajakduikelen. Source unknown, pp. 17–23.

—Enkele proeven over het ei als broedobject. *Ardea*, **23**: 82–9.

—Abweichendes Verhalten eines Haussperlings. *Ardea*, **23**: 99–100.

—*Eskimoland*. Van Sijn & Zonen, Rotterdam.

1935

—Een boomvalknest. *De Levende Natuur*, **39**: 143–50.

—Field observations of East Greenland Birds. I. The behaviour of the red-necked phalarope (*Phalaropus lobatus* L.) in spring. *Ardea*, **24**: 1–42.

—Über die Orientierung des Bienenwolfes (*Philanthus triangulum* Fabr.). II. Die Bienenjagd. *Zeitschrift für vergleichende Physiologie*, **21**: 699–716.

—Over de betekenis van 'territorium' in het leven der vogels. *Vakblad voor Biologen*, **16**: 95–106.

1936

—Waarnemingen en proeven over de sociologie van een zilvermeeuwenkolonie. I and II. *De Levende Natuur*, **40**: 262–80, 304–8.

—Eenvoudige proeven over de zintuigfuncties van larve en imago van de geelgerande watertor. *De Levende Natuur*, **41**: 225–36.

—Zur Soziologie der Silbermöwe, *Larus a. argentatus* Pont. *Beiträge zur Fortpflanzungsbiologie der Vögel*, **12**: 89–96.

—The function of sexual fighting in birds, and the problem of the origin of 'territory'. *Bird Banding*, **7**: 1–8.

—G. Schuyl, L. Tinbergen, and N. Tinbergen. Ethologische Beobachtungen am Baumfalken

(*Falco s. subbuteo* L.). *Journal für Ornithologie*, **84**: 387–433.

—J. J. ter Pelkwijk and N. Tinbergen. Roodkaakjes. *De Levende Natuur*, **40**: 129–37.

—H. L. Booy and N. Tinbergen. Nieuwe feiten over de sociologie van de Zilvermeeuwen. *De Levende Natuur*, **40**: 325–34.

1937

—Über das Verhalten kämpfender Kohlmeisen (*Parus m. major* L.). *Ardea*, **26**: 222–3.

—Margaret Morse Nice – Studies in the Life History of the Song Sparrow I. Transactions of the Linnean Society of New York, 4: review in *Ardea*, **26**: 210–13.

—Bloedende berken. *De Levende Natuur*, **42**: 1–7.

—J. J. ter Pelkwijk and N. Tinbergen. Eine reizbiologische Analyse einiger Verhaltensweisen von *Gasterosteus aculeatus* L. *Zeitschrift für Tierpsychologie*, **1**: 193–204.

—N. Tinbergen and L. Tinbergen. Roofvogels en vogelbescherming. *Jaarboek 1929/36 van de Nederlandse Vereeniging tot Bescherming van Vogels*, 180–8.

1938

—De Noordveluwe. *De Levende Natuur*, **42**: 330–7.

—De Bijenwolf (*Philanthus triangulum* Fabr.). Lecture for *Instituut voor Arbeidersontwikkeling Amsterdam*. 1 March 1938.

—Ergänzende Beobachtungen über die Paarbildung der Flussseeschwalbe (*Sterna h. hirundo* L.). *Ardea*, **27**: 247–9.

—Bespreking van F. Fraser Darling: Bird flocks and the breeding cycle: a contribution to the study of avian sociality. *Ardea*, **27**: 249–51.

—Why do birds behave as they do? (I). *Bird-Lore*, **40**: 389–95.

—K. Lorenz and N. Tinbergen. Taxis und Instinkthandlung in der Eirollbewegung der Graugans. I. *Zeitschrift für Tierpsychologie*, **2**: 1–29.

—R. J. van der Linde and N. Tinbergen. Über die Orientierung des Bienenwolfes (*Philanthus triangulum* Fabr.) 4. Heimflug aus unbekannten Gebiet. *Biologisches Zentralblatt*, **58**: 425–35.

—N. Tinbergen and W. Kruyt. Über die Orientierung des Bienenwolfes (*Philanthus triangulum* Fabr.). III. Die Bevorzügung bestimmter Wegmarken. *Zeitschrift für Vergleichenden Physiologie*, **25**: 292–334.

—M. Boeseman, J. van der Drift, J. M. van Roon, N. Tinbergen, and J. J. ter Pelkwijk. De Bittervoorns en hun mossels. *De Levende Natuur*, **42**: 129–36.

—N. Tinbergen and R. J. van der Linde. Über die Orientierung des Bienenwolfes. IV. Heimflug aus unbekannten Gebiet. *Biologisches Zentralblatt*, **58**: 425–35.

1939

—Vogelbeschermers beschermen zich tegen hun beschermelingen. *De Levende Natuur*, **43**: 102–8.

—De Schutkleur der takspanners. *De Levende Natuur*, **44**: 230–4.

—Bespreking van M. M. Nice. *The watcher at the nest*. *Ardea*, **28**: 51–2.

—Review: A. F. J. Portielje: *Dieren Zien en Leeren Kennen*. *Ardea*, **28**: 111–13.

—Field observations of East Greenland birds. II. The behavior of the snow bunting (*Plectrophonax nivalis subnivalis* (Brehm)) in spring. *Transactions of the Linnean Society of New York*, **5**: 1–94.

—On the analysis of social organisation among vertebrates, with special reference to birds. *American Midland Naturalist*, **21**: 210–34.

—Over de betekenis van 'territorium' in het leven der vogels. *Koninklijke Nederlandsche Academie van Wetenschappen*, 95–106.

—Why do birds behave as they do? (II). *Bird-Lore*, **41**: 23–30.

—N. Tinbergen and J. J. ter Pelkwijk. De kleine watersalamander. *De Levende Natuur*, **43**: 232–7.

—N. Tinbergen and D. J. Kuenen. Über die auslösenden und die richtunggebenden Reizsituationen der Sperrbewegung von jungen Drosseln (*Turdus m. merula* L. und *T. e. ericetorum* Turton). *Zeitschrift für Tierpsychologie*, **3**: 37–60.

1940

—Die Übersprungbewegung. *Zeitschrift für Tierpsychologie*, **4**: 1–40.

—Elk vogeltje zingt zoals het gebekt is. University Lecture, Leiden. Leiden, Luctor et Emergo.

—De schutkleur der takspanners. *De Levende Natuur*, **44**: 230–4.

—Die Ethologie als Hilfswissenschaft der Ökologie. Voordracht gepubliceerd in *Journal für Ornithologie*, **88**: 171–7.

1941

—Ethologische Beobachtungen am Samtfalter, *Satyrus semele* L. *Journal für Ornithologie*, **89**: 132–44.

—Over de waarde van het populariseren van de biologie. *Vakblad voor Biologen*, **22**: 106–9.

—Wat brengt een zilvermeeuw ertoe zijn prooi te laten vallen? *De Levende Natuur*, **46**: 119.

—Een hommel die de weg wist. *De Levende Natuur*, **46**: 119.

—Over de 'taal' der dieren. I, II, and III. *De Levende Natuur*, **46**: 82–8, 107–12, 125–9.

1942

—Signaalbeweging bij dieren: functie, veroorzaking en homologie. *Vakblad voor biologen*. **23**: 1–6.

—Een bliksembuis. *De Levende Natuur*, **47**: 87–92.

—An objectivistic study of the innate behaviour of animals. *Bibliotheca Biotheoretica D*, **1**: 39–98.

—De staartmees als bouwkunstenaar. *De Levende Natuur*, **46**: 215–18.

—Boekbespreking. *Geslachtsverandering bij Gewervelde Dieren*: G. J. van Oordt. *De Levende Natuur*, **47**: 159.

—N. Tinbergen, B. J. D. Meeuse,
L. K. Boerema, and W. Varossieau.
Die Balz des Samtfalters, *Eumenis
(= Satyrus) semele* (L.). *Zeitschrift für
Tierpsychologie*, **5**: 182–226.

1945

—Bespreking van J. A. Bierens de Haan:
Instinct en intelligentie bij dieren.
Vakblad voor biologen, **26**: 70.

1946

—Bespreking van A. F. J. Portielje:
dieren zien en leeren kennen. *Ardea*,
34: 252–6.

—G. J. Tijmstra. *Ardea*, **34**: 400–1.

—J. J. ter Pelkwijk. *Vakblad voor biologen*,
26: 2.

—*Inleiding tot de diersociologie*.
Noorduijn, Gorinchem.

—De Schoenpoetsers. In *Beekvliet,
gedenkboek gijzelaarskamp St.
Michielsgestel* (ed. P. Geyl *et al.*),
pp. 231–2. Roelants, Schiedam.

1947

—*Kleew: the story of a gull.* Oxford
University Press, New York.

—Orientatie en orientatievlucht bij
Bembex rostrata L. *Tijdschrift voor
Entomologie*, **88**: 435–8.

—Waarom kakelt een kip na het leggen
van een ei? *De Levende Natuur*, **50**: 57.

—Waarvoor gebruikt de geelgerande
watertor zijn ogen? *De Levende
Natuur*, **50**: 71–3.

—1. Wouwen. 2. Rumoer om een
kiekendief. *De Levende Natuur*, **50**:
131–2.

—De Levende Natuur, Vijftig Jaar. *De
Levende Natuur*, **50**: 133–4.

—Der Struktur der
Wirbeltiergemeinschaften. *Revue
Suisse de Biologie*, **53**: 427–31.

—De Natuur is sterker dan de leer, of
de lof van het veldwerk. *University
Lecture, Leiden*. 25 April 1947. Luctor
et Emergo, Leiden.

—N. Tinbergen and J. van Iersel.
'Displacement reactions' in the three-
spined stickleback. *Behaviour*, 1:
56–63.

1948

—*Klieuw*. Boucher, The Hague.

—Jan Joost ter Pelkwijk, 24 October
1914 – 2 Maart 1942. Foreword. In
J. J. ter Pelkwijk, *Deze mooie wereld*,
pp. 7–16. Ploegsma, Amsterdam.

—Sperwer en mezen. *De Levende
Natuur*, **51**: 16.

—Dierkundeles in het meeuwenduin.
De Levende Natuur, **51**: 49–56.

—Wat prikkelt een scholekster tot
broeden? *De Levende Natuur*,
51: 65–9.

—Grote Sterns. *De Levende Natuur*,
51: 111.

—Hoe komen vogels aan zoogdierharen
in hun nest? *De Levende Natuur*,
51: 111.

—Vogelfotografie. I. Vogelportretten.
De Levende Natuur, **51**: 113–14.

—Pijlstaarten. *De Levende Natuur*,
51: 114–15.

—Pauwoogpijlstaart. *De Levende Natuur*,
51: 127.

—Vogelfotografie. II. Trekvogels. *De
Levende Natuur*, **51**: 161–3.

—Social releasers and the experimental
method required for their study.
Wilson Bulletin, **60**: 6–51.

—Physiologische Instinktforschung.
Experientia, **4**: 121–33.

1949

—Introductie. In Hans Warren,
Nachtvogels, p.1. Brouwer, Arnhem.

—Zebrarupsen. *De Levende Natuur*,
52: 41–3.

—Vogelfotografie IV. De vogel in zijn
milieu. *De Levende Natuur*, **52**: 101–3.

—Hoornaar op jacht. *De Levende
Natuur*, **52**: 120.

—Een gelukkig snapshot. *De Levende
Natuur*, **52**: 141–3.

—Muggen en vleermuizen. *De Levende
Natuur*, **52**: 160.

—Vogelgeluiden. *De Levende Natuur*,
52: 181–3.

—Jac. P. Thijsse en de biologische
wetenschap. In *In het voetspoor van
Thijsse* (ed. A. F. H. Besemer, K.

Hana, N. Tinbergen, and J. Wilcke), pp. 15–17. Wageningen, H. Veenman & Zonen.

—De functie van de rode vlek op de snavel van de zilvermeeuw (*Larus a. argentatus* Pontopp.). *Bijdragen tot de dierkunde*, **28**: 453–65.

1950

—Een meeuwenraadsel. *De Levende Natuur*, **53**: 80.

—Nog een meeuwenraadsel, tevens een kraaienraadsel. *De Levende Natuur*, **53**: 99, and *Amoeba*, **26**: 101–3.

—Het tiende Internationale Ornithologencongres. *De Levende Natuur*, **53**: 216–18.

—Afweervertoon van de Dagpauwoog. *De Levende Natuur*, **53**: 220.

—Grimbeert thuis. *De Levende Natuur*, **53**: 221–4.

—Kraaien en schelpdieren. *De Levende Natuur*, **53**: 239.

—The hierarchical organization of nervous mechanisms underlying instinctive behaviour. *Symposium of the Society of Experimental Biology*, **4**: 305–12.

—Einige Beobachtungen über das Brutverhalten der Silbermöwen. In *Ornithologie, als biologische Wissenschaft. Journal für Ornithologie Supplement* (Erwin Stresemann Festschrift), pp. 162–7.

—N. Tinbergen and A. C. Perdeck. On the stimulus situation releasing the begging response in the newly hatched herring gull chick (*Larus argentatus argentatus* Pont). *Behaviour*, **3**: 1–39.

1951

—Schoonheid die niet gezien wil worden. *De Levende Natuur*, **54**: 61–4.

—De Grote parelmoervlinder. *De Levende Natuur*, **54**: 139.

—Een gestrande watertor. *De Levende Natuur*, **54**: 141–3.

—De feilbaarheid van het instinct. *De Levende Natuur*, **54**: 181–90.

—Recent advances in the study of bird behaviour. In *Proceedings of the 10th International Ornithological Congress, Uppsala* (ed. L. von Haaften), pp. 360–74.

—*The study of instinct*. Clarendon Press, Oxford.

1952

—*The tale of John Stickle*. Methuen, London.

—When instinct fails. *Country Life*, 15 February: 412–14.

—Welke wesp vliegt 's nachts? *De Levende Natuur*, **55**: 40.

—Schorrengeur en zonneschijn. *De Levende Natuur*, **55**: 41–5.

—Een kwikstaartroest. *De Levende Natuur*, **55**: 78.

—De gemaskerde Meeuw. *De Levende Natuur*, **55**: 101–5.

—'Derived' activities: their causation, biological significance, origin and emancipation during evolution. *Quarterly Review of Biology*, **27**: 1–32.

—Over nestbouwen en broeden. *De Levende Natuur*, **55**: 141–7.

—'Operation Kittiwake'. *De Levende Natuur*, **55**: 161–9.

—On the significance of territory in the herring gull. *Ibis*, **94**: 158–9.

—A note on the origin and evolution of threat display. *Ibis*, **94**: 160–2.

—The curious behavior of the stickleback. *Scientific American* (December), pp. 22–6.

—N. Tinbergen and M. Moynihan. Head flagging in the black-headed gull; its function and origin. *British Birds*, **45**: 19–22.

1953

—Zwarte kraai met slechtvalkmanieren. *De Levende Natuur*, **56**: 120.

—Terug naar de Farnes. *De Levende Natuur*, **56**: 121–8.

—Eidereenden. *De Levende Natuur*, **56**: 141–6.

—Kegelrobben. *De Levende Natuur*, **56**: 170–1.

—Met weinig tevreden. *De Levende Natuur*, **56**: 201–7.

—Fighting and threat in animals. *New Biology*, **14**: 9–23.

—Ein ethologischer Beitrag zür Tierpsychologie. *Archive Néerlandaise de Zoologie*, **10** (Suppl.): 121–6.

—Nederlandse bijdragen tot de vogelethologie. *Ardea*, **41**: 264–70.

—*The herring gull's world*. Collins, London.

—*Social behaviour in animals*. Methuen, London.

—Over de betekenis van 'territorium' in het leven der vogels. In *Koninklijke Nederlandse Academie van Wetenschap Jaarboek 1953*, pp. 95–106.

1954

—Van 'Leeus' en 'Bobbejanen'. *De Levende Natuur*, **57**: 12–14.

—Een meeuwenkolonie tussen de aronskelken. *De Levende Natuur*, **57**: 41–6.

—De stormmeeuwen van Loch Sunart. *De Levende Natuur*, **57**: 121–30.

—Eider-invasie. *De Levende Natuur*, **57**: 161–6.

—Een week in het Krugerpark. *De Levende Natuur*, **57**: 181–7, 201–8.

—*Bird life*. Oxford University Press, London.

—The origin and evolution of courtship and threat display. In *Evolution as a process* (ed. A. C. Hardy, J. S. Huxley, and E. B. Ford), pp. 233–50. Allen & Unwin, London.

—N. Tinbergen and G. J. Broekhuysen. On the threat and courtship behaviour of Hartlaub's gull (*Hydrocoloeus novae-hollandiae hartlaubi*). *The Ostrich*, **25**: 50–62.

1955

—Zilvermeeuwennieuws. *De Levende Natuur*, **58**: 21–30.

—Some neurophysiological problems raised by ethology. *British Journal of Animal Behaviour*, **2**: 115.

—Some aspects of ethology: the biological study of animal behaviour. *Advances of Science*: 17–19.

—Autobiographical sketch. In *Group processes*. Transactions of First Conference (ed. B. Schaffner), pp. 311–12. Josiah Macy Jr. Foundation, New York.

—Psychology and ethology as supplementary parts of a science of behavior. In *Group processes*. Transactions of First Conference (ed. B. Schaffner), pp. 75–167. Josiah Macy Jr. Foundation, New York.

1956—On the functions of territory in gulls. *Ibis*, **98**: 401–11.

—Stekels – veilig en voordelig. *De Levende Natuur*, **59**: 25–33.

—Evolutie – een ooggetuigeverslag. *De Levende Natuur*, **59**: 73–82.

—The activation, extinction and interaction of instinctive urges. *Royal Institution, Friday Evening Discourses*.

1957

—The functions of territory. *Bird Study*, **4**: 14–27.

—The study of behaviour. In *The ornithologists' guide*, pp. 60–5. British Ornithological Union, London.

—De bittervoorns en hun mossels. In *Speurtocht naar het leven der dieren* (ed. E. Zandstra), pp. 235–42. Veenman, Wageningen.

—'Oogvlekken' bij vlinders. *De Levende Natuur*, **60**: 25–31.

—Van hommels, hondstong en vingerhoedskruid. *De Levende Natuur*, **60**: 73–8.

—Exodus der eiders. *De Levende Natuur*, **60**: 275–80.

—Preface. In *Instinctive behavior: the development of a modern concept* (ed. C. H. Schiller), pp. 15–19. International Universities Press, New York.

—R. D. Hoogland, D. Morris, and N. Tinbergen. The spines of sticklebacks (*Gasteroesteus* and *Pygosteus*) as means of defence against predators (*Perca* and *Esox*). *Behaviour*, **10**: 205–36.

1958

—Over de 'honingmerken' van bloemen. *De Levende Natuur*, **61**: 1–7.

—Over het nut van 'zich dood houden' bij zangvogels. *De Levende Natuur*, **61**: 167.

—Merel eet rupsen van Cucullia verbasci. *De Levende Natuur*, **61**: 215–16.

—Bauplan-ethologische Beobachtungen an Möwen. *Archives Néerlandaises de Zoologie*, **13**: 369–82.

—On anti-predator responses in certain birds – a reply. *Journal of Comparative Physiology and Psychology*, **50**: 412–14.

—N. Tinbergen and K. Lorenz. Closing speech International Ethological Congress, Freiburg 1957. *Zeitschrift für Tierpsychologie*, **15**: 377–80.

1958/59

—Nieuwe experimenten over de functie en de evolutie van kleurpatronen bij dieren. *Natuurkundige voordrachten*, **14**: 61–5.

—*Curious naturalists*. Country Life, London.

—R. A. Hinde and N. Tinbergen. The comparative study of species-specific behavior. In *Behavior and evolution* (ed. A. Roe and G. G. Simpson), pp. 251–68. Yale University Press, New Haven.

1959

—Recent British contributions to scientific ornithology. *Ibis*, **101**: 126–31.

—Obituary: Gustav Kramer (1910–1959). *British Birds*, **52**: 306–8.

—Behaviour, systematics and natural selection. *Ibis*, **101**: 318–30. (Reprinted in *Evolution after Darwin*, Vol. 1, ed. S. Tax, pp. 595–616. University of Chicago Press, 1960.)

—Einige Gedanken über 'Beschwichtigungsgebärden'. *Zeitschrift für Tierpsychologie*, **16**: 651–65.

—The Ruff. *British Birds*, **52**: 302–6.

—Comparative studies of the behaviour of gulls (*Laridae*): a progress report. *Behaviour*, **15**: 1–70.

—Film on the reproductive behaviour of the black-headed gull. *Ibis*, **101**: 503–4.

—Een slakkenraadsel. *De Levende Natuur*, **62**: 145–9.

1960

The evolution of behavior in gulls. *Scientific American* (December), pp. 118–30.

—Eidoppen zijn gevaarlijk. I and II. *De Levende Natuur*, **63**: 241–51, 265–76.

—Eidoppen zijn gevaarlijk. III. *De Levende Natuur*, **64**: 265–72.

—Kampf und Balz der Lachmöwe. *Journal für Ornithologie*, **101**: 238–41.

—On turning native. Unpublished MS. *Tuesday Talk Series*. BBC, February 1961.

—N. Tinbergen and H. Kruuk. Van den vos Reinaerde. *De Levende Natuur*, **63**: 193–203.

1961

Larus ridibundus (Laridae) – fighting between males. *Encyclopedia Cinematographica* E, 334.

—*Larus ridibundus* (Laridae) – pair formation. *Encyclopedia Cinematographica* E, 335.

—Larus ridibundus (Laridae) – agonistic displays. *Encyclopedia Cinematographica* E, 336.

—Speurzand. *De Levende Natuur*, **64**: 241–7.

—N. Tinbergen and I. J. Patterson. Ringing in sea-bird colonies. *The Ringer's Bulletin*, **1**(10): 1–7.

1962

Sub-family Larinae. An introduction to the behaviour and displays of British gulls. In *The birds of the British Isles*, Vol. 11 (ed. D. A. Bannerman), pp. 191–200. Oliver and Boyd, London.

—Behavioural research at the Cornell Laboratory of Ornithology. In *The living bird*, pp. 79–82. First Annual of the Cornell Laboratory of Ornithology.

—The evolution of animal communication – a critical examination of methods. *Symposia of the Zoological Society of London*, **8**: 1–6.

—Foot paddling in gulls. *British Birds*, **55**: 117–20.

—Work of the Animal Behaviour Research Group on Animal Behaviour in the Department of Zoology, Oxford. (Summary of lecture given to ASAB, Oxford 1962.) *Animal Behaviour*, **11**: 1.

—N. Tinbergen and H. Kruuk. Van Scholeksters en Mosselen. *De Levende Natuur*, **65**: 1–8.

—N. Tinbergen, G. J. Broekhuysen, F. Feekes, J. C. W. Houghton, H. Kruuk, and E. Szulc. Egg-shell removal by the black-headed gull *Larus ridibundus* L.: a behaviour component of camouflage. *Behaviour*, **19**: 74–117.

—N. Tinbergen, H. Kruuk, M. Paillette, and R. Stamm. How do black-headed gulls distinguish between eggs and egg-shells? *British Birds*, **55**: 120–9.

—N. Tinbergen, H. Kruuk, and M. Paillette. Egg shell removal by the black-headed gull (*Larus r. ridibundus* L.) II. The effects of experience on the response to colour. *Bird Study*, **9**: 123–31.

1963

—The shell menace – behavioural aspects of camouflage as demonstrated by gulls. *Natural History*, August/September, 28–35.

—On adaptive radiation in gulls (tribe *Larini*). *Zoologische Mededelingen* **39** (Feestbundel H. Boschma): 209–23. Rijksmuseum van Natuurlijke Historie, Leiden.

—The Ravenglass Peninsula. *Visitors' guide to the Ravenglass Bird Sanctuary*. Cumberland County Council.

—On aims and methods of ethology. *Zeitschrift für Tierpsychologie*, **20**: 410–33.

—De genten van de Bass Rock. *De Levende Natuur*, **66**: 121–35.

1964

—Review of *The natural history of aggression*. In *Proceedings of Symposium British Museum of Natural History 1963*, pp. 28–9.

—The evolution of signalling devices. In *Social behavior and organization among vertebrates* (ed. W. Etkin), pp. 206–31. University of Chicago Press.

—The search for animal roots of human behaviour. Typed MS. Lecture given in series *Social Studies and Biology*, Oxford University, October 1964. (Published 1972 in *The animal in its world*.)

—Het laatste vossenieuws. *De Levende Natuur*, **67**: 237–43.

—Een addertje in het gras – en op het zand. *De Levende Natuur*, **67**: 261–6.

—Aggression and fear in the normal sexual behaviour of some animals. In *Pathology and treatment of sexual deviation* (ed. I. Rosen), pp 3–23. Clarendon Press, Oxford.

—N. Tinbergen and M. Norton-Griffiths. Oystercatchers and mussels. *British Birds*, **57**: 64–70.

1965

—*Animal behavior*. Life Nature Library, Time Inc., New York.

—Co-existing with a crow. *Animals*, **6**: 334–5.

—Von den Vorratskammern des Rotfuchses (*Vulpes vulpes* L.) *Zeitschrift für Tierpsychologie*, **22**: 119–49.

—Some recent studies of the evolution of sexual behaviour. In *Sex and behavior* (ed. F. A. Beach), pp. 1–34. Wiley, New York.

—Veldwerk in de Serengeti. *De Levende Natuur*, **68**: 134–46.

—Behavior and natural selection. In *Ideas in modern biology* (ed. J. A. Moore), pp. 521–42. Proceedings of the 16th Zoological Congress, Washington, DC. Doubleday, New York.

1966

—The Serengeti Research Project. *Animals*, **9**: 28–36.

—Ritualization of courtship postures of *Larus ridibundus* L. (Description of three short films.) *Philosophical*

Transactions of the Royal Society, London B, **251**: 457.

—Instinct parliament (review of *On aggression* by Konrad Lorenz). *The Listener*, **76**: 736–7.

1967

—Afrikaanse olifanten. *De Levende Natuur*, **70**: 156–62.

—Adaptive features of the black-headed gull *Larus ridibundus* L. In *Proceedings of the XIV International Ornithological Congress* (ed. D. W. Snow), pp. 43–59. Blackwell Scientific, Oxford and Edinburgh.

—E. A. R. Ennion and N. Tinbergen. *Tracks*. Clarendon Press, Oxford.

—N. Tinbergen, M. Impekoven, and D. Franck. An experiment on spacing-out as a defence against predation. *Behaviour*, **28**: 307–21.

1968

—Masses on the move. *Animals*, **11**: 418–21.

—On war and peace in animals and man. *Science, New York*, **160**: 1411–18.

—Über Kampf und Drohen im Tierreich, Ausdrucksformen des Lebendigen. In *Mensch und Tier* (ed. H. Friedrich), pp. 13–20. Deutscher Taschenbuch Verlag, München.

—Book review, *Territory in the three-spined stickleback*, by J. v. d. Assem. *Animal Behaviour*, **16**: 398–99.

1969

—Ethology. In *Scientific Thought 1900–1960* (ed. R. Harré), pp. 238–68. Clarendon Press, Oxford.

—In de tuin. *De Levende Natuur*, **72**: 98–103.

—*Signals for survival*. Unpublished script for BBC television film.

—Cracking the footprint code. In *Look* (ed. J. Boswell), pp. 28–37. BBC Publications, London.

—Von Krieg und Frieden bei Tier und Mensch. In *Kreatur Mensch* (ed. G. Altner), pp. 163–78. Heinz Moos, Munich.

1970

—Ziende blind. *De Levende Natuur*, **73**: 97–105.

—Umweltbezogene Verhaltensanalyse – Tier und Mensch. *Experientia*, 26: 447–456.

—Konijnewentels. *De Levende Natuur*, **73**: 193–99.

—N. Tinbergen, H. Falkus, and E. Ennion. *Signals for survival*. Clarendon Press, Oxford.

1971

—Eco-ethology – the animal in its niche. *Abstracts 12th International Ethological Conference*, p. 103. Edinburgh.

—Plantenverspreiding. *De Levende Natuur*, **74**: 96.

—Grimbeert in het duin. *De Levende Natuur*, **74**: 145–6.

—Over Rugstreeppadjes. *De Levende Natuur*, **74**: 185–9.

—Van kraaien, eksters en lijsters. *De Levende Natuur*, **74**: 225–7.

—Clever gulls and dumb ethologists – or the trackers tracked. *Die Vogelwarte*, **26**: 232–8.

1972

—The Croonian Lecture, 1972: — Functional ethology and the human sciences. *Proceedings of the Royal Society, London B*, **182**: 385–410.

—*The animal in its world: explorations of an ethologist 1932–1972*. i: *Field studies*. ii: *Laboratory experiments and general papers*. Allen & Unwin, London.

—E. A Tinbergen and N. Tinbergen. Early childhood autism – an ethological approach. *Advances in Ethology (Zeitschrift für Tierpsychologie)*, Suppl., **10**: 1–53.

1973

—Soet Nederlandt. *De Levende Natuur*, **76**: 257–60.

—Die Verhaltensforschung und die gegenwartige Weltsituation. *Universitas*, **9**: 963–8.

—Review Rudy Kousbroek: *Ethologie*

en cultuurfilosofie. Cultureel Supplement NRC-Handelsblad, 2/3/1973.

1974

—Ethology and stress diseases. Nobel Lecture. In *Les Prix Nobel en 1973*, pp. 196–220. Norstedt, Stockholm; and *Science*, **185**: 20–7.

—In vogelvlucht. *De Levende Natuur*, **77**: 49–53.

—In de Hof van Eden. *De Levende Natuur*, **77**: 242–54.

—Een bioloog-etholoog over vragen van welvaart en welzijn. *Waddenbulletin*, **4**: 119–25.

1975

—The importance of being playful. *Times Educational Supplement*, 10 January: 19–22.

—Julian Sorell Huxley, 22 June 1887 – 14 February 1975. *Animal Behaviour*, **23**: 482–3.

—Autism, stress and ethology – reply. *Science*, **188**: 405–6.

1976

—Functional ethology and the human sciences (Croonian Lecture). *Proceedings of the Royal Society, London B*, **182**: 385–410.

—De mosseleters van Ravenglass. *De Levende Natuur*, **79**: 1–14.

—Ethology in a changing world. In *Growing points in ethology* (ed. P. P. G. Batson and R. A. Hinde), pp. 507–27. Cambridge University Press.

—Use and misuse in evolutionary perspective. Alexander Memorial Lecture November 1976. In *More talk of Alexander* (ed. W. Barlow), pp. 218–36. Victor Gollancz, London.

—E. A. Tinbergen and N. Tinbergen. The aetiology of childhood autism: a criticism of the Tinbergens' theory: a rejoinder. *Psychological Medicine*, **6**: 545–9.

1977

—Time is running out. Unpublished MS.

1978

—Onbehaaglijke co-existentie. *De Levende Natuur*, **81**: 11–21.

—Zo pienter als kraaien – I and II. *De Levende Natuur*, **81**: 49–63, 97–111.

1979

—L'enfant et le jeu. In: *Prospective santé*, **8**: 65.

1980

—Vossen en konijnen. *De Levende Natuur*, **82**: 59–63.

1981

—On the history of war. In *Aggression and violence: a psychobiological and clinical approach* (ed. L. Valzelli and L. Morgese), pp. 31–8. Edizioni St Vincent, Milan.

—Vee in het vrije veld. *De Levende Natuur*, **83**: 27–33.

—Een verse wond. *De Levende Natuur*, **83**: 40.

1983

—N. Tinbergen and E. A. Tinbergen. *'Autistic' children: new hope for a cure*. George Allen & Unwin, London.

1985

—Watching and wondering. In *Studying animal behavior* (ed. D. A. Dewsbury), pp. 431–63. Chicago University Press.

1988

—Holding therapy and prevention: Foreword. In *Holding time* (M. G. Wells), p. 1. Simon & Schuster, New York.

—Aus der Kinderstube der Ethologie. In *Wozu aber hat das Vieh diesen Schnabel: Briefe aus den frühen Verhaltensforschung 1930–1940* (ed. O. Koenig), pp. 309–14. Piper, Munich.

1989

—Foreword for reissue of *The study of instinct*. Oxford University Press.

Index of proper names

Index of subjects